THE BEST OF
THE BEATLES BOOK

EDITED BY JOHNNY DEAN

Beat Publications Ltd.

First edition 2005
Published by Beat Publications Ltd
PO Box 46297
London W5 3ZD

PUBLISHER
Sean O'Mahony

EDITOR
Johnny Dean

DEPUTY EDITOR
Peter Doggett

DESIGNER
Peter Bailey

Thanks also to Tony Barrow, Ian Gray, Pete Nash, Simon Wells, Nic Barfield, Gillian G. Gaar, Lillian Marshall, Ruth Ward and Aaron Bremner for their help in the preparation of this book

This book is dedicated to Jackie, Suzanna and Josephine

This edition is distributed exclusively in the UK by
Music Sales Ltd, 8/9 Frith St., London W1D 3JB
Visit Music Sales at www.omnibuspress.com

ISBN 0-9549957-0-8

Scanning and origination by Replica

Printed in Hong Kong by South Sea International Press

Contents

Introduction

When I rang Brian Epstein in September 1962, to ask if he'd like to promote his new group in *Pop Weekly*, the magazine I was publishing for Bob Stigwood at the time, it was just another routine call. I certainly had no idea it would change my life.

I'd never spoken to Mr Epstein before, but he turned out to be quite charming. Yes, of course he'd like an article about his group, and he'd also be quite willing to support it with an advertisement for their first record. He even told me he was pleased that I'd rung. What a nice man, I thought, as I rang journalist Peter Jones to ask for a quick 500 words on the Beatles.

And that, as far as I was concerned, was almost certainly the last I'd ever hear about the band from Liverpool with the odd name, because most new singers and groups vanished without trace after a couple of weeks. So I was surprised to see 'Love Me Do' reach the charts a few weeks later. But its success proved that I was doing the right thing. For over a year I'd been following the growing interest in beat music in the UK, and I'd finally decided – just around the time that 'Love Me Do' was climbing up the charts – that beat groups were going to be the next 'big thing' to hit the music business. So, just before Christmas 1962, I left *Pop Weekly* to start my own magazine which I'd decided to call *Beat Monthly*.

In January, I was sent a copy of the Beatles' second single, 'Please Please Me'. It grabbed my attention right from the opening bars. When it ended, I played it again, just to make sure. Yes, it was good – very good. I rang Brian as soon as I could, told him I thought the new release was great and that I would be featuring the Beatles in every issue of my new magazine. In return, I asked if he'd let me offer A Day With The Beatles as the big prize in a competition in the launch issue. Brian was always very friendly whenever I spoke to him – probably because I was the first person on a national music magazine to ring him about the Beatles – and he assured me that the boys would be quite happy to spend a day with my prizewinner.

For various reasons, the launch of *Beat Monthly* had to be delayed for a few weeks, so by the time I put the first issue to bed in March, 'Please Please Me' was already a huge hit. The fact that John, Paul, George and Ringo had been making a big impact with audiences everywhere on the Helen Shapiro tour, and

The Beatles were the obvious choice to appear on the cover of the second issue of Beat Monthly in 1963.

The Beatles Book editor Johnny Dean (sitting next to Paul) with the group in their dressing-room before a Beatles concert.

For me Brian Epstein was always the fifth Beatle.

were also attracting a fast-growing army of fans, made my competition even more attractive. The future was beginning to look very bright for the boys from Liverpool. When I came to plan the second issue of *Beat Monthly*, it was blindingly obvious that there was only one group to put on the cover, because the Beatles were far and away the most exciting new band to hit the British charts for a long time. I wanted to ring Brian right there and then, and ask him if I could start a magazine exclusively for the Beatles. But good old reality kept nudging me in the back, saying: "Don't be stupid. You can't start two magazines at the same time, it's the perfect way to go bankrupt."

A few days later, the advance promo of 'From Me To You' arrived on my desk. It was another great record, a perfect follow-up to 'Please Please Me', and certain to top the charts. The Beatles were clearly going to be enormous. If I wanted to get involved, I had to do it immediately – and stuff the consequences. So I rang Brian. In his usual calm, measured way, he said that he liked the idea of a Beatles magazine, but he couldn't agree anything until he'd talked to the boys. And that was how I had to leave it. Naturally, I became more and more concerned as the weeks flashed by, thinking that Brian was probably talking to several other publishing companies. But he finally called with the good news that the boys would like to meet me on 21st May, 1963, at London's Playhouse Theatre, where they would be recording some of their songs for BBC Radio's *Saturday Club*.

As soon as I shook hands with John, Paul, George and Ringo, I realised that this wasn't going to be one of their usual jokey encounters with the press. The meeting had clearly been arranged to suss me out. Editing their magazine meant that they would have to admit someone new to their inner circle and put up with me in their dressing-rooms, recording studios, homes – in fact, virtually everywhere they went.

Fortunately, I got on with them all from the start. When we sat down to a cup of tea in the BBC canteen I outlined my ideas for their magazine. John didn't have a lot of questions, but I got the immediate impression that he rather liked the idea of calling their publication *The Beatles Book* rather than *The Beatles Magazine*. George was very charming in an easy-going way, although he did want to know how much I would be charging for the magazine. Ringo let the other three do most of the talking. Paul asked several very pertinent questions, including: "What on earth are you going to put in it after the first three issues?" I assured him I would have absolutely no problem whatsoever filling every page twice over. A few days later, Brian rang to let me know that he would be putting a contract in the post, giving me the sole and exclusive right to publish the official Beatles magazine. The first issue finally went on sale on 1st August, 1963.

Over the next forty years – apart from a gap after the group broke up in 1969 – *The Beatles Book* covered almost every aspect of the group's extraordinary career, from the peak of Beatlemania in the 60s to their split at the end of the decade. Life with the Beatles has been one hell of a rollercoaster ride for all of us. The early 60s were a wonderful time to live through. Just being in the audience at one of their concerts was an amazing experience that none of us will ever forget.

Following many requests from readers, I have put together this special commemorative book to celebrate the lives of John, Paul, George and Ringo. I've arranged everything in chronological order, so you can relive the events in the order they happened. This anthology obviously concentrates on the years they were all together. But it also includes a number of features about important events during their solo years.

As our regular readers will know, we did return to many of the most important Beatle moments on several occasions, as more information became available, but I've solved that dilemma by merging all the best features on each topic into one major article.

Johnny with George during an exclusive Beatles Book visit to the Harrisons' home in Esher.

Johnny pictured with Neil Aspinall and Mal Evans, the two road managers who were the Beatles' closest aides in the 60s.

Right from the beginning, I decided that, whenever possible, every feature or report that was published in the magazine should be written by somebody who was actually there at the time. That's why I asked Bill Harry to give us the lowdown on the Merseybeat scene; Iain Hines to report on what it was like with the Beatles in Hamburg; Paul's father to talk about his son's childhood; and Neil Aspinall, Mal Evans and Tony Barrow to supply the latest facts about their recording sessions, tours, films, and whatever else was happening behind the headlines in the Beatles' world.

Many people have contributed to the magazine down the years, but I must single out the help I've received from Tony Barrow, the Beatles' Press Officer in the 60s. He did a lot for the magazine during the early days, and has continued to write for us ever since. I also want to thank all the readers who wrote to *The Beatles Book* over the years. I've managed to include quite a few of your letters in *The Best Of The Beatles Book* – particularly the ones we received after the deaths of John, George and Linda, which were particularly moving. I'm also grateful to everyone who wrote to me personally after the

final issue of *The Beatles Book* appeared in January 2003. Your letters meant a great deal to me, and your good wishes were very much appreciated. It's been a great privilege to edit your magazine for so many years.

It is impossible to imagine the second half of the 20th century without the Beatles' music, which has accompanied so many events in all our lives. I would like to sign off by repeating what I said in my editorial in June 1969: "I'm certain that whatever method is used to play music in the year 2000, songs like 'Yesterday', 'Eleanor Rigby', 'Strawberry Fields' and dozens and dozens of others will be played regularly." The only change that I'd like to make to that prediction is to amend the date to 3000!

Finally, I'd like to thank the five people who made it all possible: John, Paul, George, Ringo and Brian.

We will never see their like again.

Johnny Dean

Childhood profiles

Their families and friends talk exclusively about the Beatles as children

PAUL McCARTNEY

Anyone who knows Paul well would say that he hasn't changed very much from the young boy that his father describes: "Michael and Paul did everything together, especially anything that they were told specifically not to do. As children, they were inseparable. Wherever one went so did the other. I remember their friends called them the 'Nurk Twins', but I never did find out why. John and Paul used the same name for one of their first live shows.

"Paul was 18 months older than Michael, so naturally he was the leader. I remember that he always seemed to know exactly what he wanted and usually knew how to get it. He was a born diplomat. He also had the fascinating ability to do two things at once. In the evenings, he would sit at the table doing his homework and watching television at the same time. How he managed it, I don't know, but the extraordinary thing was that afterwards, he usually knew more about the programme than I did. And he got his homework right as well.

"He was a typical tearaway ragamuffin. Once Paul, Mike and another boy went apple-scrumping from a farm in Speke. They were only 12 and 10 at the time. They were just about to climb the trees when the farmer appeared. They all ran away, but Paul got stuck and Mike went back to help. The first I knew about it was when the farmer rang me up and told me that my two sons were locked up in his barn. He was very reasonable about it, so we decided to scare the boys a bit before we let them off. We stood outside the barn door and said things like, 'Do you think they will get a long sentence?' and 'Shall we just spank them now and not tell the police?' When we thought they'd had enough, we opened the barn door – only to find we'd been completely wasting our time. The two boys trotted out and greeted me with 'Hello Dad, about time you got here'. I was really amazed that both of them seemed so completely unconcerned by the whole proceedings!"

Iris Caldwell, who knew Paul when he was in his teens, says: "I met him at the Cavern, in the late 1950s. He was not really a boyfriend because I could only see him one night of the week. We used to go to the pictures or the Empire, because he was working the rest of the time. I always remember that he used to write me notes and sign them 'Pool McCooby'. He was always doing impressions of other people and whenever anyone used to stare at him he'd just stand there and grin right back. He was always joking. I remember one time we had a row, ending with the decision not to go out with each other any more. But the next night he came round with a gaudily wrapped present. Of course, we were friends again immediately. That is, until I opened the parcel and saw a pound of cheese for next week's sandwiches. But he was so likeable that I couldn't help forgiving him." Iris adds: "My house was always open to him and his friends and one night Paul brought Cilla Black round. We sat up playing word games until dawn started to break. He was always drawing silly pictures and giving odd names to things."

Beatles Book writer Peter Jones recalls one incident which shows how down-to-earth Paul remains, despite everything that has happened to him in the last few months: "It was during the filming of *A Hard Day's Night*. Paul had just been mobbed by hundreds of screaming fans. As he entered the door of the building, he turned and waved to the crowd. Then he looked at me, gave a typical Paul grin, and said: 'I'm not really big-headed you know'!"

Paul (in the foreground) with his younger brother Mike.

GEORGE HARRISON

George is very friendly and very natural. But he can be changeable. One day he acts as if he cannot understand why anyone should want to interview him, and the next he seems to positively enjoy talking to everyone. According to his mother, he certainly hasn't changed much. She recalls, "George was always full of fun when he was a child. He never caused any big trouble and the neighbours liked him a lot, which is unusual with little boys. I was very proud of the way he liked to help old people. I used to take George around with me when I went visiting elderly people in our district. I remember one day, when I took him to the pictures with me. He was only eight. When we came out there was an old tramp sitting on a wall. George immediately suggested that we give him half-a-crown. Money meant nothing at all to him then and he couldn't see why I shouldn't give money to every old person we met.

"The first time he ever got a big urge to play the guitar was when he was 13 years old. His brother Peter bought one and George promptly tried to learn. Eventually, he formed a small group with some friends and they went along for an audition at the Speke British Legion Hall. The main act did not turn up, so George's group played instead. They only knew two songs so once they had done them, they went back to the first one and went on playing the same two over and over again!"

George's father remembers: "He was always very fond of cycling. He also loved hitchhiking. I remember one day he turned up with Paul and announced that they were going to hitchhike to the South of England. The next day they disappeared. We didn't see them again for three weeks, but we kept getting postcards from places like Southampton and Torquay. They really loved that holiday and although they were only 14, I felt they were a lot older in their attitude to everything when they returned. As far as I remember, they took their guitars with them."

Singer Shane Fenton's wife, Iris, knew George very well when he was 15. She says, "George used to rehearse in a cellar, in a house near where we lived. After a time he started inviting friends of his to 'come down and use his rehearsal room'! One group who took advantage of his offer was the Quarry Men, John's original outfit. Everyone thought that George was a very good guitarist at the time. I think the main reason was, that he was one of the very few people in Liverpool who could play 'Guitar Boogie Shuffle' all the way through."

Iris's mother, Mrs. Caldwell, remembers George as "the boy who used to come round and watch television three nights a week. He and Iris used to sit there holding hands. As far as I remember, it was the first time that either of them had taken any interest in the

George showing off his first guitar in his early teens.

opposite sex. At her 14th birthday party, George turned up in a brand-new, Italian-style suit. He looked very grown-up. Like most teenage parties, they kept on playing kissing games and somehow or other, George and Iris always ended up together."

George's own style of humour is, and always has been, the deadpan, surreal kind. Here's what he wrote to Iris's mother when the Beatles were in Hamburg in 1962:
"To: Mrs. Violent Stubb
Darling Vi,
    We are all missing you very much. To caress your teeth once more would be just heaven. Also to hold your lungs in mine and drink TB. John sends you his lunch, also Paul and Ringworm greet you too. It's not much fun here but only one week to go now, so it's not so bad now. Have tea ready on Sunday 18th. Cheerio, love from George and friends."

JOHN LENNON

"Dear Fater Xmas, will you please bring me a water pistol with love from John, and do not forget a money box with a key, and a pair of gloves, and have you any books and would you try to get some dinkies please, also a pair of skates."

So went one of the very first literary efforts of five-year-old John Winston Lennon. His beloved aunt, Mimi Smith, raised him from the age of five, after the marriage between his dad, Freddie Lennon, and his mum, Julia, fell apart. Mimi describes the schoolboy John as "a lovable rebel. He hated any kind of conformity, and those who wanted to make him conform, especially his school masters. When he was at art school he had a lot of homework to do, and I had to lean over him all the time to make sure that he did it. If George or Paul came round to see him it became quite hopeless." Mimi adds: "He loved animals, especially our cat, Sam, which only died last year. He was really heartbroken when I told him the sad news. He was a very handsome little boy, with silver-gold hair and big brown eyes. I don't think he minds people looking at him now, because they used to do it when he was a child. He got so used to it that if they didn't look at him he would go up to them and say 'I'm John Lennon, I am'.

"He had this little house built in a tree in our back garden. From the spring onwards it was impossible to see through the leaves, and he used to hide in there for hours. He called it his 'den', and used to sit there drawing and making up rhymes, just like those in his books. I used to get annoyed because he kept stealing all my clothes lines to make alterations to his tree-house. When he was naughty, I sent him to his room, but he was so quiet that I decided to see what he was doing. There he was, sitting very comfortably in an easy chair reading a book. He was perfectly happy, and all the time I thought I'd been punishing him. He always loved reading, but only classics. I never saw him look at a comic or a novel. His favourite books were all about painting and painters."

Mr. Ballard, John's art school tutor at Quarry Bank School during the 1950s, paints a different picture of the teenage Lennon: "Compared with other students, he was very reticent and quiet. I don't remember him as a leader. At first I didn't think he had any particular talent, but that was before I found his sketchbook, his private one. Inside were loads of drawings and satirical comments about the staff and pupils, which obviously formed

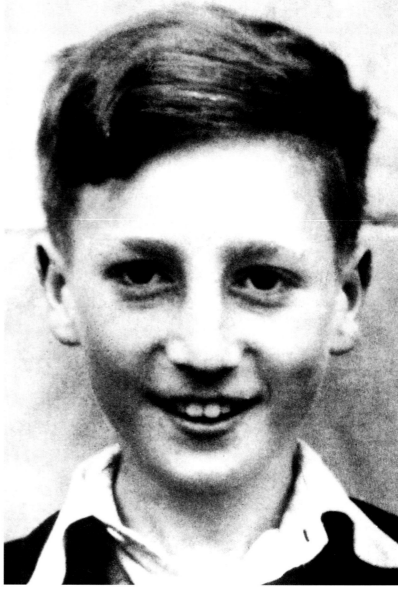

A school photo of John in his football shirt in the early 1950s.

the basis for his first book. To say that they were brilliant would be an understatement. They showed a brand new John Lennon. His girlfriend Cynthia Powell also helped him a great deal at this stage, as far as I was concerned. She was his guiding light, and even though she was the top girl in her class, she always managed to spare time for John. Even in those days they were really made for each other.

"I was convinced that John could become a brilliant graphic artist, so I recommended him for the Graphic School of Art. Unfortunately, John was already getting a reputation as a rebel, so the Graphic School refused to have him. I kept trying like mad, and finally they did accept him, but in the painting school. His graphic talents just faded out and after about six months he left.

"The last time I saw John was at the Liverpool Rag Day in 1960. I was driving through the crowd, which had got completely out of control, when suddenly the car was pelted with fruit and tomatoes. I peered out, and there was John with some of his friends, grinning all over their faces. He came over and apologised, and we parted the best of friends."

John outside his Aunt Mimi's house in Menlove Avenue, Liverpool.

RINGO STARR

Ringo's success with the Beatles since he joined the group in the final months of 1962 is all the more remarkable when you discover the tremendous difficulties he had to overcome. He was dogged by ill-health during his childhood, and his illnesses had a big effect on his life. His mother says: "He was in hospital so much that he didn't have the chance to do all the usual things that young boys get up to". His physical training instructor at Dingle Vale Secondary Modern School, Mr. Dawson, recalls: "He always wanted to do the same things as the other boys. I remember one time when the class were jumping over the vaulting-horse in the gym. When it came to Ringo's turn, he was pretty doubtful whether he would get over the obstacle because he had never done it before. He ran up to it, jumped, and just managed to clear it. When he realised he'd succeeded and not fallen flat, his face burst into a really broad, satisfied grin."

Ringo's mother remembers the first time he took an interest in drumming. "It was in 1957", she says. "He was working in Hunt's Sports Equipment store in Speke, and he had just started the Ed Clayton Skiffle Group with his only really close friend at the time, Roy Trafford. Later Ringo joined with the Darktown Skiffle Group, and met Rory Storm at a 6.5 Special talent contest. Ringo found out that Rory needed a drummer, and soon he became a permanent member of the group."

Iris Fenton recalls the time that the boys were booked to appear at Butlins' Camp in Pwllheli, in Wales, and the others decided they would look more professional if they wore make-up. But Ringo refused point blank to "put that muck on my face". In the end, however, he gave in to stop the argument and smeared his face with a thin layer. She adds, "I remember that he was very popular with the girls staying at the camp. They all loved the grey streaks in his hair, even though Ringo hated them. He did not grow his beard until their second season at the camp. I think it was to try and draw attention away from the streaks in his hair."

Iris's mother, Mrs. Caldwell, remembers Ringo's first swimming lesson: "Rory found out that Ringo could not swim a stroke, so he decided to try and teach him. It was fine at first, but then they decided to try underwater swimming, which almost caused a tragedy. Rory told me that suddenly a pair of hands appeared from beneath the waves, desperately searching for something to grab on to. Luckily Rory saw what was happening and pulled him out." She adds: "In 1961, Ringo was going very steady with a girl called Jerri. They went everywhere together and the only reason they broke it off was because Ringo refused to give up show business. I remember that Ringo's moods used to vary a lot. Sometimes he'd be very happy and animated, and other times miserable and depressed. But he had a very strong effect on the others. If he was feeling happy they all ended up feeling great. If he was sad, they all felt down too.

"He always seemed to be getting into scrapes. I remember when he went to Hamburg for the first time. He travelled alone on the train and had to change in Paris. During the usual scramble he lost track of his drumkit. As he couldn't speak a word of French, he stood on the platform and tried to explain what had happened in sign language. The French people thought he was mad and called the gendarmes. Fortunately, one of them did understand English, and realised what had happened.

"I know that Ringo always admired John, Paul and George very much, and it was the biggest moment of his life when they asked him to join them. Looking back at all the troubles that Ringo went through as a child, I'm very glad that he has become so successful and famous." (TB)

Ringo (left) and friend dressed up for a local fair.

The Quarry Men

Pianist John Lowe reveals the story behind John, Paul and George's first group

John Charles Duff Lowe was the original piano player with John Lennon's first band, the Quarry Men. Among the other original members of this 1950s skiffle outfit were George Harrison and a boy from the same form as John Lowe at the Liverpool Institute, Paul McCartney. Together they recorded the now legendary 1958 acetate, 'That'll Be The Day'/'In Spite Of All The Danger', at a studio in Liverpool's Kensington district – where a cluster of new streets were named after the Beatles a quarter of a century later. When Lowe announced that he was ready to sell this priceless rarity to the highest bidder in 1981, it was bought by none other than Paul McCartney. More recently, Lowe has renewed his acquaintance with several of his old colleagues in the reformed Quarry Men.

JOHN LOWE: About ten years ago, I saw a photograph taken when Paul and I both auditioned for the Liverpool Cathedral choir when we were ten, just before we went to the Institute. We both failed on that occasion. I got in six months later, but Paul never tried again. I think he went on record as saying he'd tried to make his voice break, because he didn't really want to do it! If he had, he'd have received the same musical training that I did, with music theory being pumped into you every evening and weekend, and services on top of that. As a result, you tended to grow up apart from your mates. But in 1958, my voice broke, and I stopped going straight from school to the Cathedral every night.

Q: What was Paul like in class?
He was a very amusing cartoonist. His drawings – of things like the master who was taking the lesson – would appear under your desk, and you'd pass them on. But I don't remember him, or John and George, being anything special. They were just mates at school.

Q: How did you come to join the Quarry Men?
Paul was already a member, and he asked if I could play the beginning of 'Mean Woman Blues'. I could, so he invited me to his house in Allerton to meet John. It wasn't a particularly momentous encounter – though when you're 16, anyone 18 months older can be a

bit intimidating. John used to dress in what you'd loosely describe as Teddy Boy gear. Paul's father, like all parents then, was paranoid that his children were going to turn into Teddy Boys, pushing bottles into people's faces and creating mayhem in the clubs. The uniform indicated someone who was looking for trouble. John gave the impression of being like that, but was actually quite a nice guy.

I lived in West Derby, on the opposite side of Liverpool to all the other Quarry Men. Whereas Paul could easily bike round to John's house, it was a journey on two buses for me. So I didn't tend to get involved during the week. We'd rehearse on Sunday, and perform the following Saturday if anyone would have us. In 1958, it was all jazz bands, and we mostly played at intervals, during their beer breaks. We were always warned not to play too loudly.

Q: Who else was in the group?
George came in a week or two after me. Prior to us joining, the band had Rod Davis on banjo, Pete Shotton on washboard, Eric Griffiths on guitar, Colin Hanton on drums, Len Garry on tea-chest bass, John Lennon and, right at the end of the skiffle era, Paul McCartney. John wanted to put more rock'n'roll into it – which meant that Pete, Rod and Len had to go, because you didn't need a washboard, tea-chest bass and banjo to play rock'n'roll. I can't remember us doing any skiffle after that. It was all Gene Vincent, Buddy Holly and Chuck Berry.

Q: How long did you stay with the Quarry Men?
Only for 1958. It wasn't a big deal, but I just got fed up with the hour-long journey from West Derby to rehearsals, and my girlfriend used to moan about it. Also, A-levels came along, plus parental pressure. It was only after the exams were out of the way that John and Paul got together again. Meanwhile, George was playing with other groups.

Q: What's the story behind the most famous Quarry Men original of that era, 'In Spite Of All The Danger'?
That was written by Paul. Some say that he was inspired by a favourite record of his,

'Tryin' To Get To You' by Elvis Presley, which was in the charts when Paul went to Boy Scout camp in 1957. John used to sing it with Paul harmonising. We rehearsed quite a long time for that recording session. 'That'll Be The Day' was the A-side.

Making the record was John's idea, but we all chipped in to pay for it – John, Paul, George, Colin and I. It cost something like a pound. The studio was just a back room of a house, with these huge machines on the table – no overdubs, just one microphone in the middle of the room, and a piano. The guy who ran it, Percy Phillips, cut the acetate, there and then, and we walked out with one copy. It didn't even have a proper sleeve; it was put in a Parlophone 78rpm sleeve. Nobody used it for anything much, so I ended up with it. Even after the Beatles had become well-known, none of them bothered to try and get it back. So it lay in my linen drawer for years, though I did play it to a few people.

In 1981, I put my head above the parapet, and spoke to Sotheby's to see what the acetate was worth. It got into the newspapers, and Paul immediately took out an injunction stopping me from selling it, because it had an original song of his on it that had never been published. A letter from his solicitors arrived, saying that he wanted to settle the matter amicably. Paul and I had a couple of telephone conversations, and he suggested that I come up to London for a chat about the old days. I told him that we ought to get the business about the acetate out of the way first. He sent his business manager and solicitor to see me in Worcester, where I was working at the time. I was perfectly happy with the deal we agreed, so I handed the acetate over, and that was that! (AC)

John on stage with the Quarry Men — on the day he met Paul for the first time.

Liverpool Days

'Mersey Beat' editor Bill Harry looks back at the birth of a legend

The basic Fab Four line-up of John Lennon, George Harrison, Paul McCartney and Pete Best first started performing together in 1960 at the Casbah Club, Haymans Green, which was run by Pete's mother, Mona. But at this time the Beatles were still small potatoes on a scene dominated by bands such as Rory Storm & The Hurricanes, Howie Casey & The Seniors, Cass & The Cassanovas and Kingsize Taylor & The Dominoes.

Back then, I reckon that Cass & The Cassanovas were actually Liverpool's most popular local band. After all, this was almost two years before the *Mersey Beat* readers' poll that established the Beatles as top dogs locally. The Cassanovas ran their own club, and drew large crowds to their gigs at such jive hives as Knotty Ash Village Hall. They were even on the bill of the Gene Vincent concert at the Liverpool Stadium.

Stuart Sutcliffe and John Lennon were in the audience that night, and after the show Stuart asked promoter Allan Williams why he hadn't booked the Beatles. After all, they had been playing at Allan's own club, the Jacaranda. But the Jacaranda was a small coffee bar with barely enough room to fit in a couple of dozen people. It was almost the bottom rung of the ladder in a scene with venues that were large enough to contain hundreds of fans.

My first memories of seeing the Beatles are still vivid. I descended into the basement, conscious of the insistent throb of the music, and squeezed my way into the mass of people, some crowded beneath the arches. The place was dimly lit but the atmosphere was exciting and almost overpowering. On stage, the Beatles were performing a set of high-energy rock'n'roll numbers.

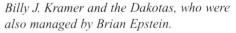
Billy J. Kramer and the Dakotas, who were also managed by Brian Epstein.

No, it wasn't the Cavern. I saw the Beatles perform on stage for the first few times at Liverpool College of Art dances in the late Fifties and the beginning of the Sixties. The venue was the college canteen and the group were regarded as the college band. I had already seen the boys rehearsing in one of the art college 'life rooms' (where the models posed). Apart from the college gigs, I also saw them performing at the Jacaranda Club, a small coffee bar on the premises of a former chandler's shop in Slater Street. In that small, cramped cellar room they played for pennies rather than pounds. They had no proper equipment, and their girlfriends sat on chairs holding broom handles to which their mikes were attached.

During the course of the next few years I saw hundreds of Beatles performances: in the local jive hives, at the Cavern sessions, at concerts in the larger Merseyside halls,

The Searchers, Liverpool's best-selling group of the 60s after the Beatles.

during their initial British tours and at the filming of television shows. The jive hives were the venues in which Merseybeat was born and where the Beatles served their musical apprenticeship. The venues probably derived their name from Doug Martin's Ivamar Promotions at St. Luke's Hall, Crosby. Doug advertised the venue as "The Jive Hive" when he began his twice-weekly (Wednesday and Saturday) sessions there in May 1959. The other "jive hives" included Hambleton Hall, Aintree Institute, Litherland Town Hall, Parr Hall, Knotty Ash Village Hall, Wilson Hall, St. John's Hall, Blair Hall, The David Lewis Theatre, The Plaza, The Co-op Hall, The Winter Gardens, Rialto and Baths Hall. At these places, local promoters presented several local bands each night for an admission charge in the region of 2/6d (12p).

Although the jive hives were the breeding ground of the Mersey sound, the range of venues open to the young groups was quite extensive, including the Palace Ice Rink, the New Brighton Pier and aboard the Royal Iris ferryboat; at established ballrooms such as the Grafton Rooms and the Locarno; at small clubs such as the Casbah and the Basement; in pubs such as the Cross Keys (where the Searchers enjoyed their first residency); and

in the 300-plus social clubs affiliated to The Merseyside Clubs Association.

The Casbah was situated in West Derby and was opened by Mona Best in the basement of her house. The Beatles became resident at the club when they stood in for the Les Stewart Quartet, the band originally booked to open the club. George Harrison

and drummer Ken Brown were members of the quartet, but following Les Stewart's decision not to play at the Casbah, they quickly enrolled John Lennon and Paul McCartney and took over the residency there. The initial entrance fee was 1/6d (7p). Later, when Ken fell ill and couldn't play, there was a dispute within the group about whether he should continue to receive a fee. The upshot was that he never played with the group again.

Brian Kelly was an astute promoter who recognised the immense potential of the Beatles after local luminary Bob Wooler had brought them to his attention. They'd been appearing at the Jacaranda and Bob suggested that Brian should pay them £8. He offered them £6 and booked them to play at Litherland Town Hall on Boxing Day, 1960. At this time, they were called the Silver Beatles. He recognised their dynamism, placed a couple of his bouncers at the dressing room entrance to prevent other promoters from talking to them, and booked them for an extensive series of dates. Following their Hamburg trip, Brian Kelly displayed posters with the phrase "direct from Hamburg" beneath the Beatles' name. The local kids thought they were a German group who spoke excellent English and went berserk over the leather-clad rockers.

The Merseybeats (later known as the Merseys) enjoyed a run of hit singles.

Before he joined the Beatles, Ringo played with Rory Storm & The Hurricanes.

Meanwhile, Ringo was happily drumming for Rory Storm's group, the Hurricanes. Already well-established locally, the Hurricanes were led by one of the most engaging personalities on the scene. Bob Wooler was correct to dub Rory 'Mr. Showmanship'. During one gig at New Brighton Pier he climbed to the top of the glass dome – and fell through it!

From 1961 onwards the proliferation of new venues on Merseyside was incredible. In the heart of the city, the Cavern had turned to rock – as had the Iron Door, the Mardi Gras and the Downbeat. The Silver Blades Ice Rink also presented groups each week, and opportunities for gigs were increasing at venues such as Vale House, the Riverside Ballroom, the Borgia Club, the Red Door, Heaven and Hell, the Avenue

Cinema, Fazakerley Jive Club, Barnston Institute, Prescot Jive Hive, the Peppermint Lounge, Savoy Hall, the Top Hat, the Contrast Club, the Witch's Cauldron, the Hole In The Floor, the Cassie, Maggie May's, the Orrell Park Ballroom and the Kraal Club.

Despite the fact that it has gone into history as the centre of the Merseybeat boom, the Cavern didn't want to know about the local beat groups when Alan Sytner originally opened it in 1957. It was primarily a jazz venue, with support provided by skiffle groups. At one time, beat music was actually banned in the Cavern, and Rory Storm & The Hurricanes were fined for playing 'Whole Lotta Shakin' during a gig there. Eventually, after the Cavern had passed into the hands of ex-accountant Ray McFall, the cellar became a legend. Ray switched to a policy of using beat groups exclusively, not only every evening, but at lunchtime

sessions as well. The Iron Door followed suit, and soon there were groups performing each lunchtime and every night of the week. An entire city was throbbing to the sound of hundreds of groups. The Cavern became the home of the Beatles; the Orrell Park Ballroom (the OPB) was the residence of the Undertakers, Ian & The Zodiacs and Mark Peters & The Silhouettes; the Iron Door played host to the Searchers; the Mardi Gras was the home of the Swinging Blue Jeans, Earl Preston, the Escorts and Cy Tucker – and so on. Despite the fact that the Cavern was winning hands down because of its coup in securing the Beatles, the other venues never lacked for full houses either. Tens of thousands of youngsters were now religiously pouring into the halls and cellar clubs to support their local favourites.

But although the Merseybeat scene had made an incredible impact on the city of Liverpool, no group on Merseyside ever

A very early picture of top Mersey group Gerry & The Pacemakers.

magical, there were often outbreaks of violence. Liverpool has always been a tough city and although the venues mainly served soft drinks, gangs often got tanked up at pubs before going to the dances. There was a constant need for "bouncers", those tank-like figures who could control potential outbreaks of violence. Among them was the Cavern bouncer, Mal Evans, who went on to play his own part in the Beatles' story.

When the Beatles first hit the charts at the end of 1962, the Mersey scene began to change. The great god Mammon raised his head and groups began to toughen up in their attitude to their fellow musicians as they competed for fame and recording contracts. For instance, promoters sometimes received telephone calls cancelling gigs – only to discover later that the calls were hoaxes. The big groups were siphoned away and resettled in London and a lot of heart went out of the scene. But for a couple of glorious years, Liverpool was arguably the rock'n'roll capital of the universe.   (BH)

considered that they would be fortunate enough to make 'the big time'. The prospect of getting a recording contract seemed very remote. The groups were happy to be playing the music they loved and earning a few extra pounds every week, which they usually spent in after-hours haunts such as the Blue Angel and Joe's Cafe, enjoying a drink with fellow musicians. They helped each other and co-operated in an atmosphere of friendly rivalry.

A gig on October 19th, 1961 at the Litherland Town Hall saw a perfect example of this comradeship, with the appearance of the Beatmakers. This was a hybrid band made up of members of the Beatles and Gerry & The Pacemakers. George wore a hood, Gerry wore George's leather outfit, Paul wore a nightie, and Freddie Marsden and Pete Best played one drum each. Numbers performed that evening included 'Whole Lotta Shakin' Goin' On', 'What'd I Say', 'Red Sails In The Sunset' and 'Hit The Road, Jack'. Although the music and atmosphere of the clubs and halls was

The Four Mosts changed their name to the Fourmost and scored several hit singles.

The Cavern and the Casbah

Two Liverpool beat clubs played a vital role in the Beatles' early career

The name of the Beatles will always be linked with the Cavern Club in Liverpool's Mathew Street, where they appeared more than 270 times over a period of two-and-a-half years. Their first lunchtime session was on February 21st 1961, when they were paid £5. Their last was on August 3rd, 1963, for which they received £300.

The Cavern was a bare, uninviting and badly ventilated basement warehouse in a run-down back street in Liverpool's central business district. It consisted of a series of long, narrow, arched, tunnel-like sections, and was completely unsuitable for live shows. Only those in the centre part had a clear view of the stage. The seating in the central tunnel was made up of second-hand wooden chairs sold off by local church halls. The most prestigious spots were in an archway to one side of the stage – special territory defended vigorously by a small bunch of regulars who saved places for their mates. This is where local office workers such as Cilla Black and actress Sue Johnston spent most of their lunch breaks watching their favourites at midday sessions. The Beatles performed at such close quarters to their fans that the girls in the front row could pass their love letters to Paul by hand, or touch John's boots without leaving their seats.

The lighting was primitive and included a string of bare coloured bulbs stretched across the front of the stage. These and the rest of the club's inadequately serviced and improperly protected electrical circuits were totally unreliable, and failed very frequently during shows, because of the condensation that dripped constantly from the brick walls. When this happened to the Beatles, they played on regardless using acoustic guitars. Nicknamed 'the best of cellars' by DJ Bob Wooler, the Cavern actually stank of disinfectant from the toilets and stale onions from the hot dog and hamburger counter. Despite the installation of a makeshift ventilation shaft and a few electric fans, the vile stench and the wet slime still used to linger on visitors' clothing long after they had spent a hot night in the Cavern. Quite clearly, nobody went there for the décor or the ambience of the premises. They filled the place to overflowing solely because the Cavern offered the greatest live music on Merseyside.

Paul remembers the Beatles' sessions at the Cavern Club with affection, saying that each one was more like a party than a formal performance. He recalls how they used to do DJ-style request numbers for anyone who asked for a dedication. At almost every show, Paul would leap off the front of the stage and sing straight into the blushing faces of a few favoured girls, while John would often do his spoof impression of Bill Haley's double-bass player by lying flat on his back on the stage. The boys' battered old amplifiers doubled as refreshment tables, littered with stale sandwich crusts, beer and Coke bottles, or with soup cans at lunchtime if the lads were still getting over a hard day's night. Ciggies lit between numbers were left to smoulder away, and each amplifier had a row of cigarette burns along the top.

Bob Wooler recalled that the first evening performance by the Beatles in March 1961, a month after their initial lunchtime session there, "turned a modest night into a bomb". He added: "It took me a while to persuade them that a Cavern appearance would be a good thing. They were really down in the dumps, and disappointed with other bookings elsewhere. They were even talking about packing it in completely. Eventually I talked them into doing the Cavern's Tuesday guest night." By July, their Cavern following had grown so much that they were given their own Wednesday night residency, in addition to appearing two or three other times each week.

One real highlight in the Beatles' Cavern Club calendar came on June 9th, 1962, when the venue's attendance record was broken. Fans had gathered to welcome the boys back from a trip to Hamburg, and the street outside was crammed end to end with people queuing to get in. It was a hometown version of the outbreak of Beatlemania that swept the whole country in 1963. The boys had to battle through hundreds of Cavernites to reach the club's only entrance, as the place didn't have a stage door. It was a night Bob Wooler would never forget: "Although the national newspapers didn't invent the word Beatlemania until the following year, I would say that the Cavern reception given to John, Paul, George and Pete Best was just as enthusiastic as the nationwide acclaim which was to come. I thought the Beatles might be tired after their strenuous Hamburg season. Instead, they gave one of their finest performances

Paul, Ken Brown and John performing on the opening night of the Casbah.

Paul and John in their leather gear on stage at the Cavern in 1961.

and seemed to draw extra inspiration from the feverish reaction they got from the hundreds of fans who filled the place." After that, whenever the Beatles were billed to play, early morning queues formed outside the Cavern and competition for the front seats grew ever more intense.

The majority of stories about the Beatles on Merseyside have always centred around the Cavern. But as Paul points out in his introduction to Roag & Pete Best's book *The Beatles: The True Beginnings*, "People know about the Cavern, but the Casbah was the place where all that started. We looked upon it as our personal club." During the months before the Casbah opened for business in the summer of 1959, Paul was very impressed by what he heard about this proposed new club, which was to be launched in a labyrinth of rooms underneath a large Victorian house. "I remember coming along this tree-lined avenue in West Derby thinking, very posh! Wow, they've got a club in the basement of this house!" Paul and a few of his friends, including John, volunteered to help out with preparations for the opening, lending a hand with the painting of the walls and ceilings, and transforming the bare, dark rooms into a more comfortable setting for a night club. John painted pot-bellied figures with long scrawny legs on the ceiling of the main dance room, but the

owner, Mona Best, made him get rid of them, so he did his impression of African art instead. Paul painted a rainbow design above the stage area, and George joined them to put stars on the ceiling around the coffee counter.

Just like the Cavern, music was the main attraction at the Casbah. Neither place served alcohol or boasted lavish decorations. Both were located underground in dimly-lit, windowless rooms with minimal ventilation and only the most basic and inexpensive furniture and fittings. But while the Cavern was beneath a warehouse, the Casbah was in a leafy-green suburban residential area of Liverpool that was once the HQ of the West Derby Conservative Club. The driving force behind the Club was drummer Pete Best's mother, Mona. Imagine the joy of any teenage rock'n'roll fan at having a mother who was prepared to open up part of her home as a place where youngsters and musicians from local groups could come to drink coffee and listen to the latest singles. Paul says: "Some grown-ups are different. Mo was one of them. You could go to Mo's place late at night when you'd finished a gig. She understood what kids were going through. I wouldn't mind betting that the reason she wanted to run a coffee bar was to help all the kids who would otherwise have been getting up to bad things."

The very basic poster used to promote the Beatles at the Casbah.

But Mo had another motive for offering her hospitality to the up-and-coming Liverpool groups. She was ambitious for her son, Pete, and she knew that it would help his career as a drummer if he had a chance to meet other local musicians. She recognised that the Casbah would provide a perfect opportunity for networking and might well help Pete to get into one of the more popular groups. She was proved right when Pete was asked to go and play with the Beatles in Hamburg as a direct result of meeting George at the Casbah.

For the first year or so, Mona pumped out the latest rock'n'roll releases on a basic Dansette record player, with the volume

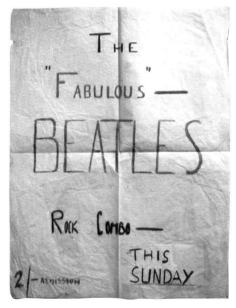

The Beatles at the Cavern in 1961:
George, Pete Best, Paul and John.

turned up as high as it would go. When the Casbah membership list grew, she installed a powerful Wurlitzer jukebox. The head count kept rising, especially at weekends, when members crammed into the club and spilled over into the front and back gardens for the Casbah's live music nights. Early in 1960, the number actually topped 1350 people on one extraordinary occasion.

John, Paul and George became regular visitors at the club. The deal for Pete Best to join the Silver Beatles, as they were known at the time, was clinched when they saw him in action at the Casbah with the Blackjacks. Pete remembers an informal audition at which John said simply: "Do you know 'Ramrod'?" He adds: "We only played about six numbers, so it wasn't too difficult." The group rehearsed like mad at the Casbah with their new drummer for their first Hamburg stint. This meant that Pete didn't have to haul his drumkit around Liverpool in taxi cabs.

Back in Liverpool again when the first Hamburg booking ended, the Beatles appeared at the Casbah in the week before Christmas. Mona billed them as 'The Fabulous Beatles Direct From Hamburg: Admission 1/-" (5p!). Pete recalled the dramatic musical change that had taken place while the group was undergoing its vigorous stage training in the colourful German clubs: "I think it was Paul who kicked off with 'Red Sails In The Sunset' or 'Long Tall

Left: George pictured on the stage of the Cavern Club.

Sally'. We belted it out exactly as we had been doing in Hamburg, and you could physically hear the crowd gasp. We took the roof off the place." According to Roag Best, it was at the Casbah that Brian Epstein and the Beatles signed their original contract – a second one, including amendments, being signed later in January 1962 at Brian's office at NEMS. Roag writes: "The boys had asked Mo to look over the management contract before they signed it." I don't recall hearing this before either from the Beatles themselves when I was their publicist or in any books published since, but I'm quite sure that Eppy would have intensely disliked the idea of having Mona Best breathing down his neck. Maybe her hovering presence in 1962 gave him an extra hidden reason for agreeing so readily to the sacking

of her son from the group that summer.

Mersey Beat editor Bill Harry claims that in some ways, the Casbah has more right to be called the birthplace of the Beatles than the Cavern, which didn't book them until they had already become established locally: "The Casbah played an important part in the career of the Beatles. If it had not opened, there would never have been any Beatles." And it is undeniable that this was the club where the group had its first (albeit brief) weekly residency; where George first met Pete Best, and asked him to join the group; and where Brian met the boys at least once to discuss their management contract.

But if the Casbah loomed so large in the Beatles' legend, why did they virtually ignore the place when telling their story to reporters and authors after they became famous, and why does it get so little attention in the *Anthology*? I think the answer lies in the controversial and unpopular sacking of Pete Best and his replacement by Ringo Starr in August 1962. From that time on, Pete represented a negative facet of the group's history. Most of what had happened at the Casbah belonged to a chapter of their youthful development that the Beatles wanted to forget as much as they could. They couldn't discuss the Casbah at any length in public without referring to Pete and Mona, and that would have forced them to open a can of worms that they preferred to keep permanently closed!   (TB)

John and Paul pictured with one of their rock'n'roll heroes, Gene Vincent.

With the Beatles in Hamburg

Fellow musician Iain Hines recalls his time in Germany with the Beatles

I was lucky enough to be playing with a band called the Jets in Hamburg in the early 60s – sharing the bill, plus plenty of drinks and much more besides, with the Beatles. Looking back at those fantastic, crazy times, one thing becomes clear: everything the Beatles learned in Hamburg showed up in the music they played later in their career.

The drive and sheer energy that took them to the very top has been attributed by some people to the fact that they had to play loud and fast to make themselves heard above the cacophony of the Hamburg club crowds. That's not quite true, though. Nobody ever talked much while the Beatles were on stage at the Star-Club, the Indra, the Kaiserkeller and the Top Ten; their music was far too good for that. The audience danced, for sure, but they saved all the noise until after the number in question had finished — and then all hell broke loose! I suppose that the strange mixture of students, gangsters, prostitutes, tourists, shop girls and office workers were the first real fans the Beatles ever had, apart from the few dozen Liverpudlian girls who used to follow them at the Cavern.

Having to play for anything between six and eight hours at a stretch, non-stop, with only an occasional five-minute 'jukebox' break, was what gave the Beatles their sheer exuberance. They developed terrific

The Beatles larking about on stage in Hamburg.

stamina. The German club owners were hard taskmasters, who wouldn't let the groups slacken up for a second. The name of the game was attracting punters, getting them going with driving music so that they danced their feet off and sweated their guts out and ended up buying gallons of booze – at club prices! All the bands had to create an all-night party atmosphere and it was not uncommon for a tray full of 'Cola-Rum' and 'Prellies' to arrive on stage, "compliments of the management" – anything to keep the music coming hard and fast.

The first time I set eyes on the Beatles in Hamburg was shortly after their arrival. They arrived on the doorstep of the Indra Club in the Grosse Freiheit. Looking back, one thing strikes me now that didn't occur to me at

Stu Sutcliffe and George taking it easy.

the time: the Beatles were endowed with a quiet confidence that almost amounted to arrogance. They knew just where they were going; maybe they didn't know how or when, but they certainly knew they'd get there. They knew they were good and that they had something special, they were that confident, so perhaps they saw Hamburg as a quick apprenticeship.

There were certain weaknesses within the band at that time. I don't wish to appear unkind to Pete Best, but Ringo was, after all, the most driving drummer in the 'Pool at that time, and he hadn't yet joined the Beatles. He was with a different group, Rory Storm & The Hurricanes, and Peter Eckhorn possibly delayed the Beatles' rise to success slightly by taking Ringo over to Hamburg with him to join the Top Ten Club's house band, with Tony Sheridan and Roy Young. But it was clear that the Beatles wanted him – and on his return they got him. All I can say is, poor Pete Best!

All hell broke loose in the Reeperbahn on the day the USS Fiske, officially designated as a 'Destroyer Radar', whatever that means, hit town, or rather dock! I don't know how long the crew had been at sea, but from the way they acted it must have been two thousand years or more, for they came trooping off that ship as though it was on fire. It didn't take long for the Beatles at the Indra, and the Jets at the Top Ten, to make friends with the American sailors.

Naturally all the seedy members of Hamburg's clubland and the owners of the striptease clubs and bars thought that the seamen would head straight for their doors. But when they walked past the Top Ten and the Indra, they couldn't believe the fantastic rock'n'roll sound coming out of the doorways. Furthermore, they couldn't believe

their eyes when they went in and saw that the sounds were not being produced by jukeboxes, but were actually coming from live bands like the Beatles.

Eventually they started to chat to us, and ask for requests. It nearly knocked them back on their heels when they realised that the Jets came from London, and the Beatles from Liverpool! They really couldn't do enough for us. Two guys in particular, Red and Bob from Boston, became fantastic buddies with us all – and how they didn't end up before a court martial, I don't know. They used to get us to meet them at the Harbour, as they came off ship for the evening, and down the gangplank they would come, uniform trousers bulging with goodies, causing them to walk so stiffly that they looked like a couple of Frankenstein's

monsters. We would have a taxi waiting, to take them to the club, where they would start shaking their trousers, and out would pour literally hundreds of Pall Mall Kingsize cigarettes, which were like gold dust to us! In fact, I don't think that they were even on sale in the UK at that time.

Eventually, Red and Bob – and the dear old USS Fiske – had to set sail, and we returned to the business of making music, and making ends meet on 30 marks a day. Paul wanted to play the latest American sounds in his leisure time – Little Richard, Fats Domino, the Everly Brothers and all the others – but he didn't have a record player. However, he and I used to know a couple of

George, John, Pete, Paul and Stu strike a pose in their teddy boy outfits.

The Beatles and one of their German friends during a rare off-duty moment.

obliging barmaids, Liane and Gerda, who took us up to Liane's flat after the Top Ten closed at three in the morning. We had a great time there, playing records on Liane's 'machine' while she and Gerda prepared coffee and Deutsche Bifsteak (alias hamburgers).

A lot has been said about the way the Beatles behaved in Hamburg when they were there . . . but I really don't intend to go into that. We worked hard, and we played hard, and the play sometimes became a bit boisterous. But I should like to say that as far as the story concerning what John is supposed to have done over a balcony is concerned, I never saw him do it, and don't personally believe he ever did. They would certainly dress up in outrageous costumes, and freak about all over the Reeperbahn, but they did nothing harmful.

'Pilzen' in German means 'mushrooms', and 'kopf' means 'head', so it is safe to assume that 'Pilzenkopf' means 'mushroom head' . . . which is how the Beatles were affectionately known in Germany in their early days. Actually, the first person I ever saw with the early Beatles hairstyle, which

was so different to the 'Tony Curtis' they sported when they arrived from Liverpool, was a photographer friend of Astrid Kirchherr, whose name was Peter Penner. The Liverpool lads loved his great new haircut, so when he revealed that it had been done by his friend Astrid, they asked the lovely lady to do theirs, and the famous 'mop-top' style was born.

Any group who have been residents in a club for quite a while come to a point where they feel like a change of scene. Towards the end of 1960, some of the members of my group, the Jets, were getting a trifle restless and Herr Peter Eckhorn got to thinking that it was maybe a good time to get a different band into the Top Ten. So it was with much regret that I had to disband the Jets and put an end to our Top Ten gigs – leaving the way clear for another rising young group to try their luck! In the Beatles at that time, Paul played piano, doubling on rhythm guitar, while Stu Sutcliffe played bass, and Pete Best drums. The members of the Jets who didn't really want to go home were myself, our bassist Colin Milander, and singer Tony Sheridan. For Colin, there was no chance at all of playing with the Beatles, as one very seldom sees two bass players in one band, but Tony was so popular with the Hamburg crowd that Peter Eckhorn asked him to stay

anyhow. After a session the two bands shared at the Top Ten, Paul asked me if I would play piano with the Beatles, leaving him free to concentrate on rhythm and vocals with John, but by then I had got used to the idea of going home for a while. So the Beatles auditioned at the Top Ten on the night the Jets were due to finish, with Paul doing a Little Richard act at the piano, then changing to guitar, and doing some fantastic vocal harmony numbers with the others. Needless to say, they passed their audition with flying colours! However, playing at the Top Ten before their previous contract had ended eventually proved to be their undoing.

The next day, young Colin Milander, heartbroken at having to go home to the UK and leave behind his German sweetheart, Antje, begged me to stop in Hamburg with him, and play as a duo at a very small restaurant called the Fleurs Schanke. I agreed, we went to an audition, and we passed. So we were in extremely high spirits when we returned to the Top Ten, where the Beatles were already in full swing with Tony Sheridan. Tony and Paul invited me up on stage, and we had one of the wildest sessions I have ever taken part in – doing all the old favourites, including a 70-minute version of the Ray Charles classic, 'What'd I Say'. If only I'd taped it!   (IH)

Astrid Kirchherr

An interview with the photographer and Hamburg friend of the Beatles

Every Beatles fan worth his salt knows Astrid Kirchherr. In the early 1960s, as a fashion-conscious Hamburg photographer, she was not only the fiancée of fifth Beatle Stuart Sutcliffe, but the style guru who invented the Beatles' world-beating 'mop-top' hairstyle and who dressed them in the collarless jackets which later symbolised a new era for British pop music. Right? Wrong! According to Astrid, these supposed facts are gross distortions of the truth.

"That stupid Beatles haircut," she exclaims at the beginning of our interview. "That's still going on and on! I didn't invent that style. It's a complete misinterpretation. The style was already there. All my friends from art school were wearing it. We got all our influences from France. OK, they may have worn it shorter, but even so . . . And I only cut Stuart's and George's hair. I never touched Paul's and the others'. But people just don't listen, they keep saying that I invented the Beatles' hairstyle. And that drives me crazy. Was I just sitting there telling them what to wear? It's absolute rubbish!" She goes on to explain the extent of her influence over the Beatles' style. "We inspired one another," she says. "What they gave to me in return was so much. And I still have got it all here, inside. They changed my life completely. They gave me this wonderful friendship. That's what I mean by people misinterpreting me. I can talk and talk until my voice is gone, and still they write in their papers that I did all the clothes for the Beatles. People just make a big deal out of it.

"I admit they got the idea for the collarless jacket from me," concedes Astrid. "I had one, and Stuart wanted it. So I made one for him, and when he went to the Top Ten wearing it, John would say, 'Hey, have you got your mum's jacket on?' But they were all like little kids. They didn't have any money and soon they'd all be saying, 'I want one of those'. I said, 'They take ages to make', and they said, 'So what, you're our mate!' So I made the jackets for them, because I loved them."

Astrid's romance with Stu Sutcliffe formed the basis for the hit movie Backbeat.

"All this fuss about Paul and Stuart not having a very nice relationship," she says, "I know that if I'd had to play with Stuart, I would have gone crazy! I think Paul was very brave, putting up with Stuart for so long. He never practised. Never! But John would say, 'Oh he looks rock'n'roll, that's enough!' Whenever Stuart wanted to talk to me, he would just hand his bass guitar to Paul, and Paul would take over. Or if Paul was on the piano, Stuart would give the bass to Klaus Voormann, and Klaus would play with the Beatles. This would usually be in the early morning when there was only about ten people in the club. Klaus would just sit on a table playing the bass. And they had fun!" Ringo wasn't with the band then, of course, so did she know Ringo? "Yes, I knew Ringo when he played in Rory Storm's band." What about Pete Best? "Pete was so lovely. I loved Pete." Did she have any contact with him after he left the group? "No. But he was always very quiet and liked to be by himself, and I respected that, and the others did too." Didn't she think that the film *Backbeat* paints Pete in rather a bad light, though? "No, I thought it was great. That's how he was. He never talked!"

Astrid came to terms with Stuart Sutcliffe's death a long time ago, and she is still very grateful to the remaining Beatles for their continuing support. "Of course it was a tragedy, and it was initially very hard for me. I was terribly sad and lonely, but you can't just leave it like that, because I had the love I received from my friends. I always see the wonderful side of life. I have the Beatles, these great friends who helped me get over Stuart, and I have my German friends, including Klaus, and my mother. It means so much when you've got friends. That's all that counts." (AD)

Brian Epstein

More than anyone, claims Tony Barrow, 'Eppy' deserved the title of 'the fifth Beatle'

There were no showbusiness connections in Brian Epstein's family background. His family owned a string of furniture stores in Liverpool, and they firmly expected Brian to follow his father into the business. But Brian had a restless sense of ambition that led him to pursue a number of different avenues – until he discovered the Beatles, and found the direction that he had been looking for all his life. At school, he had always shown a lot of interest in the stage, and in 1956, when he was 22, he enrolled at the Royal Academy of Dramatic Art, in the hope that he might be able to forge a career as a professional actor. But he had only been there three terms when his father persuaded him to leave.

A new branch of the family company, NEMS (North End Music Stores), was opening in the centre of Liverpool, and the rather reluctant Brian was put in charge of the record department, handling both classical and pop releases.

Between 1957 and 1962, Brian swallowed his other ambitions and became an exceptionally enthusiastic record retailer. He introduced his own NEMS Top 20 charts to stimulate business. What's more, he attempted to cater for specialist tastes by diligently ordering single copies of records that were not held in stock. He actually encouraged people to ask for stuff that was not amongst the best-sellers. It was one such request, now chronicled as a landmark of pop history, which led Brian to Liverpool's Cavern Club cellar and hence to the Beatles in 1961.

Why did Brian sign the Beatles? A variety of reasons have been advanced. Certainly the larger-than-life magnetism of John Lennon's potent personality played a large part in the matter. If Brian had not been so greatly attracted by Lennon the man and the musician, NEMS might not have gone into the management business at all. At the same time, he fancied getting closer to showbusiness than record retailing was ever likely to take him. Like so many other successful 'backstagers', Epstein was a frustrated performer who was prepared to settle for second best by bathing in a little reflected glory. Brian always claimed that he knew from the beginning that there was going to be an awful lot of glory about as far as the Beatles were concerned. "As big as Elvis" was his confident cry at one of the earliest meetings I had with him. This had been modified to "bigger than Elvis" even before 'Please Please Me' gave the Beatles their first chart-topper!

The very fact that Brian approached the business as a novice played a key role in his establishment as Britain's best-known pop entrepreneur. As a newcomer to the London showbiz scene, he tackled everything in his own way instead of accepting any status quo situations. He was one of the first managers to recognise the value of encircling his

Brian and the Beatles going through immigration at Le Bourget Airport in 1964.

artists with all the expert guidance that they could possibly require. Instead of relying upon the freelance services of outsiders, he brought experts into NEMS on a full-time basis. Apart from setting up my side of things to take care of publicity, he hired his own producer/director to handle the actual staging of NEMS presentations and to groom each group in stagecraft.

Towards the end of 1962, between the release of 'Love Me Do' and 'Please Please Me', Brian decided to put a PR consultant on the payroll. Billy J. Kramer & the Dakotas and Gerry & the Pacemakers had already been signed up, as Brian realised that the depth of talent in Liverpool went far beyond the Beatles, and several other Merseysiders, like the Big Three, the Fourmost, Tommy Quickly and Brian's only songstress, Cilla Black, were anxious to join his stable. At that time, I valued the security of my regular job as a sleevenote writer with Decca Records, so I turned down Brian's

first offer of a full-time job at NEMS. A little later he returned with a richly improved offer, which finally persuaded me to leave my Decca desk. My parents urged me to be very cautious. They reckoned I was living a bit dangerously even to consider forsaking the warm protection of a widely respected firm like Decca Records to work for some Liverpudlian record retailer who had signed up a pop group or two. It was amusing to watch history repeating itself about five years later, when I resigned from NEMS to launch my own PR company. Again, my parents warned me against acting in haste. Was I really doing the right thing to abandon an excellent organisation like NEMS for the total insecurity of my own independent business?

That was the measure of public esteem in which NEMS Enterprises was held during the second half of the 60s. Brian's efforts, plus the extraordinary international interest shown in his roster of acts, had raised the

Brian talking to Paul and George backstage in Brighton in 1964.

NEMS name from nothing to the highest level of professional acceptance within the entertainment industry.

One of my first – and totally misguided – bits of advice to Brian concerned the group's name. "It's going to be a hell of a difficult job to sell a name like Beatles," I told him. "They need more than that. They need a lead name. Think of Cliff Richard & the Shadows, and Brian Poole & the Tremeloes. Why don't you talk to the lads about calling themselves John Lennon & the Beatles, or Paul McCartney & the Beatles?" I made this suggestion before I'd met the four Beatles or watched them in action on stage.

Of course, Brian was quite adamant that the name should stay as it was. He drew attention to the fact that the group was

Ringo puts his feet up as he chats to a journalist in his manager's office.

the negotiations before agreeing to anything. This was interpreted by the cigar holders as a sign of great strength and acute business acumen. In fact, Brian simply wanted to check out the figures with someone he could trust – like lawyer David Jacobs, who offered him substantial guidance in contractual and financial matters. By the time Brian came to his next meeting, better offers were already being thrust under his nose. This helped Brian to achieve some truly remarkable deals for the Beatles.

Brian seldom used the power of the Beatles to promote other acts. But he did persuade John and Paul fairly forcefully to provide songs for his other artists. Mostly these were pieces of material that the group had discarded as unsuitable for their own use. There were very few occasions when anyone got a custom-penned Lennon & McCartney original. The exceptions included Paul's made-to-measure numbers for Peter & Gordon, and 'Step Inside Love' for Cilla Black.

Brian was very conscious of the jealousy generated among the Beatles by the success of the other NEMS acts. Despite the superficial friendliness between all the Liverpool groups, there was a fierce rivalry between them. Because they were by far the most successful, and also the first to be signed up, the Beatles expected priority attention from Brian at all times. But he tried to be everywhere at once, attending every important function involving his artists. For the first couple of years, he kept up his direct and personal supervision of every act by sheer hard work. He was very bad at delegating, but some of NEMS' failures marked occasions when Brian found himself forced into delegation situations against his better judgement.

Brian was often called 'the fifth Beatle' – and he deserved the title more than anyone – but he was never one of the lads. As their personal manager, he accompanied John, Paul, George and Ringo around the world all through the touring years between 1963 and 1966. Yet they invariably went their own separate ways during their leisure hours. Vastly different things amused them. Their ideas of personal ecstasy were poles apart. But what they did share from the very start was a steadfast determination that the Beatles would be money-spinning monarchs of the pop industry. I don't think they ever knew or fully appreciated exactly what he did on their behalf. They cared (each to a

already locally famous as the Beatles, even in the unlikely event that either John or Paul had been willing to be billed as the frontman of the group. Although he was thoroughly versed in the ways of running a retail operation, Brian had much to learn about entrepreneurial tactics within showbusiness. The

swift success of the Beatles quickly swept him into top-level negotiating, where he was bartering the group's services with some of the fattest and longest cigars in the business. Key agents and bookers with decades of know-how under their braces would throw figures at Brian that would have made the average manager jump for joy. But Brian would refuse to do a deal at most initial meetings, preferring to go away and sleep on varying extent) about the outcome of their labours in terms of cash gained and comforts provided, but they were not greatly interested in business affairs. When they did start delving into that area after his death, their lack of business talent became abundantly obvious.

On the other hand, Brian was neither a musician nor a composer, never even writing a B-side or picking up an instrument. So in creative affairs, the fifth Beatle was far from close to the four moptops. He knew he could rely upon his group to produce highly commercial new songs, and to turn them into best-sellers in the recording studio. He didn't advise, or push, or criticise, in areas where he knew he would be out of his depth.

As time went by, there were two levels of relationship between the Beatles and Brian. One was a 'group and manager' thing, and it was very solid. The group turned down the advances of other managers whatever carrots were dangled. There was no way they wanted to split from Brian. The other was the more flexible 'one to one' relationship between Brian and each Beatle. A temporary falling-out on that level never threatened the invincible 'group and manager' bond.

On a 'one to one' basis, the closest friendship that developed was between John and Brian. Some witnesses have been confused about this, because John shouted at Brian quite a lot in the early days, and later on whenever an on-tour crisis lit his blue touchpaper. Those who saw such fury translated it as dislike, even hatred. But it was not. John would vent his feelings (and those of the others) without pulling any verbal punches. That was the way he was made. Yet he had a much less violent side, a quieter, almost poetic half which was the true John Lennon when he wasn't hurt or annoyed or afraid. Partly because John had appeared to be the group's leader and spokesman from the beginning, Brian used to sound out the Beatles via John. He'd try to assess group reactions to policy changes by discussing them with John before having more formal talks with the group as a whole. If Brian got John on his side at that stage, he could be sure his opinions would prevail generally.

Ringo was the least complicated of the four. He was also by far the least involved in policy-making discussions. This stemmed jointly from the fact that he was the last to become a Beatle, and the fact that his musical talent was less complex. Ringo and Brian were never really close, although Ringo was an excellent social companion, a very witty drinking partner, and a wise observer of human nature generally.

George was always a thoroughly genuine guy, sincere in his beliefs and refreshingly ordinary in his attitudes. Although they could not find common ground on musical matters, he and Brian talked intelligently about the Beatles' finances. Later on, George was the first one to fight Brian over touring, which he thought should end. Brian would have taken the Beatles round the world's largest concert venues for several more years if George and the others had not stopped him in 1966.

Paul approved of Brian's suave social sophistication. The two shared playboy aspirations of one sort or another. Brian could also rely upon Paul to play the role of the group's genial ambassador. He always knew that he could introduce Paul to somebody very important and rely on the charm being turned on generously without any prodding.

If I had been asked to predict a life expectancy for Brian at any time during our working relationship, I might well have said he would be dead within five years. He lived at a frighteningly furious pace all through the middle 60s, and I honestly felt that his health must suffer in the end. I did not think he could avoid some sort of serious breakdown. But I do not believe that Brian intended to kill himself. I believe that his untimely death, several weeks before he was due to celebrate his 33rd birthday, was a tragic accident. When he died, there were those who felt that the challenge of further ambition had left Brian now that the touring days were over. On the contrary, I would say that Brian was finding fresh fields to explore, and new segments of the entertainment world to conquer. But sadly all that promise was cut short when he was found dead in the bedroom of his luxurious Chapel Street house over the August Bank Holiday weekend in 1967.   (TB)

Brian examines possible artwork for the next American Beatles LP in 1966.

Decca and EMI

It was only Brian's constant pushing that won the Beatles a recording contract in 1962

In January 1962, the Beatles were auditioned and turned down by Decca Records. The man who conducted their New Year's Day test session and eventually decided to sign up Brian Poole & the Tremeloes instead of the Beatles was Mike Smith, a young newcomer to Decca's pop production team.

The boss of Decca's A&R (Artists & Repertoire) Department in control of the label's pop output back then was Dick Rowe, the man often cast by authors and journalists as the pantomine-style villain in the Beatles' scenario. He's been made to carry the can for rejecting the group in the wake of their Decca audition. Rowe was certainly partly responsible, but it was Mike Smith who made the actual decision. Shortly before Christmas 1961, Decca's A&R managers began to hear about the Beatles from several different sources. I was working for

Decca as an LP and EP sleevenote writer at the time, but I was also writing a weekly column called 'Off The Record' for the *Liverpool Echo*, which had caught the eye of local record retailer Brian Epstein. A few days before the Beatles signed their management deal with him, Brian paid me a visit at Decca to gain my support. I told the marketing department that one of the company's best customers in the North West, Brian Epstein of NEMS , was trying to get a recording contract for a group of his. I told them: "He's promising to buy at least 5000 copies of their first release (worth around £1000 to Decca), to sell in his own shops!"

Brian had also been pestering Decca's sales people in Liverpool about the Beatles, so the pressure was on for someone from their A&R Department to audition the Beatles. Eventually Dick Rowe was pushed into taking notice, although he was

unwilling to make a personal trip to Liverpool just before the Christmas break. Instead, he sent his young assistant, Mike Smith, to see what was happening at Liverpool's bustling Cavern Club.

Mike recalls: "Someone at Decca House had to show interest because Epstein ran NEMS, which was an important account for the sales people. I went to Liverpool on December 13th and met with Brian, who took me for a splendid dinner. Then we headed for the Cavern. I was very excited when I saw the Beatles on stage, and on the strength of that and the reaction from their local fans I had no hesitation in telling Brian that we'd fix an audition as soon as possible."

Decca A&R man Mike Smith (centre), with bandleaders Edmundo Ros and Ted Heath next to him and arrangers Bob Sharples and Johnny Pearson.

Dick Rowe was away from his office over the Christmas and New Year period so he gave Mike a free hand to check out new acts in his absence. When Neil Aspinall saw the state of the weather that New Year's Eve, I'm sure he regretted agreeing to drive the Beatles from Liverpool to London for their audition at Decca's West Hampstead studios. Sub-zero temperatures had covered Merseyside with a thick white carpet of frost and re-frozen the residue of the previous week's snow. At this time, the Beatles didn't have a full-time roadie let alone a regular chauffeur. Most of their bookings were in and around Merseyside and the boys either drove themselves or relied on friends who had cars. Breakdowns sometimes delayed their arrival at venues, a habit that 'Eppy' vowed to stamp out by fixing them up with more reliable transport and a roadie. Meanwhile he made sure that Neil rented a decent van for the round-trip to the recording test: "Decca will expect punctuality and we must not get off on the wrong foot by earning black marks."

The 200-mile journey proved to be a 10-hour nightmare, twice as long as the trip would take an average driver today even in bad weather. Somewhere near Wolverhampton in the Midlands, less than halfway to London, 'Nel' and the Beatles hit a blizzard that made driving conditions horrendous. Huddled among their equipment, the boys did their best to stop guitar cases and amps from bashing into each other as the van slithered about in the driving snow. Imagining 'Eppy' reclining comfortably in a well-heated First Class train compartment with a glass of Scotch in his hand only served to intensify the boys' growing disgruntlement. They knew their manager could look forward to a fine dinner and a

good night's rest at the home of some Epstein family relatives while they stayed in cheap digs near Russell Square. Finally, having been mis-directed more than once by uninterested and/or inebriated pedestrians when they lost their way in north London, the Beatles arrived at the Royal Hotel in Woburn Place, weary and very hungry. Their attempts to find somewhere nearby to eat with prices that would fit their limited budget ended disastrously – they couldn't even afford the soup let alone a main course – so eventually they consoled themselves with single measures of Scotch and Coke instead. According to Neil Aspinall, they walked to Trafalgar Square and "saw all the New Year's Eve drunks falling in the fountains". It was a memorable New Year's Eve for all the wrong reasons.

Writing down his version of the audition day's events later on, Brian recalled: "At 11am on January 1st we arrived at Decca in a bleak wind with snow and ice afoot. Mike Smith was late and we were pretty annoyed about the delay. We were being treated as people who didn't matter." Seething inwardly but keeping a weak smile fixed on his face, 'Eppy' told the Beatles: "I'm sure it's not Mike's fault, he'll be stuck somewhere in this appalling weather on his way in." Looking back now, Mike laughs at this suggestion. "I was always late for everything so it was no different that morning except that most probably I was well hung over from New Year's Eve." The audition was a big disappointment to Mike compared to the standard of performance he'd heard in

Dick Rowe, Decca's head of A&R in 1962, who later signed up the Rolling Stones.

Brian Poole & the Tremeloes were given a Decca contract instead of the Beatles.

Liverpool. "Maybe I should have trusted my instincts and signed them on the strength of their stage show. In the studio they were not good and their personalities didn't come across. Maybe they were in awe of the situation." Mike let the boys off gently and made some kind noises to Brian before they left West Hampstead.

Back at Decca House the next day, I asked Mike to sum up the audition session so that I could report on it for my one million-plus *Liverpool Echo* readers. He was sufficiently enthusiastic for me to write: "Decca disc producer Mike Smith tells me that he thinks the Beatles are great. He has a continuous tape of their audition performances that runs for over 30 minutes and he is convinced that his label will be able to put the Beatles to good use." The truth was that Mike's hands were tied until Dick Rowe returned to London. He could recommend, but he couldn't actually sign up fresh talent without specific authority from above – something that Dick confirmed to Johnny Dean during a conversation at the start of 1964. Mike remembers: "As soon as I was able to pin Dick down at his desk I took my audition tapes to Decca House. I also had to take a tape machine from the studios because, believe it or not, there wasn't one in Dick's office!" According to Mike, Rowe gave him a hard time: "From the acts I'd seen while Dick was away, I wanted the Beatles AND Brian Poole & the Tremeloes but he said I couldn't have both. He hadn't done either of the auditions but he was the guv'nor, I was very much his junior."

In the 60s, the building in the centre housed Decca's recording studio in West Hampstead.

Most remarkable is Mike Smith's claim that Dick Rowe did not even want him to play the audition tapes so he could weigh up the merits of the two groups. Mike told me: "I hoped he'd say which of the two sounded better to his experienced ears, but he didn't express any opinion. It was simply a numerical thing, like a child being told he can have one sweetie but not two. He left the decision to me. It was crazy for Dick to suggest afterwards that either Brian Poole & the Tremeloes or the Beatles sounded like the Shadows – who didn't even sing for a start! I believe Dick was simply pulling rank on

me, proving his superiority in terms of his status at Decca." The root cause for the Beatles' failure to gain a Decca contract was the unexpectedly poor quality of their New Year's Day performance. They were simply not in the mood to give of their best and the strength of their showmanship did not come across in the recordings. Their singing lacked power and conviction, the playing was loose and undisciplined, maybe needing a heftier backbeat to drive it along. They raced through their songs in an hour and felt under pressure to finish as soon as possible.

Mike believes that the Beatles' bad choice of original material – 'Love Of The Loved', 'Like Dreamers Do' and 'Hello Little Girl' – contributed to their downfall. He says now: "Of course I kicked a lot of furniture in the year or two afterwards when the Beatles started to happen. Meanwhile Dick Rowe would tease me by saying stuff like 'I've just spent an hour with the Chairman but I still haven't told him it was you who turned down the Beatles'. If I had signed the Beatles, without question it would have been to exploit the songwriting of Lennon & McCartney. At that time the song was always paramount. But I liked only one of the three original songs they did for me. I would like to have auditioned the group when they had a better range of songs to offer, but NOT after they fired Pete Best. In my humble opinion he was a better drummer than Ringo!"   (TB)

Mike Smith says that most of the criticism of himself and Dick Rowe was unfair.

THE LONG ROAD FROM DECCA TO EMI

Once he'd recovered from Decca's decision, Brian picked himself up and started to pursue every other record company in London. He put all the pressure he could on their Northern sales offices, and every so often he would get his tapes and discs together and disappear to London to see somebody. He tried every major company, but the answer was always the same. EMI were not interested, Les Cox of Pye refused an audition, Philips just didn't want to know, and Oriole could not be bothered. In the end, Brian even considered the Woolworths label Embassy, which produced a series of cheap copies of recent Top 20 hits for their stores. But Embassy never actually signed anyone up, so even they wouldn't take his boys.

During one of his many visits to London in 1962, Brian began to wonder if it would be better to leave a record rather than a tape at the record companies. As he walked along Oxford Street, he stopped at HMV's shop near Bond Street tube station. A sign in the window offered to turn tapes into discs. Brian went in, and waited for his tapes to be copied onto black acetates. The engineer was immediately impressed by the quality of the Beatles' audition tapes, probably because most of his customers brought in very poor recordings for him to work on. When he heard some unfamiliar songs, he asked Brian where they came from. On learning that they had been written by the group who made the tape, he offered to ring

Syd Colman of publishers Ardmore & Beechwood, who had offices in the same building. Brian was pleased to accept any help at all. At long last he could play his tapes to someone who was actually prepared to listen to them all the way through. Syd Colman was always on the lookout for new songs, so he asked if the group had a recording contract. When he found that they hadn't, he offered to try and interest one of EMI's A&R men in the Beatles, as his publishing company was a subsidiary of EMI.

His assistant Kim Bennett told me a few months later that Syd went through the recording managers to work out who would be best to approach. "Let's see," he said. "Norrie Paramor's got the Shadows, Wally Ridley's also got a group and so has Norman Newell. The only one who hasn't is George Martin. I'll give him a ring." George wasn't very keen to listen to the tape or meet Brian Epstein, and it took a lot of persuasion from Syd Colman before he agreed to give Brian an appointment. When George finally met Brian he wasn't terribly impressed with the Decca tape at first, but he did agree to audition the group. Over the next few months, Brian worked very hard to maintain George Martin's interest in the Beatles. He had naturally hoped that the meeting would quickly result in an audition, followed by a recording session and a record release. Eventually a combination of great persistence by Brian, coupled with pressure exerted through EMI's salesmen, culminating in a threat by Brian not to buy any more records from EMI Manchester, did the trick. Alistair Taylor remembered one occasion when Brian was reduced to tears by his inability to get things moving.

Only George Martin knows exactly why it took from May to September before he agreed to give the Beatles a recording contract. He certainly didn't think much of John and Paul's songs at first, otherwise he wouldn't have tried to get them to record 'How Do You Do It'. I also find it very hard to believe that George Harrison's remark about George Martin's tie at the first audition would have attracted him to the group. There were only a small number of all-powerful A&R men in 1962 and they alone could give the magic recording contracts to new groups and singers. They were very much the gods of the recording world. Certainly they didn't expect to make a world-shaking discovery in Liverpool. They knew America was the fount of all great new things in pop and all they hoped for at the

most was another Cliff Richard & the Shadows. To them, the Beatles were just another unimportant group with an inexperienced manager, who was unfortunately able to exert a bit of pressure on them from the sales side – not the sort of situation that would have endeared a new group to any A&R manager. But there was one other indication of what EMI and George Martin thought of 'Love Me Do' when it was first released.

The company had a plugging system. If you got the top plug – I think it was called A2, and was only awarded to stars like Cliff Richard and Frank Ifield after they had had a big hit – your new record would receive up to seven plays a week on EMI's own Radio Luxembourg show, at a time when that station was a very powerful plugging medium for pop singles. The lowest plug, B2, actually meant no plugs at all. Kim

Bennett insists that this is what the Beatles were given for 'Love Me Do' – meaning they weren't promoted regularly on EMI's Luxembourg show.

No one can say what would have happened if Brian had given up the struggle after two or three months of slogging around the record companies with nothing to show for it. Would the Beatles have stayed together? Would another, more influential manager have stepped in? Would Brian have used his money to make some more recordings? No one will ever know. Certainly the persistence and effort he put into selling the Beatles was vital, even though it was actually quite foreign to his rather shy nature, and it must earn him the thanks of every person who admires the Beatles' music today. (JD)

George Martin supervising the recording of 'Love Me Do' in 1962.

1962

LOVE ME DO HITS THE CHARTS

Despite very little national publicity, 'Love Me Do' actually made the singles chart for the first time this month. In *NME* it entered the charts at No. 27, while it turned up in *Melody Maker* at No. 48. NME ran a small feature about the Beatles to celebrate their success, under the heading: "Liverpool's Beatles Wrote Their Own Hit". But only one national music paper bothered to review 'Love Me Do' in their new release column. The October 6th edition of *Disc* rated the single as "ordinary" and said: "The Beatles sound rather like the Everlys or the Brooks according to whose side you're on. But in 'Love Me Do' they have got a deceptively simple beater which could grow on you. Harmonica backing. 'P.S. I Love You' weaves a little Latin into itself as the boys sing a letter ballad of everyday sentiments."

The last few weeks have seen the Beatles featured in all of the music papers. Brian has also started advertising the group as available for bookings in the *New Musical Express*, while the same paper now carries a national advert for the Beatles' Fan Club. Both are signs that things are definitely looking up for the Beatles all over the country! (October 1962)

NEXT STOP – HAMBURG!

Before long, the Beatles will be on their way to Hamburg for another season at the Star-Club, where they've already become firm favourites. Ringo is no stranger to the Star-Club, as he often used to play there with his previous group, Rory Storm & the Hurricanes. (October 1962)

EXHAUSTED!

Reporter Jean Carol spoke to the boys just 12 hours after they returned from Hamburg. "We're very tired," said John, leading the magazine to print the interview under the heading "Beatles Find Showbiz Isn't All Fun"! The trip had its consolations, however: "This time they put the red carpet out for us because our record was beginning to hit the charts." George confirmed the rumours about the boys' new single: "We've got a stack of stuff like 'Love Me Do' and our next disc may be a remake of the demo we first cut for Parlophone. It's called 'Please Please Me' but our manager, Brian Epstein, is not too keen on the title so we may change it." Paul chipped in with a word about the Beatles' sessions: "You know they say that Ray Charles can record a number in one take. That's not us. Ours start at about 7am and don't finish until a whole day later!" (November 1962)

RADIO MIMING

The Beatles turned up at a small EMI studio in Manchester Square in London to record a programme in the EMI-sponsored *Friday Spectacular Show* on Radio Luxembourg. In fact, "record" isn't really the right word, for all the Beatles did was mime to both sides of their 'Love Me Do' single before an invited audience. If you listened to the show at home, you'd just have heard exactly the same versions of the songs as the Parlophone single, which I'm sure you all bought a long time ago! (November 1962)

RICHARD JOINS FAN CLUB

In Hamburg, where the Beatles spent the first two weeks of November, they've been playing their usual exhausting schedule at the Star-Club — several hours every night, with only short breaks for refreshments and a rest! They shared the Star-Club bill with rock'n'roller Little Richard, who says that the more he sees of the Beatles, the more he likes them. He's going to spread the word when he gets home to the States, so maybe the biggest record market in the world may get a taste of the Beatles before too long. (November 1962)

One of the first publicity photographs of the Beatles' taken in 1962.

OFF-BEAT TEAM

Since 'Love Me Do' made the Top Thirty at the end of last month, the Beatles have received a lot of coverage in the music press. In *New Record Mirror*, Norman Jopling introduced the boys to his readers, describing them as "a very off-beat team"! The interview revealed a few secrets about the Beatles. Paul explained how they were always sure of a great reception on their dates outside their hometown: "When we played outside Liverpool, we would often hire a couple of coaches and take an audience with us!" Paul also said how much the Beatles enjoyed playing at the Cavern: "But surprisingly, groups from outside Liverpool don't like it. It's small and cramped but we're at home there. We play the frantic beat numbers, and the R&B stuff, like 'Some Other Guy' and 'If You Gotta Make A Fool Of Somebody'. We improvise on the original thing — not to improve it but because we can't get the sound of the disc. Once we've performed it, it's kept in that same form. We won't change it at all."

The Beatles apparently reckon that 'Please Please Me' is the most likely choice for their next single. Jopling says: "It's a more catchy number than 'Love Me Do' which, incidentally, was first performed by the boys in the Buddy Holly style. And if their new disc is anything like the first by this high-class rock team, it will certainly please us." Let's hope he's right! (November 1962)

LIVE CAVERN LP?

The boys are due to record their first LP next month. Their recording manager, George Martin, may tape the record during a live session in Liverpool's Cavern Club. Then they're off for their fifth visit to Hamburg, where they'll be staying over Christmas. (November 1962)

PLEASE PLEASED THEM

Everyone at the Beatles' second EMI recording session was delighted with the way that John and Paul's 'Please Please Me' came out. The boys actually recorded a rough version of the song at the 'Love Me Do' sessions, but George Martin said that it sounded too much like Roy Orbison, so they worked out a different arrangement.

The Beatles recorded three more songs as well. 'How Do You Do It' was a Mitch Murray composition which the boys tried out in September, but apparently they weren't too happy with the results on either occasion. Two more Lennon/McCartney songs were taped at the same time: 'Ask Me Why', a ballad which the boys have been including in their set for several months, and 'Tip Of My Tongue', a bouncy uptempo number which John and Paul wrote more than a year ago. They're in no danger of running out of material, however, as they already have more than one hundred original songs stockpiled, and more are being written all the time! (November 1962)

BEATLES FOR HELEN?

Rumours in London suggest that the Beatles are set to join Helen Shapiro on her British tour early in the New Year. Helen, whose latest single on Columbia, 'Keep Away From Other Girls', is being outpaced in the charts by 'Love Me Do' at the moment, is apparently expected to tour Britain in three stages, at the start of February, the end of February and in mid-March. It is thought that the Beatles will take part in at least two parts of Helen's tour. Negotiations are also under way with the promoters of the forthcoming Tommy Roe British tour, for which the Beatles are again being considered as a support act. (November 1962)

TELEVISING THE BEATLES

Proof, if any were needed, that the Beatles are really starting to make an impression on the pop world is provided by their recent TV appearances. They have already appeared on Granada TV's *People And Places* show twice, including a memorable film from the Cavern Club soon after Ringo joined the group. But other local TV companies have also featured the Beatles in recent weeks. TWW's *Discs-A-Go-Go* show gave the boys a chance to plug 'Love Me Do' on December 3rd, while the next day AR-TV's *Tuesday Programme* also featured the group. But the best news of all is that the Beatles are set for their first appearance on ATV's very popular *Thank Your Lucky Stars* show on January 12th — just as 'Please Please Me' will be appearing in the shops. They are also pencilled in for Brian Matthew's popular radio show *Saturday Club* at the end of the month. (December 1962)

STILL CLIMBING

'Love Me Do' is still creeping slowly up the charts all the time. It has actually been around in the various charts printed by the pop papers for almost three months now. In *Melody Maker* the boys' single is still hovering in the lower reaches of the Top Thirty, having peaked at No. 22 on (appropriately enough) December 22nd. *Record Mirror* had the Beatles at No. 17 last week, the highest position they've reached in any of the national charts so far.

American star Roy Orbison.

The strange exception to all this chart activity is the *New Musical Express*, where 'Love Me Do' came in at No. 27 at the end of October and promptly disappeared. Every other music paper reports that the single started climbing again at the end of November, but so far the *NME* chart compilers have managed to overlook the Beatles' steady sales over the last few weeks. Let's hope that 'Please Please Me' sells so well that they won't be able to ignore it! (December 1962)

TAPED AGAIN

Back in Hamburg, the Beatles are sharing the bill at the Star-Club with the top American instrumental outfit, Johnny and the Hurricanes. Also in Hamburg at the moment are Liverpool's Kingsize Taylor and the Dominoes, and Cliff Bennett and the Rebel Rousers. Apparently Adrian Barber has made reel-to-reel tape recordings of all the bands playing at the Star-Club. It will be interesting to compare the results with the live recordings that George Martin is planning to make at the Cavern for the Beatles' first album! (December 1962)

CAMPAIGN BEGINS

The promotional campaign for the Beatles' second single has already begun. The decision to couple 'Please Please Me' with 'Ask Me Why' as the follow-up to 'Love Me Do' was taken last month, and since then EMI have been preparing for the official release date of January 11th. Around 300 white label copies have already been sent out to disc jockeys and journalists, and there has been an incredible response from everyone who has heard one of these initial pressings. (December 1962)

Love Me Do

Did Brian Epstein buy the Beatles' first record into the charts?

The rumour that Brian Epstein surreptitiously helped the Beatles into the UK pop charts in 1962 by creating bogus record sales for their debut single, 'Love Me Do', has been raised persistently down the years. The boys always stoutly denied that any skullduggery went on, but as one journalist remarked at the time: "Maybe Brian didn't tell them". In an interview, John emphatically dismissed the suggestion that it had taken unfair hype to get 'Love Me Do' into the charts: "Everyone thought it was a fiddle because our manager's stores ordered loads of records and everybody down south said they were being bought by Brian himself. But it wasn't true."

Ever since the release of the record in October 1962, however, this question has gone unanswered. Did the group's personal manager use his position as the boss of Liverpool's NEMS store to buy up thousands of copies of 'Love Me Do'? Or did the fans give the Beatles' first single a perfectly legitimate chart entry by purchasing it simply because they liked it? The rumour that emerged was that 'Eppy' ordered a total of 10,000 copies of 'Love Me Do' to make quite sure that the Beatles' first release enjoyed reasonable sales.

In the autumn of 1962, I was writing a weekly record column for the *Liverpool Echo*. The column included a list of Liverpool's Own Top Five, reflecting each week's best-selling singles in the city and suburbs. I got sales figures from key city-centre retail outlets such as Beaver Radio, Rushworth's and NEMS, and also from the main Merseyside record 'factors' or wholesalers, the people who supplied the shops. Although I hadn't met the Beatles in October 1962, I helped to launch their first single by compiling a press kit for Brian.

Because of my freelance PR connection with the group, I was determined to avoid any accusations of favouritism when I put together my Top Five for my October 5th column. I bent over backwards in my efforts to be fair and deliberately failed to get sales figures from NEMS. Even so, I found that every other retailer I spoke to was reporting extraordinarily heavy demand for 'Love Me Do', which clearly indicated it was the week's No. 1 best-seller on Merseyside. The Beatles also shot straight to No. 1 in the local Top Twenty published by Bill Harry's *Mersey Beat* music paper.

George Martin discussing a playback of 'Love Me Do' with the boys.

After I joined NEMS in 1963, Brian admitted to me that he HAD ordered far more copies of the 'Love Me Do' single than he eventually sold in his shops. He put this down to an error of judgement and denied that it had been done with any idea of hyping the single into the national charts via falsely inflated figures. He said he'd been over-optimistic in assessing the number of copies his regular customers would buy. Considering that the Beatles were already the North-West's most popular group, according to the poll in *Mersey Beat*, he expected the demand to be even greater than it was. He added: "I wasn't the only one in Liverpool to burn his fingers. A number of the other Liverpool stores also had piles of unsold records tucked away gathering dust on shelves in the back room. We hadn't reckoned that many of the group's most faithful followers made a point of not buying 'Love Me Do' because they felt that Liverpool would lose the Beatles if the single was too big a success!"

The week after it was released, 'Love Me Do' went into the *Record Retailer* national Top 50 singles chart at No. 49. The title's highest position in that chart was No. 17, during the last week of 1962. According to Brian, he didn't tell the boys that he'd bought so many singles. But Paul joked to one insider that he was "starving hungry, because someone has to pay for those 10,000 records Brian bought"! Brian stuck to his version of the story, telling ghost writer Derek Taylor, who scripted his autobiography *A Cellarful Of Noise* in 1964: "There was a rumour which lingered until it became acceptable currency that I had bought the disc in bulk to get it into the charts. Possible though this would have been had I the money, which I hadn't, I did no such thing, nor ever have. The Beatles, then as now, progressed and succeeded on natural impetus, without benefit of stunts or back-door tricks and I would like to make this quite clear. The kids of Liverpool bought it in thousands."

Both Brian and the Beatles were angered and upset by Parlophone's almost total lack of promotional activity for their first release. EMI did almost nothing to get it away after it was released. The record company's reluctance to pay any attention to the single almost certainly stemmed from their own producer's lack of enthusiasm. George Martin declared with refreshing honesty: "As I couldn't find anything better, I reluctantly agreed to release 'Love Me Do' as the first single. It got to No. 17 and I never thought it would do much better because I didn't think the song had much to offer." Even *Mersey Beat*, for which Brian wrote a regular column, gave it a decidedly lukewarm write-up. Under the headline "BEATLES HEAD MERSEYSIDE POPS", the (unnamed) *Mersey Beat* reviewer wrote: "Although 'Love Me Do' is rather monotonous it is the type of number which grows on you and I have found that whilst I felt disappointed when I first heard it, I enjoyed it more and more each time I played it." He added that he liked the B-side, 'P.S. I Love You', better.

One celebrity fan of 'Love Me Do' was contemporary chart-topping teenage songstress Helen Shapiro. She bashed the ear of her tour promoter Arthur Howes, who eventually added the Beatles to the supporting bill for her next UK concert tour. Meanwhile, the boys themselves were absolutely over the moon at the fact that they had a record in the shops, whether it was a best-seller or not. As Ringo remarked later: "That was the most incredible scene, that we had a record out, a bit of plastic

George sporting the black eye he'd been given by a Pete Best fan.

with us on." John revealed: "The truth is that we were more thrilled about the little bit of success we had with that first single than the fact that later ones raced up to the top right away. I'm sorry to say that we became blasé about topping the charts; it was something that began to happen automatically with everything we released, without much effort on our part."

John went on: "When 'Love Me Do' crept in at the bottom of the charts and rose just a little each week we were happy, happy, happy. There was a feeling of deep delight that was never repeated because everyone around us expected the later releases were going to be hits and we couldn't help believing all the publicity we were being given. Personally, I found it nicer at the beginning. I loved the buzz I got then because it was a new sensation. We'd worked hard for several years to become known outside the Liverpool clubs, and finally we were making it."

Paul summed up the way he and John felt before they found national fame: "One of the things we were always trying to find was the next beat, the next craze. Everyone was talking in the music press about rock calypso or Latin rock, saying this or that would be next, while we used to sit around undecided among ourselves about what was going to be the next big thing on the music scene. The minute we stopped trying to find it, the newspapers said, 'It's Mersey Beat!' We found we'd discovered the next sound without even trying!" Brian attempted to counteract EMI's distinct lack of interest by pumping out his own publicity, centred on the biographical press material he'd paid me to provide. On the day that 'Love Me Do' became available in record shops all over the country, he wrote personal letters to a list of top London and provincial booking agents enclosing the press pack and asking: "Have you been able to find any more engagements for the Beatles?"

Three weeks later, Brian phoned round and spoke to as many concert promoters as he could reach, inviting them to come and see the Beatles in their debut appearance at the vast and

John and Paul rehearsing their harmonies for 'Love Me Do'.

professionally prestigious Liverpool Empire theatre. Actually the Beatles were at the bottom of that Empire concert billing, featured fourth on the advertised list after Little Richard, Craig Douglas and Jet Harris, but Brian was confident that his Fab Four would go down a storm with hometown fans. He figured that if agents and bookers saw them steal the scene from a heavyweight bill-topper like Little Richard, they would be mightily impressed.

One impresario he called was Arthur Howes, who had already heard Helen Shapiro singing the praises of the Beatles and happened to need a supporting band for her upcoming tour, which was scheduled to start less than four months later in February 1963. He booked the Beatles for a try-out gig in his own home-town of Peterborough, on a one-nighter bill headed by Australian balladeer Frank Ifield. This Peterborough date at the beginning of December clashed with one of the Beatles' Cavern dates but Brian pulled them out of it without a qualm. His decision gave a little credence to the fear already expressed by many

Liverpudlian fans that wider success would take John, Paul, George and Ringo beyond the reach of their local followers. But Peterborough proved to be one of Brian's earliest management mistakes. With one single crawling up the charts and few radio or television appearances to their credit outside the North-West of England, the Beatles were not ready to face a Frank Ifield concert audience in a town which had never heard of them.

Local critic Lyndon Whittaker wrote that the Beatles 'quite frankly failed to excite'. His review continued: 'The drummer apparently thought the job was to lead, not to provide rhythm. He made far too much noise and in their final number, 'Twist And Shout', it sounded as though everyone was trying to make more noise than the others. In a more mellow mood, their 'A Taste Of Honey' was much better and 'Love Me Do' was tolerable."

Fortunately, Arthur Howes still booked them for his next Shapiro tour – one of the best moves he ever made. 'Eppy' bit his lip when he read the paper, knowing that not only had he made a mistake but that he had misjudged the potential reaction of Peterborough fans by actively encouraging Whittaker to 'be sure to write about the Beatles as well as Frank Ifield'.

In November 1962, I saw the Beatles on stage for the first time and then subsequently met them over drinks at the Devonshire Arms, a small pub off London's Manchester Square, which was where the headquarters of EMI Records was located. The stage appearance was not a 'live' gig but the recording of an EMI-sponsored show for Radio Luxembourg. It took place each week in office space converted for the purpose and filled with invited fans who watched their favourite EMI recording acts and a few favoured newcomers miming informally to new releases.

One of the programme's presenters, Muriel Young, started to introduce the Beatles using only their first names. She got no further than "John, Paul, George . . .", when the crowd broke into spontaneous applause laced with more than a few excited screams. The fact that these London kids recognised the first names of three Beatles instantly and reacted so positively convinced me that the

By the time the boys came to record 'She Loves You' a few months later, they were completely at home in the studio.

group was on the brink of big-time popularity. People have said to me many times since: "Those kids were taught to react that way – there were EMI people there practically ordering them to applaud." But I saw quite a few of those radio show sessions and I can assure you there was a very big difference between the normal welcome given to most newcomers and the fiercely loud reception that the Beatles received. It was obvious that 'Love Me Do' was only the first step on what would prove to be a remarkable journey to stardom.

(TB)

Their very first interview

Peter Jones recalls the day he reluctantly interviewed a new group from Liverpool for *Record Mirror* back in September 1962

As far as the Top Thirty charts were concerned, the summer of 1962 was just one long yawn. At No. 1 for the whole month of August was Frank Ifield, yodelling his way through 'I Remember You'. The charts back then covered a wide range of music (or so-called music). There was room for the established talents of Ray Charles ('I Can't Stop Loving You') and Nat King Cole on 'Let There Be Love', the Shadows ('Guitar Tango') and even Elvis Presley – who was, by then, seen as something of an old-timer.

But generally prospects were bleak. For pop writers such as myself, nothing seemed to be happening, at least musically. We got piles of no-hope singles every week of the year. We were invited to meet countless solo singers, most with outrageous personalities or garish wardrobes or ear-jarring names. With no obvious potential superstars coming through, and no clear-cut musical direction, the pop industry was simply a rat race. Never mind about talent: just buy, beg or borrow space in the pop papers and let's hope a new name gets a hit on publicity alone.

In mid-September 1962, a group turned up in the *Record Mirror* offices in Shaftesbury Avenue, London – and the three-man staff, including myself as editor, weren't exactly excited to meet them. This was no carefully planned promotional visit laid on by their record company. Instead, a Hungarian photographer called Dezo Hoffmann, who worked round the corner, had rung us up and said, in his fractured English: "I've pictured four nice boys who come from Liverpool. They would love to meet you all. I think they have interesting stories to tell."

Haven't they all? This would make the tenth new group this week alone. OK, we're a soft touch, Dezo – tell us what the group is called. Huh? You gotta be kidding. The Beatles? Oh come on, Dezo, you must have heard it wrong. But no. In his role as pop's principal photographer, Dezo had completed several sessions with the four Beatles, including the classic poses which pictured the boys as being clean-cut, round-collared, smiling and grouped in various permutations around chairs.

So the Beatles pattered up the stairs of 116 Shaftesbury Avenue, with the quiet-mannered Brian Epstein out front. The confrontation was tough on both parties. As far as we were concerned, we had been lumbered, albeit by a friend. We hadn't heard of the Beatles and there was no evidence that this lot were anything different to all the other no-hopers. And it was tough on the visiting Liverpudlians because this was their first interview outside their home territory. Their local newspaper *Mersey Beat* rated them, and they'd won popularity polls in that neck of the woods. George Harrison even brought along some chewed up newspaper clippings to prove it.

Anyway, the Beatles shuffled in as though they were on the way to a mass execution – except Paul. There were only three seats in the room, so George sat on the floor, John on the table, and Ringo continued shuffling over to the door. Brian Epstein filled in the personal details, but there was no doubting that Paul McCartney was, even then, very much the public relations executive in the team. He managed to look happy, chatted amiably and really tried to remember little details which might bolster up what looked like being a very short story indeed . . . if it ever got written.

What we weren't told, and this is where Brian was particularly astute, is how many record companies had rejected the Beatles in the eight or nine months since he had signed them to a management deal. If we'd known that they'd been turned down by Decca, Pye, and even EMI at first, the aura of failure would have flattened the Beatles. So 'Eppy' contented himself by apologising profusely for "not knowing much about the pop business" and explained briefly that he'd got the boys an audition with George Martin in June and that he'd liked what they did, especially some of their own compositions, like 'Love Me Do', 'P.S. I Love You' and 'Hello Little Girl'.

This was pretty routine stuff. Nobody seemed to remember just why the group called itself the Beatles – though there were quite a few explanations offered once the band took off. But in individual terms, the boys came across as follows. First, there was a kind of resigned arrogance about John. He seemed somewhat surly, disbelieving and distant. He certainly didn't offer any samples of his caustic wit. But he seemed to relish having quick arguments with George about early incidents in Beatle life. Paul, clearly, saw himself as the front man – the one working hardest to try and earn the group a good write-up in the paper. He really did have the innocence of a choirboy. George, when pressed into action, was the memory man of the group, despite the arguments about factual matters with John. Ringo simply didn't say a word.

Now, as an interview, this was fast going nowhere. Nothing worthwhile was emerging. Maybe we writers should have taken the time to check with Liverpool sources, do some homework, and get to grips with the background. But we just hadn't had time. We were merely doing a favour for our photographer mate (who was proving he had influence with the press!), so that the group could at least feel we were interested to an extent, even if we didn't actually write a story.

So our interview limped along. George grew more and more silent, though he worked out some guitar chords via some nimble finger work. John grew gruffer, as if he would much rather have been somewhere else. Paul, brow furrowed as he tried to think of something interesting, smiled a lot, but that became more and more forced. From Ringo: nothing. The one bit of humour was attributed to George, though he couldn't actually remember it himself. When the boys went for their first real session at EMI, George Martin told them to let him know if there was anything they didn't like, so George said he didn't like George Martin's tie. That's part of Beatle folklore now, but it meant nothing much in that smoke-filled room in Shaftesbury Avenue years ago.

A waste of time? Pretty much . . . though Brian Epstein did have a copy of their first single, 'Love Me Do', in 12-inch acetate form. So we gathered round the record-player and gave it a spin. Now obviously it was vital to the Beatles that we liked the record and that we'd recommend it to the readers.

But there is nothing worse than sitting in a small room and either playing a record by somebody in the same room, or having that person sing live. The truth is that you just don't know where to look, particularly if the music isn't all that thrilling. 'Love Me Do' did not have instant appeal for any critics in the South of England. John Lennon's harmonica touch early on seemed reminiscent of quite a few American hits of the day. At first hearing, it was just another song. But we did congratulate the Beatles for going for original material on their debut single, as most groups in those days just copied an American hit and rushed it out double-quick to try and beat the Statesiders to the Top Ten. When the last notes died away it was our turn to shuffle around. The Beatles wanted praise, but it was hard to go overboard about the single. Brian Epstein, sensing that we pop writers had been cornered a mite unfairly, insisted: "The boys have a tremendous following in Liverpool and the record will sell well there." George said he wished he could re-record the number anyway, because there were guitar items he felt he could improve on. Paul said the song generally went down well on stage. John said they'd got some much better songs. And Ringo said nothing at all.

That first interview slumped because the interviewers had nothing to go on apart from a basic lack of interest in what seemed to be just one more British pop act trying to break into a boring scene. The general feeling that the Beatles were only average persisted through the industry – at least, outside Liverpool and the other Merseyside areas. Ted King was the first man to play the record on BBC, and even he didn't feel too sure about it. He reckoned the Beatles had talent, but doubted the appeal of the song. As for us on *Record Mirror*, we managed a little feature piece on the boys stating that the Beatles were probably the most popular vocal and instrumental group in the North.

Brian Epstein said hardly anything about his own background – his story only began to emerge months afterwards. As far as we were concerned, they were tidied up and cleaned up for the trip to London, but the magnetism wasn't there. They seemed just a bunch of nice guys, allowing for John's grunted gripes and Ringo's silence. Yet these were the guys who inside a few months were to become pop giants, idolised by millions. It all just goes to prove, once again, that first impressions are by no means the best or the most accurate, and that at the wrong time, or the wrong place, anyone can appear ordinary! (PJ)

Peter Jones did many interviews for The Beatles Book during the 1960s.

Please Please Me

Their first No. 1 sparked an argument about John and Paul's songwriting credit!

The Beatles first recorded 'Please Please Me' in September 1962, at the same time as their first single, 'Love Me Do'. In the studio, they sang the song more or less as they'd been performing it at the Cavern, taking it at a much slower pace, and rather soulfully, as a plaintive little ballad, with John and Paul sharing the vocal spotlight. The first time I heard an acetate, I asked Paul how he came to write the number. Just as he was about to reply, John interrupted: 'It's my song'. John told me that the idea for the title line, repeating the word 'please' twice, came one Sunday night when he was at his Aunt Mimi's house, listening to Bing Crosby singing 'Please' on Radio Luxembourg, the only English-language commercial radio station available in those days. I was surprised to discover that the number was John's work because, in the style the group originally performed it, 'Please Please Me' sounded remarkably like one of Paul's sentimental efforts and seemed to have the McCartney stamp all over it.

A further surprise followed four months later when I looked at an advance copy of the actual single. Beneath the title on the label, the composer credit read: 'McCartney – Lennon'. Somebody had boobed, I thought, although at least they hadn't put 'McArtney' instead of 'McCartney' like they did on the earliest copies of 'Love Me Do'!

In fact, John and Paul had agreed to let the credits for all the songs they wrote alone or together be listed as joint compositions, just as though they had collaborated equally on everything. Brian Epstein thought that this 'joint billing' idea would solve several potential problems, simplifying the accounting by giving Lennon and McCartney an equal share of all the song-writing royalties and reducing the chance of arguments between John and Paul over who should have his songs on singles. At the time, everyone also agreed the fairest way would be to show the names in alphabetical order on record labels, which is why the 'Lennon – McCartney' credit appeared so often regardless of who had actually provided the lyrics and tune. At Paul's persuasion, Brian Epstein had further thoughts about the alphabetical order thing. Eppy said: "Why don't we show the two names but indicate who really did the majority of the work on writing a number by putting his name first?"

When this proposal was rejected, Eppy's next suggestion was that the order should alternate from song to song, showing 'Lennon – McCartney' one time, and then switching to 'McCartney – Lennon'. He told me: "That ought to keep them both equally happy". As we know with the benefit of hindsight, this idea was not adopted in the long run, as both the boys and music publisher Dick James quite rightly said that it would cause confusion in the minds of fans over who was writing what. And, indeed, the first instance of confusion arose over 'Please Please Me', when Paul's name appeared first, although it was John's song!

'Please Please Me' came very close to being discarded altogether instead of making it onto the A-side of the group's second single. George Martin didn't like the tempo of the original September recording.

The boys rapidly got used to appearing on shows with stars like comic Arthur Askey.

He told John: "It needs pepping up in some way". Several of us thought it sounded more like Roy Orbison material than Beatles, and John confessed that he was influenced by Orbison's distinctive vocal style, having heard 'Only The Lonely' so often on his favourite late-night Radio Luxembourg programmes. After 'Love Me Do' entered the charts, George Martin was keen to put a follow-up single 'in the can' as quickly as possible. All the songs the boys had already recorded on tape, such as 'Please Please Me', plus Mitch Murray's 'How Do You Do It?' were given renewed consideration during this vital session.

After listening to 'Please Please Me' again, Martin said: "That could be a winner, you know, if we take the tempo up quite a lot and you really belt it out, not as a sentimental ballad but a big-sounding fast number." The boys tried it, with Lennon retaining and adapting a typical Orbisonesque element in the amazingly high falsetto voice sequences. The changes did the trick, although it actually took no fewer than 17 takes to satisfy everyone that the recording was as good as it could be.

I was up there in the studio control room at Abbey Road to hear all 17 versions. Instead of enjoying the experience, I became increasingly bored by all the 're-takes', vowing to steer clear of sessions in future unless I had essential business there. For me, a recording session lacked the excitement of a live concert or a club performance. Today the job would have been done much more quickly by merely 'dropping in' corrections or better bits where they were needed. In 1962 it was a matter of doing it all over again 'from the top', 17 times in this case, followed by an 'overdub' when John's harmonica was added. The true reason for adding the harmonica was that in 1962 the recording business liked continuity between singles. If an artist's first hit had some sort of special sound, an instrumental or vocal gimmick, it would almost certainly be repeated on the next release.

George Martin turned to me, and asked: "What do you think?" I was cautious. Having written a weekly record review column for the *Liverpool Echo* since I was 17 years old, I'd taught myself to listen only once or twice to each new disc I received from the companies. I disagreed with the idea of letting a recording 'grow

Norman Smith, the sound recordist on 'Please Please Me' and all their early hits.

on you'. My theory was that even rubbish could sound like a smash hit single if you played it over often enough and I felt I couldn't give a proper professional judgment on a record I'd just heard 17 times in a row!

But Martin was convinced. He told the boys over the intercom speakers as they climbed the long steep flight of stairs from the studio floor to his control room: "I've just heard a number one record. Come and listen." When I sent out the press release for 'Please Please Me', I wrote: "Here's the first big chart-bustin' bombshell of '63!!!!"

Cheekily, since January was only days old at the time, I added: "The Beatles have made THE record of the year. Please, please make sure you listen to 'Please Please Me'." In the charts published by *Melody Maker* and *New Musical Express*,

which were used by the national newspapers, the single zoomed to the top of the pops — as it did, indeed, on the BBC's chart rundown on *Pick Of The Pops*. But it never did make Number One in *Record Retailer*. For this reason, 'Please Please Me' is never listed as a chart-topper by the authors of the various Guinness books of hits because they always went by the *Record Retailer* chart.

'Please Please Me' also marked Ringo's first appearance as the Beatles' regular drummer in the recording studio, beginning an incredible era of record-splintering achievement for the group, as consecutive releases raced straight to the top, selling faster than anything else had ever done in the history of popular music.   (TB)

Introducing the group in 1963

On lead guitar:
GEORGE HARRISON

George and barbers don't get on well. He constantly says that his pet hate is having his hair cut. He first met fellow Beatle John Lennon in the fish-and-chip shop by his school and his immediate reaction was: "He's a good lad. He doesn't get his hair cut, either." George operates on lead guitar but is also efficient on drums and piano. Guitar is the main hobby of his life, though, and he says: "One day I want to sit down, give it a lot of thought and come up with a completely revolutionary idea for a new guitar. They could call it the Harrison guitar!

"Chet Atkins is, for me, the greatest instrumentalist of them all. But I'm also very fond of the Duane Eddy group. That's how I spend most of my spare time, just listening to records by favourite artists. They inspire me to get out my own guitar and play to an audience of only me." At school, George found it easy to express himself in art classes but slumped badly when it came to marks for subjects like

mathematics or history. At Dovedale Road Primary School in l.iverpool, he was a sports fanatic — any sport: soccer, cricket, athletics, and swimming. Had he persisted, he could have reached quite a high standard. "But, by the time I went to Liverpool Institute High School, I'd lost all interest in sports,' he says.

"I suppose I quite enjoyed those schooldays — though what a long time ago they seem now! But I must say my version of the school uniform didn't go down very well with the masters. I used to do myself up in tight trousers, waistcoat and suede shoes. I reckoned it was all very fashionable, but obviously the people in charge had a different view of what boys should be wearing."

George is just short of six feet tall, and weighs in at 10 stone 3 pounds. He has a sister, Louise, and two brothers, Peter and Harry. He was born on February 25, 1943, eight months after Paul McCartney. "Apart from girls, and listening to records with girls, I put driving as my big hobby. I thoroughly enjoy a long drive, but though I rate myself as good behind the wheel, I'm not so sure the police agree!

"Now the money is coming in, I can indulge myself that bit more than before. But I'm not a big spender. One day, I'd like to buy a big house somewhere quiet, but for the meantime I just buy whatever I like in the way of clothes and records." When it comes to romance, George adds: "It's funny. Once I just used to date girls and that was that. Now people seem interested in why I like certain types of girls and they ask for tips and hints and that sort of thing. Well, my own tastes run to small blonde girls who can share a laugh with me. That sense of humour is all important to me, but I do like her to be able to switch moods as quickly as I do. Anyway, I date as often as we get a night free, which doesn't add up to many dates these days! No, there's nobody regular. It wouldn't be fair on her, not with us being as busy as we are right now."

George cops at least his fair share of the fanmail for individual Beatles. His taste for jelly-babies – which he shares with John Lennon – caused panic at one time. Hundreds of pounds of 'babies' poured in for him. He once sang a song called 'Three Cool Cats', and was besieged by parcels containing china cats. And teddy bears – he gets plenty of those too. "With so much travelling, I sometimes get behind on answering fan-mail," he confesses. "I don't seem to get marriage proposals through the post, but I do try and answer any letters that really need an answer. Lotsa girls ask what age I feel is best for marriage. The truth is there is no such age – it's just when you feel you ought to."

George lavishes praise on his parents, Harold and Louise Harrison. Though not particularly musical themselves, they helped him a great deal, he says, "simply by not complaining about the racket I kicked up when I first started learning to play. I think they're very proud of all of us now." Though R&B music figures very strongly on the Beatles' scene, George likes listening to C&W and to Spanish guitar, as long as both are well played. He's a perfectionist. He's a key figure in the Beatle sound. He's thoroughly likeable. And he's only unhappy when he HAS to get a haircut!

On rhythm guitar:
JOHN LENNON

John, who's brown-eyed and brown-haired, also plays harmonica, drums and tinkers on the piano. He's short sighted – so much so, that unhappy rumours have been circulated that he is slowly going blind. This is untrue, but John admits: "For rehearsals, and most of the time off-stage, I do wear heavy glasses. On stage, without them, I can't see very far into the audience. Maybe this is just as well, as it means I can't pick up any expressions on the faces of those who aren't digging our act. That helps me to feel self-confident. I only know an audience is there by their noise, like screams and all that". At 5 ft. 11 in. ("well, let's settle for six-foot"), John is the same height as both Paul and George. He's also the heaviest at 11 stone 5 pounds, just one pound heavier than his longtime mate Paul.

John was educated at Dovedale Primary School, Quarry Bank Grammar School and then at Liverpool College of Art. Art, in fact, was the subject at which he really shone. "Maths and science proved my downfall on more than one occasion," he recalls. "Anything to do with figures had me baffled." He grins: "Now I can say that figures are one of the chief interests of my life!"

His interest in music really started with his mother, Julia. Unfortunately, she died in a car accident in the 1950s, before John reached stardom, but she played an important part in his early musical days by teaching him banjo. John now lives with an aunt, Aunt Mimi, who is "knocked out" at the way the Beatles have hit the top. "My mother used to accompany her songs on banjo," said John. "Dad sang, too. But there isn't much time for family get-togethers nowadays – I've really only got Julia and Jacqueline, my step-sisters. But though my spare time is pretty sparse, I don't think I'd change anything about life at the moment – except to try and avoid that horrible business of getting up at five o'clock in the morning sometimes, to go off on long-distance dates. People often ask what I'd do if I couldn't earn my living as a musician any more. It'd be a nightmare to me if that DID happen, but I'd definitely go on writing. I spend most of my spare time writing material and I guess my main aim is to keep on writing hit songs. But I must produce a stage musical one day. That's definite. It'd be a big challenge, but I'd enjoy it. I honestly enjoy writing . . . writing anything. It makes me laugh, if you see what I mean."

John is always fast with the wisecracks, and equally speedy to pick up a new musical idea. For example, if a radio producer asks him for an immediate ad-lib, John is always happy to oblige. His agile mind ploughs quickly through several alternatives, then he picks out the right one for the occasion. He talks fast, always with that hint of good humour. He can deliver a crushing retort with a deadpan face so that the full importance doesn't sink in immediately.

"This new craze for the Beatles is fantastic," he says. "I've met such a lot of interesting people in the past few months. Of course, the money is very nice to have, too. One day, maybe, I'll branch out away from the music business, in the sense of financing something different – maybe some high-class clothes shops. I spend most of my money these days on clothes so if I owned the shop I'd be able to give myself a discount. My own tastes in clothes run from suede to leather, or cord, or denim. The only thing I don't like is anything in a really bright colour."

John's birthday is October 9th. He's still only 22, a one-time art student who has now written over 100 songs with Paul McCartney. Sonny Terry is his favourite musician and he listens admiringly to discs by Little Richard, Chuck Jackson, Chuck Berry, Mary Wells and, among the groups, the Miracles, Shirelles, Chiffons and Marvelettes. He doesn't analyse his tastes: "I just like that style of singing". He sometimes relaxes by going to the cinema, especially if Brigitte Bardot is in the movie. But sleeping occupies him deeply. Driving, cars – they leave him cold. John Lennon is uncomplicated, yet complicated. But he's determined to become a first-rate writer, maybe even to outdo his present reputation as a singer and musician.

On bass guitar:
PAUL McCARTNEY

James Paul McCartney is often regarded as the elder statesman of the Beatles, but the fact is that he didn't see the light of day until June 18th, 1942, and that he is therefore the second youngest of the batch. He's a left-handed bass guitarist, a prolific songwriter, an enthusiastic conversationalist, who lists his favourite off-stage hobbies as writing and bird-watching. Paul is brisk, business-like and alert. He looks taller than the others but is actually precisely the same height as John Lennon and George Harrison, He weighs in at 11 stone 4 pounds, with an athletic sort of frame, topped by dark brown hair. His eyes, always on the move ("from bird-watching!"), are hazel in colour, and deeply intense.

Paul's mother, Mary McCartney, is dead. But his father, James, can take credit for some of Paul's interest in music. Some thirty years ago, he led his own group: Jim Mac's Jazz Band. Says Paul: "Dad always encouraged me to take up music. I think he likes our sound, but sometimes he says we're away from home a bit too much. He put up with my practice sessions for years, which shows he's a brave man!" Sometimes Paul's career seems studded with things back to front. His main childhood memories are of writing back to front, a habit he's got out of. And of pedalling his bicycle back to front, on the theory that he was actually doing it the right way!

Paul originally played rhythm guitar with the group, and once filled in on piano during one of the Beatles' trips to Germany. He took over on bass when former member Stu Sutcliffe died. "Give me any time to myself and you'll find me listening to American records, specially rhythm 'n' blues," he says. "Anything by Chuck Jackson, the Miracles, Ketty Lester, Little Richard, or Margie Hendrickson of the Raelettes. You can mark down Juliette Greco for me, too. She looks fab as well as singing so well."

At school, Paul was a useful student of English literature but was pretty hopeless at geography and mathematics. A feeling of helplessness when confronted with simple sums is something common to all four Beatles. They have always leaned towards the more artistic subjects. And while John Lennon hates haircuts, Paul opts out on shaving whenever he can. Once he said he shaved with green toothpaste and was inundated with complaints from fans who'd tried it and found it didn't work!

"I suppose I've become a bit of a big spender," said Paul, serious for a moment. "One day I'd like to buy a house and set everybody up in it but just at the moment the money seems to run away on the little things, like clothes and food. I kinda relax with food. Otherwise I just sleep, or play guitar, or smoke cigarettes. Films? Yes. I'm a fan – I go for Marlon Brando, Belmondo, Sophia Loren. Peter Sellers, Oh yes, and Juliette Greco."

He adds: "These hit records have done a lot for us. Somehow we always felt we'd make it big one day. But this has been very sudden. We owe a great deal to Brian Epstein, you know. He's good, astute and sympathetic . . . even when he's driving us very hard, we call him a good lad."

Since his days at Liverpool Institute High School, Paul has been very matey with George Harrison. They've developed a fast-chatting gag exchange style of conversation that can prove baffling at first hearing. He says he taught George his first guitar chord.

Marriage, one feels, will certainly be for Paul one day. He admits that the idea of domesticity appeals to him, but he won't be committed as to what would be the best age for him to get married. "It'll just happen. I suppose", he says, and leaves it at that. "I get about 70-odd letters a week," he says. "And, believe me, some of them are very, very odd. I try to answer as many as I can, but it does take time. I hope the fans realise that. It's terrible to disappoint them, but we can only do so much in any one day."

Paul also dabbles on drums and banjo but there's no doubt that bass guitar is his principal interest. It's just that he likes to see how other instruments work, so he can understand their problems. "Songwriting is very important to me," he says, "and John and I work well together. We don't seem to have any shortage of ideas. What knocks us out is the way some of the top Americans are so interested in recording our material."

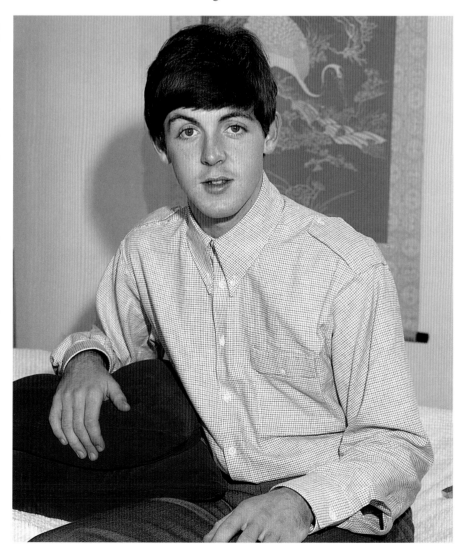

On drums:
RINGO STARR

Ringo was the last to join the Beatles. He's a drummer of really ferocious efficiency. The shortest (at 5 ft. 8 in.) in the group; also the lightest (9 stone 6 pounds). The only blue-eyed one of the four. A happy-go-lucky type . . . who still remembers with horror his first appearance at the massive Liverpool Empire, when the curtains swirled back to reveal Ringo still in the process of setting up his drum kit!

Ringo is also the only Beatle to have changed his name for show business purposes. Starkey is his family name, and his parents, Elsie and Harry, gave him the first name Richard, which they soon shortened to Dick. 'Ringo' came about because he wears a minimum of three highly colourful rings on his fingers.

He has an expressive face, and expressive hair, too, dark brown in colour and flop-happy as soon as he attacks his drum kit. It crinkles down towards his eyes, which mirror the excitement of the rhythms he pounds out.

During his schooldays, Ringo journeyed from Saint Silas Infants' School, to Dingle Vale Secondary Modern, to Riversdale Technical College. His school interests? "Not many," he admits. "I was pretty good at handicrafts – any sort of thing just so long as I could make something, or use my hands to create. Don't talk to me about the more usual subjects. I was terrible at maths and English. Sporting things didn't really appeal to me. Even now I don't find myself following any special club or team. I don't even bother to read the results. Music is a full-time business and I wouldn't change it for the world.

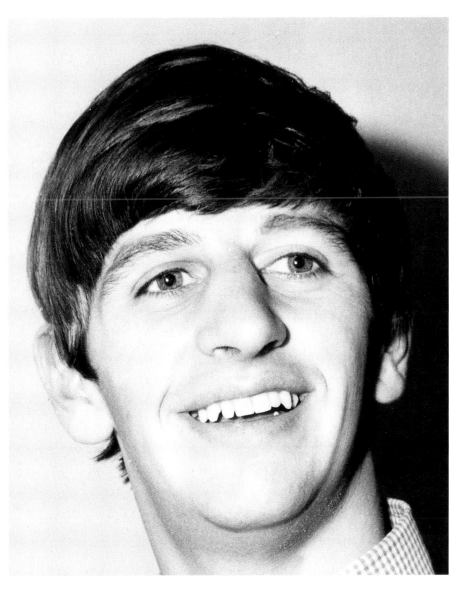

"If it hadn't been for music, I would have been an engineer, I think. I learned enough to return to it, if this music business ever folds up on me. And yet I also nurse this crazy ambition to become a motor racing driver. I'm crazy about driving especially night driving. Would I be good enough to make the grade as a professional? I dunno. All I can say is that I haven't had any convictions yet!"

Ringo, who was 23 on July 7th 1963, is a thoroughly experienced drummer. Once upon a time he appeared in the Liverpool area with the Darktown Skiffle Group, then for three years he went round with Rory Storm and the ever-popular Hurricanes. Three seasons at Butlin's Holiday Camps, where he had to cope with anything and everything, added to his experience.

Watch him at rehearsals. When he's not actually playing, his hands and sticks are seldom still. He taps out incessant rhythms on his knees, or his snare drum – on anything that doesn't make any distracting noise. He's a real professional, able to pick up a cue instantaneously, and improvise at the drop of a rim-shot. Yet he says: "I've built up my confidence over most things to do with drumming.

But my main ambition now is to be able to play everything with either left or right hand. It's hard, and needs plenty of practice, but it's coming along."

Ringo first met the other Beatles in the Jacaranda Club in Liverpool. He doesn't remember much about them individually, except there was a certain sadness about the occasion because their original bass guitarist, a talented young man named Stuart Sutcliffe, had died tragically earlier that year. "I recognised immediately that they were all good musicians and that I'd be more than happy with them."

Now the money is pouring in and Ringo is a star. He is thinking in terms of investing some of his loot in a business. He mentions a ladies' hairdressing salon as a possibility. His parents always thought that would be a good line for him, despite his own unruly locks. Or perhaps he'd dabble in a car hire firm. His love of cars and driving is never far from his mind. Relaxation? Ringo admits: "Sometimes I find it hard to unwind, specially after a series of one-nighters. I don't go mad with my free time, though. Maybe I'll just stay at home and listen to records or watch TV. Musically, I go for R&B or C&W. I also get a great kick out of listening to singers like Brook Benton, or Dinah Washington, Della Reese or Patsy Cline. I collect discs by the Shirelles too – they've got a very fine feeling for their sort of music." And so has Ringo Starr for HIS sort of music. (TB)

1963 UK tours

Johnny Dean reports on the year they took Britain by storm

As soon as 'Love Me Do' entered the charts towards the end of 1962, Brian Epstein started to get phone calls from agents and impresarios. He wanted the boys to be seen by as many of their fans as possible, so he started to line up a load of appearances for 1963, including a series of four lengthy one-night concert tours of the UK As the Beatles were newcomers with only one minor hit, they started off as one of the supporting acts on the Helen Shapiro tour. They moved on to back up American singing stars Chris Montez and Tommy Roe for their next series and followed it by taking second billing to Roy Orbison for their third series of one-nighters.

The actual performances became more and more difficult for the headliners once the Beatles' popularity started to soar. Helen Shapiro and the visiting Americans might have been top of the bill, but the fans saw things differently, and they almost screamed the roof off the theatre the moment the Beatles appeared, which made it very hard for the 'star of the show' to go on after them.

Every performance was greeted with massive enthusiasm by local fans. At the start of the year there were usually only a few dozen fans waiting outside the theatres they were playing. But it rapidly became hundreds and, by the autumn, thousands. Just to get the Beatles in and out of a theatre or cinema anywhere in England became a huge exercise. They often walked off stage and straight into a waiting car in order to get away before the fans realised what was going on.

The national press ignored the Beatles at the start of 1963. When 'Please Please Me' and 'From Me to You' hit the charts, they began to give them the odd mention. It was only when they saw the massive crowds lining the streets around the London Palladium Theatre in the autumn that they realised their huge potential. Immediately they started giving them massive coverage. They've always claimed ever since that they were the ones who made the Beatles. The truth, of course, was that pretty well every man, woman and child in the country knew about the Beatles long before the national press climbed onto the bandwagon.

I visited the boys with my photographer Leslie Bryce in July 1963 in Margate, where they were playing their first week in variety at the Winter Gardens. I found them enjoying life after years of playing hundreds of one-nighters and sleeping in grotty rooms. The Beatles loved the luxury of staying in a good hotel and sleeping in the same bed for a whole week. They also enjoyed taking advantage of all the hotel's facilities. Billy J. Kramer & the Dakotas, who were appearing

---

The boys pictured in their collarless suits on stage at the Margate Pavilion in the summer of 1963.

on the same bill as the Beatles, were staying in a place without a pool, so they often used to take advantage of the one in the Beatles' hotel.

The excitement that greeted their appearances in Margate was repeated that season in dozens of other theatres, dance halls and cinemas in English and Welsh seaside resorts where the Fab Four performed for holiday crowds, doing two shows a day for anything from two to six consecutive evenings in each town. The venues ranged from the Odeon in Llandudno and the Gaumont in Bournemouth to the Ritz Ballroom on the promenade at Rhyl and the Odeon at Weston-super-Mare.

While the boys put on their well-pressed stage suits, roadie Neil Aspinall would carry out all the final checks on their equipment, placing guitars precisely beside the appropriate amplifiers on stage and tucking a spare pair of sticks into the side of Ringo's drum kit. Each time he went back into the dressing room a volley of questions would be fired at him from four directions. "Where's my spare set of strings, Nel?" "Did you get that Scotch to go in this Coke yet?" "Have you got the clean shirts for the second show?" "What's happened to my bacon sarnies?" Coping with their musical instruments, their stage outfits, their personal wants and professional must-haves, as well as plotting their late-night getaway plans, was proving a bit much for the extraordinarily efficient 'Nel', who soon demanded that he be given an assistant before the summer was up.

Concert audiences may have imagined John, Paul, George and Ringo lying peacefully asleep in their luxurious hotel beds for most of the day, getting up just in time for a late-afternoon brunch of eggs and chips before showtime. But life by the sea wasn't all that easy for the four mega-busy young musicians. Sometimes they had to shoot back to London for a few hours during the day to squeeze in a BBC radio session or a three-hour visit to the EMI recording studios in Abbey Road. Even when they didn't have to make the round-trip to the capital and back, there was usually a photo shoot on the beach or a few press interviews in the hotel lounge. The group had very little free time.

Their diary in 1963 was so full of gigs that it was relatively easy for anyone to get hold of concert tickets. Many fans followed the

Two lucky fans posing for a once-in-a-lifetime photo opportunity in 1963.

Beatles around the resorts that summer, attending show after show. They didn't have to book tickets in advance because there were plenty of seats to be bought at the box office when they arrived at each new place. The country's top-circulation teenybopper fanzines of the day were packed with colourful pin-up pics of John, Paul, George and Ringo and fascinating scraps of fresh information. For example, they used to give Ringo's dad five bob (25p) each week to put on the football pools! The Beatles loved every moment of their new-found fame. They were grateful for the encouragement and loyalty their fans gave them. As George told me at the time, "We feel flattered. If the screaming fans weren't there, then we wouldn't be here, would we?" Relative newcomer Ringo, who had only joined the group the previous year, was still receiving less attention from interviewers than the rest of the group, but he was gradually becoming more confident.

Each of the four boys soon realised that everything they mentioned to magazine writers, whether supposedly off the record or not, might well finish up in headlines. In one interview, Paul happened to tell a journalist that he used a particular brand of green toothpaste, and cartons of the stuff poured in. Paul quipped: "Next time I'll tell everybody I like Jaguar cars!" The years of slogging away at all-night sessions in Hamburg's clubland had given them tremendous stamina and hardened them up to face what less experienced bands might have

thought of as a punishing schedule. But they thoroughly enjoyed their one-nighter tours and all the other shows they did in 1963.

Apart from the shows in the summer, there was a short run of nine concerts in Sweden at the end of October and several other special dates, including a guest spot on the star-packed bill of the 1963 *New Musical Express* Poll Winners' Concert in April. To round off a truly amazing year, the group opened in their own Christmas show at the Finsbury Park Astoria in North London on 24th December.

Paul met his first long-term lover, actress Jane Asher, during a BBC concert called *Swinging Sound '63* at London's Royal Albert Hall in April. The media eventually revealed something that all their fans had known for ages (that John was married to Cynthia and they had a son named Julian). *The Times* concluded that "the outstanding English composers of 1963 seem to have been John Lennon and Paul McCartney, the talented young musicians from Liverpool whose songs have been sweeping the country since last Christmas, whether performed by their own group, the Beatles, or by the numerous other teams of English troubadours that they also supply with songs". When *The Times* deigned to give a write-up to a new pop group, you knew they'd truly arrived! (JD)

BEATLE NEWS

1963

VEE-JAY SIGNS BEATLES FOR U.S.
The Beatles have an American recording contract! Traditionally America has been the toughest nut for British pop acts to crack, although the Tornados recently topped the US charts with 'Telstar'. Now the Beatles have their chance in the biggest record market in the world. (January 1963)

MAJESTIC RESPONSE
Frantic scenes greeted the Beatles on January 17th when they arrived at the Majestic Ballroom in Birkenhead for their regular concert date. Several hundred fans turned up for the show, to find that all the tickets had already been sold! Police had to be called to restore order after many of the fans tried to take the Majestic by storm.

While all the Beatles' fans on Merseyside are delighted with their recent success, some are worried that national success might take the boys away to the bright lights of London. The Beatles are adamant, however: Liverpool is their home, and Liverpool is where they're going to stay! (January 1963)

BEATLES ARE NO. 1
They've done it!! 'Please Please Me' has made it to the top of the *NME* charts, giving Liverpool's most popular group a No. 1 hit record with only their second release. Not surprisingly, the boys are absolutely ecstatic. They got the news just before they joined the second part of the Helen Shapiro tour in Mansfield. (February 1963)

LONG DRIVES, SHORT SHOWS
Whoever worked out the schedule for the Helen Shapiro tour? He had better not get too close to the Beatles, as they aren't too pleased at having to travel several hundred miles for some concerts, only to find themselves almost back where they started the following night! Luckily, the tour format means that the group only have to play for about 20 minutes at each performance – a far cry from their exhausting schedule in Hamburg! (February 1963)

MARATHON SESSION
No title has yet been fixed for the boys' first album, recorded in a marathon session at EMI on February 11th. But George Martin apparently favours *Off The Beatle Track*, and as he is their recording manager, what he says usually goes! (February 1963)

FLU BUG BITES JOHN
Flu-stricken John Lennon was forced to miss several dates of their tour with American stars Chris Montez and Tommy Roe, but he was fit enough to rejoin the group for their show in Sheffield. In the meantime, the boys struggled on as a three-piece, but Paul, George and Ringo were relieved when his doctor pronounced John fit to join them again! (March 1963)

NO. 1 AGAIN!
It's another Number One hit for the Beatles! Their third single, 'From Me To You', rocketed into the charts at No. 6 just days after it appeared in the shops – and the following Friday it was No. 1. Meanwhile, the lads' first long-player has been climbing steadily up the album charts. It has now reached No. 2, and advance sales predictions suggest that it could start May off on a great note by giving the Beatles double chart-toppers! (April 1963)

BEATLES WOW NME SHOW
The boys were a big hit at the *NME* Pollwinners' Concert, held at the Empire Pool, Wembley. The organisers slotted them in at the last minute, although they hadn't won any categories in the recent poll, realising that two No. 1 singles on the trot makes them Britain's hottest pop talent of 1963. The Beatles played four numbers at the all-star show: 'Please Please Me', 'From Me To You', 'Twist And Shout' and finally 'Long Tall Sally' – introduced by Paul with the words, "Here's a song immortalised by that great gospel singer Victor Silvester"! (April 1963)

MEN AT WORK
John and Paul are sorting through their old songs, in the hope that, as John says, "we might be sitting on a goldmine"! They are also writing new songs ready for their second album. Meanwhile, Brian Epstein's latest protegés, Billy J. Kramer and the Dakotas, are being launched with no fewer than two Lennon/McCartney songs: 'Do You Want To Know A Secret' and 'I'll Be On My Way'.

Neil Aspinall at the wheel of the van that carried the Beatles to their early concerts.

A third Epstein group, Gerry & the Pacemakers, are debating whether to follow their own No. 1 hit, 'How Do You Do It', with John and Paul's number 'Hello Little Girl'. (April 1963)

NOT FOR SALE

Liverpool is apparently the source of the rumour that the Beatles have released 'Some Other Guy' as their new single. Last autumn, Granada TV visited the Cavern and recorded the Beatles singing the song for their *People And Places* show. Apparently, the TV company had several singles pressed up featuring the Beatles' performance, and a couple of these have turned up in Liverpool record shops. One report suggested that as many as 400 copies are in circulation. The rumour is quite untrue, as the Granada singles were made only for their own use, and sadly you can't order 'Some Other Guy' in the shops. (May 1963)

TWIST & SHOUT BATTLE

There's a real battle at the moment over who will have the biggest hit with that Beatles stage favourite, 'Twist And Shout', which the boys included on their LP. The reaction to their version has been so great that the original recording of the song, released by the Isley Brothers a year ago, has entered the charts this month. And this week, another version of the song has been issued by Brian Poole & the Tremeloes. To cap it all, the Beatles' version of the song is contained on their first EP, called *The Beatles No. 1*. It will be interesting to see which version comes out on top chart-wise, although you have to remember that the Beatles start with a real disadvantage – their EP will cost almost as much as the Isleys' and Tremeloes' versions put together! (June 1963)

LP SETS RECORD

The Beatles notched up another remarkable record this month when their *Please Please Me* LP became the longest-lasting No. 1 of all time. It has now been at the top of the charts for an incredible 21 weeks in succession, outstripping the previous record of 19 weeks, held by the film soundtrack to *South Pacific*. (August 1963)

FINAL CAVERN?

The Cavern Club once more resounded to the sound of the Beatles on August 3rd – their first show there for months. No further dates are planned at the club for the immediate future, as the venue is simply too small for the sort of crowds that the Beatles are attracting these days. (August 1963)

GEORGE AND RINGO WRITING

There are now four songwriting Beatles! We know all about John and Paul, but George and Ringo are getting in on the act as well. George has written a song for the boys' second album, while Ringo has come up with a number called 'Don't Pass Me By'. "There," he says, "it even sounds miserable. And every time I play it to the lads, they just laugh!" (August 1963)

RINGO BRANCHES OUT

Ringo apparently has plans for a new career – dancing! The boys are looking for a way to incorporate Ringo's talent into their act. Says Paul: "It would only be for certain numbers, but it's an idea we're working on. We all mess around on drums a bit and we could take his place now and then. Mind you, we could never be as good as Ringo. He's the best drummer we've ever had. He's fitted into the group like a glove. We have heard rumours that he's leaving, but there's absolutely no truth in them. Besides, if he went, we'd miss his morning dance sessions!" (August 1963)

BEATLES BREAK

All four boys flew off on Monday 16th September for two weeks' well-earned break from the pressure of being Britain's top pop stars. George and his brother Peter went to see their sister Louise in St. Louis, USA. "I've wanted to go for years," George said, "but I could never afford it before."

John has gone to Paris: "My reason for going there is that I did the trip two years ago when I was near broke. I hitched most of the way and stayed in pretty low dumps. Now I want to see what it's like being there with money in your pocket."

Finally, Paul and Ringo have gone to Greece, Paul "to have all my teeth out" and

Wherever the Beatles went in 1963, hundreds of fans were always waiting for the group to arrive.

Ringo "to get my toenails tattooed"! (September 1963)

TOPPING THE BILL

The boys were the stars of TV's *Sunday Night At The London Palladium* recently, supported by Des O'Connor. The audience reaction was ecstatic, and even more overwhelming were the scenes outside, as hundreds of fans screamed for a glimpse of their idols. The national press picked up the story, and coined a new word – 'Beatlemania' – to describe what happened. But the scenes at the Palladium were only a continuation of what has been seen across the country all this year. (October 1963)

WHAT A MONTH!

It's been an amazing month – in every way! Top of the bill at the Royal Variety Show; a new album, *With The Beatles*, straight into the charts at No. 1; an old single, 'She Loves You', climbing to the top for a second time; riots around the country as they play their latest UK tour; and most incredible of all, a million sales of their new single, 'I Want To Hold Your Hand' – in advance! (November 1963)

AWARDS PRESENTATION

November 18th saw a special ceremony at which the Beatles were given gold discs for their latest releases. Sir Joseph Lockwood, the chairman of EMI, made the presentation. At one point, he stumbled slightly over his words, and John butted in: "You're fired!" Only artists with a couple of million sales behind them can get away with treating their boss like that! (November 1963)

Fan club conventions

Two incredible events when thousands of lucky fans met their idols in the flesh

In 1963, several thousand fan club members from all over the South of England were lucky enough to win a lottery organised by the Official Beatles Fan Club, which gave them the chance to spend a remarkable day with John, Paul, George and Ringo in South London.

Every single one of them shook hands with all four boys, while some girls managed to plant a quick kiss on the lips or cheeks of their favourite Beatle, and others even touched their hair. Most of them came away with souvenirs signed by the boys and quite a few were able to chat with the Beatle they loved for a few moments.

It all started with an official fan club announcement telling members about two very special conventions, one in the north and one in the south, which would be held during the pre-Christmas period. They were told: "For members based in the north, there will be a get-together at Liverpool Stadium on a date to be announced in October, and — for those who live in the south — another one at London's Wimbledon Palais on the afternoon of Saturday 14th December. The Beatles will attend each session and they'll meet as many members as possible. Please don't write for tickets or more information just yet because members in both parts of the country will receive full details, along

with application forms, by post shortly before the date of each convention. There will be a draw to decide who gets invited. At Wimbledon Palais there will also be a public dance featuring the Beatles in the evening after the get-together, and members will have a priority chance of purchasing the first 1,000 tickets for the dance in advance."

The Liverpool convention was eventually put back to Saturday 7th December, to coincide with an existing tour date at the city's Odeon Theatre. The venue was changed from the Stadium to the Liverpool Empire (next door to the Odeon), and the Beatles not only gave a special afternoon concert for their fans, but also allowed them to watch a recording of the BBC TV show *Juke Box Jury*, compered by DJ David Jacobs, in which the four boys formed the judging panel to give "hit" or "miss" verdicts on newly released singles. Both this special edition of *Juke Box Jury* and the concert performance, which the BBC called *It's The Beatles*, were shown on national TV the same evening.

The special treat for those invited to the Liverpool event was to see not one, but two television shows in the making. Unfortunately, there were no facilities for face-to-face meetings with the Beatles, who had to race across the street to the Odeon to prepare for their two further evening concerts.

Like Liverpool, their Wimbledon convention also involved an existing gig. The Palais appearance was destined to be the Fab Four's final ballroom date before they moved on to far larger arenas and stadium venues abroad. I went down to Wimbledon to look at the layout of the ballroom. There was a long wooden bar that the four Beatles could sit behind while the fans filed past on the other side.

On the big day, the four boys arrived in Wimbledon, looking amazingly bright and fresh considering they had just finished a strenuous UK tour. At Neil Aspinall's suggestion, they were already wearing their stage outfits to avoid spending any time in a cramped and uncomfortable dressing room.

John wore a pin-striped city-gent job, three had smart white shirts with black ties, while the fourth (Ringo) was the odd man out in a darker shirt.

When they checked the layout of the big ballroom the first thing they saw was a grim-looking steel cage-like structure erected all around the front of the stage. "This is a joke, isn't it?" asked Paul. George commented solemnly: "Do we go on before or after the lions?" "It's bloody daft!", yelled John, shaking his head. "Get hold of Eppy! I want to sort this out. Now!" But very wisely, the Beatles' manager was keeping his head down that afternoon because he didn't want to be involved in a verbal battle with either the promoters or the Beatles.

I was as shocked as anyone to see the height of the so-called security barrier the promoters had erected between the Beatles and their fans for the boys' stage show. The wall of wire and steel was in two sections, one fixed on top of the other. I argued with the Palais management people that the top half should be dismantled, because the bottom half was quite high enough to offer suitable protection for the group. But I got nowhere, even when I warned them that the Beatles might refuse to play under these conditions.

In a hastily convened huddle to discuss the crisis, the boys threatened to walk out if nothing was done about the cage, but they let me talk them round into accepting the unsatisfactory situation for the sake of their 3000 waiting fans. Paul told the others: "What we ought to do is go ahead with the show but apologise to the crowd for the cage and make it clear it wasn't our idea." George pointed out the danger of fans getting crushed against the wire mesh: "Everyone will push forward. It's not just our safety that's involved, a lot of fans may get hurt."

Meanwhile roadie Mal Evans was having problems of his own: "They've made a lousy job of extending this stage," he told me. "The extra bits they've added on are wobbling about when I walk on them, so

The boys meeting their fans in Wimbledon

This ridiculous wire cage was erected to 'protect' the boys from their fans.

what will they be like when the four lads start playing? I can see John or Paul disappearing through the floor!"

When we opened the front doors it was like the January sales at Selfridges multiplied by ten! Following a quick consultation with Neil, Mal and press officer Brian Sommerville, we all decided we'd ignore the little corps of commissionaires and take over crowd control duties ourselves. Above the din of shrieking girls, we managed to get some sort of order into the situation, lining up fans at one end of the bar so they could move along the front of the counter and meet the Beatles seated behind. At a guess I'd say that the vast majority were girls, although the fan club records showed that at least 20% of the members were boys.

The hardest part was to keep the queue moving without hurting the feelings of fans to whom even the briefest contact with each of the boys meant so much. We didn't stop any girl from stretching across the bar to feel a Beatle fringe or trying to kiss them, but we drew the line at letting anyone climb over to have a picture taken with the group, although everyone could take as many shots

as they liked from the front. We gave each fan as long as possible before urging them to move on to give the next in line a chance. It was essential to keep things moving reasonably fast if all 3000 were going to meet the boys in just a couple of hours. Magazines, concert tickets, album covers, copies of *The Beatles Book* and a wide assortment of souvenir posters were offered to the boys to sign. Few of the fans could have imagined that each signature they obtained was adding a handsome three-figure sum to the eventual value of whatever item they'd brought along.

John, Paul, George and Ringo did a magnificent job, constantly shaking hands, smiling for the cameras and writing little messages beside their autographs. Each of the four made eye-contact with each fan and held on to every hand that came across the counter. Occasionally a Beatle would shout out for a drink and we'd open another case of Coke or Pepsi bottles. A few fans asked for half-empty Cola bottles and the Beatle concerned would take one more swig before passing it across the counter.

From time to time a Beatle would be offered a really bad photo to sign, which made them wonder how on earth such rubbish had gone on sale. The simple answer

was that merchandising of Beatles gear had yet to be controlled and we had no way of checking on the quality of anything that was being produced to satisfy the souvenir hunters. Outside the ballroom, the pavements of Merton High Street were lined with hawkers selling all sorts of tatty Beatles stuff at sky-high prices. The poor kids were being ripped off but they were prepared to buy anything that they could take in with them to be signed by the Fab Four.

We thought the line of waiting fans would never end and I began to realise that some of the early arrivals might be joining onto the end of the queue for a second go. Eventually Neil, Mal and I took it in turns to stand at the end of the line to stop that happening. As soon as the final autographs had been scrawled and the last kisses were planted on the Beatles' faces, the boys made a quick exit to take a brief break before going on stage.

It has to be said that the ridiculous security cage around the stage almost spoilt the enjoyment of the fans right at the front who were constantly pressed against it by the crowd pushing from behind. Several of the white-hatted security men sat or knelt inside the cage, but they weren't able to do much apart from making ideal targets to have their white hats knocked off or grabbed by hands that came through the wire mesh of the barriers. After their show, the Beatles said they were pleased with every aspect of the gig except the metal barriers. Paul said: "The fans filed past us quite calmly at the long bar, nobody ripped off our shirts or did anything daft. What made the Palais managers believe the crowd would change into monsters when we did our show? The barriers were stupid and we're sorry we weren't able to get them pulled down before we went on." The show was given an ecstatic response and the entire afternoon was voted a huge success that generated hundreds of 'thank you' letters. Ursula Fuery of London N16 wrote: "Thank you for making my dream

come true and for inviting me to Wimbledon. I shall never forget it as long as I live – it was the happiest day of my life. I not only saw the boys performing, but I actually touched John, Paul, George and Ringo after queuing up to meet them for two hours."

Jackie Brennan from Kettering, Northants asked: "Please could you do me a favour. I met Viv, Linda and Gill at the Wimbledon get-together, but we got separated in the crush to meet the Beatles. I saw Viv later then lost her again at the evening dance. Please ask them to write to me as I would love to hear from them." A club newsletter to members after the two conventions said: "We met something like

6000 of you in Liverpool and Wimbledon. We didn't like having to refuse so many thousands of other members whose applications for Get Together tickets were unsuccessful but, on the other hand, if we had held these sessions in larger venues it would have meant losing the informal atmosphere altogether." When Brian asked the boys afterwards what they thought of Wimbledon, the replies were unanimous: "Great!" "Fab!" "Gear!" "Terrific!" Like the rest of us, the Beatles tended to remember the best of their experiences and forget the problems.   (TB)

_____

The full-length performance that ended the Wimbledon convention.

The first Christmas show

Behind the scenes at the pantomime Brian Epstein put together in December 1963

The Beatles' very first Christmas Show in 1963 would have been recorded and released on video or DVD if the technology had been in place 40 years ago. What a collector's item it would have been, preserving for future generations not only the acting debut of John, Paul, George and Ringo but also raw newcomer Cilla Black's spot in the second half, plus appearances by Australian compere Rolf Harris, Brian Epstein's young Liverpool protegé, Tommy Quickly, the Barron Knights, the Fourmost, and Billy J. Kramer with the Dakotas closing the first half.

The Beatles' theatrical acting debut was seen by 100,000 people who flocked to the Finsbury Park Astoria between December 24th 1963 and January 11th 1964. Unfortunately, though all their dialogue was pre-recorded and played back to audiences through the PA system, most of what the Fab Four had to say was drowned out by continuous high-pitched shrieking. This was the age of Beatlemania and the mere sight of the Beatles dressed up in fancy costume was enough to start the screaming. Producer

Peter Yolland did his best to help people follow the story of the Beatles' sketch. Besides having the boys' lines blasted out over banks of giant loudspeakers, Yolland put up the words on a series of slides, silent movie style, on a screen suspended above the stage.

One week into the Beatles' late-autumn tour of Britain, Yolland brought them scripts for the couple of brief sketches he'd come up with for the show. When the boys read that they'd be expected to come on more than once during each performance, they reacted in different ways. John said they ought to stay out of sight until their own spot at the end of the second half. "I'm not sure that we're ready to clown around on stage in front of 3000 people," he said. "It's one thing to tell a joke or two between songs with a guitar in your hand. It's quite another to go dressing up and trying to do a proper play, even a comedy piece."

Paul said he liked the idea of the entire cast being seen at the beginning and the Beatles popping in and out from time to time. He told the others: "After all, we've

got to find ways of making this a proper production as against an ordinary concert." Epstein gave them a little lecture: "Paul's right, you know. This isn't just another concert, it's a new concept altogether so far as a pop show is concerned. It has to have a theatrical atmosphere, comedy and lots of laughter along with the songs." So John, Paul, George and Ringo obediently agreed to everything and Yolland fixed an appointment when the dialogue for the Victorian melodrama sequence could be put on tape.

In one respect, the personal wishes of the Beatles prevailed without any argument. Paul made the point to Eppy: "It's all very well doing a Christmas show for Londoners, but what about our fans up north. Why not do it in Liverpool as well?" The truth was that the Beatles could not be in two places at once over the holiday season but Brian's compromise was to preview the show for single nights in Bradford and Liverpool. Brian Epstein told me that Yolland instantly rejected the idea of any pre-Christmas provincial dates on the grounds that it would be impossible to shift all the scenery hundreds of miles at a time of year when travelling conditions might cause disastrous delays. Without consulting the Beatles, Brian said: "Forget the costumes, the scenery and the sketches. Bradford and Liverpool can just be glorified final rehearsals for the music side of the show. We'll do them just like concerts and it'll give us all the chance of making sure the other acts fit in."

Peter Yolland found Paul the most attentive Beatle throughout the preparatory stages when there were costume designs and little models of the stage sets to look at. Formal rehearsals for the sketches never really took place until everyone moved into the theatre. Poor old Peter had to be content with grabbing the boys here and there to tell them where they'd move on this line and where they'd need to look on that line. Ringo told me: "It's pointless him asking me to remember these things without seeing the

Before the dress rehearsal the Beatles posed for the press in costume.

actual stage. I won't carry any of this in my head until I do it at Finsbury Park." The others reminded him that since the dialogue was all recorded in advance, it wouldn't be necessary even to memorise any lines. After all, it wasn't as though there'd be TV camera close-ups to reveal miming mistakes. Who'd see their lips moving from the front row of the stalls, let alone the seats in the back circle? Brian Epstein's main concern was that the sketches should be in the right places in the show's running order. He told me: "If someone like Cilla has to come on just after the audience has been roaring away at the Beatles, she'll be petrified. Everyone must be given a fair chance."

Everybody was nervous on Christmas Eve, despite the fact that the show had run successfully for two nights in Bradford and Liverpool, minus the theatrical moments. Cilla was looking worried, the Beatles were on edge, even seasoned performer Rolf Harris had the jitters just before showtime. The place was crawling with newspaper people. Beatlemania had become big front-page news since *Sunday Night At The London Palladium*, the Royal Variety Performance and the recent concert tour, all of which had produced spectacular press pictures of crowds of fans filling the streets.

As the safety curtain went up on the Beatles' Christmas Show, a colourful cloth was revealed with a giant cartoon Christmas cracker painted on it and photographs of the four hairy heads of the Beatles. On a screen, a series of speeded-up silent movie sequences depicted a car chase, then a channel swimmer and eventually a vintage Wright Brothers aircraft. "By land, by sea and by air come the stars of Brian Epstein's fabulous Christmas show." When the drapes parted, a big cardboard BEA helicopter could be seen, accompanied by appropriate sound effects. One by one, the acts emerged, brought down the steps by Rolf Harris who was dressed in an airline pilot's outfit and peaked cap.

Harris went through the routine of thoroughly teasing his audience, almost letting the helicopter leave without delivering John, Paul, George and Ringo, then bringing it back to the ground: "Ladies and gentlemen, boys and girls, introducing the stars of our show . . ." But the rest was lost in a tidal wave of screaming as the Beatles climbed down from the helicopter, waved and raced off the stage. Then came a quickfire sketch that passed by so swiftly that its point was

The climax of the comedy sketch, with Ringo in the silent role of 'Snow'!

lost on most of the audience. They saw the Beatles huddled together in long white coats at the front of the stage. "News flash!! Three out of four doctors . . ." (at which point three Beatles left the group and disappeared into the wings) ". . . leaves one." John, suddenly realising he's the one, also leaves the stage. There was no laughter, just screaming. The quick visual joke didn't really work, but it didn't matter – it was a pretty weak punch-line, anyway! The only thing that did matter was that the crowd had caught their second glimpse of the Beatles! Now they'd listen to the Fourmost more readily!

In the blackout which followed the Fourmost, the movie screen dropped back into view. "Beatlerama Productions present, in breathtakingly colourful black and white Beatlescope, What A Night!, starring Sir John Jasper and Ermyntrude, Our Heroine." Lennon appeared as the villainous top-hatted Sir John, wielding a vicious bullwhip and twirling his curly moustache. As you might have guessed, John loved all that. Ermyntrude was George, a maiden in distress, in a shawl, spotted headscarf and embarrassed grin. Ringo was the Snow, scuttling to and fro as he scattered paper flakes from a large bag whenever the screen subtitles said: "And the snow continued to fall . . ." Inevitably, as in all good Victorian melodramas, Ermyntrude had to be saved from her fate worse than death, tethered to

the railway lines to await the express train, and the chap to do the heroic deed had to be Paul the Fearless Signalman, clad in wide-peaked cloth cap, striped shirt, braces and baggy trousers tied up with string around the thighs.

How could Billy J. Kramer & the Dakotas follow that? Answer: with great difficulty! The Beatles returned to fill the final 25 minutes of the second half with their usual concert performance. The numbers included 'Roll Over Beethoven', 'All My Loving', 'This Boy', 'I Wanna Be Your Man', 'She Loves You', 'Till There Was You', 'I Want To Hold Your Hand', 'Money' and 'Twist And Shout'. Then, with the audience still crying out for more, the Fab Four were off and running, with towels round their sweat-soaked heads, dashing for tonight's secret exit where their getaway car was waiting, engine already running. By the time the emerging audience realised that the sleek limousine lined up outside the stage door was only a decoy, John, Paul, George and Ringo were miles away from Finsbury Park, racing through the night towards their favourite West End club, combing back their hair, smacking their lips and ready to tackle the first round of Scotch and Cokes at the beginning of another hard day's night. (TB)

Great news in Paris

Neil Aspinall reports how the Beatles learned that they were No. 1 in America

Paris waved the white flag of surrender after only a few blasts of artillery that sounded very much like 'She Loves You'. The fabulous, international Beatles had struck again and infected a whole country with Beatlemania. They took a little time to settle in. But I was there to watch the excitement grow among their French fans, until the Beatles finally left Paris, three weeks later.

It was pretty chaotic early on, though. In fact, they nearly didn't make it on time. The Beatles' invasion of France began on Tuesday, January 14th 1964. Ringo Starr was unable to meet the others in London, having been fog-bound in Liverpool. "I'll make my own way. See you all in Paris", he wired. And at London airport, thick mist swirled around the buildings and the planes. "We've had it, too", said Paul, looking anxiously at the sky. But the misty fog lifted just

enough to get planes aloft. One plane, a Comet 4B, was extra-special, as it had three-quarters of the Beatles aboard, plus Brian Epstein, Mal Evans, press representative Brian Sommerville, me . . . and a load of photographers and reporters. The Beatles posed for a few pictures, waved to the fans who yelled "Good Luck" and ran up the stairs into the front of the plane. 35 minutes later, at precisely 5.50pm, we coasted into Le Bourget airport, outside Paris, into a mad rush that threatened to engulf the Beatles. There were yelling photographers and questioning reporters, gabbling in French and English. Flashlights exploded all the way through the Customs as the Beatles tried to maintain resolute grins. Fans screamed, including eight-year-old Anne Maskell, from Tooting, South London, on her way to Austria with her parents. "It IS the Beatles, it IS", she yelled excitedly. Paul flashed her a quick smile.

The boys were frog-marched through Customs, and then left the arrivals building, hidden in a mass of newspapermen. The Beatles' usual Austin Princess car had been ferried across the Channel by chauffeur Bill. More flashlights popped. And off into the heart of Paris, to the fabulously lush George V Hotel, close to the Champs Elysées.

Inside: more pandemonium. Everybody craning to get a look at the Liverpool lads. More flash-bulbs erupted. The management of this dignified, super-fab hotel looked disturbed. Eventually, the Beatles were shown to the comparative peace of their suites. John saw the tapestries and Louis XIV furniture, and said: "It looks like a museum". There should have been a rehearsal that evening, but without Ringo, there was no point. Said George: "It's odd without Ringo. We sort of feel we've lost a limb". The missing limb was actually in Liverpool, making final preparations to catch a plane to London and then Paris the following day. John and Paul took that first night easily, relaxing in their suite, calling for 'ciggies' and Cokes. George wandered off with a news-paper man, ending up in an expensive club, watching a high-charged (in both ways) cabaret. "It's a smart place", said George. "But the music was pretty standard sort of swing. Nice as background to a chat, though."

John and Paul thought back to the time they'd been in Paris before – flat-broke, unable to afford a taxi, without funds for a decent meal. "Maybe we'll buy the Eiffel Tower this time", said John with a grin. The boys made friends easily. Bruno Coquatrix, the guv'nor of the Paris Olympia theatre, called round to see his latest signings. So did a representative of Odeon Records, who release the boys' discs in France.

When the room was finally cleared, the McCartney and Lennon partnership talked about songs. George Martin was coming to Paris and wanted to hear some brand-new material from the boys. John and Paul had agreed to write six songs for their first film, plus one for Billy J. Kramer and the

Arriving at Le Bourget airport in January 1964 for their first French concerts.

swarm backstage. Fans danced in the aisles and chanted "Les Beatles". One boy aged about 17, dressed in a red sweater, shimmied his way to the front of the stalls. Rocking in time with the solid Beatle beat, he couldn't restrain himself any longer. He jumped up on the stage and tried out a dance routine with John. John kept on singing, but couldn't help a quick grin. Then on came big Mal Evans to clutch the offender in his arms and cart him off into the wings.

It was noticeable, though, that the audience actually let the Beatles be heard. You could pick up the words of songs. And, unlike all their previous shows in Britain, there were more boys than girls in the audience. Everybody joined in the clapping, and one girl cried out in plaintive French, "I just can't anymore, my hands are hurting me." The boys made a hectic get-away just in front of a crowd of fans. Ringo barely had time to observe: "The audience was so different to those in England. They don't seem to scream."

The Beatles had another huge surprise to come. They made their way back by fast car to the George V Hotel and up to their suite. Two of the boys took a quick bath in the marble-walled bathrooms. Then they sat talking. And then the news arrived. Direct from London came the message: "The Beatles are top of the American Hit Parade." The boys went mad. Said Mal Evans, who happened to come into the suite immediately afterwards: "They always act this way when anything big happens – just like a bunch of kids, jumping up and down with sheer delight. Paul climbed onto my back and I gave him a piggy-back around the room. They felt that this was the biggest thing that had ever happened – and who could blame them? Gradually they quietened down, ordered some more drinks, and sat down to appreciate fully what had happened. It was a wonderful, marvellous night for all of them. I was knocked out."

Celebrations went on until five o'clock in the morning. Somebody else rang through to say that 'I Want To Hold Your Hand' was the fastest-rising disc ever by any British artiste in the States. Capitol Records had never known anything like it – just three weeks to hit the top spot. The boys had plenty to talk about: their night in Versailles, and their forthcoming trip to America.

Dakotas and another for Tommy Quickly. They also hoped that one of the songs they'd just written for their first movie would be released as their next single. But time was against them.

"We'll get a piano moved into the suite" said Paul. "That'll help speed things up." John and Paul shared a large room so they could keep working on their new numbers. George and Ringo shared another huge room, though the two rooms had communicating doors and were on the same landing. Top stars from all walks of life stay at the George V Hotel. For the first few days, film star Burt Lancaster was there – and yes, he HAD heard of the Beatles.

On Wednesday morning, the Beatles were late getting out of bed. Nothing unusual! In a sense, they are night people, rarely waking up properly before lunch. Said George: "I think we're gonna like Paris. I only hope the French people like us." But the boys delayed showing themselves. They'd said they'd be up at twelve noon. Instead it was around three o'clock in the afternoon when they finally made an appearance along the

Champs Elysées, with photographers following their every move. Cries of "It's the Beatles" followed the boys in German, French and English. Scots teenager Inez Uthington was heard to say: "It's marvellous, I'd not seen the boys before. I feel weak at the knees!" But before the crowds got out of hand, the Beatles were driven back to the Hotel George V.

Ringo arrived at Le Bourget at five o'clock. He was picked up by a British car that was entered in the Monte Carlo Rally and driven by Stuart Turner, and was rushed to join the others at the hotel. Many fans from Liverpool had heard that Ringo was driving all the way to Paris in one of the competition cars, and they flooded the switchboards, wondering about his route. "Please, please, let me talk to a Beatle," came the calls. "We want to wish them luck." All four Beatles eventually made their way to the Cyrano Theatre in Versailles, some ten miles from the centre of Paris, for a try-out performance. The show started at nine o'clock and went on until well after midnight. Gendarmes held the young audience back as they tried to

The next morning – which, for the Beatles, started sometime after two o'clock in the afternoon – they had to prepare for their opening night at the Olympia, the top music-hall in France. Every season there starts with a 'stuffed-shirt' audience on the first evening, with plenty of minks and diamonds filling every other seat, and dinner-jackets filling the rest. The Beatles arrived in their Austin Princess, leapt out and hustled into the dressing-room – a tiny room for the four boys, with barely space to swing a guitar. At their hotel, they'd been used to a bigger bathroom EACH than the area they now had to share. Also on the bill were US star Trini Lopez and French songstress Sylvie Vartan, plus a full variety programme, including the inevitable juggler. Trini closed the first half, while Sylvie preceded the bill-topping Beatles.

Fortunately, lots of fans turned up for the afternoon show. They were clearly intrigued by the Beatles. Later, in the evening, as expected, lots of sophisticated Parisians filled the seats. Again the boys did well, despite three failures in amplification which had Mal Evans leaping onstage to repair the damage. There was no squealing, no screaming, but the audience clapped in time, appreciating every number. "Merci beaucoup", said Paul, the only French they attempted. The cameramen, who were everywhere, mobbed the stage, firing off at every movement the boys made. But the real drama was going on backstage. Fists flew, in that confined space. Mal Evans said the trouble started when a French photographer wasn't allowed in to take exclusive pictures. But there were other outbreaks of trouble. Paul called out for order. Nobody listened. George had to protect his guitar from swinging fists. The gendarmes arrived on the scene to try and sort things out. They only added to the chaos.

On subsequent evenings, the backstage area was declared no-man's land. The police positively refused to let anybody through. But the initial damage was done. In the rush of Beatlemania, many people who held genuine tickets were kept out of the theatre. Some who did manage to get through found their seats had been taken, and had to watch the show from the back of the stalls. Outside were crush barriers, manned by truncheon-carrying policemen, to curb the enthusiasm of the fans. Brian Epstein and George Martin were in the audience and heard the

applause and the wave of enthusiasm. One felt sorry for Sylvie Vartan, blonde and shapely, who had her act interrupted by cries of "We want Les Beatles." And an ironic note was struck when part of the interval music at the theatre was a gramophone record of the Shadows!

Though the French press were not particularly kind to the Beatles, the audience liked them and so did the fans waiting outside the theatre. French stars like Francoise Hardy, Johnny Hallyday and Richard Anthony, plus Britain's Pet Clark were there to cheer them. The Beatles' exit was hectic, and a few more punches were exchanged between photographers. Eventually they made it back to the hotel for a few hours' kip before the papers came out. The press was frankly mixed. One paper said it "was daddy's rock'n'roll stuff. Nothing very new." Another suggested that it was Trini Lopez who had triumphed. But one influential voice said the

Beatles must have caused jealousy among French pop idols, because hands had never been beaten in time so loudly before at an Olympia opening. As the stay in Paris continued, the police had bigger and bigger crowds to deal with outside the theatre. And still the fans from England spared no expense in ringing the George V Hotel in the hope of getting a few words with the boys. I watched the interest grow. I felt proud for the boys. World interest in the Beatles had gone a step further forward.

But the year was only just starting for the Beatles. Before them were America and their first big film. There were a million more photographs to pose for, a thousand interviews to give, and hundreds of vitally important shows to perform. The Beatles are wonderful ambassadors for Britain in any part of the world where pop music is important, which is now most of the world. And this is only the beginning!   (NA)

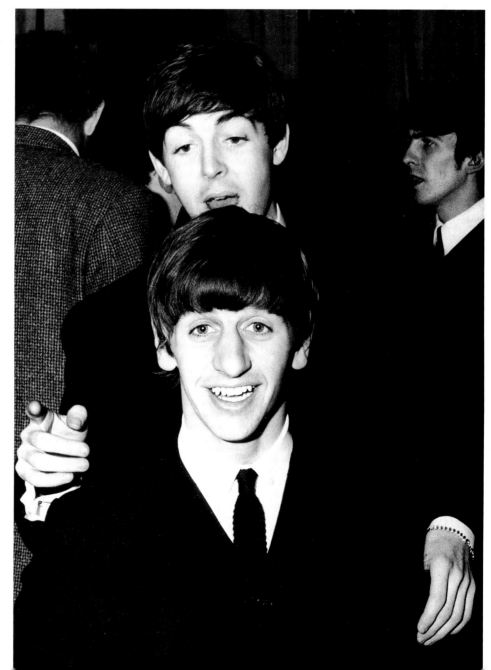

Ringo and Paul react to the news that they've reached No. 1 in America.

First American visit

A day-by-day on-the-spot diary of the Beatles' triumphant conquest of America

Friday, February 7

The Beatles, Brian Epstein, Neil Aspinall, Malcolm Evans and the rest of the touring party leave London Airport at 11 am. There are over 3000 fans waiting at John F. Kennedy Airport on a cold and clear day, and 100 photographers watching as the Boeing 707 jet touched down. Their first duty is a press conference in a room much too small for the job. Photographers wrestle with each other for pictures, TV camera lights glare, and reporters cup their hands to their ears to try and pick up a Beatle reply. The conference is a scream. "Are you just a bunch of British Elvis Presleys?" "It's not true, it's not true", the four reply, and start dancing like Elvis.

There is a battle to get into the cars – one Cadillac for each Beatle. A top journalist travels in each car, to snatch an interview. The convoy is followed to the plush Plaza Hotel by car-loads of fans, who mob the Cadillacs at traffic lights, but fortunately the doors are locked. "We ARE welcome", observes George, dryly. On to the hotel, where the management make it clear that they'd never have accepted the bookings for Messrs. Harrison, Lennon, McCartney and Starr if they hadn't thought they were English businessmen. The Beatles go to their 12th-floor rooms, on a corridor sealed off by guards from the Burns Detective Agency. Plain-clothes men patrol the back stairs. Every time the Beatles leave the hotel, there are 100 New York City cops on duty, backed by a squad of mounted police.

Saturday, February 8

The boys tape an interview, with the Ronettes asking the questions. A croaky George complains that he has a sore throat. Dr. Gordon arrives and says: "I'll have to get you fit, otherwise my young relatives will blunt all my needles." He insists on a signed picture before starting treatment. George's sister, Louise, who's married to an American and living in Illinois, moves in as nurse. At 10am the others head for Central Park, with newsmen tagging along. Limousines are left at the front of the hotel as a decoy, while the boys climb into a small red car belonging to one of the guards. But there's a police car in front to clear the way, siren wailing, red light revolving. More chaos! Mounted police seal off part of the Park, as the Beatles ride in a horse-drawn hackney carriage, "mounties" following at a gallop.

Then a limousine arrives to take them to rehearsals of the *Ed Sullivan Show* at CBS Studios. Massed police are unable to stop fans surging forward. An amazing "cavalry charge" eventually breaks up the crowd – a nasty, worrying moment. Inside the studios, masses of newsmen are waiting, holding up the rehearsals. Neil Aspinall stands in for George Harrison during a run-through. Later, George makes a dramatic recovery, arriving at the studio to be greeted by cheers and applause from technicians, newsmen and Ed Sullivan.

John, Paul and Ringo are entertained to dinner at the exclusive 21 Club. Capitol executives select pheasant and other high-priced food, but the Beatles go for chops and mashed potatoes! There are curious glances from diners but only one asks for an autograph. Paul tackles crepes suzettes; Ringo, on being shown round the wine cellars, observes: "What, no Cokes?" With the food finished, the boys set off to find New York night life, and see Times Square, Broadway, the UN Building and the Empire State, but it is too risky to leave the car. They return to the hotel to find George, throat improving steadily, taking phone calls from all over America. He talks to a DJ, then listens to himself on his portable radio. Everybody joins in, for the rest of the night!

Sunday, February 9

It's dress rehearsal day for the *Ed Sullivan Show* which is going out live that night. Ed Sullivan threatens, "There shouldn't be too much noise, or else I'll send for a barber!" The show is a tremendous success, with only one problem: John's microphone is switched off during one number. The boys wish they'd been allowed to say something as well as sing. With work over, it's time to go out on the town. George decides to go back to bed, but the others walk from the Plaza to 59th Street and the Playboy Club. It's a risky stroll, but the boys are too fast for the waiting fans.

In the penthouse lounge of the club, drinks and food are being served by attractive girls dressed up as 'bunny rabbits'. The music is soft and sweet, just piano and bass. Says John : "This is the stuff we really like. We only do rock for money!" Something more lively is called for, so it's off to the

Brian Sommerville (left) tries to keep order at their first press conference on US soil.

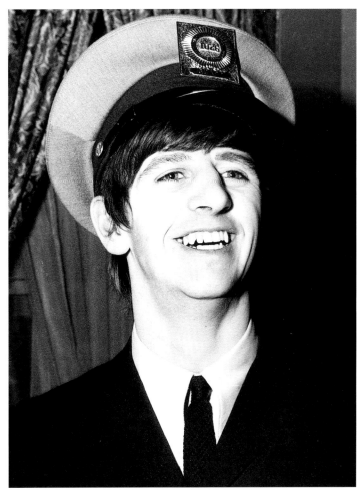

then the Improvisation in Greenwich Village – it's full of teenagers so used to seeing celebrities that no-one even asks for autographs.

Tuesday, February 11

There are snow-storms before the trip to Washington. Instead of flying, the Beatles decide on a train trip. At Penn Station, the railway coach is already full of newspapermen. It's non-stop press encounters on the train, while every stop finds photographers poking cameras at the windows. In Washington, it's straight to the Coliseum for a press conference. The boys have a snowball fight in the street; the cameramen are delighted. At the Shoreham Hotel, the whole seventh floor is put "off limits" by the Beatles' party. One family refuse to be moved. Eventually, the hotel management switch off all the central heating, light, radio, TV and hot water, saying there's been a power failure. The family finally move!

The show at the Coliseum could be the best the boys have ever done, with the atmosphere of a world championship fight, as the boys walk out to a "ring" stage in the centre. The reception is deafening, with 8600 throats screaming for the boys who have captured the greatest country in the world. Brian Epstein, standing at the back, is congratulated by everybody. Brian Sommerville unashamedly cries tears of joy. Incredible scenes – perhaps THE biggest moment of the whole tour. After the show, the boys meet promoter Harry Lynn in his office. Ringo jumps into the big swivel-chair, and starts giving orders. "Mr. Who? Oh, Presley. Has he an appointment to see us? Ask him to wait!"

On to the reception and ball at the British Embassy, where they're received by the Ambassador and Lady Ormsby-Gore. Sir David gets the Beatles' names wrong. The boys confuse him more: John: "No, he's George. I'm Fred and that is Charlie." In the ballroom, it's chaos – debs, duchesses and society ladies all trying to grab themselves a Beatle. One 'lady' snips off a lump of Ringo's hair, from behind his left

Peppermint Lounge, New York's Cavern, the home of 'The Twist'. Four boys in the show do a take-off of the Beatles and Paul, John and Ringo laugh louder than anybody. The press take pictures for hours from every conceivable angle, and it's impossible to get near the floor when expert dancer Ringo decides to twist with one of the girls from the show. Autograph hunters bear down on the boys, so at 4 am the party make for the Plaza Hotel.

Monday, February 10

It's press day: conference after conference, interview after interview. Question: "Who is the sexy one?" George: "Our manager, Brian Epstein". Question (girl reporter): "Who chooses your clothes?" Beatles: "We choose our own. Who chooses yours?" Girl: "My husband". Later, the same girl: "Are there any subjects you prefer not to discuss?" John: "Yes, your husband!" Question: "Which do you consider the greatest danger to your careers, nuclear bombs or dandruff?" Ringo: "Bombs. We've already got dandruff!" Asked why

he said so little, George said: "I'm the anonymous Beatle – but I don't mind as long as they split the money with me."

That evening, it's another round of the New York rock clubs. First, the Headliner,

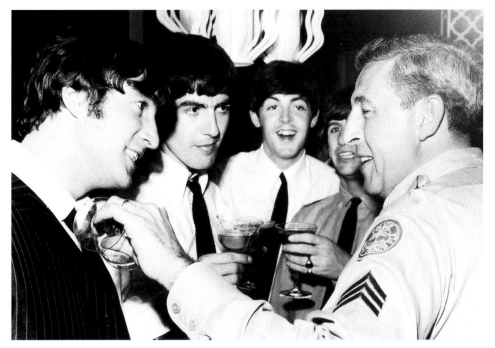

The Beatles with their personal bodyguard, Sgt. Buddy Bresner.

ear. Ringo's response is definitely unprintable. One highly-important couple talk loudly about the boys. He: "Who are these Beatles, anyway?" She: "They sing or something and grow their hair." The Beatles, jostled and shoved, good-naturedly make the draw for the raffle – and beat it quickly back to the Shoreham Hotel.

Wednesday, February 12

Today it's a very amusing train journey back to New York. A reporter says: "Never mind their music, these boys are as good as the Marx Brothers". Ringo wears a ladies' fur coat and white astrakhan hat. John crawls round under swivel chairs. George, asleep at first, later dresses as waiter and serves drinks to the passengers. Ringo appears loaded down with about 20 cameras.

The arrival back at Penn Station causes difficulties. It's Lincoln's Birthday public holiday and the schools are closed. Ten thousand fans are waiting, with many more at the Plaza. The boys are eventually smuggled out of the station and taken to the hotel. The police are caught off guard, as crowds surge forward. The car driver loses his nerve and stops – a fatal mistake. It takes another cavalry charge to get the Beatles through. The police chief arrives to warn the boys that they must be more careful. He looks white and strained: "He's cracking up", whispers George.

It's decided that the boys will go down a back elevator and out through the kitchens for the evening's shows at Carnegie Hall. The plan works and they speed off in taxis.

But, near Carnegie Hall, one cop yells loudly, "There they are". Very foolish. The crowds surge through yet again. Both shows at "long-hair" Carnegie Hall are a tremendous success. Fifty seats are actually placed on the stage itself as "overflow", but management insist only older customers should be there. So much excitement is generated once again that the boys decide on an early night before the flight to Miami the next day.

Thursday, February 13

They leave the Plaza Hotel accompanied by the usual crowds. Their flight arrives in Miami at 4pm, and the reception is indescribable. All the other passengers disembark before the Beatles. Then the four emerge to face a battery of photographers and a bedlam of screaming. The crowd break through the cordons, but on a shout from Brian Sommerville, the Beatles jump from the plane into waiting cars and are whisked off with a strong police motorcycle escort.

The drive to the Deauville Hotel at Miami Beach is a thriller, with a convoy of three black limousines, and police outriders in front, alongside and behind. They go through the red lights and on the wrong side of the road, but even 'offended' motorists smile and

wave when they see who the visitors are. The streets outside the hotel and lobby inside are packed with cheering, smiling and clapping fans. Paul notes the difference between New York (dirty streets, skyscrapers) and Miami (clean, suntanned folk, palm trees, sunshine).

DJ Murray The K is with the boys all the time. He takes them out the first night to see Hank Ballard appearing at the Miami Peppermint Lounge. The boys are besieged by requests for autographs and pictures so they only stay a couple of hours. Then it's back to the hotel to talk about the excitement of the day and to discuss their coming appearance on another *Ed Sullivan Show*.

Friday, February 14

Mr. Bernard Castro offers the boys his luxury houseboat so they can escape the crowds and relax in the bright sunshine. But first they have to go to a private house in Miami Beach to have pictures taken in a private swimming pool for *Life* magazine. Then the houseboat is handed over, complete with captain and crew – and, inevitably, pressmen. So it's pictures all round before the trip round the Bay of Miami. The rest of the day is spent sunbathing and swimming. Ringo isn't so keen on swimming so he stays aboard most of the time. Paul takes over a piano for a while and runs through some ideas for a song he and John are working on.

The Beatles have been assigned a personal police bodyguard, Sgt. Buddy Bresner, who

The Beatles made a huge impact on every aspect of American society in 1964.

pm and queues of people form at breakfast-time. The 'Stamp Out The Beatles' brigade have moved in from Detroit and threaten to demonstrate against the boys. But they cancel their plan after they see the size of the crowds! After the rehearsal, John can't be found; he is asleep behind a curtain. Paul says: " I thought he'd been kidnapped by the Detroit crowd." Not too late back to bed, to prepare for the important show the following day.

Sunday, February 16

The show is broadcast direct from the Deauville Hotel. CBS issue 3,500 tickets though the theatre holds 900 fewer than that. More riots are caused outside when people are turned away even though they have proper tickets. Brian Epstein watches the show closely, and says afterwards: "Definitely the best television appearance and performance by the Beatles yet". A big party is thrown for the boys afterwards by Maurice Lansberg, owner of the Deauville Hotel. Only about forty people attend, and for once the Beatles are not mobbed.

The boys finally decide that they simply must take the opportunity to stay on and get a few days' complete rest, even though they are worried about missing a big Oxfam charity luncheon in London. But reports that Harold Macmillan, host at the lunch, "fully understands" make them feel happier. There are reports, too, that Sir Alec Douglas-Home, the Prime Minister, has praised the boys. He'd said "I think the Beatles are great". They reply: "He doesn't know we've taken Number 11 Downing Street, for rehearsal rooms." He said: "They are the biggest dollar earner we've got". They say: "Little does he know we are putting it all in a Swiss bank".

Monday, February 17

Bob Hope announces in Miami: "Of course I dig the Beatles. My kids would take away my television set if I didn't." Richard Rodgers, top-dog composer, tells Ed Sullivan before he leaves: "The Beatles are the healthiest thing to happen to show business since the discovery of penicillin." The boys discover that there had been a bomb scare during the Miami Sullivan show. The police search their hotel but nothing is found.

The Beatles run through a number while the crew rehearse their camera angles.

has often looked after celebrities. He invites them to his home and the Beatles gratefully accept, going off with Buddy to meet his wife, Dottie and his children, Barry, Andy and Jeri. They sit down to a meal of roast beef, green beans, baked potatoes, peas, salad and a tremendous strawberry iced cake. The Beatles sign autographs and pictures for their new friends.

They're back at the Deauville Hotel by about 11pm to see the floor shows in each of the hotel night clubs. First is Don Rickells, a comedian who gets his laughs by insulting members of the audience. He says about the Beatles: "Look at this. A police sergeant guarding four Zulus when all over the city there's fighting and burglary going on." He keeps up this sort of humour for an hour at least, but the whole audience (especially the Beatles) laugh them-

(Left) The boys in front of the Capitol building in Washington DC.

selves under the table. John feels tired after this show and returns early to bed, but the others go on to see Myron Cohen, another comedian, and singer and dancer Carol Lawrence.

Saturday, February 15

Rehearsals all day for the following day's *Ed Sullivan Show*. The dress rehearsal, before an audience of 2600, is timed for 2

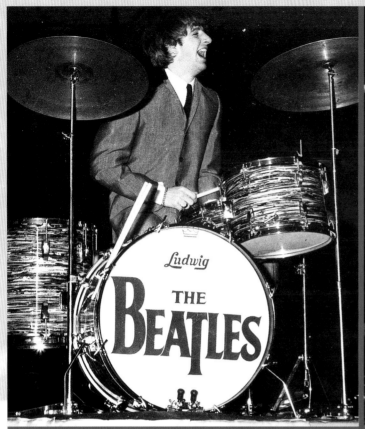

A photo opportunity in the Florida surf.

Now the boys can concentrate on water-skiing. Paul is a good water-ski pupil, and can stay upright longer than the others, and John does well too. George prefers fishing, staying in the shade and not getting too sun-tanned. The boys notice that "love messages" have been scrawled in the sand on the beach outside their hotel rooms.

Tuesday, February 18

The day has been left completely clear for whatever the boys want to do. They decide to visit Cassius Clay (alias Mohammed Ali) in his training quarters. It's utter chaos, as usual. Newsmen are everywhere, furiously taking photos as Cassius pretends to land a left-hook against all four Beatle heads, and then picks up Ringo as if he weighed only a few ounces.

Asked who would win the big heavy-weight fight, Ringo says: "I'll wait till I get out of this gymnasium!" Paul says:

(Left) The scene as the Beatles conquered America. Note the jelly beans on stage, thrown at the group by their fans.

"Cassius, 'cos he's the funniest." Cassius himself hails them as the world champions of singing and says how much he enjoyed meeting them. A big barbecue is laid on in the grounds of a millionaire's home and the Beatles have to cope with "the biggest steaks we've ever seen". Then they go to a drive-in cinema, mainly to see what it's like. The film is *Fun In Acapulco*, starring Elvis Presley. Elvis had earlier sent the boys a good-luck telegram for their visit.

Ringo tries his hand at steering a speed-boat, but abandons ship after losing control as he was trying to park it. The boys still find time to send back picture postcards to their journalist friends in Britain. Meanwhile, television technicians on the *Sullivan Show* are quoted in various American papers as saying they've never worked with such a friendly, co-operative bunch of people as the Beatles – and all the top stars have been on this show. Ringo takes a fancy to a hat worn by one camera-man and asks where he could get one. "You'll have to go to police HQ", is the reply. It was a convict's hat!

Wednesday Febuary 19 – Friday Febuary 21

For the last three days, the Beatles make the most of the sunshine and the opportunity of doing nothing much. There's fanmail from Britain to read that has been forwarded to the boys – and they read the lot! The consensus is that it has been a "fab" trip, all the way.

Finally, it's time for the plane back to Britain. There's an early morning arrival at London Airport, to find thousands of fans, many of whom had stayed out all night to greet the conquering heroes. The Beatles wave from the plane's steps, and John says: "America was great, but this reception tops everything".

The most sensational visit ever made by British stars to America is over. If their US fans had their way, the boys would have stayed on in the States for another year, but they wanted to get back to their fans at home. But more than 200 million people have been exposed to the full force of Beatlemania in three amazing weeks. (TB)

Back in the USA

Their August 1964 US tour broke box-office records from coast to coast

When the Beatles first invaded America in February 1964, hardened journalists there declared that scenes like that could never happen again. Now they ruefully admit that they got it hopelessly wrong, because the Beatles' second trip across the Atlantic has led to scenes so incredible, sensational, fantastic and unbelievable that those hardened journalists are actually inventing new adjectives to get the point across! We'd need a full-length book to include all the highlights of this whistle-stop tour round the States, on a Lockheed Electra jet airliner, with the fab foursome and their entourage. But one thing stands out: it didn't make any difference whether we were in San Francisco, Las Vegas, Canada or New York, the scenes were exactly the same in terms of fan frenzy. The boys were mobbed in hotels, theatres and cars. And through it all they kept up a marvellously serene approach – the sort of attitude that has carried them head-and-shoulders above any other ambassadors from Britain in recent years. Here's a series of quick snapshots of some of the most memorable moments on this amazing tour.

On August 18, the Beatles left behind a tearful, fan-laden London Airport on a Pan-American airliner for San Francisco, some twelve hours away, where they received a real ticker-tape welcome. On their arrival, they heard that actress Jayne Mansfield had 'discovered' one George Ringo (supposedly born in Liverpool, New York), who had a Beatle haircut and was going to appear on a wrestling tour of the same towns as the group. 17,000 people paid £30,000 to see that first show at the Cow Palace in Frisco. "It was incredible," said Paul. The management of the Milton Hotel in San Francisco said that if the fans behaved, they would give them towels, ashtrays and other things handled by the Beatles. At the obligatory press conference, John said, "We get haircuts regularly, but with others you notice it more". Shirley Temple's daughter Lori Black (10) was photographed with the boys, who were showered with jelly-beans and stuffed animals during the concert. They only escaped from the venue by suddenly leaping off the stage, dashing into a car and leaving before the audience realised the show was over.

Their US shows attracted many big stars, such as Pat Boone, Liberace, and leading ventriloquist Edgar Bergen. A 12-year-old blind girl met the boys on stage one night, and was overcome with emotion. Police officers often vanished under a mass of fans. At another press conference, Ringo had to deny strongly that he was having a romance with actress Ann-Margret, the co-star of the latest Elvis movie. As they moved on to Seattle, Vancouver, and Los Angeles, there were similar scenes all the way. Fans threw peanut shells on stage and recovered them as souvenirs after the boys had stamped on them. A gallery of 'Beatle Art', featuring hundreds of drawings of the boys, was opened at the New York World's Fair.

A radio station sponsored a contest to find the best fan-artist. Along the way, Brian Epstein met Elvis Presley's manager, Colonel Tom Parker. "Elvis very much likes the Beatle records," reported the Colonel. The two managers talked long and hard about the early days of their respective stars. Meanwhile, journalist Chris Hutchins arranged for Paul to speak to Elvis Presley on the phone. Elvis said he'd bought a bass guitar and was practising but getting blisters on his hand. "Keep on working at it," advised Paul. Ringo asked a policeman where he could get a genuine police holster, and soon each of the boys was presented with one. At one Canadian date, the boys had to escape in an ambulance because their own car had been badly damaged by fans. There was a ban on Beatles looking round the World's Fair in New York, because the organisers didn't want it "totally destroyed". American teens were divided into "Beatle Maniacs" (those who dig the boys) and "Beatle Saniacs" (those who don't)! There were very few "Saniacs". New box-office records were created all the way. In Cincinnati airport, the Beatles sang 'Hello Dolly' to the crowd.

But the Beatles did get upset at some of the stories in the American fan magazines. They included the rumour that John was about to become a father again, that George would soon be leaving the group, that Ringo was a sick man, and that Paul was married. And despite all their denials, the rumours kept coming. Particularly upsetting was the dreadful story that 'The Seer of the Capital', Mrs. Jeanne Dixon, had forecast that three of the Beatles would shortly be killed in a plane crash. Later Mrs. Dixon denied the story, saying: "The boys are an inspiration for the good to our teenagers." One woman in Wisconsin advertised two Beatle tickets for sale, and her phone didn't stop ringing for two days! Crazy scenes occurred outside hotels throughout the tour. In New York, hundreds of fans screamed as long-haired figures appeared for a second at the windows, but it was merely ordinary guests in the hotel, who were wearing Beatle-wigs. After that, US police banned the boys from ever waving from hotel windows, even though it hadn't been them in the first place. Three of the Beatles went to a night-club with Jayne Mansfield, and three of them also managed a fairly comfortable trip to a clothing store. Mostly, though, they stayed in their hotel rooms, often having late-night parties with a few friends. Columnists commented on "The Beatles' enormous energy".

Show-biz papers worried that the Beatles tour would leave a permanent mark on the business: "They get 150,000 dollars for a show at the Kansas City Municipal Stadium, and maybe other entertainers will decide to raise their prices." Brian Epstein said: "The boys have triumphed totally in the States. I doubt if this impact and excitement will ever be matched again." And Jack Good met up with our party; he's coming back to Britain to produce a TV show with the Beatles this month. Along the way, the boys took in Atlantic City, Philadelphia, Indianapolis, Milwaukee, Chicago, Detroit, Toronto, Montreal, Jacksonville, Boston, Baltimore, Pittsburgh, Cleveland, New Orleans, Dallas, and finally New York again – an incredible, never-to-be-forgotten tour. The boys said: "It was so very tiring. The hot weather added to the strain. Apart from two days in a private house in Bel Air, it's been all go, go, go." Their whistle-stop tour was one of the most hectic ever arranged. Jackie de Shannon, the blonde singing star who appeared on the Beatles' bill, summed it all up in a single word: "Phew". For everyone lucky enough to be along for the ride, it's been a devastating experience.   (BS)

Their fan club

From small beginnings, it soon grew into a huge operation, as Tony Barrow reveals

The very first Beatles Fan Club was run by Roberta ('Bobbie) Brown from her home in Buchanan Road, Wallasey. Bobbie put together a list of local Fan Club members and sent them regular info about the activities of their favourite group in 1962. The most famous Fan Club secretary, Freda Kelly, became involved after she met Bobbie at the Cavern and quickly became a fan of John, Paul, George and Pete. Freda told me: "It wasn't just their music. It was the easy-going way they acted all the time. They made the Cavern stage seem like their own front room and the crowd were all friends they'd invited round. They chatted to individuals in the audience."

In the months that followed, Freda began to share the increasing Fan Club workload with Bobbie. When Brian Epstein opened a NEMS management office above his family's record store in Liverpool's city centre, he took on Freda at £6 10s a week to type letters. She recalls: "I shared this poky little room without any windows with another girl named Beryl. Before I worked for Eppy on a full-time basis, my only contact with the Beatles was at the Cavern where they used to relax in a tiny bandroom after the lunchtime session ended at 2.15pm. I was always after money, so that I could buy more stamps to reply to their fan mail! Paul used to have a whip-round amongst the lads and

hand over what I needed. After I went to work at NEMS Enterprises, Eppy said that if Bobbie and I handed over the fan club subscription money to him, he'd start paying all the bills for postage and duplicating. I didn't have to go cadging from the boys after that, but I did see them more often when they had their management meetings in the office."

When *The Beatles Book* was launched in August 1963, publisher Sean O'Mahony gave the Fan Club a couple of pages in each issue. This was good for both the magazine and the Club. New readers became Club members, while existing members found a new monthly newsletter in the magazine (more up-to-date than anything mailed out to them earlier). I decided in June 1963 that the Club should have a National Secretary based in London at our Monmouth Street address. Until then, fans in the South had kept in touch through Bettina Rose in Surrey whilst Freda had looked after the top half of Britain from Liverpool. The name of the new National Fan Club Secretary was listed as Anne Collingham. In fact no such person ever existed. The 'Collingham' surname was based on my secretary's home address in Earls Court, while Anne was my wife's middle name. This wasn't done in order to deceive the fans.

Clearly, as the membership grew, a full-time office staff of clerks and helpers would be needed. There was little to be gained from confusing members by letting them receive replies from an assortment of people, especially as staff came and went all the time. So the simplest answer was to have 'Anne Collingham' as the regular signature on all letters, newsletters and printed stationery. There was another massive advantage. The press office and the Fan Club shared a single telephone number, COVent Garden 2332. As the publicity side of things became busier, the telephone lines were being used more and more heavily. Therefore it was convenient to know at once if a caller wanted the press office or the Fan Club. If the caller asked for 'Anne Collingham', they were passed straight through to the right room.

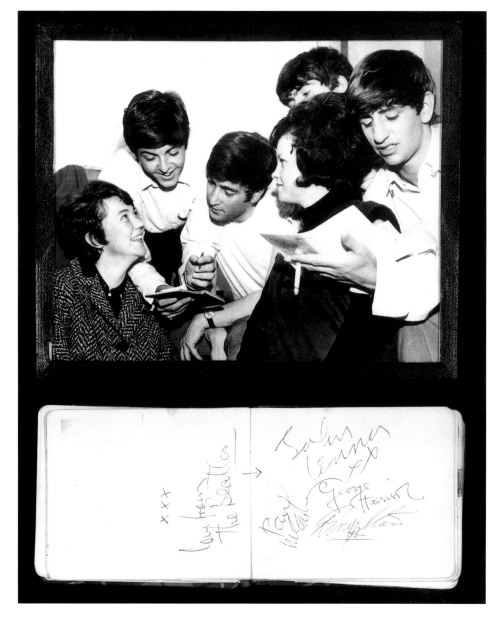

The Beatles meet two of their fans – and the valuable autographs they signed.

Personal callers at 13 Monmouth Street always found themselves talking to 'one of Anne Collingham's assistants'. Ms. Collingham herself was permanently unavailable to meet her visiting members!

Brian Epstein usually refused to sell souvenirs via the Fan Club, but he did make exceptions to that rule – for instance, to help a relative of his who ran a firm called Weldons Of Peckham. They produced a two-tone Beatles badge embroidered in gold and red, which they stitched onto a black polo neck sweater made of 100% Botany wool. It was a quality product and one of the few items ever sold directly through the Official Fan Club. Put on sale at Christmas 1963, it cost £1.15.00 (£1.75) which included postage and packing. Fan Club worker Mary Cockram, a pretty little brunette with an out-going personality, was used to model the Beatles Sweater, but the caption beneath the photograph read: 'Anne Collingham wears the Official Sweater'.

Even before the end of 1963 the onslaught of 'Beatlemania' brought an enormous increase in Fan Club membership. Clearly the personal link between the Beatles and their fans was in danger of being lost forever, despite the heroic efforts of our full-time employees slaving away trying to deal with the mountains of mailbags on the second floor of 13 Monmouth Street.

Two things helped to regain the confidence of Club members, who were disappointed at not getting prompt or comprehensive replies to their letters. The first was the mailing out of the Beatles' first Christmas record. Bettina Rose and Anne Collingham reminded their Newsletter readers: "We emphasise that ONLY Beatle People whose subscriptions are received by our office BEFORE DECEMBER 1st will qualify for this specially produced Christmas gift from our fabulous foursome." The second morale-boosting feature for Beatle People was announced later in the same Newsletter: "We are looking forward to meeting something like 6000 members at the two December Fan Club Conventions – at the Liverpool Odeon on Saturday, December 7th, and at Wimbledon Palais on Saturday, December 14th". The two big conventions, and the exclusive free flimsy disc, left 30,000 Fan Club members relatively happy again by Christmas 1963.

In 1964 the membership of the Fan Club reached its peak. There were 80,000 officially enrolled Beatle People in the UK. But the Club still failed to make any profit. On the contrary, it still required substantial sums from NEMS to keep it ticking over. The actual subscription money scarcely covered the printing and mailing out of three or four Club Newsletters each year, plus the manufacture of the free Christmas record, which became an annual affair after 1963.

To be truthful, the Beatles seldom visited the Fan Club offices. They were occasionally persuaded to climb to the second floor at Monmouth Street to pose with sacks of mail for publicity pictures. But that was about all. Usually they climbed no further than the first floor, where they used to do all their press interviews in my office. But there was one occasion in April 1964 when the Beatles did make a memorable visit to the Fan Club. For one particular scene during the making of *A Hard Day's Night*, a mountain of fan mail was required. So the production people asked me to organise the real thing rather than a load of phoney letters. They borrowed actual fan club mail from the Monmouth Street offices. I think the sight of all those letters reminded John, Paul, George and Ringo of what the fan club was doing to help them, as they immediately suggested a visit

The Beatles with NEMS receptionist Maureen Payne and PA Valerie Sumpter.

to Monmouth Street. With the rest of the NEMS staff having joined forces with the office in Argyll Street, I was very aware that our Fan Club workers might be feeling left out. A visit from the Beatles was an excellent PR move, and a morale boost for the secretaries and their helpers. It was also a chance to have some photos taken while the boys sorted through all the mail.

"This is incredible! There's a girl here inviting all four of us to her big sister's wedding on Saturday." "I've got one that says, 'Dear George, I hope these lozenges cure your sore throat.' I had a cold for three or four days and they've all been sending pastilles and pills to the office ever since!" "Here's one for you, Ringo. Can I have one of your rings, it says." "This letter from L.A. is 50 pages long. It looks as though it's been written with her foot." John couldn't resist that one: "All Americans write with their feet, it keeps them on their toes".

None of the letters was unusual. What was unusual was that the four Beatles should be spending so much time at the Fan Club offices, digging their way through sacks of incoming mail from all over the world, when they were supposed to be making a movie!

Even with a full-time office staff, disasters occasionally happened. There was one crisis point in the Club's history where a huge backlog of mail had built up. The Monmouth Street offices were so full of sacks containing unopened letters that the staff weren't able to start opening them, let alone get on with all their other work. In my absence – I was away on an overseas tour – the chap in charge at Monmouth Street took an emergency decision. Of course he should have checked it with one of my deputies in the press office at Argyll Street, but unfortunately he didn't. He went ahead and arranged for a waste disposal firm to ditch many thousands of unopened letters. Some contained subscription payments and Postal Orders. Others included queries about the Beatles. The whole lot went to a waste tip.

Not surprisingly the press got hold of the story, after some eagle-eyed member of the public spotted some undestroyed fan mail at the tipping site. The papers had a field day. I went crazy when I heard what had happened. I issued instructions that this should never happen again – and to my knowledge it never did.

My memories of the Fan Club include enough humorous anecdotes to fill a book. There was the time when George Harrison celebrated his 21st birthday and we were all swamped with silver keys – plus an actual DOOR! Someone sent a full-sized door, saying here was something for George to open with all his keys! Then there was the occasion in the spring of 1964 when an American fan sent a letter to her favourite pop group in England, addressing her envelope simply: 'The Beatles, c/o H.R.H. Prince Philip, Buckingham Palace, London'. Eventually it reached the Club's offices – but not before someone had scrawled boldly across the envelope: 'NOT KNOWN AT BUCKINGHAM PALACE'.

Fans waiting outside Abbey Road studios in London for the Beatles to arrive.

Eventually the Club ceased to have a London headquarters altogether. Freda's address became: The Official Beatles Fan Club, PO Box 12, Liverpool 1. Once it became obvious that the Beatles were no longer going to work together as a group, the Fan Club was wound up in March 1972 and Freda Kelly's involvement with it came to a natural and inevitable end.

She recalls: "We had a final meeting, just Ringo and George and me with some of the Apple people. John was out of the country. The time was right for the Club to close down then. We were not getting any new group photographs any longer. And, in any case, I was six months pregnant and knew I would have to make the break sooner or later." When Brian took most of his Liverpool NEMS people to London in 1964, Freda had stayed behind. But in the end the whole Fan Club came back home to her in Liverpool!   (TB)

The Beatles were thoroughly amused when I showed them this envelope. After all, they had appeared in the 1963 Royal Variety Show the previous November and Beatlemania had been claiming headline space in the newspapers for at least six months!

After the touring days were over, Freda Kelly continued to play a key role in the Fan Club's operation. In October 1966, she was appointed the Joint National Secretary of the organisation, and the elusive 'Anne Collingham' was quietly phased out of the whole situation.

John and George at a special Fan Club showing of Magical Mystery Tour.

LETTERS from BEATLE PEOPLE

1963-1964

SCREAMING AT CONCERTS

Dear Miss Collingham,

In your next Fan Club newsletter, could you please ask members to reduce their screaming when going to one-nighters, etc. because their yells must upset the Beatles – they certainly looked very worried when they played Walthamstow. Admittedly, it must be nice to know their fans are there, but I was sitting about five rows from the front and about six seats away from the loudspeaker, which, incidentally, was loudspeakering extra loud, and I could hardly hear The Group at all above the noise.

Valerie Payne,
Leyton, London.

CASBAH/CAVERN

Dear Johnny,

When the Beatles first appeared in the Cavern, we would go down about half-an-hour before the session began, to make sure we got a seat at the front. The Beatles mainly used to play numbers that were requested by the audience. But they also fooled around a lot on stage, playing pieces like 'Bill and Ben' and 'Torchy'. When they had a break you could always talk to them in the band-room by the stage, and at the snack-bar at the back.

Then they became more famous, and we used to queue all day for front row seats at an evening session, and sometimes even from the night before. Everyone going past The Cavern could see us all huddled in jeans, rugs and blankets in the doorway! We have many early memories of Our Boys, but they've probably forgotten all about us now.

From: the original Beatlettes,
LIVERPOOL, of course!

The Beatles reply: Of course we haven't forgotten the early days and everyone who helped to start us going. We wish sometimes that we could go back to the Cavern and play around like we used to do, just for a few days.

JAM BUTTIES

Dear Johnny,

Help ! Please, I must have the recipe for "jam butties".

Kathy Heard,
London N21

The Beatles reply: "Take two slices of bread, butter them, add jam and munch away". Butties is Scouse for sandwiches.

MY BEATLE-DIGGING MAMA:

There are Beatles on the staircase
And Beatles in the hall
Four Beatles in the bathroom
On every nipping wall.

There is Ringo on the landing,
George, and Paul McCartney's head,
John Lennon's place of honour
Is the wall above her bed.

Her mind is filled with Beatles
She 'Twists and Shouts' and sways
She renders 'All My Loving'
And walks like in a daze.

At times when I address her
She looks at me – Oh heck!
The Beatles stare at me as well
They're dangling from her neck.

She used to care for knitting,
Debussy, Gershwin, Trad –
But now she digs John Lennon
The woman's Beatle-mad!

Is this my loving Mother
Who once nursed me on her knee?
I think her 'Taste of Honey'
Needs a dash of D.D.T. . . .

Peter Crane, 13 Harehills Place, Leeds,

WHO WRITES THEM DOWN?

Dear Johnny,

Please tell me who arranges and writes down the music that John and Paul compose, as I have heard that neither of them can read music.

Lesley King,
12 Bew Court,
Lordship Lane,
London SE22

John and Paul answer: We don't usually bother to write the music down, just the words. When we get into the recording studio we usually change bits before we get it right. Then afterwards someone else does the donkey-work for us.

BEATLES IN SWEDEN

Dear Johnny and Beatles People,

I'm sure you've heard that the Beatles have been in Sweden. Yeah, yeah, yeah! The 'gear, fab, smashing' Beatles! Before their first performance here (I saw all their performances), I sat quite calmly talking to my

George, Paul and John during one of their final performances at the Cavern Club.

friends. Then suddenly they came up on the stage! I found myself jumping into the air, then crawling on the floor with my tongue hanging out of my mouth like a red tie and my eyes nearly fell out of my head! (Recognise yourself, girls?) After the show I flew home singing "You really got a hold on me".

At home my mother met me and she said very angrily: "Who has put a picture of George Harrison over our wedding-photo?" I tried to hide behind a big heap of Beatle-pictures and answered innocently: "Must be the cat . . ."

PS: Why do they have seats at Beatles shows? No one is sitting down!

Marie Selander,
Hasselquistvagen 1, Johanneshov,
Stockholm, Sweden.

KIND GEORGE
Dear *Beatles Monthly* people,
We want to tell you what great fellas the Beatles are. About three weeks ago, we wrote to George Harrison's address, saying that our friend, Anne, was very ill, and requesting a pic (signed) to be sent to her. Within a very short time, she received a pic of the lads, signed by not only George, but by every single Beatle! We think they are the kindest boys in showbiz.

Ann and Jane, York.

IN HIS OWN PRINT
Dear Johnathan Lennon,
May I conjugate your worthly self on your idiotic Block aptly called "Jon lonely in his own print". I fondled it quite nilaptuous in its dwarfings and funnily stories. But how do you think of it. It took me ages to make a weak attempt at this miserable sentence. How about another one as, to quote a phrase, "it was the most wonderfoul larf l've ever ready".

Yvonne E. Tingle,
56 Alexander Street, Kettering, Northants.

John Lennon answers: I never think of it. The words righted themselves acrobatically on the paper all alone.

TRANSLATION FROM THE GREAKLE
Dear Johnny,
I would like to congregate John Lennon on his most wonderfoul correction of short writty. It circusly is a famous larf. I would like to felicitate him most on the furrowing:

'At the Denis', 'About the Awful', 'You might well arsk', 'The Finglctoad Resort of Teddiviscous', 'Alee Speaking', unt 'Liddypool'. But please could you require him not to publifie any more writties as I am a bit long of Ice at the perfect monument. I think he is baf (no office superintended) with him (hope none is taken) little guitar. If he apopoletics (I have no idea what that means) this let, could you ask him to send me a stabbed undressed evelope contaminating a life sizzle panel of litel Jackie Lemmon automated of corse. Tell him hc has a shoal reporter in IV Middle W of my schule wot shall remain nameless. Mainly me. From a penned-in, restricted, disciplined Johnny Lennon fan.

P.S. Give my best fishes to the other three, the love is superintended for him belonely.

Love, Margaret A. Jones,
15 South Drive, Sandal,
Wakefield, Yorks.

A SCHOOL MORNING
Interrupted Thoughts during a normal School Morning. Can't buy me love-You can't do that. "You – take off that Beatle hat!" "Sit down. you idiotic child". Ringo really drives me wild. Latin first, at half past nine . . . I wish that George were really mine . . . Oh no, amo-amas-amat . . . I like John Lennon's leather hat . . .

Inde et quo, Capulus. Can't buy me love is fabulous . . . English now-oh no-Shakespeare. If music be the food ... oh dear! I've got to sing some stupid song. . . Why can't we have It won't be long. The teacher jumps out of her chair. "Karen, are you listening?" Now it's maths, what fun, I think. What is the Beatles' favourite drink? Coke ... thc volume of a sphere? . . . I wish that Ringo could be here. Pythagoras' wretched square . . . I wonder, how long's George's hair . . . Ten centimetres no, not so quite . . . Oh, er-my answer's not quite right. Chemmy now, sulphuric acid . . . Paul always looks so mild and placid. His eyebrows . . . add potassium How did Ringo learn to drum? Now history, and the Civil War. Which battle? 1644? I fear I don't recall the date . . . The things they say are simply great. They're full of laughter, and of wit. And every record is a hit. I love the Beatles, they are great. KAREN, WILL YOU CONCENTRATE!

With (frustrated) love, Karen Blyth (13)
37 Walmsley Road,
Broadstairs, Kent.

Another nutty pose from John.

BEATLE POEM
Dear Johnny,
On looking through a book of poems I came across this one (slightly adapted).

Address to the Beatles (With apologies to Robert Burns)
O thou, whatever title suit thee,
Auld hairy friends, I'll never doubt ye.
Wha in yon Cavern grim and sootie
Closed under hatches,
Wi' guitars and drums ye sing To please poor wretches.
Hear me auld Beatles for a wee
And never let poor bodies be,
I'm sure sma' pleasur you can gie
To sing and thrill poor folks like me
Great is thy pow'r and great thy fame.
Far kent and noted is thy name,
And tho' yon Liverpool's thy hame, Thou travels far,
But faith! thou never stay too lang, For Britain none can mar.
Hope you like it!

Evelyn Grant,
Glasgow.

A Hard Day's Night

An exclusive look by Peter Jones behind the shooting of the Beatles' first movie

The scenes with the police were filmed on the streets of Notting Hill in West London.

John Lennon took a deep breath and said: "Who's that little old man over there." And Paul McCartney replied: "What little old man?" This dialogue doesn't mean much out of context, but it was very important indeed for the Beatles – because these were the opening sentences from their first movie.

The early days of filming were strange for the boys. They were knocked out by the friendly approach of all the technicians and production staff, but baffled at the apparent waste of time, when they simply had to sit around and do nothing while the lighting, cameras and scenery were set up just right. And there was something else that they positively *hated*: getting up so early in the morning. They usually had to be on the set by 8.30am, a time which the Beatles normally regard as the middle of the night. The job of getting them out of bed fell, as ever, to road manager Neil Aspinall. After the first few days, he was telling friends: "I'm wearing myself to a shadow! It means I have to get up at five o'clock to call the boys. They can't keep their eyes open. I try to get them breakfast, but they don't want to know. They're night people, that's the trouble. For them, the day doesn't start until mid-afternoon."

But gradually Paul, John, George and Ringo got into the rhythm of the film studio's day. Only once in the first few weeks of filming were they late, and that was less than half-an-hour. They spent their entire first week on a train. They left from Paddington, went to Minehead, and then came back. Every single newspaper in the country wanted to get pictures of the boys embarking. The first day, another problem was revealed: crowds of fans who slowed things down. Film-making can be a very expensive business, and delays cost money, so from then onwards the boys got aboard at Acton station, a little way down the line from Paddington. But there was no way they could avoid the crowds of Beatle fanatics who were waiting at every other station all the way down to the West Country.

Ringo said about the early days of filming: "We were tempted to go out in the evenings and relax, because they *were* pretty long days. But we realised it was important to be as fresh as possible early in the mornings. So we normally just hung around our own flat. We were probably a bit scared, because at the back of our minds was the thought of Neil coming round at the crack of dawn. It would have been fatal to be late."

The boys always turned up on the set together. The explanation was simple: it meant there only had to be one tremendous effort to get them through the crowds of fans. Meanwhile, the business of learning their lines didn't really cause any problems. The boys got a shooting schedule every day, notifying them which scenes would be included the following day. As all four of them had equally big parts, it meant that each individual Beatle had rather less to learn. They'd just read through the scripts in the evening, and maybe glance at them again (if their eyes stayed open long enough) in the car on the way to the set in the morning.

The scriptwriter Alun Owen was often around on the set. Sometimes the boys would disagree about some of the words he wanted to put into their mouths. For example, George had to say, "Oh, get away", when he would normally say, "Oh, gerroff". Alun didn't mind the changes a bit. He'd lived with the boys and got to know their ways of talking, and all that mattered to him was that the dialogue was as accurate as possible.

The film's producer, Walter Shenson, took time off during the first week's shooting to tell me: "The vital thing here is to do nothing to damage the boys. They are great personalities in their own way and we want to present them exactly as they are, day in and day out. It's better if the American audiences don't understand all the things the boys say, than we change anything about the Beatles just for the sake of it." Mr. Shenson, quiet-spoken, balding, with constantly expressive hand gestures, added: "We're certainly not going to build one of the boys bigger than the others. They complement each other – you can see that after watching them for just a few moments. It's equal shares for all. To be honest, you can't call this film a 'musical'. There are only six numbers in it, all written by John and Paul. It's really a Beatle story with music added."

In the film studio, getting the right sound level is easy, but it's much harder on a rolling train. So, for the dialogue inside the compartments, the Beatles had to wear special neck microphones inside their shirts, with the leads running down their trouser legs and being strapped to their usual-style Beatle boots. Even then, they had to do many re-takes because the level of their voices didn't come through loud enough. The hardest thing for the boys was listening to other actors giving their cues. They'd been used to 'feeding' each other with lines and sometimes it was difficult for them to let the others get a word in edgeways.

Norman Rossington – a popular actor for his role in TV's *The Army Game* – plays the boys' road manager. In real life, of course, Neil Aspinall, takes that role. I cornered Neil one morning, and asked him: "How does it feel to see yourself being played by somebody else?" Neil grinned. "Oh, it's great," he said. "But Norman has some lines to say that make me laugh a bit. He says things to the Beatles . . . well, if it had been me saying 'em, I'd be fired on the spot. Like when he takes in a great pile of fan mail and tells the boys: 'Get on with that lot, right away'. Honestly, I know what they'd say to me if I tried that lark on them!" Neil has been on permanent call during the filming. He copes with queries and picture requests, and helps the boys in a dozen different ways. And he's seen some of the scenes shot so many times, he's memorised most of the script.

Then Norman Rossington came over for a chat. An experienced professional actor, he summed up the individual Beatles as they'd struck him on the sets. "I think Paul really was the most self-conscious one of the four in the earlier days. He clowned around sometimes, but I think he was hiding a little

bit of embarrassment. After all, filming is a difficult sort of medium. You shoot a scene, then go through it all again just to get different camera angles. At first, it's hard to tell why something is being done, and you keep feeling that all those hard-bitten technicians are looking straight at you.

"John and George don't seem to worry how the next scene will go. They leave it all to the director and just do as he tells them to. When they've got nothing to do, they just

relax. The scriptwriter has decided to make Ringo play the dumb one of the four – like Harpo Marx, of the Marx Brothers. He's doing very well indeed, but in a different way to the others. And of course, when you get them all together, anything at all can happen!" In fact, Ringo had his own day of glory when he was in a scene all by himself, in a pub. In the script, he'd got lost and

Norman Rossington and John enjoyed a real test of wills – and strength – in the film

didn't know where John, Paul and George were, so he crammed on a cap as a disguise and darted into the pub for a drink. He admitted feeling a bit shaky, all by himself, at first, but soon he was working like an experienced star.

Once the railway sequence was out of the way, the boys had a day clear and then moved on to Twickenham Studios. This was much more like the film-making they'd expected. There were four chairs, very prominently placed: with their individual names written in large black letters! George rushed straight over, sat in the canvas-backed seat and tugged at a huge cigar. "Might as well act like a film star now I've got my own chair," he said, grinning hugely. The boys had two dressing rooms – two Beatles in each. John and Paul shared one, and George and Ringo the other. And, in between takes, they listened to some playbacks of the new songs in the film. Paul grimaced quizzically once or twice, but generally they seemed pretty happy with the end products.

The scene in the guard's van featured some co-stars, in the shape of dogs and chickens. The song in that scene is called 'I Should Have Known Better', and comes right at the end of the scene. It's not the first number in the film, but it was the first one the boys shot. "That's another thing that's odd about filming," said George. "You do everything in such a strange order. You've got to keep checking with the script to find out what the actual story is all about!"

This particular sequence has the boys sitting around on some boxes in the guard's van, while they play cards. Paul sings and plays bass; John sings and plays harmonica; George is on twelve-string guitar; and Ringo just plays snare drum and cymbal. It was another case of the boys speaking out about something in the original script that they thought was a bit corny. In dialogue with the grandfather character, they were supposed to be asked: "Well, what can YOU do?". In response, they were meant to pick up their guitars, etc., and sing. But the Beatles felt that was a bit cliched, so they started off playing cards and then, with a touch of fantasy, the picture fades into them holding their instruments instead of the cards. The next day, things looked a bit brighter for the boys. Because they'd worked late the previous evening, they didn't have to report to the studios until nine o'clock. A few weeks before, they'd still have regarded this as being "the middle of the night", but gradually they were realising that some people actually did work in the mornings! And this second day in the studios was a riot. Ringo was featured most, in a scene in which he found an old man, a waiter, in a cupboard at the hotel. The Beatles had their first change of costume for this scene – though that merely meant wearing their indoor casual stuff instead of their travelling clothes!

Poor Ringo kept getting things wrong. For example, he forgot his opening line, which made the others laugh. Then he got it wrong again the next time – though you couldn't blame him, with George, Paul and John trying hard to keep straight faces. Each time it had to be re-shot, the laughs got louder and louder. Soon, even the technicians joined in the giggles. It all took more than twice as many takes as usual. But, after a break when things quietened down just for a moment, Ringo eventually emerged triumphant, and another scene was in the can.

Within a few days, the boys were completely at home at Twickenham, but they often found the whole thing very frustrating. One Thursday, for example, they had to be up at the crack of dawn in order to be driven to the studios in time to go on the set when shooting started. On this particular day they found they spent the first couple of hours just walking up and down the corridors! "My feet are killing me," moaned George, putting on a greatly exaggerated limp. Then it was time for a mad dash to the Dorchester Hotel, where the Beatles were presented with their awards as outstanding entertainers by the Variety Club of Great Britain. "Thanks for the Purple Hearts", John quipped. George said: "We're grateful for being given four separate awards. Normally we have to cut them into four quarters."

Then they had to rush back, as quickly as possible, to the studio. For the rest of the day, they were still marching up and down the corridors, along with Norman Rossington. Ringo got off lightly, because he wasn't wanted for this particular scene. The story had him storming off in a huff because he'd been upset by Paul's grandfather (Wilfrid Brambell) in a canteen sequence. But if Ringo had a rest, it wasn't for long, because the boys had to rush over to the BBC in the evening to record *Top Of The Pops*. In between all their hard work, the boys managed to come up with a title for the film. Suggestions from the various produc-

ers included *Moving On*, *Travelling On*, even *Let's Go*. But the boys wanted something really different. They'd already rejected *Beatlemania*. Then Ringo hit on *A Hard Day's Night*. He often comes out with strangely worded quotes. Earlier, he'd been asked if he'd had a haircut, and replied, "No it's the same difference"! After a long day's work, as the hands on the clock reached into the early hours, he said casually, "Boy, this has been a hard day's night". It clicked naturally into place.

Ringo didn't realise what he'd said at first, but you should have seen his grin of triumph when everybody accepted that it was the best possible title they could have for the movie. John says: "There were times when we honestly thought we'd never get the time to write all the material for the film. But we managed to get a couple finished while we were in Paris, during our stay at the Olympia. And

All the concert sequences in A Hard Day's Night were filmed at the Scala Theatre in London.

three more were completed in America, while we were soaking up the sun on Miami Beach." In came Paul to add: "The only real panic was over the title number. For a long time, there wasn't a title at all. So that had to be a bit of a rush job."

All the boys agreed on one thing. They *hate* those films where the songs become part of the story. They spend a lot of time taking the mickey out of the usual run of musicals. "These are just songs," they say. "They've been worked into the action in as natural a way as possible. You don't see us suddenly whipping out instruments in a plush restaurant as a 40-piece orchestra creates heavenly sounds from nowhere!" (PJ)

From Europe to Australia

As their first world tour began in 1964, one of the Fab Four was missing

The build-up could hardly have been more dramatic. With just hours to go before the boys set out for a lengthy trip across Europe and then to the other side of the world, Ringo went down with a serious throat complaint. The doctors said there was no way he could travel, so the Beatles had to find a replacement – and fast. Top session drummer Jimmy Nicol was available, and after a hasty rehearsal to make sure he knew their repertoire, the makeshift line-up of the Beatles was ready to roll.

John, Paul, George and Jimmy Nicol drove into London Airport on Thursday, 4th June with their chauffeur Bill behind the wheel of their Austin Princess. After a quick stop for customs, it was straight on to the plane to embark before the other passengers. They were immediately stopped by members of the crew and asked for autographs. The boys obliged, but the co-pilot didn't seem to realise that Ringo was in hospital and kept asking for his signature. Finally, he convinced himself that Paul was Ringo. George immediately stepped in. "Go on, Ringo", he told Paul, "give him your

The Beatles toured through Amsterdam on a canal boat so their fans could see them.

signature". The Beatles love this sort of situation and can never resist pulling somebody's leg. The other passengers filed aboard and the plane zoomed off the runway, heading for Denmark.

They got a terrific reception from over 6000 fans in Copenhagen. But something different was happening. Unlike most of the other welcomes that the boys have had, with girl fans leading the chorus, it was the boys in Denmark (and later on in Holland) who did all the yelling, while the girls stayed shyly in the background. The fans were wearing the latest styles which they gleaned from the British newspapers, as they all follow Britain very closely on the Mods and Rockers kick. The boys were booked into the Royal Hotel in Copenhagen,

Their 1964 world tour set new box-office records wherever the Beatles went.

opposite the Tivoli Gardens, where they were appearing that evening. The first thing they discovered was that they were staying in the same suite of rooms as Russia's president, Mr. Krushchev, had booked for his visit two weeks later. George, in fact, was sleeping in the same bed that was reserved for the Russian leader. George quipped: "Right, I'll be leaving a note for him under the pillow!" Inside the Tivoli Gardens was the KB Hallen sports arena owned by the local football team. The boys worked out their set-list, with drummer Jimmy Nicol paying particular attention. Road manager Mal Evans always writes out the titles of all the songs they are going to play on slips of paper and sticks them on their guitars with Sellotape!

The boys kept rehearsing with Jimmy Nicol, telling him when to speed up and when to slow down. Our photographer Leslie Bryce watched, and said: "I didn't realise how difficult it was to be a Beatle until I saw a new man among them." He's right. The Beatles have a special way of saying and doing things, and understandably, Jimmy found it hard to fit in. But he was obviously very excited, and very proud. The British Ambassador in Copenhagen visited the boys – and 4400 fans packed the theatre for each of two performances. As usual, there were riots at the end of the second show, especially when the master of ceremonies announced that the boys would not be coming back on stage. One Danish lad picked up a pot of delphiniums and threw it at him!

After the show, Jimmy Nicol went outside to meet somebody – and stood there completely unmolested, as he watched the crowds yelling for the Beatles. Incidentally, Jimmy wore Ringo's suits during the tour – though the trousers were too short for him. A telegram that Paul sent to Ringo read: "Hurry up and get well, Ringo, Jimmy is wearing out all your suits". Back at the Royal Hotel, a call came through from Brian Epstein, who reported that poor Ringo had a temperature of 103 but was improving.

Next day, it was on to Amsterdam. Girls presented the Beatles with bunches of flowers and traditional Dutch hats. The boys went straight to a television rehearsal at the Tres Long restaurant in Hillegom, some 26 miles from Amsterdam – and what a show! Members of the audience jumped up onto the stage and sang into the mikes along with the Beatles. Again, it was boys who were the

most fanatical, and Neil had a tough job getting them off the Beatles! On Saturday, there was a highly publicised hour-long trip through the canals of Amsterdam in a glass-topped boat. Huge, shouting crowds crammed every yard of the banks, and we noticed big banners saying, in English, "Ringo, Quick Recover". Some fans dived into the canal, which upset the Beatles because the police certainly weren't gentle

Paul waving to the crowds who lined the route their boat took through Amsterdam.

in fishing them out again. "I've got to protest about this," John Lennon said, and he did. He couldn't understand why the police were being so tough on the teenagers. Then they went to the Exhibition Hall, Blokker, about 36 miles from Amsterdam, for two concerts. They travelled in style in two white

complete with white hoods. The boys had a break between the two shows, but because of the crowds outside, they had to stay in their dressing-room, so they tried to curl up and go to sleep, the screams still ringing in their ears.

John pulled off their suit covers, made himself a comfy little bed and went off to sleep without much difficulty at all. Jimmy Nicol slid under the dressing-room table and was left undisturbed. This is a trick often used by groups on the road, as most dressing-rooms are tiny, and under the table is the only place you can avoid being trodden on by intruders. George also found himself a handy corner to catch some kip. But this rare moment of rest actually caused the boys a lot of trouble. It turned out the boys had been expected to attend a civic reception at a big restaurant and were also meant to have visited a traditional Dutch village. The problem was that nobody had told them about the arrangements. So while they were slumbering fitfully, the papers were preparing knocking stories about how the Beatles had let people down, which was completely unfair, of course.

But this was the only black cloud in a tour that was a howling success from start to finish. The boys liked the Dutch countryside and what they managed to see of the scenery. They liked the food and they loved

Cadillacs, with motorcycle escort. The bikes had side-cars, which leaned over dangerously as they roared round the corners, and it reminded the Beatles of Brands Hatch on a race day. Local groups, usually featuring girl singers, made up the rest of the bill. The one just before the Beatles wore startling stage garb like members of the Ku Klux Klan,

the reception given them by the fans. Said Paul: "Sometimes we thought they were going to get out of hand, but nobody ever started any real trouble." It just shows how much the Beatles do worry about their fans.

Cynthia Lennon linked up with the boys in Amsterdam, travelling with them from the airport for their brief return to London – where they were joined by Aunt Mimi, that wonderful lady who was responsible for bringing up John Lennon. Both were going

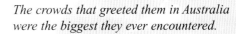

landed in the wrong country", said George. And to top it all they had to drive round the airport on an open-top truck! Everyone was absolutely soaked to the skin. It completely ruined the terrific welcome that the Sydney fans had lined up for the boys. Even so, about 2000 of them braved the drenching rain to say a very wet hello. In Sydney, they headed for the safety and shelter of the Sheridan Hotel. News had already got around that they had arrived and hundreds of fans made their way to the hotel to catch a glimpse of the famous Beatles. The boys wanted to wave to the crowd from their hotel window, but first of all they had to get out of their wet clothes. Their luggage was still at Sydney Airport, so a frantic search was made for dry togs. John and Paul managed to find some, but George couldn't get hold of any trousers, so he finally ended up wrapping a towel round his lower half and dancing onto the balcony like that! "I thought their winter was just like our summer", commented John, "but it's freezing. Come on, turn on all the electric fires," as the boys tried to get the blood moving through their veins again.

But they had to launch straight into a round of press conferences, photo sessions and meetings with all the local big-wigs. In London, Ringo had finally been passed fit by the doctors at University College Hospital, and he was discharged on Thursday, 11th June. Everyone was a bit concerned about him flying straight off to Australia, as he really should have had at least a week to convalesce. But Ringo insisted that he must join up with the boys again. So, the following day, he left with Brian Epstein, flying to Australia via San Francisco. Back Down Under, John, Paul, George and Jimmy Nicol started their Australian tour with riotous concerts in Adelaide on 12th and 13th June.

Then they flew across the great Australian desert to Melbourne, where the four Beatles finally joined up together again, and the group said farewell to Jimmy Nicol, who flew home alone. Ringo looked a bit worn out after his long trip, but the very next day he seemed back on his usual top form. Ahead of the already exhausted Beatles lay concerts in Melbourne, and then a trip to New Zealand, before they made it back to London on 2nd July – with just a couple of days' break before they had to go back to work again!   (TB)

with the party to Hong Kong, that isolated, hustling little island, and slice of the mainland, sitting right on the edge of Communist China. The Chinese promoter had decided to raise the price of seats for the two shows in the Princess Theatre, and the result was that many of the local teenagers, who gave the boys a rapturous welcome at the airport, were unable to afford to see them perform. The cheapest seats were £2 a time, which is a lot of money in low-wage Hong Kong. But the theatre was still almost full for both shows. The busy streets of the city were so congested with shopping housewives, street traders and beggars that John, Paul and

George hardly ventured out. It would have been too dangerous if they had been recognised. The city is notorious for its excited mobs rapidly getting out of control and the boys might have been torn to pieces. So only Mal went out to try a rickshaw ride.

After Hong Kong, it was time to get back on a jet for Sydney, the biggest city in Australia. The Beatles were all looking forward to that beautiful hot sun for which Australia is so famous. So they got the shock of their lives when they flew into Sydney Airport in one of the heaviest downpours they had ever seen. "We must have

Shindig!

Behind the scenes of one of their best TV performances, in October 1964

The old Granville Theatre in the heart of Fulham used to be a top London variety house, featuring acrobats, jugglers and red-nosed comedians. Many Saturday evening audiences lifted the rafters when they joined in the community singing. But the rafters were never stretched as high as on the Saturday afternoon that the Beatles called in. That day, the walls and the roof fairly bulged. The Granville is now a television studio, and it was used by ace producer Jack Good to record a special British edition of his wham-bam US show, *Shindig*! The Beatles topped the bill in front of a jam-packed audience, and the excitement was intense. George Harrison ambled over for a

John wore a pair of dark glasses for the Shindig! rehearsals.

chat with *The Beatles Book* team. "It's no good, I'm not really awake yet," he said, slowly rubbing his eyes. "The choke isn't out – that's the trouble!"

Next I bumped into Paul McCartney, and asked him what the Beatles were going to do in the show. "Oh, we've lined up 'Kansas City', 'I'm A Loser' and 'Boys'. Just the three." How come "Kansas City" is included? That's a bit of a surprise. "Well, Jack Good asked John what we would be starting with and John came out with 'Kansas City'. Jack said 'Great – so it's IN.'"

The Beatles went on stage, through the maze of cameras, trailing wires and odd bits of scenery. Up went the yell: "John, Paul, George, Ringo." The boys yelled back:

John provided the extra pair of hands at the top to create this shot.

"Tom, Harry, Fred". John sidled up to a spare microphone and sang, sexily: "Could I Forget You". Someone shouted: "I could". John put on a *very* hurt look. As the engineers balanced odd bits of sound through the microphones, John strummed an acoustic guitar and launched himself into 'House Of The Rising Sun', very close to one mike. As he came to the word "down", he suddenly roared it at the top of his voice. Everybody jumped about a foot in the air with the shock of it all. John just grinned back at them.

Immediately, Jack Good rushed onstage, stuck his face about twelve inches from John's and said, with dignity: "You rang,

TV producer Jack Good (above left) in deep discussion with his star guests.

sir?" The pre-show fun was hotting up. There was lots of chat among the Beatles about what clothes to wear. They had what they call "our *old* Palladium suits and our *new* Palladium suits". They tend to argue a lot about clothes, but they settled on the new suits, as they felt the trousers didn't match properly with the old jackets. Also in the show were Sounds Incorporated, Sandie Shaw, P. J. Proby, and the blonde ex-Vernon Girl, Lyn Cornell. It turned out that Lyn is now married to drummer Andy White – who played on 'Love Me Do'. She used to live very near Paul in Liverpool, so they had a happy fifteen minutes talking over favourite memories and remembering some of their mutual friends.

Jack Good buzzed about energetically, checking final details, encouraging the artists, cajoling the audience. In the tiny space by the side of the stage, about twenty of us were standing, including the artists. A yell went up for the Beatles. Paul, putting on his ripest Cockney accent, said: "Come on Beatles, where ARE you?". It was a good, big, brash show, with the Beatles turning in a marvellous act. The American critics loved it, and they weren't the only ones. It was a lotta fun just being there, watching the whole process through from start to finish. It's just a shame that we won't be able to see the show in Britain.   (BS)

Top right: Paul and Ringo came up with this unusual pose for our cameraman in the corridor outside their dressing room.

1964

THE NEWS FROM AMERICA IS TERRIFIC!

'I Want To Hold Your Hand' is racing up the American charts. That one appearance on the Jack Paar show was all that was needed to start a mad rush to the record shops. It could well be right at the top by the time the boys arrive in the States on the 7th February. (Johnny Dean's editorial, February 1964)

NO. 1 IN AMERICA!

It's unbelievable – but true! The Beatles have made No. 1 in America, and they have three other records in the US chart at the same time. Reports from the States suggest that Beatlemania is already in full flow across the nation, even before the boys have arrived for their first US visit. DJs, pundits and industry executives are astounded. But all of them agree that the Beatles are America's biggest pop sensation for years!

The Beatles are only the fourth British artists to top the American singles chart, following in the footsteps of Vera Lynn, Acker Bilk and the Tornados. None of them was ever able to follow up their initial success, but with 'She Loves You' and 'Please Please Me' already racing up the American Hot 100, it looks as if the Beatles are all set to make pop history again! (February 1964)

LIVE ALBUM SOON?

It seems very possible that one of the boys' shows at Carnegie Hall in New York will be recorded by George Martin for a possible live album. The taping is dependent on the boys having written sufficient new songs to make an album worthwhile, as neither the group nor George Martin are keen to issue a live recording made up entirely of songs they've already released. (February 1964)

AMAZING US SALES

The Beatles were apparently responsible for 60% of all the records sold in America during February! Since then, sales of 'Can't Buy Me Love' have been breaking more records. It sold 1,250,000 copies in Britain during its first week of release, while in America the million mark was passed on its second day in the shops, and total sales have now reached two million! (March 1964)

NOW IT'S TOP FIVE!

News is coming through from New York that the Beatles have captured all the top five places in this week's singles chart! The records in question are 'Can't Buy Me Love', 'Twist And Shout', 'She Loves You', 'I Want To Hold Your Hand' and 'Please Please Me'. The group also have another seven titles in the Hot 100. It all adds up to the most remarkable chart domination in history.

The figures are even more incredible on the other side of the world, in Australia, where the Beatles have nabbed all the top six positions in the chart! (March 1964)

FANTASTIC BEATLE MAIL

The post has become quite amazing. When I was in New York I found Brian Sommerville, the Beatles' Press Officer, sitting in the middle of 100 sacks of mail, so imagine the sticky time that Anne Collingham and Bettina Rose are having in London. If you haven't had an answer to your letter, or if you've sent in a subscription to join the fan club and haven't received a membership card yet, now you know the reason. So, please wait a little longer 'cos they're doing their best and they've only got one pair of hands and one tongue each!
(Johnny Dean's editorial, March 1964)

BEATLES FOR BOND

This must be the final confirmation that the Beatles have made it. Apparently they are going to be mentioned in the script of the next James Bond movie, which is now in production. (April 1964)

OUR CELEBRATED AUTHOR

John Winston Lennon has caused a big stir with his fantastic book *John Lennon In His Own Write*. The fab title was thought up by Paul, by the way.
(Johnny Dean's editorial, April 1964)

Ringo, Paul and John in New York during their famous debut trip to the USA.

PHOTOGRAPHERS GALORE

Here's a quote from a scene painter on the Beatles' film: "I've worked on hundreds of films with most of the big-name stars, like Errol Flynn, Alec Guinness, Laurence Olivier and Peter Sellers, but I've never seen so many press photographers around as on this one."

Meanwhile, American comedian Bob Hope recently offered the boys the chance of a guest appearance in his next movie. Unfortunately, they had to turn him down, because they are already fully booked for the rest of the year! (May 1964)

BEATING ELVIS

Apart from topping the British and American charts the boys are also No. 1 in Canada, Australia, New Zealand, South Africa, Holland, Germany, Denmark, Sweden, Norway, Brazil, Belgium, Japan and the Philippines. The latest country to ask EMI in London for all their tapes to release is Mexico. Total world sales of Beatles records are racing towards Elvis's total of approximately eighty million. Bing Crosby, of course, still holds the record with over 250 million. (May 1964)

ALL OVER THE WORLD

There are Beatle People in Europe, America, Canada, Africa, Australia, New Zealand, and pretty well every country in the world. And every single one of them very naturally wants John, Paul, George and Ringo to make a personal appearance in THEIR own hometown. Mind you, the boys are doing their best. Last month they flew over 30,000 miles giving concerts to Dutch, Danish, Hong Kong, Australian and New Zealand fans. But how can they please everyone? Put yourself in their shoes – or rather, boots – it's very difficult to appear in ten different places at once!
(Johnny Dean's editorial, July 1964)

MONEY TALKS IN KANSAS

American businessmen have been flocking around the Beatles in the hope of getting a slice of the action. One Kansas City entrepreneur was carrying round a cheque for $150,000, made payable to the Beatles. "I offered them this to do one show for me in Kansas," he explained. "They wouldn't take it."

Another questioner told the Beatles: "To get the money back, the Kansas promoter would have to charge $4 and 83 cents a seat, and even then he'd lose 33 cents on the show. What do you have to say to that?" Paul's reply? "We'll lend him the 33 cents." But the story has a happy ending for the man from the Kansas City. Brian Epstein

Paul relaxes in a New York hotel during a rare break from the frenzy of Beatlemania.

has accepted his offer (which amounts to just over £50,000) and a show in Kansas City has been scheduled for one of the 'rest days' on their US tour. (August 1964)

BEATLES 'MONSTER'

The music critic of the *New York Times* had some harsh words for Beatles' fans following the boys' shows in that city. "They have created a monster in their audience," he wrote. "If they have concern for anything but the money they are earning, they had better concern themselves with controlling their audiences before this contrived hysteria reaches uncontrollable proportions." If the hysteria stopped overnight, guess who'd be the first ones to write that the Beatles were finished! (September 1964)

PRESSURED PAUL

Paul has been talking between dates on the US tour about the pressures of being a Beatle. "A friend of mine – he's been a mate since schooldays – got married recently in Hull and invited me to the wedding. I was dying to go, but how could I? It would probably have ruined the whole day for the poor bloke.

"A lot of people probably think we're big-heads because suddenly we're famous, but we're not, truly! Character never changes whatever happens to a person. But people's attitude towards us changes, because they think, 'Oh, he's famous now, so he won't want to know us'." (September 1964)

POWDERY RECEPTION

The boys had a shock when they played at the Colston Hall in Bristol this month. As they finished their ballad 'If I Fell', and got ready to move into the finale of their act,

four students sitting above their heads among the lighting gantries tipped bags of flour down on top of them!

The boys burst into fits of hysterical laughter, Ringo tipped up his drums to get rid of the flour, and John, Paul and George had to shake the powder out of their guitars. Then, eventually, they were able to carry on, to the delight of the audience.

Colston Hall manager Ken Cowley was fuming after the incident, but the Beatles took it the way it was intended – as a joke. The group also had to withstand an invasion from some members of the audience, with George the target of most of the girls in question. (November 1964)

CONGRATS, DAD!

Congratulations to Paul's father, Jim McCartney, who married widow Angela Williams last week. James has been a widower himself, of course, for many years following the death of Paul's mother, Mary. (November 1964)

ADVANCE ORDERS

Advance sales for the boys' new single hit the three-quarter million mark this week – not quite up to the record of a million orders for 'Can't Buy Me Love', but still 150,000 clear of the total for 'A Hard Day's Night' back in the summer. These sales will ensure that 'I Feel Fine' enters the charts at No. 1. Meanwhile, 650,000 orders have so far been received for the group's fourth album, *Beatles For Sale*, another guaranteed chart-topper. (December 1964)

Beatles For Sale

The boys' fourth album had to be recorded at breakneck speed between two major tours

George Martin, John Lennon and Johnny Dean sharing a joke.

In late September 1964, the Beatles returned from their second visit to America – the most successful tour in pop history up to that point. But after only a few days' rest, they had to go back to work. At the top of their agenda was an exhausting schedule of recording sessions. The boys were also booked to begin another UK tour on John's 24th birthday, October 9th. But, before that started, they had to come up with two songs for their new single and enough material to fill their fourth album. So it's not surprising that when *Beatles For Sale* was released, the group looked rather tired when they did the shoot for the front cover photo.

'I Feel Fine' was chosen as the most suitable song for their next single. The Beatles were surprisingly doubtful about its commercial potential, but of course it raced straight to the top of the charts around the world. When it came to the LP, they had to pull together as many Lennon/McCartney originals as they could, and then fill the rest of the record with some of their favourite rock'n'roll oldies. Despite the haste with which it was recorded, the album still had a distinctive sound. "The numbers on this LP are different from anything we've done before," John told us after the sessions were over. "You could call our new one a Beatles Country & Western LP."

There certainly was a hint of the Nashville sound on several of the tracks, but the boys also experimented with a folky approach on 'I'm A Loser'. *The Beatles Book* camera was there to document the session for one of the best tracks on the album, the waltz-tempo 'Baby's In Black', which was a true Lennon and McCartney collaboration. *Beatles For Sale* was released on 4th December 1964, and went straight into the UK chart at No. 1, knocking *A Hard Day's Night* off the top! With 650,000 advance orders in the books, it was a guaranteed chart-topper even before anyone had heard a note. Not surprisingly, the LP picked up some excellent reviews along the way. Derek Johnson set the tone in the *NME*. "Believe me, the latest package from the Liverpool quartet is worth every penny asked. It's rip-roaring, infectious stuff, with the accent on beat throughout. The LP is overflowing with absorbing and distinctive Beatles trademarks." Derek singled out 'No Reply', 'I'll Follow The Sun', 'I Don't Want To Spoil The Party' and 'Mr Moonlight' ("perhaps the most ear-catching track on the LP") for particular praise. Meanwhile, in *Disc* Paul McCartney himself 'reviewed' the LP, adding his comments on every track.

(Right) Candid shots taken during the recording of 'Baby's In Black' at Abbey Road.

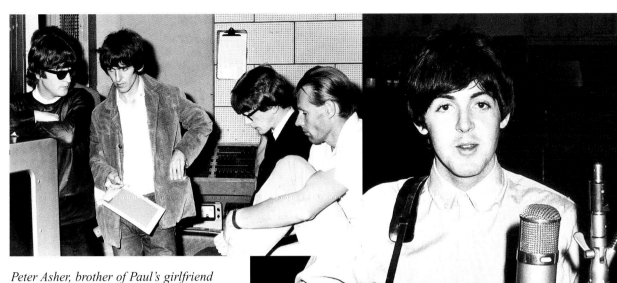

Peter Asher, brother of Paul's girlfriend Jane, joined the Beatles and George Martin to listen to the playbacks.

"We think there are some interesting sounds on the LP," he said. He explained that two of the songs, 'Every Little Thing' and 'What You're Doing', were written on the same day in Atlantic City during their last US tour, while 'I'll Follow The Sun' was an old song slightly rewritten for the LP. *Disc*'s Nigel Hunter added: "Their best yet. There's an enormous amount of variety and contrast in all respects."

Unlike the boys' previous LPs, *Beatles For Sale* only stayed at the top of the charts for about a month. Some critics took the opportunity to claim that the group were on the way out, after they were knocked off the No. 1 spot by the second album from the Rolling Stones. But what the critics failed to mention was that the Beatles had crammed a record-breaking number of sales into the three weeks before Christmas. The same thing happened in the States, where Capitol's equivalent release, called *Beatles 65*, sold no fewer than three million copies in its first month. It was soon acknowledged as the biggest-selling LP of all time in the States – at least, until *Sgt. Pepper* was released less than three years later!

In retrospect, *Beatles For Sale* very much marked the end of an era, as it was the last of the group's albums to be filled with their favourite cover tunes. But several of its original songs, such as 'Eight Days A Week' and 'Every Little Thing', looked ahead to the more sophisticated pop sounds that would rule the world in 1965. Once again, the Beatles were leading the way.   (PD)

More exclusive Beatles Book shots from the 'Baby's In Black' session.

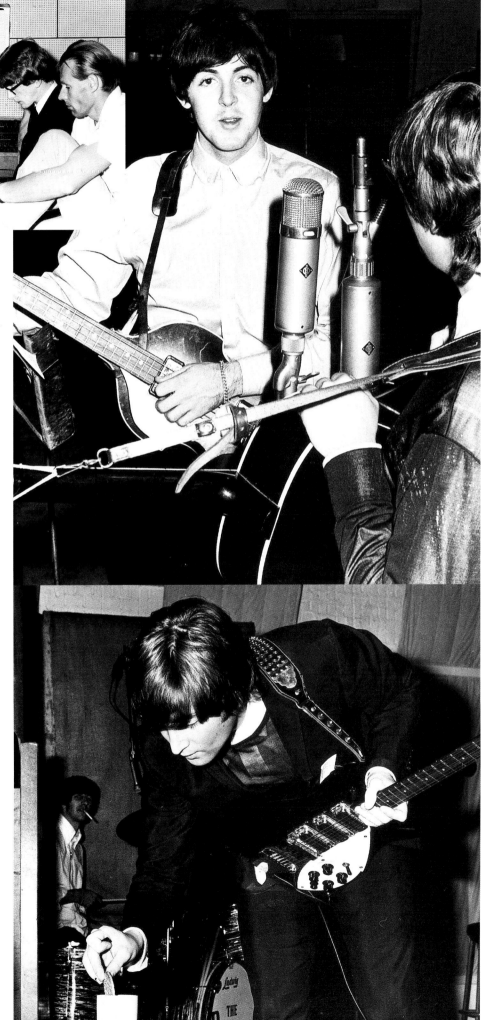

Backstage at Brighton

Johnny Dean reports from inside their dressing-room during the autumn 1964 UK tour

The enormous contrast between America and Britain must have really hit the Beatles when they started their autumn tour of the UK in October 1964. In just a few weeks they had exchanged huge venues like the Cow Palace in San Francisco, the Municipal Palace in Seattle and the Hollywood Bowl in Los Angeles, for comparatively small cinemas and theatres which seldom seated more than 1500–2000 people. But on that opening night of their autumn tour the crowds surrounding the Gaumont in Bradford, were just as wild and enthusiastic as ever. The Beatles were back and every local fan was there to pay homage. Whenever they were interviewed the boys went out of their way to tell reporters how glad they were to be home. They'd wanted to play in the States very badly but five weeks had been far too long for that kind of tour. Next time they'd make it shorter.

Any London appearance by the Beatles was always marked by a constant stream of photographers, reporters, other groups and people from show business who had either persuaded the powers that be – or the theatre doorman – that they should be allowed into the Beatles' dressing room. The number of visitors always dropped quite dramatically when they appeared outside London, so I decided to wait until their Brighton concerts to visit the boys for our October photo and interview session.

The boys only had one other visitor that afternoon. Chris Hayes was a *Melody Maker* reporter who had the job of finding out the details of all the instruments and equipment that hit groups were currently using. Although the Beatles were interested in equipment they didn't want to be asked to supply details of all the wattages and knobbages of their latest amps and guitars. But Chris persevered and kept going until he had a fairly complete list of everything. Towards the end I noticed a rather wicked glint in John's eyes when Chris asked him for details of the mouth organ he played. John replied that it was made by some bloke in Liverpool. "It's not a Hohner, then", Chris asked him. "No, there's this geezer up in Liverpool who makes them specially for us". When Chris pursued the matter, John came up with a name, which was duly printed in the *Melody Maker* the following week. It was all rubbish, of course: John played Hohner mouth organs like everyone else!

When Chris finally left I asked the Beatles about their new single. For once they were unusually reticent and I began to realise they were actually just that little bit worried about their next release. I found it quite incredible. Here was the most famous group in the world, who had just finished an amazingly successful first tour of America and who were playing to packed houses everywhere they appeared in England, and yet they had doubts about the recording they had just made. Paul eventually picked up a guitar and played 'I Feel Fine'. Despite my assurances that their fans would love it, the boys still seemed strangely doubtful. It was an extraordinary moment at that particular stage of the Beatles' career, which is hard to believe now. Every star has doubts from time to time but I never thought the Beatles had any until that day.

Shortly afterwards the mood was broken when Neil came in and insisted that they had to change for their first performance on stage. We left the boys to get ready and our photographer positioned himself in the wings to take some shots of the boys on stage. We also saw some of the other acts on the bill going through their performances. The excellent line-up featured several proteges of Brian, including Tommy Quickly, Sounds Incorporated, Michael Haslam, the Remo Four, the Rustiks and Bob Bain. The special guest star was Mary Wells who had been brought over from America following her big hit with 'My Guy'.

Every artist who went on before the Beatles always had a difficult job. They knew only too well that everyone in the audience was waiting to see the Beatles on stage and that every other act was a bit of an anticlimax. Mary Wells had a difficult job closing the first half as the audience weren't familiar with any of her material apart from 'My Guy'. Sounds Incorporated were always good fun and their lighthearted approach won them a lot of genuine applause at Brighton. Brian Epstein's new protegé, Tommy Quickly, also made quite an impact in the second half when he came on

The Beatles didn't always welcome unexpected guests to their dressing-room.

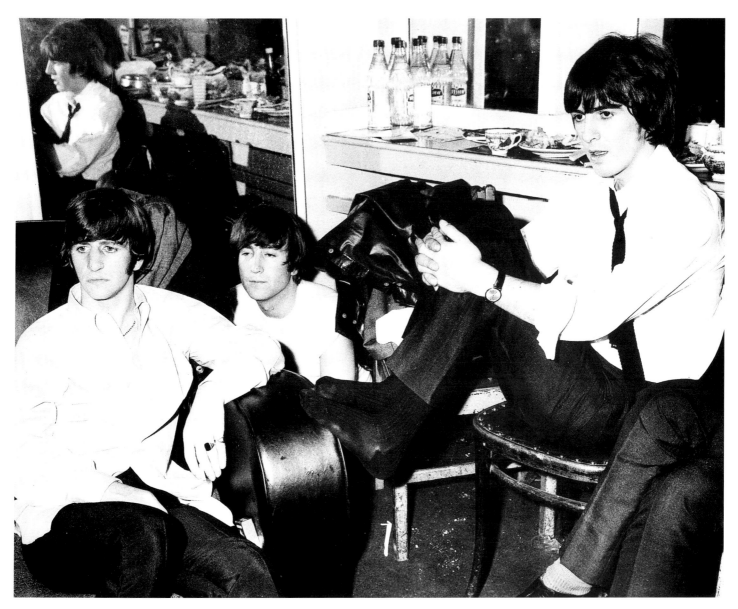

just before the Beatles, but even he was swamped by the enthusiasm for the four people who were due to follow him. When compere Bob Bain finally introduced the Beatles, his words were drowned by an enormous roar which continued and then increased as the Beatles finally walked on stage looking tremendous in their black mohair suits.

They opened with 'Twist And Shout' followed by 'Can't Buy Me Love' and then moved to four newer numbers, 'Things We Said Today', 'I'm Happy Just To Dance With You', 'I Should Have Known Better' with John on harmonica and 'If I Fell'. Ringo then took the spotlight to sing 'I Wanna Be Your Man'. John sang 'A Hard Day's Night' and then Paul went into his tremendous closing number, 'Long Tall Sally'. Although I'd seen the boys perform many times over the previous two years I'd never seen them look slicker or more polished. But the marvellous thing about every

Beatles performance was the way they enjoyed themselves so much. The looks they exchanged and the little things that they did between songs at Brighton clearly indicated that they were having fun. It was a typical barnstorming performance, which the packed audience enjoyed immensely. If they'd had their way the Beatles would never have left the stage.

Once the Beatles had cooled down and relaxed a bit, we rejoined them in their dressing room. They had time on their hands before their second performance around 9.45pm, but, as always, more visitors started arriving. The first was a local fortune-teller who wanted to reveal their futures. Only George offered his palms to be scrutinised by the bouffant-haired lady, who proceeded to examine the Harrison hands for those tell-tale lines which would reveal how many children he'd have, how long he would live and how lucky in love he'd be.

After Richard Harris and his wife left, John and George sat up again to watch TV.

George wouldn't let us listen to any of the secrets that were imparted over the next five minutes but by the expressions on his face we gathered that some of them were very welcome, while others were merely intriguing. After the fortune-teller had departed, the boys settled down to watch the television but, after only a few minutes' rest, Neil walked in and announced that film star Richard Harris and his wife wanted to pop in to see them. Paul and Ringo agreed but John and George decided that they weren't in a visiting mood. George promptly flopped onto the sofa and pretended to be asleep while John wrapped himself in a green plastic mac and lay down behind it.

The scene that followed was good enough to grace any modern stage farce. Enter Mr and Mrs Harris. Mr Harris: Hello, do you mind if we come in? Paul & Ringo: Yes, of

course. Mr & Mrs H: We just popped round to say hello. Paul: Hello. Mr H: How's it going then? Paul: Great! Mr H: (looking at George sleeping in the chair) What's the matter with George? Paul: He's tired. Mrs H: Where's John? Paul: He's there (pointing behind them at John wrapped in the green plastic mac) Mr H: What's the matter with him? Ringo: He's tired too. Mrs H: We just wondered if you could give us an autograph for the children. Paul: Yes, of course. Mr H: (handing over a paper) You must have signed thousands of these. Ringo: Yes. Mr H: I suppose you're so used to it you just sign anything that's put in front of you. How about a cheque, then? Paul: O.K. Mr & Mrs H: (realising that they were not exactly getting anywhere and deciding to make a graceful exit) Goodbye and thanks for the autographs. Paul & Ringo: Bye.

As soon as Richard Harris and his wife had exited, John and George sat up and resumed watching the television. Then the food arrived. Almost every time I saw the Beatles eating backstage they seemed to be consuming the same meal – steak, peas and chips. Neil explained that one of the main reasons for their rather monotonous diet was that it was one of the few reliable meals that could be churned out by almost any pub in England.

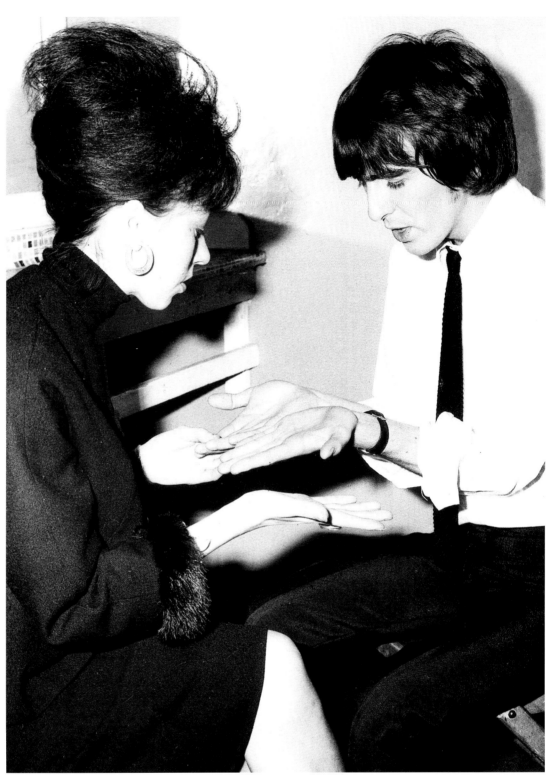

The eating conditions were rather cramped, to put it mildly. All the Beatles had to perch in front of the dressing table, facing themselves in the large mirror. But if the conditions were poor the cutlery was very decorative. Promoter Arthur Howes turned up in the middle of the meal and a big discussion ensued about the forthcoming tours that he wanted the boys to do. I'd brought along a pile of photographs that we had taken during previous sessions, plus some copies of *Beat Instrumental*, the leading group magazine at that time, which I also published.

The boys flipped through the magazines and then moved on to the pile of photographs, laughing uproariously at some of the faces they'd pulled during past sessions.

A short while later Neil came in to tell the boys to get ready for their second performance of the night, and we left to join several other reporters and photographers who were clustered around backstage, waiting for the Beatles to appear. One of the fascinating things about visiting the boys in 1964 was that you never knew what was

George having his famous palms read in their dressing-room at Brighton in 1964.

going to happen next. After all, when I set out from London that morning, I had no idea I was going to hear the Beatles give a private performance of their next single; photograph George having his fortune told; or end up trying to keep a straight face while John pretended to be asleep, wrapped in a green plastic mac in the corner of the room, as one of the world's most famous actors looked on! (JD)

The second Christmas show

By December 1964, the boys just wanted to play their music on stage,
and didn't enjoy the comedy sketches they were asked to perform

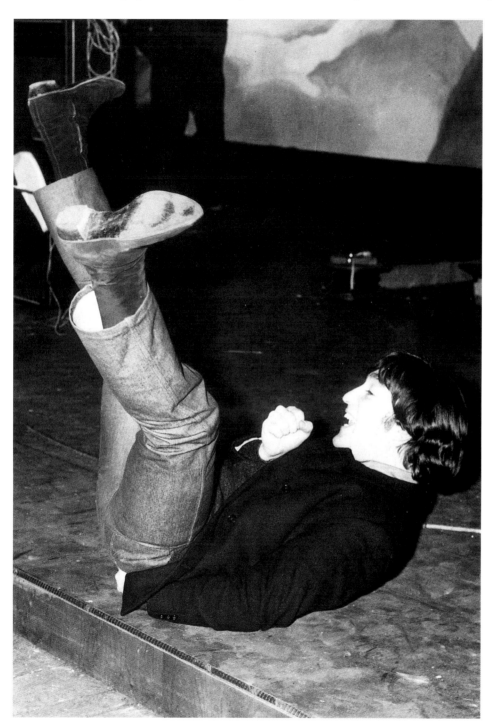

*Rehearsals for the Christmas Show
allowed John to show off his zany humour.*

The boys turned up casually dressed having enjoyed a well-deserved and long-overdue break for the previous few weeks. George had spent his time in Nassau, in the Bahamas, and early in the Hammersmith Odeon season, he received a bronze medal in the post that he'd been awarded for his fishing! He had caught a 30-pounder in a competition while he was on holiday, and had presented it to the fishing-boat's captain. Paul had gone back to Liverpool to spend a quiet few weeks with his father and stepmother. Ringo was in hospital having his tonsils out, while John was concentrating on the building and furnishing of his new house.

But now there they were, back at work again. On the first day of rehearsal, the boys made friends with everyone and wandered about the stage mimicking various people, taking everything in, and generally getting used to the place that would be their home for three whole weeks. The opening night was Christmas Eve and utter chaos prevailed backstage. Understandably everyone was apprehensive and people were running in a dozen different directions.

The Beatles' dressing room was the centre of attention, as it was every night. If the boys weren't recording taped messages for transmission in Australia, Canada and the States, then Jimmy Savile would be knocking on the door with several fans who desperately wanted to meet the boys. The stage door man regularly brought in an armful of autograph books, plus the inevitable stream of journalists and photographers. When they got a rare break, the Beatles ate. You might imagine that such stars would enjoy lavish spreads, but you would be wrong. A typical Beatles meal was simply egg, sausages, chips and peas! John joked that in the old days they used to virtually live on steak,

BBC disc jockey Jimmy Savile played the role of the Abominable Snowman for one sketch. That's the show's director, Peter Yolland, next to Jimmy (bottom right).

For the last three weeks (24 December 1964 to January 16) thousands of Beatle fans have crammed into the Hammersmith Odeon twice a night to watch the Fabulous Four appear in their highly successful Christmas Show. Little has changed since last year. The minute the Beatles were due on stage each night there was a mass rush to the front of the theatre, and the local police had to work overtime to prevent the fans from climbing onto the stage itself. The old Beatlemania atmosphere was still there, for the boys are now recognised as having conquered the world, which made their presence eagerly awaited not only by younger fans, but also by the adults in the audience.

As usual, Paul was very happy to pose for photographs.

eggs and sausages, and now, two years and many successes later, they were still eating the same stuff! Apart from a brief and rather lame comedy sketch in Abominable Snowman costumes, the boys' appearance was reserved for the end of the show. After some patter from compere Ray Fell, and an appearance by Jimmy Savile, they were on! Dressed in midnight blue mohair shirts the Beatles leaped into 'She's A Woman', accompanied by shrieks from every girl in sight. Paul introduced the next number "By Gracie Fields . . ." as John Lennon sang 'I'm A Loser' with appropriate gestures into his microphone. George, who had spent the last two numbers alternating between deep concentration on his guitarwork and a few typical grins at the people in the front row, now moved up to the mike and announced his big vocal of the night, 'Everybody's Trying To Be My Baby'.

Then there was a handful of "Sha la la's" by John Lennon into the mike, and he was joined by Paul for 'Baby's In Black'. Ringo followed by performing his usual impossible feat of providing drumwork at the same time as singing 'Honey Don't', while the others moved back to let him take the spotlight. John took centre-stage to sing 'A Hard Day's Night' with harmony from Paul, and George, and then returned to the front to announce 'I Feel Fine' and thank everyone who had bought the disc. After their chart-topper came a raving version of 'Long Tall Sally', an appropriate finale to a dynamic act. The crowd cried out "don't go!", but the Beatles were already on their way backstage and then straight out to their limousine. Another night of their show was over.   (JE)

*****

In retrospect, none of the boys looked back on their second Christmas show with any great enthusiasm. Brian Epstein did his best to persuade them to try it again in 1965, but was greeted with a unanimous refusal, so instead the group staged a more orthodox UK tour. What had been mildly amusing the first time round, in 1963, came to be seen by all concerned as rather hackneyed when it was repeated a year later. From this point on, the group decided to reserve their comedy and acting routines for films, when at least they knew that their audiences would be able to hear them!

Norman Smith

A rare 1964 interview with the recording engineer who worked on all their early hits

Creating a million-selling Beatles disc is essentially a team job, involving the Beatles themselves, of course, their recording manager George Martin, and studio engineer Norman Smith, a backroom boy who deserves his time in the spotlight. So who is Norman Smith? He's 42, tall, married, and greying, and he lives in Edmonton, North London, where he was born. He started playing drums at the age of seven, went on to trumpet and other brass instruments, and then took up vibes.

"I came out of the RAF in 1947," he says, "did the usual round of auditions, but got nowhere." Eventually he got a production job at the BBC. Norman says he was disappointed with the general balance of music programmes, as the rhythm sections never sounded right. He got his chance to improve that situation, especially when he joined EMI, and then played a very important part in changing the way recordings were made when he started working with the Beatles.

"It was just before we recorded the Beatles for their first release that I'd become established enough to try out my own ideas in the studio. I suppose I had a bit to do with the birth of the Mersey Sound. For starters, we kept their recordings 'dry', as I was fed up with the sound of echo chambers. Let's be honest. When I first met the Beatles, they didn't strike me as being a musical group. They didn't have a clue about sound production. In fact, they were an absolute headache. But what really came across was their sense of humour, and their sense of calm. I suppose it was just their star quality. Their simplicity is appealing. They're just very likeable chaps.

"When George Martin and I started to talk about the technicalities of recording, the boys began to send us up. Actually, John Lennon calls me 'Normal' Smith. George Martin and I had talked about getting more bass from Paul, and I'd said, 'We can't stand more than two D-B's, or decibels'. So the boys sent me a pair of gold cuff-links at Christmas, addressed to 'Two D-B Smith'! The Beatles soon showed they had some definite ideas of their own. But they'll always listen to somebody who has some-

Paul and Norman Smith in the control room of Abbey Road's No. 2 studio.

thing new to offer. At that first session, we didn't know we were at the start of a phenomenon. When I first heard about doing a session with them, they were completely new to me. I thought to myself, 'Oh, they're probably a shaggy-dog group, wet behind the ears, a run-of-the-mill lot'. But their attitude and keenness soon got rid of that idea.

"We really did have troubles with them, though. We took a rough take of 'Love Me Do', then played it back to the boys. But their own equipment was all wrong. So we fixed Paul up with our own bass speaker and amplifier, and tied bits of string round John's equipment. There were crackles and pops, and then troubles with the cymbals. I remember thinking that we were going to have a lot of difficulty getting a good recording out of this lot. But, of course, it all worked out perfectly in the end!

"These days, the boys often really send us up. As a matter of fact, we've recorded some of their jokes and wisecracks, and the tapes have gone into the archives at EMI. One day, I suppose, they'll be part of the history of pop music. I've been on all their sessions. I even went to Paris with them, as they recorded 'Can't Buy Me Love' there. How have they changed? Well, I think they're much more fussy these days, more hit parade conscious, if you know what I mean, in terms of sound. They're absolutely deter-

mined not to duplicate tempos or ideas. They want to come up with something different each time. If we put forward a suggestion the boys don't like, they'll try it just the same, even if they've turned up their noses. Then they'll do it as badly as they can . . . until we get the point!

"Paul has a lot of musical ideas, though he's not that good at expressing them. Ringo doesn't have a lot to say. He'll start out with one sort of rhythm, then John and Paul will tell him the way they 'hear' it in their head. Usually, they make the point by referring to some American disc that I've never heard of! Ringo then comes up with the perfect rhythm. The closeness of the group is fantastic – the way they're all on the same wavelength and read each other's thoughts is truly amazing.

"The Beatles don't like working in the mornings. They always want to get some 'play time' in, and that's usually at night. So if they have to turn up in the mornings, you don't get much done. It's really just loosening up. And of course, they make jokes. I think Paul is probably my favourite joker: some of the things he says tickle me pink. My own favourite song? It's hard to say, but 'This Boy' rates very high. I remember that as a thoroughly enjoyable session. The boys didn't think it was all that great at the time. But I think they've got a sneaking regard for it now, after all our plugging for it.

"The 'Twist and Shout' session was a tremendous day . . . an all-time record for the Beatles. We did thirteen titles in ten hours, all for the first LP. Their voices must have been rasping. But John suddenly thought of 'Twist and Shout' and said he wanted to do it. We felt sure his voice would never stand it. But it was done in one 'take', with no overdubbing. The Beatles certainly seem to know what they want. In that sense, they've really improved since their very first session. I don't know what to say about their songs. I mean, nobody could have foreseen just how important they would become in the world of music." (PJ)

The making of Help!

The Beatles' second movie nearly turned out to be a tragedy, not a comedy

When *A Hard Day's Night* was released in 1964 it was a massive success, and everyone assumed that Brian Epstein and the Beatles would bank a huge slice of the profits. But Brian was out of his depth in the film business, and he found it difficult to drive a hard bargain, even with the mild-mannered producer Walter Shenson. When he came to negotiate the contract for their second movie, he pushed for a better deal, but he still found it difficult, because he knew that the Beatles' acting abilities were very limited, so they would need maximum goodwill from Shenson to bluff their way through another movie. It was finally agreed that the film would be a Walter Shenson/Subafilms production, Subafilms being a company Epstein set up in 1964. To protect the Beatles' image, Brian insisted that the storyline depict the boys as squeaky-clean – with no sex and nothing criminal. He also proposed that Shenson should re-hire Richard Lester as director because all the Beatles got on well with him. Brian also wanted Ringo's flair for silent comedy to be developed in the screenplay. Finally, he suggested that United Artists should increase the budget and make the new movie in colour. George's first reaction to the idea was memorable: "I don't mind colour in a film if it doesn't mean dancing about in a red shirt, like in one of Cliff's."

Confident that John and Paul could come up with as many new songs as the soundtrack might require, Brian promised at least 10 titles on their behalf. The Beatles actually produced 14 recordings for *Help!* and Brian handed over a tape containing nine of the best for the producer to choose from. Shenson welcomed the idea of shooting the new film in colour because, as he pointed out to colleagues, it would divert attention away from any weak acting: "If we shoot in glamorous locations against picturesque backdrops we stand a better chance of covering up a multitude of sins."

It was agreed that the budget should be double that of *A Hard Day's Night*, providing enough cash to shoot the new picture in colour and send the cast and crew to exotic locations. Shenson told Lester that he wanted him to keep the dialogue to a minimum and concentrate instead on plenty of slapstick action sequences, with Ringo playing a central role. The creation of a suitable script proved to be quite difficult. An initial draft script was put together by director Richard

The boys joined forces with an Austrian brass band for this scene.

Film director Dick Lester (above left) discussing the next scene with the Beatles.

Lester with TV producer Joe McGrath, telling the tale of a depressed doctor who believed he was dying, but it was rejected because it was too tragic for a Beatles film. Lester attempted to modify the story, making the central character seriously stressed rather than terminally ill, but the idea was quietly shelved. Finally, Lester brought in Charles Wood, who had just finished working with him on a comedy called *The Knack*, and a script quickly took shape. In less than a fortnight Wood presented the team with an outline in which Ringo acquired a priceless sacrificial ring that a bunch of thugs belonging to a religious cult were keen to re-possess at all costs.

Paul called the screenplay "pretty higgledy-piggledy", adding that they just browsed through it rather than taking it very seriously and learning their lines. Regardless of its literary quality, the plot gave adequate scope for a series of wacky races between the baddies and the goodies using all manner of international backdrops. It led the Beatles from the ski slopes of Austria to the silvery beaches of the Bahamas, calling in on Salisbury Plain and Lord Astor's home at Cliveden along the way.

A wide range of seasoned professionals joined the Beatles this time, including such stage and screen stalwarts as Leo McKern, Eleanor Bron, Warren Mitchell, Victor Spinetti, Roy Kinnear, Bruce Lacey, Patrick Cargill and Dandy Nichols. Additionally, Frankie Howerd and Wendy Richard were cast in cameo roles, but their scene was cut from the final version of the film. As an 'in joke' for buddies, pals and mates, the Beatles' roadie Mal Evans was seen briefly as a channel swimmer and there was even a bit part for New York DJ Murray (The K) Kaufman as a tribesman. Paul told me afterwards: "The Queen Mother was nearly in one scene – but that was unintentional. She was driving by on her way to the airport after touring Jamaica."

All the boys had to learn the basics of skiing for the filming of Help!

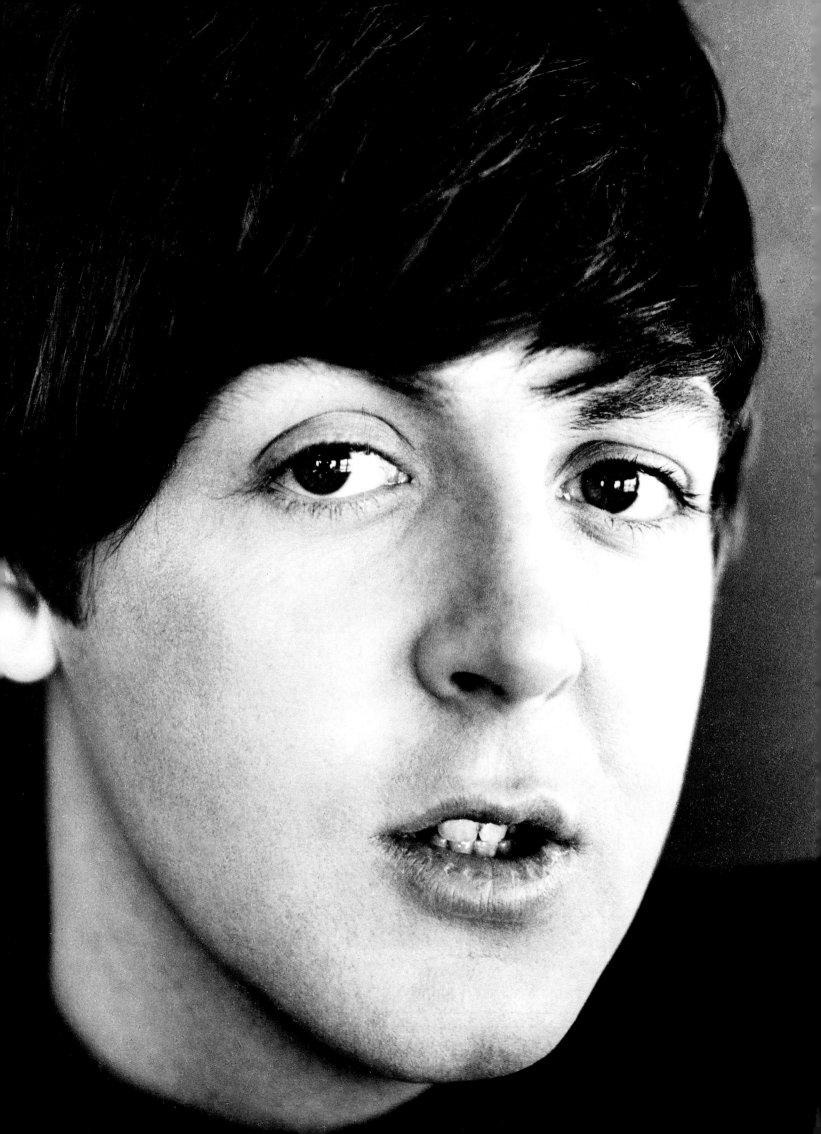

The filming of the curling scene in Austria, when one of the stones turns out to be a bomb!

While the story was being revised, Epstein, Shenson and Lester were forced to be economical with the truth when they spoke to the group. The boys were baffled by the vague answers they got, but Paul conceded: "If we are forced to write the film songs without seeing a script, it could be a good thing. Instead of us having to tailor each song to their script, they'll have to fit our songs into suitable slots. That gives us more scope." In the weeks immediately before shooting started, the Beatles recorded 'The Night Before', 'You've Got To Hide Your Love Away', 'I Need You', 'Another Girl' and 'Ticket To Ride'. They also started work on 'You're Going To Lose That Girl' but were unable to finish the recording before leaving for Nassau.

When the boys asked Walter Shenson about the new comedy thriller, he assured them that they would be playing themselves and would not have to 'get into character'. He said: "You'll be the Beatles in fancy dress, you'll have fun." He and scriptwriter Charles Wood suggested that there would be a hint of Marx Brothers about the picture, and that the thriller content could also be played for laughs. This cheerful information, plus the prospect of spending time on ski slopes and sun-drenched seashores, led the Beatles to take a carefree attitude to the 11-week shooting schedule. Shenson described the locations as "from calypso to yodel with a lot of yeah, yeah, yeah thrown in". By the time they took off for Nassau on 22nd February 1965 for the Caribbean segment of the shoot, the Beatles were substantially less fearful than they had been when *A Hard Day's Night* went into production. At this stage it hadn't sunk in that sunbathing in the Bahamas would be out, because most of the scenes were being filmed out of sequence and tanned skin would look wrong

All four Beatles had screen doubles for the more complicated skiing scenes.

on the ski slopes at Obertauern during the six-day snow shoot which was to follow! Furthermore, February is not the hottest season in the Bahamas, so there were no long days of blazing sunshine to look forward to. The main source of night-time amusement proved to be a pair of Nassau limbo dancing clubs.

One of the first scenes to be shot had Victor Spinetti – playing Foot, a crazy scientist – trying to cut the precious ring from Ringo's finger. As part of the action, Ringo had to dive into the sea. Production people kept a careful watch for sharks, which were spotted swimming nearby. The scene was repeated a number of times, first for rehearsal purposes and then to get the camera angles right. Each time Ringo dried himself off and wrapped his goose-pimpled body in a large beach towel. Richard Lester kept asking for just one more shot until Ringo cried unhappily: "Do we have to do it again, because you do know I can't swim, don't you?" Lester and Spinetti both went pale and looked at one another in horror, imagining Ringo thrashing about in the water unable to escape from the jaws of a hungry shark. "Why didn't you warn me?" said Lester. "You didn't ask me," replied Ringo. During another scene Ringo was in trouble again when a smoke bomb went off more violently than expected and Ringo inhaled enough fumes to send him into a fit of coughing. He told me later: "There were so many people around with cine cameras whenever we shot a scene I shouldn't be sur-

The boys had to cope with bitterly cold weather during the Salisbury Plain shoot.

prised if there are 20 different versions of the film available as pirates!" George told me that autograph hunters held up shooting: "They didn't bother to wait until the end of the scene, they just walked straight up to us, even when we were in front of a rolling camera!" The least appealing locations were left until last. After the spectacular scenery of the Bahamas and Salzburg the producers obviously thought that Salisbury and Twickenham would seem a bit tame. But Paul enjoyed filming on Salisbury Plain: "We had a fabulous four days surrounded by tanks and troops on loan from the army." The boys stayed at the Antrobus Arms pub in Amesbury, where they drank with the locals, and Paul and Ringo enjoyed regular poker sessions with Leo McKern.

It wasn't just the script that kept being revised during the filming; the title of the film was also changed several times. Richard Lester was happy to release the film under its working title of *Beatles 2*, but Ringo came up with an alternative, *Eight Arms To Hold You*, which was still being used in the middle of May, during the final week of location shooting on Salisbury Plain, although the boys had recorded John's song, 'Help!', three weeks earlier.

One reason why *Eight Arms To Hold You* was abandoned is that John and Paul disliked it as a film title. They also felt they would have difficulty writing lyrics around it at short notice. According to Walter Shenson: "*Eight Arms To Hold You* sounded corny. The one thing that the Beatles weren't was corny, so they rejected the title and I was delighted. I think it was Dick Lester's

wife who suggested we call it *Help!*". Richard Lester has claimed that *Help!* became the official title in the second week of April and "within 30 hours the Beatles had written and recorded" the song. He also claimed that "they wrote most of it in the back of the car on the way home from the studio". In fact, the song was almost 100% John's work and the recording was completed at a single four-hour session on April 13. Through the years John expressed mixed feelings over the song, sometimes refusing to talk about it at all and at others declaring that it was one of his first 'message' numbers, a genuine cry from the heart. Others have blown up this claim out of all proportion making it sound as though the song contained some deeply emotional plea on John's part. In my view it was nothing of the sort, but merely a hastily penned film title song and I think John had his tongue planted firmly in his cheek when he went along with interviewers who wanted to make a bigger issue of it.

The 92-minute movie had its world charity premiere at the London Pavilion, Piccadilly Circus, on Thursday 29th July 1965. John commented at the time: "The first half of the film is much better than the end. It's a bit of a letdown when it gets to the Bahamas. We've decided that if we win Oscars, we're all going to send them back!" Walter Shenson said many years later: "I think the Beatles liked *A Hard Day's Night*, as everybody did, but I don't think they were as pleased with *Help!*". John's last word on the movie: "All the best stuff is on the cutting room floor with us breaking up and falling about all over the place." (TB)

At the premiere

The first showing of *Help!* in 1965 brought central London to a standstill

"Stop worrying, HELP's here!", proclaimed the souvenir programme. The approach to the London Pavilion was crowded with fans aged from eight to eighty. No fewer than 10,000 had assembled in Piccadilly Circus on this steamy summer evening to greet the Beatles. Of course, the foyer of the cinema was packed. Titled ladies and monocled men mingled with a surprisingly large number of 'debs' in long dresses, who I suspect were all secretly Beatle fans at heart. Flashbulbs popped, programme sellers shouted, the crowd outside screamed deafeningly, and spirits were high. The attendants tried hard to clear the foyer: "The Royal party is expected any minute! Please take your seats now, madam!"

As the crowd filed reluctantly into the cinema, I recognised several faces. Dick James was there, and Walter Shenson stood smilingly at the doorway, welcoming friends – and suddenly, it happened. One moment you could hear yourself; the next, a mighty yell arose from the ranks of screamers gathered outside, the clanging of fire-engine bells harmonising with the tinkle of ambulance bells as they rounded Piccadilly Circus, preceding the Beatles. A large black Rolls appeared, seemingly from nowhere, and, as the aged buildings shuddered at the noise, the four Beatles, dapper in their dinner-suits, leapt out of the car and bounded into the cinema, fringes shaking, jackets shining, the epitome of switched-on elegance. Cyn Lennon and Maureen Starkey were there too, looking happy and proud of their husbands who were so obviously the apples of the public eye this evening. The flashbulbs popped like miniature machine guns, the boys smiled and gagged for the cameras.

Pandemonium reigned in the Dress Circle of the cinema, as the people lucky enough to be there waited for the Royal party and the Beatles. I noticed a girl with her leg in plaster, who had hurt her leg in a car crash. "I hope George will autograph it", she whispered. When George entered the room where the Beatles would meet the Royal party, she asked him to sign. George's normal grinning face contorted in an expression of sympathy: "Yeah, on the way out, I will, wait a sec, could you?" George left behind him one very happy, albeit beplastered, Beatle fan. The rest of the Beatles, grinning broadly at all and sundry, trooped into the room, and then Princess Margaret appeared, accompanied by her husband, Lord Snowdon, and a few officials. The door marked 'Private' was solemnly closed, and we waited. After what seemed like an eternity, the door opened, and the Royal party came out. I looked inside and saw that the crowd in the room was definitely thinning out and it looked as if only the Beatles were left, posing for the photographers. The girl with the leg plaster asked me to go in with her. Gathering together almost all my (non-existent) pluck, I took a deep breath, and in we went. We had been right (for once!). The Beatles were posing for the cameras and George had recognised us. He pointed us out to Ringo. Ringo stared at the plaster, and his highly expressive features puckered in a grimace of sympathy. To cut a long story short, *all four* Beatles signed the girl's leg in the end (boy, was I envious!), as she posed for the papers with them.

Finally I found my seat. Jane Asher was sitting a few rows in front, looking shy and demure. The curtain went up on the first film, a travelogue on Venice, to the accompaniment of an avalanche of screams. I felt quite sorry for its director! However, the much anticipated moment was not far away. As the black censor's certificate appeared on the screen, ready for the first public showing of *Help!* anywhere in the world, the teenaged section of the audience emitted a long and satisfied sound. It was "yeah"!

The film was a roaring success, naturally. The Beatles left the cinema, to go to the celebration dinner party at the Dorchester Hotel's Orchid Room, with the cheers of the fans who had remained outside the cinema all evening still ringing in their ears.   (ES)

Yesterday

Paul claimed his most famous song came to him when he woke up one morning

The tragedy of Linda McCartney's death instantly gave a powerful new significance to the poignant, if deceptively simple, lyrics of 'Yesterday' – not just for Paul but for his millions of fans. This most famous of all McCartney songs was responsible for establishing, perpetuating and grossly exaggerating Paul's ongoing image as the writer of exclusively soft-centred, emotional and romantic ballads. It set him in the minds of most fans at the other end of the musical spectrum from Lennon, with his far tougher, more ferocious and dangerous style. Dismissing the idea that the song's great popularity typecast him somewhat inaccu-

(Left): Paul singing 'Yesterday' for the very first time during rehearsals for ABC Television's Blackpool Night Out show.

rately, Paul said: "I don't think I've got a particularly soft image. It all depends on whether you know my work or not. Songs like 'I'm Down' are certainly not soft."

As it happened, Paul and the Beatles recorded 'I'm Down' on the morning of the same day in 1965 that he did 'Yesterday'. But Paul had to admit that, of all the songs he ever created, 'Yesterday' was the one that did most for him and his writing career: "Certainly it's the one that's been recorded the most, and it's become one of the most widely recognised all over the world. When an audience sang the song to me in Yugoslavia, I realised it had really got around!" Most people who worked with the Beatles between 1963 and 1965 can remember where or how they first heard 'Yesterday', either as work in progress or in

its finished form. Certainly, immediate members of the McCartney family circle, including Paul's step-mum Angie and step-sister Ruth, heard him doodling away on the piano in the lounge of their Wirral, Cheshire home where the song had been given the unlikely working title of 'Scrambled Eggs'. Paul used to walk around the house from room to room singing to himself: "Scrambled eggs, Oh you've got such lovely legs, Scrambled eggs, Oh my baby how I love your legs". What family members recall most vividly is that Paul kept going back to this one song over a period of a year or more, as though it was already a bit special to him and he was determined to make it work.

Paul says that the initial musical idea for the tune came to him in a flash one morning towards the end of 1963, while he was

The boys preparing to go on stage to record the Blackpool Night Out TV show.

staying at girlfriend Jane Asher's London home: "I just fell out of bed and the bones of the melody were there. I had a piano by the side of my bed and just got up and played the chords." The ease with which the basic tune came to him as he was waking up from a night's sleep caused Paul considerable concern at the time, because he feared it must be a piece of music he'd heard elsewhere that had stuck in his head without him realising it. He was so worried that he might have unwittingly nicked an existing piece of work from some other composer, that he even began whistling the tune to those around him, asking them to name it.

Nobody could come up with a title, although some agreed that it did sound strangely familiar. One of the first people to be treated to an audio preview of the unfin-

ished tune, straight from Paul's head, was songstress Alma Cogan, a close friend of both Paul and the Beatles' manager Brian Epstein. When Paul played her the melody at her West London apartment in Kensington, she said it was lovely, she hadn't heard it anywhere before and she was perfectly convinced it was an original.

The truth is that 'Yesterday' was that sort of tune: the first time you listened to it, you believed you'd heard it somewhere before. Paul finally decided to play it to the other Beatles as an entirely new composition he'd just come up with: "It was like handing in something you'd found at the police station and waiting to see if anyone claimed it." Record producer George Martin remembers being given a live performance preview of 'Yesterday', still known only as 'Scrambled Eggs' at that point, by Paul on a grand piano that had been installed in the Beatles' Paris hotel suite in January 1964. According to

the producer, Paul was already toying with 'Yesterday' as the song's final title but needed a second opinion: "Paul wanted a one-word title except that he thought the word 'Yesterday' was perhaps too corny. I persuaded him that it sounded fine to me." George also suggested that day in Paris that the song should not be recorded in the group's usual way, with all four boys taking part together, but ought to remain a stand-alone solo vehicle for Paul. Paul did not agree at once, maybe because he was embarrassed to be singled out for a solo spotlight and wanted to put on at least some token show of being keen to involve John, George and Ringo in the recording.

The Beatles' movie director, Dick Lester, heard Paul playing 'Scrambled Eggs' constantly on a piano during the shooting of the group's second feature film, *Help!*, at Twickenham Film Studios. This became so irritating and disruptive to Lester's train of thought that he told Paul: "If you play that bloody theme one more time I'll have the piano taken off the set. Either finish the song properly or give up on it."

Music publisher Dick James also heard Paul's new song at Twickenham, played on a Hammond organ and still without lyrics. James told Ray Coleman: "It was an amazing song, even then, as great as any of the Cole Porters or Noel Cowards. Just a magnificent melody." Paul made it clear to the publisher that he wanted all the stops pulled out when the time came to promote the new song. He made such a point of this that Dick James later asked Brian Epstein how the promotion should be angled, and whether or not it should be publicised as a Paul McCartney solo record. Eppy, anxious to keep all four boys equally happy, replied: "Don't be absurd, Dick. It's a Beatles record, but with Paul singing." I believe George Martin posed the same question to Brian and received a similar response. But to my personal knowledge Dick ignored the instruction in at least one instance, revealing excitedly to a top BBC radio DJ: "I've got an advance copy of Paul McCartney's very first solo recording for you, just him and a string quartet, no Beatles, and it's sensational!"

The Beatles Book editorial team heard 'Yesterday' for the first time in Blackpool, when the Fab Four did an ITV *Blackpool Night Out* television appearance which was transmitted live at the beginning of August 1965. That afternoon, sitting in a darkened auditorium, they watched the Beatles learn a few basic dance steps under Lionel Blair's tuition, and photographer Leslie Bryce took some shots of the boys in action with Lionel's girls. Then it was Paul's turn to practice 'Yesterday' on his own. *Beatles Book* editor Johnny Dean sat in the stalls close to comperes Mike and Bernie Winters and the other three Beatles, and watched Paul in solitary rehearsal on the stage, singing the song to his own guitar accompaniment.

At the end, everybody heard John's loud and decidedly sarcastic comment. He made no secret of the fact that he thought 'Yesterday' was a slice of sentimental rubbish, and this led to several heated exchanges between John and Paul in the privacy of the group's dressing room after the rehearsal. Meanwhile, when he was asked to introduce 'Yesterday' on *Blackpool Night Out*, George Harrison couldn't resist a bit of dry humour: "We'd like to do something now that we've never, ever done

before. It's a track off our new LP and this song's called 'Yesterday'. So, for Paul McCartney of Liverpool, opportunity knocks!"

Throughout the Beatles' 1965 summer concert tour of North America, Paul avoided doing the number on stage, partly in order to avoid further unpleasant conflict with John and partly because he knew that capacity crowds in those large, open-air stadium venues would never have quietened down sufficiently to listen to such a sensitive ballad. He compromised when it came to television, although he reported later that he did not feel at ease doing the song with a trio of violinists on *The Ed Sullivan Show*. But he had to admit that this plug on such a top-rated broadcast gave American sales of the 'Yesterday' single a big boost. Paul also sang 'Yesterday' during the group's final series of stage concerts around the world in 1966.

As everyone had feared, the expected backlash was that sectors of the international media saw 'Yesterday' as Paul's way of hinting that he planned to leave the Beatles altogether in the near future and was paving the way towards a solo career. Reporters repeatedly asked the same questions: "Is Paul writing more stuff on his own now?" "What have the others got to say about 'Yesterday'? Do they see it as a betrayal?" Rather than letting Paul get into pointless debate with the press on this, we chose to limit his interviews for a while until people saw for themselves that he did not intend to split from the Beatles or make a regular thing of solo numbers.

But it was the danger of giving added strength to the 'Paul is leaving' rumour that helped to prevent 'Yesterday' from being released there and then as a single in the UK. As Paul knows, it could have been a smash hit at home as well as all over the world but it would have annoyed the rest of the group, and their hostility in such circumstances would have caused him a lot of personal grief which he didn't need. Personally, I think he'd have loved to see it soar to No. 1 in Britain, inevitably shifting the unofficial leadership of the Fab Four from John to him. In later years, Paul was to call 'Yesterday' "probably the best, the most instinctive and the most complete song I've ever written". He was particularly pleased when Mick Jagger said, "I wish I could sing

---

John's mischievous comment about 'Yesterday' upset Paul for several hours.

like that". Clearly impressed by the global scale of the ballad's extensive and prolonged popularity, and its acceptance by such a wide spread of singers and musicians who put the title in their repertoire, Paul rated 'Yesterday' among his favourite self-written songs, putting it at the top of his list alongside 'Here, There And Everywhere'. He used to tell an anecdote about a pre-Christmas West End shopping trip which had taken him into a Regent Street clothing store, where a pianist was tinkling away in the foyer. "He was playing all Noel Coward hits and I thought he was doing a grand job, so on the way out I just leaned over and said 'Thank you' because I thought he might appreciate that. He recognised me, and as I was leaving he played 'Yesterday'. I was dead chuffed that he'd picked 'Yesterday' out of all the Beatles tunes he might have chosen. It made my day!"

This incident contrasts interestingly with one which John and Yoko experienced during the early 70s in the Palm Court of New York's Plaza Hotel. The little house band there used to go into 'Yesterday' whenever the former Beatle walked in, unaware that this made the hairs on John's neck bristle almost visibly with annoyance!   (TB)

115

1965 US tour

A day-by-day diary of their third visit to America

It's almost a month since the Beatles touched down at London Airport after their third American concert tour – the most thrilling and spectacular Beatles' tour on record. Visiting ten cities, they played to well over 300,000 Beatle People at sixteen terrific concerts. Here's my day-by-day diary of the whole trip, transcribed specially for *The Beatles Book* from tapes made on the spot at every stage of this historic third US tour.

FRIDAY AUGUST 13

It's 3.00pm, and we've just arrived at Kennedy International Airport outside New York City. There's a big battery of press, radio and TV people here, but the boys are disappointed because the authorities landed our aircraft in a remote area of the field two miles from the terminal building, where hundreds of fans have gathered to welcome the foursome. Their first stop is the Warwick Hotel. We're shown into a long, bowling-alley-type room designed to accommodate 90 persons. Nearly 250 representatives of the press are there, some by invitation, the others demanding the right of entry on the basis of their press cards. In they surge, equipped with cameras, tape recorders, television cameras, microphones, and an overwhelming curiosity about the Fab Four. The questions that were put to the boys were like those you'd expect from teenagers, not hardened reporters. For example: Q: What do you think of girls from Brooklyn? A: We've never met any.

Their top-floor hotel suite is in a state of utter confusion, with people dashing in and out and phones ringing. Each time the door is opened, the guards in the hallway outside peep in for a glimpse of the boys. The Beatles had requested cans of air spray to keep the rooms free of cigarette smoke. Due to a slight error in understanding, they had received six cans of HAIR spray, and John packed one in his case without noticing the difference! By 6.00pm the boys are tired after facing the press, so they spend a quiet evening watching telly. Their only visitor tonight is Bob Dylan.

SATURDAY AUGUST 14

This morning's move from the Warwick to

Ringo poses with the moptop dolls that were given to the group by some US fans.

the CBS television studios on Broadway is a precision-planned police operation. City cops clear busy main streets of traffic for the Beatles' limousine convoy. Rehearsals for *The Ed Sullivan Show* are extended through the afternoon, as the boys are deeply concerned about the sound balance. They play the same six-title programme that they used a fortnight ago on *Blackpool Night Out*, including a repeat of John's 'elbow run' on the electric piano!

SUNDAY AUGUST 15

The day of the Shea Stadium concert, which is described elsewhere in full detail.

MONDAY AUGUST 16

A free day held open in case rain postponed last night's show. The boys sleep late, and tape interviews with some DJs. Their famous visitors include the Supremes, the Exciters, the Ronettes, Del Shannon and Bob Dylan. During the afternoon, the girls from Beatles USA (Ltd.) meet the Beatles. John and Paul suggest a game of Scrabble with them. John's inventiveness quickly comes to the fore, and he suggests such intriguing words as "Freduck", "runer" (one who "runes", of course), "er" and "daz". Paul makes an equally thought-provoking contribution, "shwegeg". (Ringo divides his attention between the game and a western on television featuring that well-known

cowboy, Johnny Ringo!) John wins the game easily, even after he's restricted to a more conventional vocabulary.

TUESDAY AUGUST 17

The boys travel to Toronto by charter aircraft for two concerts at the Maple Leaf Gardens. 35,000 Canadians watch the shows. Travelling everywhere with the group are twelve top DJs from stations all over America.

WEDNESDAY AUGUST 18

The Electra flies us from Toronto to Atlanta, where another 35,000 Beatle People watch a single concert at the mammoth Atlanta Stadium. For the first time in three years I hear a complete Beatles' performance – not because the audience reaction is anything short of wildly enthusiastic, but because of a very fine loudspeaker system, which lets every note and every word come over clearly. Tonight the boys have given one of their best-ever shows and as we fly out of Atlanta and head for Houston, they can't stop talking about that fabulous sound system. Although it is two in the morning at Houston Airport, an uncontrolled crowd swarms over our aircraft as we taxi to a halt. This is dangerous: many of the older youths

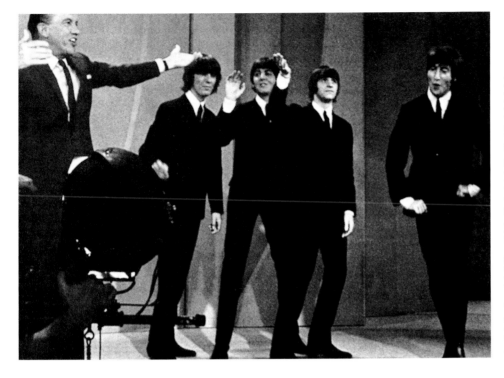

are climbing over the outside of the plane with lighted cigarettes, which could spark off a tragic explosion. We are imprisoned in the plane until a fork-lift takes off the four boys and Brian Epstein. The rest of our party reaches the hotel around 3.00am, tired and a little shaken.

THURSDAY AUGUST 19

Two concerts are seen by 25,000 fans at the Sam Houston Coliseum today. For some reason these are the least exciting to date, although the crowds are good. Maybe it's the stifling heat and general backstage chaos. There are no dressing room facilities and the boys race to and from their hotel by armoured van between shows.

FRIDAY AUGUST 20

We arrived in Chicago early this morning after a night flight in the Electra. Two shows are seen by 50,000 people at the huge Comiskey Park venue. I must mention here how well Sounds Incorporated are doing on this tour. They kill early cries of "We Want The Beatles" and hold the total attention of these enormous audiences by giving knockout performances that just can't be ignored. This is the only act I've ever seen that can precede the Beatles so successfully.

SATURDAY AUGUST 21

This afternoon we flew from Chicago to Minneapolis for a single evening show seen by 22,000 Beatle People. Today's press

The girls responsible for making the moptop dolls pictured with their heroes.

conference is broadcast live in its entirety by a local radio station. The highspot comes when George is presented with a brand-new guitar, which he uses in tonight's show!

SUNDAY AUGUST 22

To reach Portland early this afternoon we flew in through a gorge with towering rocks reaching into the clouds on either side of us. "Do you see anywhere we could land?" Paul asked me blankly as we looked out at the panorama of trees and cliffs. At length we reached Portland Airport and there were dramatic moments as one of the Electra's four engines caught fire and belched smoke. If that engine trouble had started ten minutes earlier, we might have been in severe difficulties! In the boys' dressing room this evening, Beach Boys Carl Wilson and Mike Love visited on their way home to Los Angeles. 20,000 Beatle People saw today's two performances at Portland Coliseum.

MONDAY AUGUST 23

For our overnight flight from Portland to LA, a Constellation aircraft was substituted for the out-of-service Electra. This lengthened our flying time by hours and the boys didn't reach their mountainside Beverly Hills house until a few hours before dawn. It took less than 10 hours for the secret address of their rented home to become public. Newspapers and radio stations blasted out the vital information and a steady stream of fans headed for the hills. Ready for a rest after their hectic week, the boys took it easy inside 2850 Benedict Canyon. They lay beside the swimming pool entertained by blaring music from outdoor and indoor radio loudspeakers scattered around the house.

TUESDAY AUGUST 24

This afternoon John went swimming with his sunglasses on, Eleanor Bron and the Byrds came visiting, and a dozen cops plus a Burns Agency battalion helped to maintain the Beatles' privacy, as more and more Los Angeles Beatle People surrounded the approaches to 2850 Benedict Canyon. Capitol Records boss Alan Livingstone threw a mighty party for the boys this evening. The guest list included Gene Barry, Tony Bennett, Richard Chamberlain, Jane Fonda, Rock Hudson, Groucho Marx, Dean Martin, Hayley and Juliet Mills, and James Stewart. John, Paul, George and Ringo watched a private showing of *What's New Pussycat?* but Paul and George missed all but the end reels of the film, as they sneaked out to attend a Byrds' recording session. Even the guards at the gate of the house didn't realise they had gone out and returned!

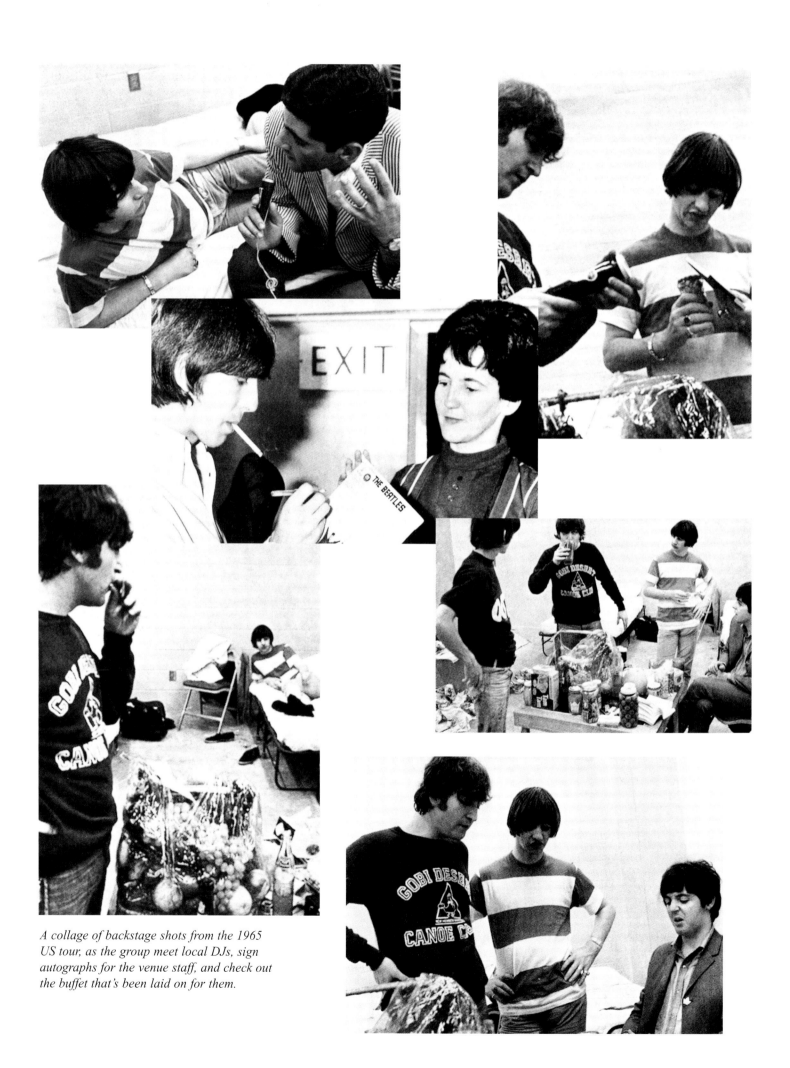

A collage of backstage shots from the 1965 US tour, as the group meet local DJs, sign autographs for the venue staff, and check out the buffet that's been laid on for them.

WEDNESDAY AUGUST 25

Paula (17), Mikki (17), Sue (18) and Kay (17) must be four of California's most ingenious Beatle People. They each lobbed in £10 to hire a single-seater helicopter, which flew them, one by one, over 2850 Benedict Canyon this afternoon. From the air they shouted down greetings to four sun-bathing Beatles. A local newspaper says they are members of "English Groups Inc., an amateur spy ring that track down imported singers". An exiled English housewife brought some packets of English tea to the house but the thoughtful catering staff were one jump ahead of her and had stocked in plenty of tea at the beginning of the Beatles' stay. George, munching a late-night bowl of cornflakes before retiring to bed, denied another local report that the house chef had created a Beatleburger out of hamburger enriched with cornflakes!

THURSDAY AUGUST 26

The daily routine at Benedict Canyon follows a set pattern now. Breakfast is around two in the afternoon, then it's sunbathing and swimming for the boys until dinner, and private screenings of new feature films in the evening. The house, set high above Los Angeles with a magnificent view across the canyon, is a paradise setting for the boys' brief break from work. Meanwhile mail is piling up and there are gifts, cards and telegrams from all over America filling two whole corners of the main living room.

FRIDAY AUGUST 27

Late this evening the Beatles left their house as unobtrusively as possible and drove over to Bel Air to Elvis Presley's house.

SATURDAY AUGUST 28

The vehicle used to carry the Beatles from Beverly Hills down the Pacific coastline to San Diego looked like an ordinary bus. Inside, however, it was the last word in luxury. There were ten seats, a fridge containing food and drink, wardrobes and a bathroom containing a shower. The 120-mile trip took two hours and the boys listened to the bus radio blasting out "Welcome To San Diego" messages as they rode. 20,000 people filled the Balboa Stadium for this evening's concert. As we left, I watched fans rush across the field to tear up souvenir blades of grass, all along the path the boys had used to run from the stage to their super-bus! There was a minor delay on the return trip: the bus broke down and the boys had to stop at a mortuary to transfer into limousines for the final part of the homeward journey!

SUNDAY AUGUST 29

At one of the largest and most efficient press conferences of the tour this afternoon, Capitol Records president Alan Livingstone presented the Beatles with gold discs for their fast-selling *Help!* album. Then the boys drove from Capitol Tower to the famed Hollywood Bowl by armoured truck for the first of their two concerts in this picturesque setting. A young married Beatle fan gave birth to a son in the car park of the Hollywood Bowl this evening but another 17,999 fans saw the performance through to its conclusion.

MONDAY AUGUST 30

Tonight is the last night in Beverly Hills and the boys are reluctant to leave their lovely canyon home. Their second Bowl concert was another resounding success. Beforehand, the Beatles invited round the dozen or so DJs and pressmen who have accompanied them throughout the tour for a last poolside party.

TUESDAY AUGUST 31

The Beatles' charter aircraft flew its last lap today, bringing the boys up the coast from LA to San Francisco for concerts before 30,000 wildly excited fans at the massive Cow Palace. As always the boys went through twelve numbers: 'Twist And Shout', 'She's A Woman', 'I Feel Fine', 'Dizzy Miss Lizzy', 'Ticket To Ride', 'Everybody's Trying To Be My Baby', 'Can't Buy Me Love', 'Baby's In Black', 'I Wanna Be Your Man', 'A Hard Day's Night', 'Help!' and 'I'm Down'. The shows made headline news across America, because scores of over-excited Beatles fans fainted in the incredible crush when they rushed towards the stage during the performances. Loose seating in front of the stage allowed those behind to push forward and move the seats aside. These incidents apart, however, everyone agreed that it was a terrific finale to a thoroughly exciting tour. (FJ)

Shea Stadium

Tony Barrow explains why the Beatles' 1965 New York extravaganza is still remembered as their most successful concert of all time

The voice of Ed Sullivan, one of America's best-known television personalities, rang out around New York's Shea Stadium. "Ladies and gentlemen, honoured by their country, decorated by their Queen and loved here in America, here are the Beatles!"

This was the cue for John, Paul, George and Ringo to emerge from a dugout tunnel beneath one of the tall stands, led by several uniformed NYPD cops. Smiling broadly and waving frantically in recognition of the high-volume screams of welcome that rose up from the fans as soon as they appeared, the Fab Four began to run out across the grass towards a platform which had been put up specially for their one-night stand. As all four members of the group came into view, the entire audience got to its feet, waving union jacks and banners, souvenir brochures, sticks of candy floss, anything that might attract the attention of a favourite Beatle.

The boys were showing off smart new stage outfits for the first time — black trousers worn with fawn-coloured collarless jackets which were unbuttoned and blowing open in the breeze as they ran. John, Paul and George carried their own instruments, each of the guitars slung over one shoulder and held closely to their sides by the bridge with one hand. Sweating profusely in the oppressive New York summer heat and panting from the strenuous race out across the field, Paul arrived first at the side of the stage, followed by Ringo and John, with George bringing up the rear. By now the screams of the crowd had reached an ear-shattering climax which echoed round and round the stands. Already up on the stage, having set out the gear, roadies Mal Evans and Alf Bicknell beckoned to Paul, urging him to bring the rest up some steps. As George climbed he reached out and up to grasp Mal's supportive hand and asked the big man if the spare guitars were in place and if they had all been tuned. The

legendary but very pompous Ed Sullivan, who hosted a weekly TV variety show, was still standing at the microphone, bathing in the reflected glory of the welcome the boys were receiving. Looking grandly groomed in his dark blue suit and almost visibly oozing self-importance, Sullivan waited to shake hands with the Fab Four before letting Alf assist him on his way down the steps.

An electric sign at one end of the field flashed up a warning sign in the hope of persuading the fans to sit down: "FOR SAFETY'S SAKE PLEASE STAY IN YOUR SEATS". The majority remained standing and cheering wildly at the slightest gesture or movement from the stage. It would take more than an electric sign to dampen their spirits. John, George and Ringo plugged in their instruments and tried to check if they were in tune. George cupped one hand over

The legendary Shea Stadium in New York as it is today.

an ear and twiddled the knobs on the top of his amplifier while Ringo clambered up to his drum rostrum at the rear and took hold of some sticks that Mal handed him. John tested his mike: "Hello! Hello!" Then Paul tried his: "One two. One two." Each provoked the same screaming response from the stands, where the continuous output of decibels just doubled. Then, quite suddenly, they were into 'Twist And Shout' and the show was on.

What helped to make the Beatles' concert at New York's Shea Stadium so very special was the sheer size of the audience, coupled with the massive space between the temporary mid-field stage where the four boys stood and the tiered stands which held some 56,500 fans (including Mick Jagger). John, Paul, George and Ringo reacted instinctively to this unprecedented situation by giving a show that was twice as large as life – and twice as exciting for all of us who were lucky enough to be there. The chemistry between the group and the crowd was amazing and the atmosphere had a magical quality about it which made the evening of Sunday 15th August 1965 the most memorable of any I can remember from the Beatles' touring years.

The Beatles were used to playing Britain's Odeon, ABC and Granada cinemas but the biggest of these places only held around 3000 people. The front row of seats in the average cinema was no more than a few metres away from the footlights that ran across the front of the stage. As they played and sang, each Beatle could look into the eyes of the closest fans. By contrast, at Shea the American fans were collected in huge stands set along the far side of a baseball field and the distance between the musicians and their audience had a remarkable influence on the way the group performed. Instead of staring directly into a sea of faces at close quarters they exaggerated every

bodily gesture and facial expression in an extra effort to bridge the unprecedented gap and make some real contact with the crowd.

The Beatles always agreed, long after the event, that this show represented the pinnacle of their success as a touring band. But few would rate the Shea Stadium concert as one of the group's finest efforts. Most, if not all, of their stage shows during the Beatlemania years were flawed vocally or instrumentally by sub-standard amplification or by actual faults in the way the Beatles played and sang under such stressful conditions. Shea was simply an extraordinary experience for the four boys and for all their aides and associates who were on the road with them that August.

For us the excitement and drama of the day had started long before the show was due to get underway. From the Warwick Hotel, at West 54th Street and the Avenue of the Americas, we were driven in a tight convoy of limousines across the city to Manhattan's waterfront heliport. This in itself proved to be a spectacular ride because the authorities broke with tradition by clearing the route. Motorcycle traffic cops were at every intersection to hold back traffic so that we could speed through red lights and along empty streets. At the heliport we raced from the limousines and ran across the tarmac towards our waiting aircraft, a long twin-rotor helicopter. As we ran, a senior-looking police officer boomed out from

John was highly amused by this portrait of Ringo that had been sent in by a fan.

somewhere behind us in a voice of authority: "Hey, which of you guys is Mr Epstein? I need the group's manager right now before you leave!" Brian stopped in his tracks, blushed, and took off his sunglasses, wondering what terrible offence he had committed to warrant such public embarrassment. "I am me, I am him, I am Brian Epstein," he stammered. "Good, I gotcha!" said the cop with a triumphant grin, and he handed 'Eppy' an autograph book. "Get your four boys to sign this here book for my daughter before you go, OK?" The helicopter was longer than any we'd seen before, with eight passenger windows down each side and a steep metal ladder up to the door, just like a full-sized commercial plane.

Once on board we sorted out our seating, each claiming one of the single seats beside a window. I took the front one on the right with George immediately behind me, and Ringo behind him. On the other side were Paul, Neil, John and Brian, who was still clutching the cop's unsigned book. Our big white craft rose into the air at an angle, tilted to the right and flew out over the river, following the waterfront coastline along the edge of Manhattan and giving us a magnificent view of the city's tallest buildings. This was a perfect vantage point from which to view the famous skyline. Cine cameras came out and jaws dropped with amazement

George borrows some untypical Beatles headgear backstage at Shea Stadium.

as we moved slowly through the air and gazed in awe at the impressive sight. Neil, Brian and Paul stood up and leaned over to our side to get the best view. Our escort from the General Artists Corporation, the giant showbiz agency, which had set up the US tour with Brian, confirmed that we had time to spare, so the pilot circled Manhattan one more time before heading out towards Shea. The original plan had been to land inside the stadium on the actual field but the authorities had vetoed this for safety reasons and we came down instead at the World's Fair site.

Before we reached the ground, our pilot circled Shea Stadium and far below us, as we flew around, hundreds of fans pointed their flash cameras into the sky to try and capture the moment on film. I doubt if anything came out but they tried all the same, encouraged by the DJ on stage: "Here they are! The Beatles are coming! Look up there right now and you'll see their helicopter!" George, never too keen on any sort of air travel, commented afterwards: "The only thing I didn't like was the fact that we were hanging up there in the sky. I like my feet to be on the ground." From where we landed on the roof of one of the World's Fair office buildings, we were driven the short final stretch to Shea in the back of a Wells Fargo armoured van. We felt absolutely anonymous behind the thick metal-plated walls of the bullet-proof truck, totally hidden from the strolling passers-by, who had no idea they were just a metre or two from the Beatles.

Meanwhile, New York DJ Murray The K was on stage hyping the crowd but also relaying the warning he'd been told to stress in the interests of security: "Welcome to what will probably be the biggest concert ever in the history of pop music. The Beatles are here, they are changing into some very snazzy

looking outfits for you but I want to tell you one thing. It's gonna be kinda difficult in this outdoor show with close to fifty, sixty thousand people, and we've got a long night to go. So scream and shout as much as you want, but whatever you do take care of yourselves and go home safely." Installed securely in the baseball team's dressing-room, which was to be their sanctuary for the next few hours, the Beatles relaxed on their canvas 'cots' and chatted with the dozen or so British and American media people, press journalists and broadcasters in our entourage. Paul was telling one of the guys about Bob Dylan's visit to the Warwick two nights earlier: "It was a great honour to meet our hero and our idol. We had a crazy party." Ringo was discussing fans with another reporter: "We love them as much as they love us; without them we'd be nothing."

In another corner of the room George was talking about the fans screaming at concerts: "I think most fans want to see us, and six out of ten also want to hear us, but if one person screams, it influences others, and the ones next to them will follow suit." Question to Paul: "Do you think you are ever in physical danger during your stage shows?" Answer: "I got hit in the eye once by a cigarette lighter. Clouted me right in the eye and closed it." John took an unruffled view of the fan-mobbing problem the boys faced whenever they were on the road: "We always call it the eye of the hurricane, it's always calmer in the middle where we are." Paul suddenly realised they hadn't worked out any final sequence of songs for the concert. They had intended to do this during breaks in *Ed Sullivan Show* rehearsals, but it never happened. It seldom did – the boys often wrote out a list at the eleventh hour in dressing rooms before they went on, handing bits of paper to Neil and Mal to stick on their instruments as reminders.

Above us, monitor speakers kept us posted about what was going on outside and we heard Murray The K yelling: "Let's start the show off by introducing you to the Discotheque Dancers." We could hear the band playing 'Downtown' and 'Can't Buy Me Love'. Then the big brassy sound of the King Curtis Band accompanied black R&B songstress Brenda Holloway as she did the Four Tops' current hit, 'I Can't Help Myself', and we all sang along from the dressing-room: "Sugar pie, honey bunch!" The show continued with the locally popular Cannibal & the Headhunters and our own fabulous Sounds Incorporated from Kent.

Half an hour before they were to go on, the Beatles were stressed out, intensely nervous, feeling sick, the butterflies in their stomachs fluttering uncontrollably. It was always a tense time just before a big show, but they knew they were about to play to their biggest-ever audience, and that made things worse. The two roadies prepared to go out ahead of the boys to set things up on stage. They were bombarded with last-minute questions about guitars and amps, drumsticks and microphones. The musical equipment specialists Vox had made a special set of amplifiers for the tour, boosting the sound output to more than three times that heard at previous shows. But the boys knew that most of the crowd would be relying on the stadium's own PA (public address) system, consisting of a set of speakers intended for sports commentary, not vocals and music. Finally, the man from GAC put his head around the dressing room door: "OK boys, showtime. Time to go. Let's go to the job, let's do it." John, Paul, George and Ringo ran their fingers through their moptops and shook their heads vigorously in front of their mirrors to get their famous fringes falling down evenly over their foreheads. "Boys, let's go to the job, like NOW!" Paul lingered to give his hair a final check and then hurried through the door after the others.

Once the Beatles were on stage and into 'Twist And Shout', all nervousness disappeared and the adrenalin and the sweat flowed in torrents rather than trickles. They used every visual trick they could to increase the raw excitement and sheer enjoyment of their fans. John was in fine fettle, gagging and fooling around between numbers. "We'd like to do a slow song off

Beatles VI or something, I don't really know what it's on, I haven't got it." He laughed heartily and went on: "It's a waltz this one, remember that. Anyway the song's called, hopefully enough . . ." Then he spotted a girl running the gauntlet of five uniformed security men to reach the stage. "Ah, look at her, ah!" He finally got around to introducing 'Baby's In Black'. Twenty-eight minutes and eleven numbers raced by, the Beatles continually increasing the tempo as they often did in live performance. They'd done a wide range of stuff, from 'She's A Woman' and 'I Feel Fine' to 'A Hard Day's Night' and 'Help!'. Then they were up to their last song and the famous fringes were dripping with sweat and clinging to their foreheads. They looked as if they'd just been in a shower – fully clothed.

Appreciating that few people could hear what he was saying, Paul mimed his bit of patter: "It's the last number of the show." He looked at his watch and pointed to it, then used his hands, palm to palm under his ear, to depict sleeping. "We're going to bed after this." Actually, they were expecting a second visit from Bob Dylan before they turned in for the night, and Monday was a day off, so sleep was still a long way ahead! Paul completed his final introduction and the group plunged headlong into a frantic 'I'm Down', during which John played his electric piano

After all the hype and pressure, this was what it was all about: the Beatles on stage.

with his elbows. He explained afterwards that he hadn't quite known what to do at that point without his guitar. On the recording he'd used an organ, so he chose a Vox electric keyboard for the US tour: "It was the first time I'd played a piano on stage and George couldn't play for laughing. That's when I went a bit berserk and ran an elbow down the keyboard, just for a laugh, you know."

'Eppy' agreed after the event that he had been right to let promoter Sid Bernstein talk him into booking the band into such a large baseball park rather than the 2900-seater Carnegie Hall for their New York concert. Eight months earlier, when the gig was first offered, he had feared that Shea was a little ambitious and had warned Bernstein that he didn't want the boys embarrassed by thousands of empty seats. The astute Sid Bernstein, never short of a headline-catching quote, came back with the promise that he would pay the Beatles for every seat unsold at Shea Stadium. Apparently there was nothing in writing between the two men – each trusted the other's word and took it as his bond. The promoter sold every ticket in less than a month without paying for a single line of advertising space, bringing in well over $300,000 in box office takings.

Bernstein described this as "the greatest gross ever in the history of showbusiness". For just under thirty minutes on stage, each of the Fab Four collected around $33,000, while Brian's 25% cut came to around

$45,000. From the balance, Bernstein paid for the extraordinarily large security force of 1300 police inside the stadium on show day, hired both for the protection of the Beatles and to reduce the possibility of accidental injuries among the 56,500 fans. George told Larry Kane, one of the U.S. radio reporters who travelled around America with us on the 1965 tour: "I don't think it was over-secure. You've got to have security and you've got to draw the line somewhere. You either have good security and get back alive or you have very little and we probably wouldn't have made it!" In fact the security arrangements were wonderful; accidents among the crowd were remarkably few and the organisation of filling and later emptying the place went like clockwork.

John summed up the group's feelings afterwards when he was talking about the Shea Stadium appearances of 1965 and 1966 in the context of their decision to stop touring. He said that such vast crowds seated so far from the stage couldn't even see the Beatles clearly, let alone hear what was being played: "We're specks on the horizon. Why thousands of people paid money to be at Shea Stadium, I'll never know." Of course the rest of us knew, even if the boys couldn't understand it. The unmatched thrill of Shea Stadium was not merely the music but the spine-tingling, mind-blowing, never-to-be-repeated and never-to-be-forgotten experience of simply being there! (TB)

Elvis meets the Beatles

Tony Barrow remembers the greatest pop summit of all time

Elvis Presley bent forward across the counter of his cocktail bar and spoke confidently into my left ear: "Are these guys always as shy as this, sir?" Elvis used to call everyone 'sir' unless they were close pals or fellow pop stars.

As he passed a silver-tray loaded with drinks across the bar, I told him: "Normally I never see the Beatles lost for words but this is an evening that's a bit special for everybody. The boys have waited years for this get-together. No wonder they're tongue-tied!" Elvis moved his face closer again and the heavy scent of his aftershave filled the air all around my nose: "You think they'll loosen up a little when they get a few drinks inside them?" I told him I was sure they would and he asked if they were into heavy boozing: "I guess John's the big drinking man, am I right? Does John like his alcohol?" "No more than the rest of us", I answered and took the tray of icy glasses from him to hand round. As we walked across the room towards the corner where the Beatles sat in a semi-circle in front of a colour TV set, Elvis asked me: "Will I embarrass your boys if I get out some guitars and suggest we play a little rock'n'roll? Do they like to do that at a party?" He was doing his best to melt the ice but it was a slow process because the atmosphere was far from relaxed.

As Elvis lowered himself into the midst of the Beatles on the long settee, Priscilla Beaulieu (later Mrs Elvis Presley) floated over in my direction, which was a wondrous sight to behold. I can't remember now, many years on, what this strikingly lovely lady wore, but the main memory I have is that she looked like Cleopatra. She looked totally elegant, absolutely cool. She said to me: "Do the Beatles have all they want now? Would they like to eat something? We can fix anything special they like to eat. You only have to ask, you know, Brian." Brian? I pointed out the Beatles' manager on the far side of the room, in deep conversation with The Colonel. I turned again to face the group of superstars lounging around the settee. Elvis had produced a guitar. From time to time he used the top end to prod the buttons down the front of the massive TV set and change the channels. Colour television was still a great novelty to the Beatles in 1965, but even much less wealthy Americans than Elvis took it for granted.

He wasn't watching any particular programme. As the evening wore on, he changed the channels with increasing frequency. It was as if he needed to see a change of pattern on the screen, new colours, nothing more. It was solely a visual thing. The sound was muted throughout while a jukebox blared out non-stop rock music at top volume. I remember George Harrison commenting that occasionally the silent pictures on the telly looked as though a particular record had been matched up to them. There was no such thing as a 'pop video' in those days, but that was the effect we were getting. Elvis Presley kept cropping up in the career of the Beatles. At the end of 1961 when he proposed a management deal to the group, Brian Epstein tried to impress a very naive Fab Four by claiming he knew Colonel Parker. He didn't then but he soon did when the Beatles became international pop heroes and a direct challenge to Presley's worldwide supremacy. At one stage around the middle of 1964, 'Eppy' confessed to me that a merger between Parker's management

organisation and NEMS was a possibility. I think Brian was overwhelmed by the sheer size of American showbusiness just then and figured he needed to link up with someone as powerful as Parker on the far side of the Atlantic. Of course the whole idea was fantasy. Presley and the Beatles were in direct competition and there is no way Parker would have wanted to work with Epstein and no way the Beatles would have agreed to become part of any Presley 'stable'. On the other hand, Presley was always in Epstein's thoughts. At our earliest meeting, as I've mentioned before, 'Eppy' promised me that his Beatles would become as big as Elvis. A year later, when the first single had dented the charts, the Epstein boast had changed to 'Bigger than Elvis'. The Beatles themselves took this with a cellarful of salt. They knew they'd be big and famous but bigger than Elvis, that was ridiculous!

By 1965, both sides decided that a 'summit' meeting between the Beatles and Elvis ought to take place while the Fab Four were touring the USA. Showbusiness politics entered the picture. Would the Colonel let his client come to the Beatles? Would Epstein allow the Beatles to visit Presley on his terms and at his house? The five just wanted to get together and enjoy an evening of small-talk. The managers looked at the wider implications, particularly in terms of their own reputations! Epstein wanted some ground rules established in case the meeting was on. For a start, the press would be excluded totally, except for Chris Hutchins of the *New Musical Express*, who knew Colonel Parker quite well from previous *NME* dealings. As the Beatles' own publicist, it was my role to hand out information about the occasion to all other media people. The date of the summit was set for Friday August 27th, 1965, the end of the week's break before their final shows in California. Late that evening, the Beatles drove from their hideaway at 2850 Benedict Canyon to the Bel Air house owned by Elvis Presley on Perugia Way.

During the limousine ride from Benedict Canyon, the Beatles stayed abnormally silent. The few exchanges of chatter we had were stilted and a little unreal. At one point John said to me: "Have you brought the picnic basket?" Everyone laughed nervously but I'm not sure whether any of us knew why. Paul said: "Have you brought your tape recorder?" I said no, and Paul seemed surprised. I wished I had fetched the thing along to keep some souvenir of the evening's conversation. Brian Epstein muttered very quietly from the far corner of the car: "No cameras. No recordings." As our limousine paused outside the gates of the Presley home, George said: "Christ! My mouth's SO dry!" And Paul added: "There are no fans! Just an army of bloody cops!"

Attired in grey trousers and a startling red shirt, Elvis stood outside his own front door waiting to greet his famous guests personally. That set the scene for the whole evening. At various moments henchmen were on the point of leaping forward to hand over guitars or empty ashtrays, when Elvis waved them aside and did the slightest job himself. It was Presley's way of stressing that just for once his visitors were also his total equals. At first the Beatles were led into an enormous living room bathed in bright red and blue lights.

There was an awkward few minutes when everyone sat with clenched hands clutching knees and polite smiles. One by one, Elvis's heavies and henchmen, the famous Memphis Mafia, emerged from other rooms, some to introduce themselves to Neil and Mal, others to see if Elvis wanted anything. Elvis asked an aide to start up the jukebox. Then he went over to the machine, turned the volume way up high and selected the next half-dozen singles to be played. Lightheartedly he returned to the Beatles who were whispering amongst themselves and said something like: "Well, if all you want to do is sit here and stare at that damned television, I'm off to my bed!" The music helped to provide a better atmosphere. Hands became unclenched as fingers tapped to the beat. Ringo was first to get the party spirit, taking a couple of cocktail sticks and drumming out a rhythm on the coffee table as the records played.

Presley himself, not known for drinking alcohol in huge quantities, sipped soda but offered his guests the choice of stronger concoctions. The measures of bourbon, scotch and other spirits served by Presley's minders were four or five times larger than regular size! It was one way of getting things jollier. Not surprisingly it was music rather than words that the key people at this strange party used to communicate with, as the evening wore on. There was little conversation that would have been worth preserving on my little tape recorder but I wish the extraordinary jam session between the five stars had been documented for posterity! All the live playing was done to the accompaniment of Presley's own record collection. Elvis played his booming bass while Paul nipped to and fro between piano and guitar.

The supply of instruments seemed unlimited. Extra guitars kept appearing in the hands of Presley heavies who had been ordered to dig them out of the singer's private recording room elsewhere in the house. Presley himself took each new instrument, tuned it vaguely but not properly with all the din going on, and offered it to his guests. Some aides joined in too. Elvis and George locked themselves in conversation about one or two of the Presley guitars and George asked me to make a note of model and manufacturer names from time to time.

Jamming away so freely caused all five stars to abandon their initial embarrassment and enjoy the party. When Elvis played Paul's bass part on one number, Paul remarked facetiously: "Elvis, lad, you're coming along quite well there on the old bass. Keep up the rehearsals and me and Mr. Epstein will make you a star!" While the boys made their music, the Colonel unveiled a roulette table disguised as a coffee table and Brian Epstein gleefully joined him in a bit of a gamble. Lennon saw this happening as he passed me to go

to the lavatory. He said: "Brian has just gambled us and Billy J. Kramer against Elvis!" On the whole, however, the party was not an unqualified success. I can't pinpoint what was wrong with the set-up. I'm sure it wasn't anybody's fault, least of all our host's. Despite the music-making, the flow of drink and the noisy jukebox, conversation between Elvis and the Beatles continued to be stilted, anxious and never properly intimate, even when tales of touring disasters were exchanged.

After just over three hours we left. The Beatles invited Elvis and his men over to Benedict Canyon. "Come tomorrow night", urged Paul, completely ignoring the fact that we'd be way down the Pacific coast in San Diego for a Saturday night concert. I suggested quickly that they should make it Sunday, thinking there might be a chance of getting Elvis over for the Hollywood Bowl show and the party afterwards. John put it to Presley, who said they'd all try to make it. They didn't. "Don't forget to come and see us again in Memphis", called Elvis from the porch as we climbed into our limousine. But that was another date which was never kept. A second meeting between the Beatles and Elvis would have just led to another set of stilted exchanges. That first get together had to happen once for the sake of the participants and the world's observers. They'd talked politely about song-writing and films, about tour disasters and record sales. But everyone agreed once was enough. It had been difficult to get the words flowing freely. Nobody relished the thought of having a second go. (TB)

A very rare shot of Elvis posing with a European fan magazine about the Beatles

BEATLE NEWS

1965

RINGO MOVES
Ringo has been forced to relocate from the block of flats in central London where he has been living for several months. Other residents were complaining about the number of fans who regularly used to wait outside for the Beatles' drummer to arrive. One resident who never complained, however, was Brian Epstein, who intends to keep on living in the same block. (January 1965)

DEFENDING THE BOYS
The latest Fab Four society is the Beatles Defending Association of America, or BDAA for short. The president, Jo-Anne Carpenito of Arlington, New Jersey, says that the Association has 650 members in five different countries, all of whom have pledged to defend the boys from unfair press criticism. (January 1965)

ANOTHER RINGOISM
A lot of Beatle People have pointed out that the title Ringo thought up for the first film, *A Hard Day's Night*, was in John's book. But quite a few of Ringo's sayings are used by John when he's writing. The latest Ringoism is "Tomorrow Never Knows" – his version of the old saying, "Tomorrow Never Comes" – and it's a possible title for their next film. (February 1965)

THEY WANT MONEY!
Not one, but two sets of taxmen are after the Beatles. Much of the cash that they earned in America during their last tour has still not been given to the boys, because both the British and American tax offices are claiming that they should get their share. Says Walter Hofer, who looks after the boys' legal worries in the States, "Our position is that we await the two governments coming to a decision on the matter. We are not resisting the tax at all, but we certainly don't want to pay it twice!" It seems as if money can't buy you love when the taxmen are involved! (February 1965)

RECORDING FILM SONGS
That special atmosphere was present all through the third week of February because the boys spent every day recording the songs for their new film. It's a unique experience seeing the way they turn a song, scribbled on the back of an envelope or on an odd piece of paper, into yet another great hunk of Beatle music. And even while they are concentrating on what they are doing, they never seem to miss an opportunity for a bit of leg-pulling with whoever happens to be there at the time.
(Johnny Dean's editorial, March 1965)

PAUL'S BEST
John spent a couple of weeks learning to ski before the Beatles started their new film. But it quickly became obvious that Paul was the best skier as soon as he put skis on for the first time. "He could have been a 'champ' if he'd started earlier," said one expert in Obertauern. All the Beatles were kept very busy signing plasters covering broken limbs. Paul also added a message to the doctors in German! (March 1965)

TICKET TO NO. 1
Their new single, 'Ticket To Ride', has been a giant success all over the world. It is just ready to take over at the top of the US charts from Herman's Hermits' 'Mrs Brown You've Got A Lovely Daughter', while at home it entered the Top 30 at No. 1, and has stayed there for the past three weeks. (April 1965)

NO-ONE RECOGNISED HIM
Both the Beatles and the Stones are regular visitors to the Ad Lib Club, just off London's Leicester Square, and they often have chats about the current scene. One night last month, Mick Jagger and Keith Richard invited John and Neil back to their flat for a night-cap. They talked and played records until the early hours of the morning. Then the 'Stoney' pair disappeared off to bed, leaving John and Neil to kip down on the couch. They decided, however, to go home instead but, unfortunately, they had no transport so they walked for a mile or so then waited on a taxi rank for what seemed like a couple of hours. Finally, when no taxis appeared, they made for the Underground as the tubes were just starting to run.

"It was amazing", Neil told us. "There were loads of workmen and cleaners all over the place, but hardly anyone looked at John with the usual question mark in their eyes . . . surely that isn't, no, it can't be ... you know the sort of thing!" The oddest part of the episode was when they got off the tube at Tottenham Court Road. The escalator wasn't working so John and Neil toiled all the way up the long, long stairs while a little man watched them from the top. When they finally reached him all puffed out, he turned round, pressed a button and the escalator started moving! (April 1965)

HELP
Help! had been bandied about as a possible title for the Beatles' second movie soon after they first started shooting, but it was discarded early on in favour of *Eight Arms To Hold You* because producer, Walter Shenson, wasn't very keen on one-word titles and Paul and John hadn't come up with a suitable song.

As we told you last month in *The Beatles Book,* the boys wrote the song on April 4th after director, Dick Lester, had asked them if he could have it as soon as possible. *Help!* was finally clinched as the name for the new

Ringo in his garden with a phonograph too small to play the Beatles' records!

movie during Ringo's scene with a live tiger at Twickenham Studios, when the boys all reacted with a spontaneous cry of "Help"! (Johnny Dean's editorial, May 1965)

RUBBISH!
Paul has been amused recently to read American interviews with someone called Marlene McKeown, Miss Ireland of 1963, who is apparently telling the press that she has been Paul's steady girlfriend for the past four months. "Rubbish! I don't even know her!", is Paul's response. (May 1965)

MBE CONTROVERSY
The award of the Membership of the British Empire to John, Paul, George and Ringo has aroused a storm of controversy. Several holders of the MBE award have returned their medals to Buckingham Palace, feeling that giving the honour to mere pop singers has devalued their own awards. But as several showbiz correspondents have pointed out, there is a little to choose between winning export sales for Britain by selling records, and doing the same thing by selling machinery or other goods. It all adds to Britain's prosperity, and so it is only right that the Beatles, who have done so much to boost Britain overseas, should also be honoured.

When Paul received a songwriting prize at the Ivor Novello awards ceremony, he quipped: "Thanks. I hope nobody else sends theirs back!" (June 1965)

BUNKERED!
Weybridge Golf Club recently made it plain that neither John nor Ringo, who both now live in the town, would be invited to join their establishment. John replied: "We don't even like golf. Neither of us has the slightest interest in the sport. In fact, I nearly didn't buy the house when I heard there was a golf course at the end of the garden." (July 1965)

ON HOLIDAY
All of the boys have been having a good rest after the finish of their very strenuous American tour. The only one who went in search of the sun was George. John relaxed by painting murals in his new house. He just gets sheets of hardboard and covers them with green, black and red shapes. They are all abstracts and he hasn't decided what he is going to do with them yet. (September 1965)

TO RINGO, A SON
If you thought Ringo was an unusual name, wait till you hear what he and Maureen have named their baby son. The tiny boy has been christened Zak, though Ringo revealed that if he had been a girl, then he would have been called Lee. Mother and child are both doing well. (September 1965)

WRONG SIDE UP!
John and EMI almost came to blows over the choice of the A-side for their new single. EMI originally announced that 'We Can Work It Out' would be the A-side, but John hit back by insisting that 'Day Tripper' should be the top side. As a compromise, EMI have agreed to promote the single as a double A-sided release, so you can expect to hear both songs on the radio very soon. (November 1965)

The experts agreed that Paul could easily become an excellent skier with practice.

STREET SONGS
Paul has been telling the press about some of the Beatles' ideas which haven't yet been turned into finished songs or scripts. "We had an idea about Jesus Christ coming back to Earth as an ordinary person. But I think we're resigned to the fact that we will just not have time to work on a full-scale musical until the Beatles are finished as a group.

"We have also always wanted to write a number about the places in Liverpool where we were born. Places like Penny Lane and the Docker's Umbrella have a nice musical sound, but when we strung them all together in a composition, they sounded so contrived that we gave up!" (November 1965)

Girlfriends and wives

Two generations of women were by the Beatles' sides in the 60s and beyond

The four girls who were the Beatles' partners in the mid-Sixties were as varied in their looks, personalities and backgrounds as the Fab Four themselves. Paul broke off several casual relationships in Liverpool when the group rose to fame as a recording act and moved to London. However, for the following four years he remained remarkably faithful to one girl. Paul wanted a lover and a constant companion combined. It had to be someone who could not only accompany him into the centre of the capital's music business 'in-crowd' but also partner him in highly fashionable West End showbiz circles. He knew that his ideal mate must be a young girl who was already accepted by the set with whom he hoped to mix. Vivacious young actress Jane Asher, the talk of the town at the time, was a perfect partner. She was stylishly good-looking and sufficiently well raised to teach Paul how to improve his party manners and expand his knowledge of middle-class etiquette.

As time went by, Jane fell in love as deeply as Paul had done when they first met, but neither was keen to marry because their careers were of paramount importance. After the first few years of closeness, however, Paul took chances when Jane was out of town. He quite openly dated other people behind her back and when she didn't respond, he pushed his luck and took greater risks. If she knew what he was doing, Jane stayed silent. Who knows, maybe she was having secretive little flings of her own. In any case, Paul and Jane remained together despite his wandering eyes.

John's choice of both lover and bride was his hometown girlfriend from college days, the gentle-natured and intelligent Cynthia Powell, probably the only female he was close to for any length of time before Yoko Ono came on the scene. Cynthia was one of the few people to see beneath John's tough outer skin. Behind the bravado beat a heart of gold, a warm and kind spirit seeking constant assurance. Cyn saw this side of John and loved him for it, recognising that his aggression concealed deep-rooted uncertainties. In the earliest stages of their relationship, there was an attraction of opposites. He was wild, noisy, boisterous, openly rebellious, loudmouthed and extraordinarily creative. She was relatively introverted, even-tempered, patient and kind – all the things that John was not.

Their son Julian became used to being brought up by Cynthia and only occasionally spending time with John. It wasn't John's fault. He was the only Beatle who was also a father at the height of the group's international popularity and it was impossible for him to give adequate time to both his job and his family. So he left parental matters to his wife. Cynthia proved to be a reliable homemaker and capable mother, perfectly willing to keep a home and a bed for her frequently absent partner. When John played away from home it was with women who looked quite unlike Cynthia. He picked strong-willed, dark-haired, olive-complexioned types. By choice he put himself next

Paul and Jane Asher at the special fan club party to launch Magical Mystery Tour.

a performer. Maureen and others within his circle had to keep on telling him he was good enough to be the Beatles' drummer. Eventually he believed it, and went on believing it long after the Beatles disbanded. The relationship between Ringo and Maureen was the most ordinary, normal and provincial of the four. She fitted with ease into the so-called Swinging London scene of the mid-60s, arriving at a time when both Merseybeat and *Coronation Street* had made young Londoners aware of accents and lifestyles from north of Watford. Maureen was a 'dolly bird' who had a subdued self-assurance, much self-respect, a well-developed Liverpudlian sense of humour, a perky personality and a skin thick enough to take life's everyday knocks. For her generation, she was extremely street-wise, but she often played that down in front of others. Maureen

to ambitious, outgoing, resilient, broad-minded, well-built females who would hit back hard and fast whenever the Lennon tongue lashed out at them. Without knowing it, he was probably already heading in Yoko Ono's direction, for despite her diminutive physical appearance, she was an absolutely dominant force on his later life.

Meanwhile, Cynthia became the central figure among the girls the Beatles left behind, probably because she was the first to marry one of the boys and had the experience of motherhood. She shared the intimate confidence of the other wives and lovers within the group's small inner-circle, a situation that lasted longer than her marriage to John. Like John, Ringo chose to stay with his hometown partner, the girl he'd known before the Fab Four hit the headlines. In his

case, she was a hairdresser named Mary Cox. He had been Richie before he was Ringo, and she became Maureen instead of Mary. They were the next to get married after John and Cynthia, remaining together for ten years until their divorce in 1975. Their marriage was full of ups and downs. 'Mo' had to cope with Ringo's notorious mood swings and his undiminishing passion for clubbing far into the night with his musician mates. She was a patient, basic, realistic sort of person who was willing to listen to Ringo's troubles and comfort him when he was depressed. In private, Ringo presented an entirely different face to the one seen by fans and the general public. Never happy about his health, he also worried about his talent as

Maureen Cox, Ringo's longtime Liverpool sweetheart, who became his wife in 1965.

had a perfectly polished and hugely flirtatious personality. Many observers believed she took a strongly calculated and determined decision to gain George's attention. It may have been mutual lust at first sight but it developed into a very comfortable relationship, that she knew would lead to marriage long before George had even considered such a step. George was all for a wild and white-hot love affair, and few friends regarded him as the marrying kind. According to their different standpoints, friends have blamed either Pattie or George, or both, for the couple's eventual break-up in the Seventies.

The marriage didn't hit the rocks overnight. Rumours of George's other romantic/sexual adventures were followed and matched by equally plausible suggestions that Pattie was seeing someone else. Their relationships were all kept within a close circle of buddies, pals and mates but in the end what began to amount to an 'open marriage' policy failed to satisfy either George or Pattie, and they split up. The four boys became pop stars so suddenly and so early in their young lives that they missed out on all the traditional experiences of bachelorhood. Instead, they spent four years on the road, criss-crossing the globe on international concert tours and, while their girlfriends stayed at home, they experienced loveless one-night stands with total strangers. This taught them little or nothing about the romantic side of relationships with the opposite sex. If anything, it gave them a distorted view of female behaviour.

Subconsciously at least, they must have formed a pretty poor opinion of women, expecting little or nothing in the way of lasting love or true fidelity from their brief and solely physical encounters in hotel rooms around the world. In turn, they also felt no remorse about their own lack of fidelity to the partners they left at home, because being faithful simply wasn't a meaningful factor in their lifestyles. Maybe it's not a coincidence that both John and Paul changed partners soon after the Beatlemania era was over. Perhaps the act of ditching the girls they had been with during their most successful years was part of their change of career direction. They were no longer happy with life within the Fab Four and that discontent spread into their private lives too, encouraging them to find fresh lovers to replace the old.

George and his first wife, model Pattie Boyd, on their wedding day in 1966.

enjoyed the materialistic trappings of the Beatles' pop superstardom but she was left behind in a slower lane when Ringo raced off to mingle with the high-rolling yachts-'n'roulette crowd on the French Riviera.

The very beautiful Pattie Boyd, who attracted George's attention during the filming of *A Hard Day's Night*, was the outsider among the Beatles' partners for quite a time. Of all the women who had relationships with the Beatles over the years, she has spoken least in public about her private life and is therefore less well-known outside her own social circle. Those who do know her see Pattie as a sexy, worldly woman, with a gentle heart and a great love of life. She is

also known as being a reliable friend in a crisis, a high-spirited and passionate person with a generous nature and an even temper, but never gullible. She didn't suffer fools gladly, and knew who could be trusted and who should be shunned. Like Jane, she had a successful career of her own but, unlike Paul, George was not interested in that celebrity side of his partner. Pattie was not from Liverpool and, at first, neither Cynthia nor Maureen saw any special point in befriending her. To be frank, they didn't think she'd last.

Pattie's marriage to George actually lasted from January 1966 to June 1977, only a year or so longer than the Starkeys – although the couple had separated several years before their divorce. It was common knowledge that George was absolutely smitten by Pattie, who

(Right) John and Yoko, and Paul and Linda – two celebrity marriages that both began in 1969.

The historic reunion that took place in 1981 when Ringo married Barbara.

It's not a criticism of anyone involved to say that it isn't surprising that John, George and Ringo's first marriages didn't last. No-one in the history of the pop business has ever had to live through the incredible excitement and strain of the Beatlemania years, and although the boys enjoyed the experience immensely, it was also bound to put intolerable pressure on their nearest and dearest.

The boys really had to do their growing up in public, under the constant eye of the media. Once they reached their thirties, however, things began to change. The break-up of the Beatles eased the pressure a little, and allowed them to carry on their four individual lives. Each member of the group found lasting happiness with one woman. Linda, Olivia, Barbara and Yoko all came along at difficult times in their husbands'

lives, when they could easily have taken a decisive step in the wrong direction. Instead, all four women provided vital stability and security, and they can take much of the credit for everything good that happened to the four Beatles in the years that followed.

John and Yoko were married in 1969, and despite a year-long separation which began late in 1973, they were still together in December 1980. Paul and Linda sealed the knot in the same month as the Lennons, and their marriage flourished without the least hint of tabloid scandal until Linda's death nearly 30 years later. George and Olivia got together in the mid-Seventies, had a quiet wedding at the end of the decade, and were still happily married to the end. And the marriage which the gossipmongers were keen to predict would never last – between Ringo and the beautiful young actress Barbara Bach, in 1981 – has proved to be long and fruitful. Since John's death, the

press have had a love-hate relationship with Yoko. They've been torn between their desire to make fun of the woman who they still accuse of breaking up the Beatles, and the sympathy which most of the public felt for John's widow. The result has been an uneasy stalemate, with each negative article balanced by an affectionate piece on how Yoko brought up their son, Sean.

Linda also had problems with the press over the years – ever since Paul insisted she should join the original line-up of Wings. Never afraid to be her own woman and say exactly what she thinks, Linda was criticised in some quarters for her strong line against meat-eating and environmental pollution. Just as many people, though, respected her for her views, and admired the delicate balancing act she had to pull off, between being hidden in Paul's shadow on the one hand, and being accused of dragging attention away from him on the other.

Of all the Beatle wives, Olivia Harrison always had by far the lowest profile. Outside George's keenest fans, few people even knew what she looked like until a few years ago. Never one to seek the spotlight, she and George decided to keep their family life (and their son, Dhani) private, so they could live as normal an existence as possible. Then, of course, Olivia found a cause that she simply had to respond to: the plight of the children who were abandoned in Romanian orphanages after the collapse of the country's Communist regime. After years of keeping out of the papers, she suddenly emerged as an extremely articulate and intelligent woman, full of energy and commitment to a cause which touched the hearts of people all over the world.

As a former star in a James Bond movie, and a nude model in *Playboy* magazine, Barbara Bach was used to the public gaze long before she met Ringo. The couple got together when they were making the *Caveman* movie, and against all the odds (including a car crash and serious health problems for Ringo) they've stayed that way ever since.

What Paul and Linda, George and Olivia, and Ringo and Barbara all found was the happiness that comes from a close-knit, private, family life. All three couples raised children in circumstances that must have been very difficult – knowing that if ever any of their offspring got into any kind of trouble, it would be splashed across the front pages of every paper in the world. They all mixed with enough Hollywood stars to know the problems faced by showbiz children, so they did their best to raise their kids in a warm and loving atmosphere. They encouraged them to make the most of their talents, and allowed them to enjoy the luxuries that their parents' wealth gave them, but at the same time they made sure that they didn't grow up to become Hollywood brats, taking the family wealth for granted.

Paul and Linda coped by ignoring the superstar lifestyle, and sending their children to ordinary schools like everyone else. George and Olivia made sure that, as far as the world at large was concerned, Dhani was a well-kept secret. Finally, Ringo and Barbara faced the potential problem of bringing two families of children together, from their previous marriages. The combination worked, and

Ringo supported his kids (who are older than Barbara's) in starting their careers – not least his son Zak, of course, who has followed in Dad's footsteps and become a world-renowned rock drummer, playing with top acts like the Who!

Sadly, a series of cruel twists of fate have pulled apart some of the happiest Beatles partnerships. John's murder in 1980 left Yoko in the uncomfortable position of being a very public widow, who was completely uncertain how she would be treated by the media and by the world at large. She adopted a fairly low profile in the years immediately after his death, but slowly began to unveil a series of tastefully presented Lennon archive projects – plus some art exhibits that proved to be every bit as controversial as the work with which she and John shocked and amazed the world back in the late 60s.

The death of Linda McCartney after a long and brave fight against cancer ended

Olivia took control of George's affairs after he died. She was the prime mover behind the tribute concert to her husband at the Albert Hall in 2002.

the longest-lasting Beatle marriage. Paul was obviously grief-stricken. So his fans were delighted when, a few years later, he fell in love with the former model Heather Mills. The couple soon got married, of course, before adding to the ranks of Beatles children.

Most recently, of course, cancer has also claimed the life of George Harrison. Like Yoko, Olivia has mostly maintained a dignified silence since her husband's death, but she did help to organise the spectacular tribute concert at the Royal Albert Hall which helped to raise millions for charity. Both Olivia and Yoko are now in effect the guardians of their husbands' heritage, both in business terms and also in the way in which unheard music and unseen films are released in the future.   (TB)

Norwegian Wood

Was John's classic song a secret message to his first wife, Cynthia?

Few married men would have the blatant audacity to perform a song dedicated to a recent extra-marital fling. But this is precisely what John Lennon did when he wrote the introspective 'Norwegian Wood' for *Rubber Soul* in 1965. With its infectiously repetitive theme and strong folksy feel, 'Norwegian Wood', subtitled 'This Bird Has Flown', must rank as one of John's most memorable songs from his pre-political era. Relatively accessible to mainstream listeners, despite some cryptic lines in the lyrics, the song was allegedly John's way of recording for posterity a quickie affair with a woman journalist he couldn't get out of his head.

John never named the lover and friend, although those close to the Beatles thought they had a pretty good idea of her identity at the time, and she has never stepped forward to enjoy the public glory. The title refers to the distinctive plain pinewood used by trendy London interior decorators in the mid-1960s. The storyline of the lyrics has the singer (quite willingly) seduced by a sexually dominant female who tells him precisely when she's ready to be taken to bed. She certainly sounded like the type of playtime partner John used to rave about in real life whenever he was away from home. All he later admitted in public was that he was writing about an affair and the words depicted an autobiographical experience of going home to somebody's apartment.

In one interview John claimed: "I was trying not to let my wife know I was writing about an affair so it was very gobbledegook." The truth is that much of 'Norwegian Wood' was written right under Cyn's nose at the Lennon family's luxurious Surrey house, Kenwood, where John allowed *The Beatles Book* to take 'at home' pictures on several occasions. My opinion is that John's marriage was already going through sticky patches by the time he created 'Norwegian Wood'. He intended the cryptic lyrics to give Cyn a hefty clue that he was going behind her back, but couldn't yet face her with a full-blown confession of infidelity.

Left: John's songwriting really came into its own during the Rubber Soul sessions.

The song was published under the usual Lennon/McCartney banner, but John said to a range of people that he had received little help from Paul with 'Norwegian Wood', and actually collaborated with George over some of the instrumental details. George had acquired his first sitar and John wanted to see if its sound would fit the mysteriously romantic but slightly bizarre feel he was after. George said he hadn't fully mastered his new 'Indian guitar' but he'd have a go. Later, John described the use of George's sitar on this recording as "an accident", indicating that it was a last-minute impromptu decision which came about because George contributed just the right atmospheric backing which John wanted. John was extraordinarily painstaking over the writing and recording of 'Norwegian Wood', extending his patience well beyond its normal span, suggesting that the production was special and important to him. He became irritable at his own initial inability to produce a recording that satisfied him: "We went through many different versions of the song, but it was never right and I was getting very angry." The other boys tried to hurry him up but he insisted on taking his time and getting his way: "So they let me go on and I played the guitar very loudly into the mike and sang at the same time." Paul's account of the song's development, told to biographer Barry Miles, suggests he took a larger role in the creative process. It started, he says, during a routine songwriting session at

The Beatles experimenting with different guitar sounds at a Rubber Soul session.

Kenwood: "He (John) had this first stanza, which was brilliant, that was all he had, no title, no nothing." Paul adds that, from there, "it wrote itself", and he reveals: "Peter Asher (brother of Paul's girlfriend, Jane) had his room done out in wood, a lot of people were decorating their places in wood. It was really cheap pine. But it's not as good a title. Cheap Pine, baby."

Paul also confirms that the song was based on a real-life affair John had and claims that he (Paul) had the idea of setting the Norwegian wood on fire as a form of revenge: "She makes him sleep in the bath. In our world the guy had to have some sort of revenge." In Paul's view there was no ambiguity; the lyrics meant that the guy burned the place down. Paul's lasting impression of the writing process for 'Norwegian Wood' was "60-40 to John". Paul concludes: "The middle was mine, John never had his middle eights."

Regardless of who contributed precisely what, the finished song was a work of

Rubber Soul was described at the time as being "the Beatles' folk album".

George's acoustic guitar playing really helped the backing to 'Norwegian Wood'

genius in many respects, from the very commercial tune to the fascinating storyline of the lyrics. The first attempts to record it took place at Abbey Road on October 12th 1965. The tape was marked 'This Bird Has Flown (Take One)'. When the Beatles reworked the song nine days later, recording engineer Norman Smith was still confused over the change of title and introduced the new take on tape as "This Bird Has ... er ... er . . . Norwegian Wood". Inevitably the song's central theme caused controversy. The decade may have been known in retrospect as the Swinging Sixties, but the establishment was still full of prudish censors only too keen to pounce on the slightest references to sexual experiences. For no apparent reason, a handful of critics thought they detected a lesbian aspect to 'Norwegian Wood' and *Time* magazine linked the song with 'Day Tripper', suggesting that one was about a prostitute and the other involved lesbianism. At a Californian press conference one reporter demanded to know what the Beatles intended when they wrote these two numbers. He was told jokingly: "We were just trying to write about prostitutes and lesbians, that's all!"

With hindsight, 'Norwegian Wood' was far from being the only revolutionary song on *Rubber Soul*, an LP that had a profound effect on the music business in 1965. And even better things were still to come! (TB)

(Right) Ringo in action during one of the Rubber Soul sessions.

The last UK tour

Nobody realised it at the time, but December 1965 marked the end of an era

Nobody could doubt that the Beatles' December concert tour of the UK was one of the most action-packed of their career. £8000 had to be returned by the management of the Cardiff Capitol after all seats for their two shows had been allocated. Scores of policemen linked arms right across the front of the stalls at Hammersmith where nearly 7000 Beatle People packed the vast Odeon during the evening. The crowds, the screams, the enthusiasm of the fans and the details of the actual performances have passed into pop history via news reports.

One story they all picked up on was the smashing of George's guitar. It was fastened to the boot of the group's Austin Princess and it fell off during the drive to Scotland. According to a disappointed George, at least fourteen lorries must have run over the guitar before the boys located the battered bits at the side of the motorway. Luckily, this wasn't one of the instruments George needed on stage. He'd just been using it to rehearse. Before setting out for Scotland, all the boys got together in the West End basement flat occupied by Neil and Mal. Here they put in nearly eight hours of act-polishing practice on the new numbers for the tour. Instruments used during this session were strapped together on the back of the Princess. Mal had already left London by van with the rest of the equipment. His load included seven guitars – two each for John and Paul plus three for George.

The last time a Beatle lost a guitar was two years ago, when the boys put on their first Christmas show at Finsbury Park. John and George had purchased a pair of Gibson Jumbos towards the end of 1962. They were very proud of these, having saved up their money for the hire purchase deposits with much determination. The Jumbos were the first two spares bought by the boys. Otherwise they were using stuff bought in Germany for £40 or £60. By the time of the Finsbury Park show, the total collection of Beatle guitars had grown, but John and George were using their Gibson Jumbos in

George enjoying the vocal spotlight during their last UK tour.

the dressing room, and they were there as stand-by replacements if strings snapped during a performance. John recalls: "George and I often took a Jumbo home with us, so nobody noticed until the end of the season that one was missing. A week or two afterwards, I asked Mal where he'd put my Jumbo. It was only then that we realised the guitar had been pinched at Finsbury Park. No, I never got it back." Losing his £300 Gretsch Countryman wasn't the end of George's problems in Scotland. During the opening performance in Glasgow his amplifier ceased to function. George says: "I checked the jack plugs, twiddled the volume control, and fiddled with everything in sight. It turned out that the amplifier itself was OK, but the lead had broken somewhere along the way."

Way back in the Cavern days the boys were used to this kind of trouble. Amps and lights blew up quite regularly, and the cause was usually the excessive amount of condensation on the walls and ceiling above the stage. So much damp dripped down that electrical problems became an accepted occupational hazard of Cavern sessions! According to Neil, equipment breakdowns happened less frequently once the Beatles started to play the major theatre and cinema circuits. The last major disaster he can remember happened in Brighton one Sunday during the summer of 1963. "Mal hadn't joined us then," says Neil. "I was responsible for setting up the equipment on stage. Everything was ready – switched on, tested and working. The boys used to open with a very fast Little Richard number at that time. I think it was 'Ooh My Soul'. Anyway, George had a big guitar intro on the number. After a few seconds, *everything* went dead. It was pointless to think of continuing, so I got the stage people to close the curtains right away. I dashed on stage, and we re-checked everything."

A minute later, everything seemed to be well, the curtains were opened for a second time, and George went into his hefty intro. "Then, for a second time, everything just went dead," recalls Neil. "It was ridiculous. We thought we were all going potty. This time John ran into the wings muttering something about the whole lot blowing up at any moment!" The cause was traced to the drummer with one of the show's other groups, not to the Beatles' amps or leads or speakers! He'd been shifting his kit around behind the scenes, and had dumped a heavy bass drum on the mains supply point.

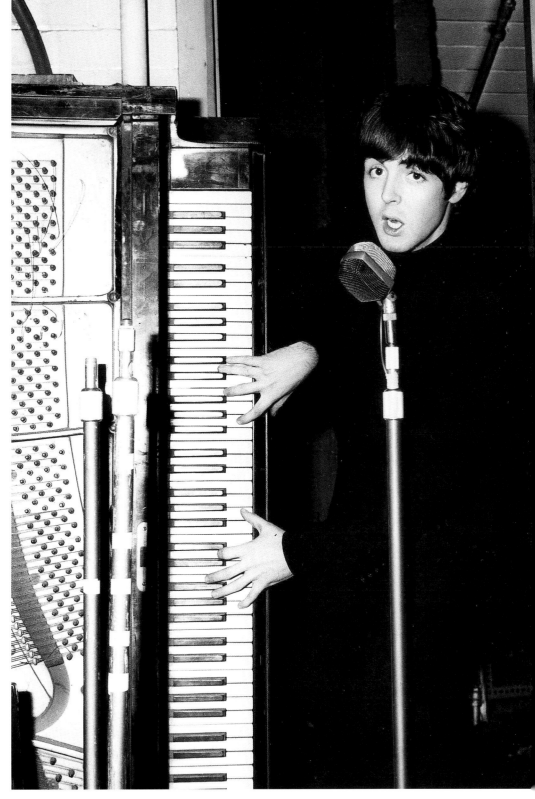

The two concerts at the Liverpool Empire must have brought back many memories for John, Paul, George and Ringo. It was at this theatre, on Sunday 28th October 1962, that the Beatles made their first major concert appearance.

They came on after the Breakaways as Item 3 in the first half of the programme. After doing just four numbers, including 'Love Me Do' and 'PS I Love You', they stayed on stage to accompany Craig Douglas. The rest of the bill included Sounds Incorporated, Kenny Lynch and Jet Harris, with Little Richard closing the show.

Paul plays around with a piano he found propped up on its side backstage in Sheffield.

At the Empire on Sunday 5th December 1965, they played to two capacity houses just as they had done three years earlier. Again the audience included friends and relatives from various parts of Merseyside. The audience also included two little girls who managed to meet the Beatles backstage to discuss their Save-The-Cavern campaign.

On their way from Liverpool to Manchester, the Beatles drove into a wall of

Moody Blues, for a highly unorthodox game of snooker. Finally, we let them relax before the show and enjoy their usual meal of steak, egg and chips.

After the meal they all travelled to the Sheffield City Hall where they were appearing that evening. While the rest of the Beatles put their feet up in their dressing-room, Paul happily obliged *The Beatles Book* photographer with a series of exclusive portrait photos that showed off his acting skills and his great sense of humour. Along the way, he took the time to impersonate a cunning spy, a short-sighted professor, and even a militant trade unionist, complete with a board saying "On Strike".

Continuing his tour through the bowels of the theatre, he messed about the massive bank of lighting controls and the internal phone system, like a mad scientist. He even put on a white coat and pretended to sweep the backstage stairs! Later, both Paul and John (who never seems to take off his Bob Dylan-style cap these days!) pulled mock-oriental faces for our photographer in the dressing room.

After that, the Sheffield stage performance was one of the most exciting of the tour. Fans were able to see two of the Beatles playing keyboards on stage. John took to his Vox organ for the closing romp through 'I'm Down', just as he did in the States earlier in the year. What was different this time, though, was that Paul also played an electric piano on stage, while the boys were performing their latest single, 'We Can Work It Out'. Maybe this is what we can expect to see more of in the future – the Beatles performing in public on an array of different instruments. Perhaps one day they could even tour with a string quartet in the wings, so that Paul could perform 'Yesterday' the way it sounded on the record!

The Sheffield fans had been forced to wait a long time for a return visit from the Beatles. Like everyone else who saw them during this final trip around Britain in December 1965, they're hoping that they won't have to wait so long next time. But the days when the group could squeeze in three or four UK tours a year, as they used to do back in 1963, are now long gone. These days the Beatles have fans all over the world – and every single one of them wants the boys to put their hometown at the top of the list!   (FJ)

fog, which started in the Manchester suburbs and brought city traffic to an all-but-total standstill. The fog was quite unexpected, as the rest of the North-West had enjoyed a bright, crisp, sunny day. For over four hours, driver Alf Bicknell steered the Austin Princess through Manchester at a snail's pace. The group arrived at the ABC Ardwick twelve minutes after they were due to appear. An extra intermission was inserted into the show while they changed and dashed on to the stage.

Producer Walter Shenson met up with the boys when they were staying in Manchester on 7th December to have a long discussion

The Beatles and the Moody Blues (with Denny Laine) at their hotel in Sheffield.

about their next film. They still haven't come to any definite decision, but all the indications are that they will plump for a cowboy script – yes, a Beatles western. If it all goes to plan (and it's still in the very early stages of negotiation), it will end up involving lots of Goons-type incidents and one very lucky leading lady.

The following day, Leslie Bryce was there to capture the tour on film for *The Beatles Book*. The fun started back at their hotel when all four of the boys joined forces with one of the other groups on the bill, the

My meetles with the Beatles

Competition winner Valerie Lloyd went backstage at the height of Beatlemania

If anyone ever asks me to name the most thrilling day of my life, I would say, without a doubt, Tuesday, November 19th. Why? Because that was the day I met the Beatles. I was lucky enough to be one of the winners of a competition run by a national musical paper. The prize was two tickets to see the Beatles' show in Wolverhampton, and the chance to meet them beforehand in their dressing-room.

The winners' names were printed on the Thursday, and I was thumbing through the paper at the tea-table, when suddenly I caught sight of my name at the top of the list. "Mum!" I screamed through a mouthful of cream cake, "I've won!" My mother picked herself up from the floor, and went straight to phone my father (who was still at work) and my brother (who lives near Wolverhampton), and just about anyone else she could think of! I tried to keep sane over the weekend, but I was suffering such a mixture of excitement, apprehension and sheer shock, that I don't know how I survived till Tuesday.

When Tuesday finally came, I didn't go to school; I would never have been able to concentrate on lessons, anyway. My parents took me down to Wolverhampton by car, and I met my brother (who was coming with me) and the other two winners and their companions, in the theatre. After what seemed an eternity we were taken to meet the Beatles. Their dressing-room was so small that we had to go in three at a time. My brother and I, and another boy, went last. The first thing I saw was an orange face (stage make-up!), almost completely veiled by a floppy mop of hair. It was George. I shook hands with him and the rest of the Beatles. Then because Ringo is rather small, he got up on a chair and started shaking hands with everyone (including John, Paul and George) all over again! Paul said, "It's still him, only he's grown a bit!" Oh, yes, and Paul, with the sexiest of voices, said "How ya doin', luv?" Well! What would *you* do? I couldn't think of anything to say, and just turned a muted shade of puce!

Paul started doing a 'Caruso' act, and someone said, "I thought John was the singer", and John, with shattering gusto, bellowed out some unintelligible tune (by no stretch of the imagination could it have been the latest John Lennon and Paul McCartney composition!). George handed round a tin of humbugs "as eaten by Ma-somebody-or-other (I think it was Cooper) in the eighteenth century".

Paul asked me what relation Christopher (my brother) and I were, and where we came from. When I told him "Shrewsbury", he said, "That's a long way, isn't it? How did you come?" I said that Dad had brought me, and he replied, "Oh, very posh, got a car!" I laughed and he repeated, in pure Liverpudlian, "A CA-A-A-AR!" What struck me about the Beatles was the way they put everyone at ease. They made us feel really welcome, and seemed really interested in us. There was nothing stuck-up about them. They were a normal, ordinary, down-to-earth bunch. I gave them a drawing I'd done of all four of them, and Paul said it was the best he'd seen. My head's never been quite the same size ever since!

By the way, Beatles, do you remember all this? I suppose it's a bit much to ask, but I've heard that you've got good memories. What became of the drawing? Have you still got it? I remember when I gave it to you, George said "Yoo've woon anoother 'oom-boog!" That made me laugh! Anyway, soon it was time to go, and after collecting their autographs (John put "The balancing dog" next to his, but I never did know what that meant!), we had our photos taken on the steps outside the dressing-room. Oh, yes, and before we went George said "Try and keep 'em (the kids) quiet". He must have been joking!

We said goodbye and went to our seats in the front row. The Kestrels, the Vernons Girls, and the Brook Brothers were on the bill. You don't need to be told that when the Beatles came on, and throughout their act, there was continual screaming. It was so loud that you had a job to hear what they were singing - and we were in the front row! When the show was over my head was spinning like a top, but in spite of that it was a wonderful evening, one that I shan't forget for a long, long time!

Valerie Lloyd (pictured left alongside Ringo) and other fans meeting the Beatles.

1965-1966

JOHN SINGING MISERY
Dear Ringo,

Just read the part in gearmost No. 17 where George says he hates groups who put on mechanical-type facial expressions to match the mood of the song they're doing at the moment, and it reminded me of the time I saw John laughing himself sick while he sang 'Misery'. Gonk! What a luv.

Ringo, I love you most of all, and I want you to know that you're the most popular Beatle over 'ere in the States. Please, please, tell me in *The Beatles Book* why you don't sing more songs: you've got an absolutely grinchy voice.

Love, Jan Wade (18),
6700 Rannoch Road,
Bethesda, Maryland, USA.

BRING BEATLES TO SOUTH BEND ON THEIR NEXT TOUR
Dear Sir,

We, the members of a committee in South Bend, Indiana, are writing to let you know of our campaign to bring the Beatles to South Bend on their next tour. We have set up petitions and posters in nearly all stores including theatres and resturants. The petitions are also circulating in grade and high schools throughout our area, and we are well on our way toward getting the number of signatures we need.

We realise South Bend is not a large city like New York or Chicago, but Beatle fans here are just as loyal as any place else. We have the stadium at University of Notre Dame in South Bend, which holds 60,000 people, which would be ideal for a concert. This is a centrally located town, and the people in surrounding areas will not have any trouble getting to the stadium. It would be really gratifying if you could hand this letter over to the Beatles so they'll know what we are doing. We know this is an unusual request and seems impossible, but your co-operation will be so important to us.

The Beatles South Bend Committee.
Mrs. A.I. Talboom (Adviser), Miss Patricia Durfec (Secretary), Linda Biber, Rosemary Aides, Rosemary Ferro, Theresa Ferro, Barbara Gudim.

GETTING AN AUTOGRAPH
Dear Mr. Dean, and especially Paul and John,

About four weeks ago I read that John Lennon and his wife would spend their holiday at St. Moritz. As my uncle has a hotel in Celerina, near St. Moritz, I took the chance to ask him whether I could come up for the weekend to see John and his wife, if possible. I had heard that John would be staying at the Palace Hotel, so I went up there the next morning. I was waiting for two hours in front of the hotel, and the hotel doorman told me that John was still asleep. Finally he came out, and with him was another gentleman – George Martin, I believe. They were obviously waiting for a taxi.

I went straight up to John, greeted him and gave him a little Beatle-doll, which I had made myself. He thanked me and I explained to him as well as I could in English that I had given my book of autographs to the doorman so he could give it to John. John said that he had seen it and I thanked him. Then the taxi arrived and he was gone. I was very happy that I had been able to talk to him, without being surrounded by policemen and hundreds of other girls. Then I discovered that the doorman had forgotten to give the book with the autographs to John, so I waited to get it after lunch.

When I came back, John had written his name into the book, but I had no opportunity to thank him for his kindness. So I would like to thank him now, for taking the time to talk to me and give me his autograph. At the same time I want to congratulate Ringo and Maureen on their marriage.

I would like to know whether it is true that a part of the new Beatle film will be made in Switzerland and if so, where? I would be happy if all the Beatles would come to Basel one day. Heartiest greetings to all the Beatles, and especially to Paul.

Christine Ramming.

A 'DIFFERENT' RELATIONSHIP
Dear Johnny,

It's funny, isn't it, how you read about the thousands of fans who saw the Beatles off at the Airport, and you think "I'm not a fan". Not a fan? You love them, don't you? But you're not a fan. Yours is a different relationship with these four – a closer relationship.

Remember how you woke up that morning and felt that something was going to happen? You didn't say anything to a soul - you couldn't put it in words – but you knew it, just the same. In the lunch-hour you went into the newsagents, and there you saw the announcement on the front page of a paper. Ringo had got married. You just stared . . . the words didn't register. Your heart was thumping as you read the article, then wandered out of the shop forgetting why you had originally gone there.

On impulse you dashed to a card shop and bought a Congratulations card for . . . for your friend and his new wife. Silly really, he probably wouldn't even see it, but you felt good sending it. Didn't your friends joke when you got back? "He's married!" "I know . . ." Yes, you knew. You thought you were going to cry, not because you were angry but because you were so happy for Ringo and for Maureen. Suddenly you felt that instead of taking him further from you, his getting married meant that Ringo was closer than before.

They may be idols, but you're not a fan. You're closer than that. You're a friend.

Jackie Easter.

FAN AT LENNON CHRISTENING
Dear John,

One Sunday afternoon, in November 1963, when I was going to confirmation classes, the vicar said he had to leave a little earlier that particular day, as he had to conduct a christening service at Trinity Road Parish Church, Hoylake. Of course we were all glad to finish a bit earlier than usual, but with a gleam in his eye he said, "I think I'd like you all to come along, you might be interested." Immediately our faces dropped again, but when we got to the church we found police outside.

I went and asked one of them what the

matter was, and he said "Don't you know who's being christened today?" Before he had a chance to tell me who it was, we were all hustled into the church, still none the wiser. The service began, and all through it I kept trying to place who the pretty blonde was with the gorgeous baby on her knee. But when the vicar got to the words, "It is unfortunate that the father cannot be here, but I christen this child: John Charles Julian", it suddenly dawned who the pretty blonde was – Mrs. Lennon! After that, I listened to the service with great interest, and afterwards talked to Cynthia and John junior. I'll never forget that day and although you weren't there, John, I'm sure everybody was thinking about you at that time.

Susan Ryall (14), Hoylake.

SHE LOVES YOU IN LATIN
Dear John, Paul, George and Ringo,
I thought you might like to see what 'She Loves You' looks like in Latin. Amat te sic, sic, sic, Amat te sic, sic, sic, Amat te sic, sic, sic, sic. Delicias tuas Vidi hesterno di-i-e, De te agit curas Hoc monere iussit me-e-e. Se te amare, Habes nihil quod plores. Se te amare, Et lactari nunc debes.

Sarah Fearnside,
Cheltenham.

This shot was taken in America in 1964 but it mirrored the reception the boys received at every airport around the world.

AIRPORT WELCOMER
Dear Paul.
I don't suppose you remember me as you've never met me. But I've done a lot for you. Did you enjoy your AIRPORT RECEPTIONS? We did! Did you see a lot of girls in white shirts with Beatles all over them? Well that was us lot! We greeted you with "IT'S GREAT TO HAVE YOU BACK BEATLES" (my fabulous brainwave). We were an hour late for school that day but we didn't care! Then when you went out to Austria we went again with our banner: "MISERY UNTIL YOU COME HOME". Then when you came home I painted another banner: "YOU'RE HERE TO STAY VIA B.E.A." but I couldn't go with the rest because my mother was in hospital and I had to 'keep house'. But from what I heard you looked over and killed yourselves laughing at our banner. THANKS BOYS!

Brenda Howard,
527 Whitton Avenue West, Greenford.

WINNER SEES BEATLES FILMING
Dear Beatles and Johnny Dean,
Thanks for sending me Ringo's fabulous drumstick. I'll treasure it 4 ever cos it's just great. Ta Ringo. Thanks also 4 the £10. I bought a suit which I wore to the Premiere of *Help!* The remainder I'll use to get your new LP, John's book, and Beatle shows.

I must be one of the luckiest Beatle fans alive 'cos I and my friend have both seen *Help!* take shape right from the beginning of the filming. At Twickenham we actually watched the Beatles shooting some scenes. We also managed to hear the song 'Help!' about 4 or 5 times while listening round the back of the studios with our ears pressed to the wall. This was in April, so we can claim to have been lucky enough to have heard it about three months before other Beatle fans.

We also spoke to John, a moment I'll never forget (even if it was only a few words). We ended up going to Twickenham on five different occasions and saw them every day.

Gill Evans, Boreham Wood, Herts.

The Beatles reply: Ta for your letter Brenda. And thanks also for coming to the airport so many times. It really does mean a lot to get a welcome like you gave us after those long nights or when we're going off on a long tour. Hope your mum's O.K. now.

AMERICAN FAN
Dear Johnny,
Every time I buy an American magazine they have articles like "John Lennon Quits the Beatles" or "Paul McCartney is Married – We Have Proof" or "The Beatles Give Up". This sort of thing makes me furious and I don't see how anyone can put up with such rubbish.

Maryanne Berlage
(A fed-up American),
RAF Station, Bentwaters, Woodbridge, Suffolk.

The 'butcher' session

Tony Barrow recalls their most controversial photo shoot of all time

On Friday March 25th 1966, in a photographic studio just off the King's Road in London's Chelsea, the Beatles did an interview for Radio Caroline – and posed for their most controversial photo session ever. The main business of the afternoon was to make a set of outrageously 'different' pictures that were destined to appear briefly on the front cover of a Capitol Records album, *The Beatles Yesterday and Today*, released in America. As it turned out, the US record company swiftly withdrew the offensive cover, but more of that later. Almost incidentally, the Beatles had agreed to spend an hour or so of that Friday afternoon doing a batch of quick-ie press interviews, including one with Caroline North's DJ, Tom Lodge. Although Radio Caroline got a useful 20-minute tape out of the session, the prime purpose of Tom's chat as far as I was concerned was to produce material for a freebie record I was making to promote *Disc and Music Echo*, a music paper in which Brian had an interest.

I used to pack in as many media interview appointments as possible whenever I was given some time with the group. There was a never-ending backlog of press requests to be satisfied, so it was a matter of selecting the most important writers and publications and keeping the rest at bay. Since we had so much to get through that day, I wanted to get all the short interview situations done first. That way we could get the studio as clear as possible before photographer Bob Whitaker went to work. I remember that there was an important Brazilian journalist for them to see. John assumed a grossly exaggerated Latin accent to give the guy staccato, tongue-in-cheek, one-line answers to everything he asked. Such journalists had a hard time with John.

While this went on, George sat in serious conversation about his sitar playing with an Indian journalist, one of the few topics he was interested in talking about by 1966. Meanwhile, Johnny Dean was standing with his own photographer, helping to pick out good camera angles and spotting suitable 'candid' situations to snap. In the middle of all this chaos, Bob Whitaker was erecting his spotlights and taking delivery of some very bizarre 'props' for his picture sessions. These included a bunch of small plastic dolls which he proceeded to mug, tearing some of them limb from limb and laying into others with a hammer until their little heads and legs and bodies had jagged, gaping holes in them. He also unwrapped four spotlessly clean butchers' coats with matching white hats, and brought in several large butchers' trays filled with cuts of meat, which were dripping blood and had spiky bones sticking through the flesh.

Lennon caught sight of these preparations and broke away from his interview with the Brazilian to inspect the dolls and the meat. He huddled with Whitaker for a couple of minutes, cackling with glee as he picked up the broken dolls and smeared them with blood from the oozing meat. John was in his element, obviously making colourful mental pictures of the photo session that was to come. Before Tom Lodge's turn came, each of the four Beatles posed for portrait shots which we would use as the next set of publicity hand-out pictures for the press to coincide with the release of the group's next record. By the time these portraits were fin-

Johnny Dean quizzing Ringo and John about the meat and dolls that Bob Whittaker had brought in for the session.

144

Photographer Bob Whitaker discussing his plans for the controversial shoot.

sight of the 'butcher' pictures and wanted the whole session scrapped to protect the group's public image. Nevertheless, a shot of four grinning Beatles draped in bloody meat and clutching pieces of damaged dolls filled the front cover of their next US album. It became a collector's item, as it was quickly withdrawn by Capitol's Hollywood boss, Alan Livingston, who announced that his company wanted to avoid controversy or damage to the group's reputation. Livingston's statement said: "The original cover, created in England, was intended as 'pop art' satire. A sampling of public opinion in the United States indicates that the design is open to misinterpretation." The dismayed Bob Whitaker took some harmlessly bland replacement pictures of the boys sitting on packing cases in Brian Epstein's office at NEMS. Later, when Tom Lodge handed over part of his tape for my *Sound Of The Stars*, I felt cheated. All I had was less than 100 seconds of dialogue, and most of that was nonsense. On the other hand, Lodge kept 20 minutes of material for his own use on Radio Caroline. Mind you, most of that was nonsense too! (TB)

ished, it was three o'clock. My main concern now was to get the voices of the Beatles on tape for the *Sound Of The Stars* flexidisc, similar to the records the Beatles sent out to their fan club members each Christmas. I had already taped material with a whole bundle of other pop stars, including Cilla Black and Cliff Richard. I had been waiting for my chance to complete the record with input from the Beatles. Tom gathered all four boys closely round him and used a single microphone to pick up what they said. He asked a string of deliberately daft questions, which triggered suitably zany replies from each of the boys.

Soon after 3.30, Tom's reel of tape was full and he knew from their ridiculous answers that he wasn't likely to get any more useful material from the boys. So he called it a day and they moved on to do their gory set of pictures with the broken dolls and raw meat. When he saw the results, Brian Epstein was upset and angered by the

Before the session the Beatles were given an award by Harpers Bazaar, which John stuck on his coat for this group photo.

Paperback Writer

"A brash insubstantial throwaway", or "One of the jewels of the Beatles' crown"?

Paul running through the basic structure of the song in No. 2 studio at Abbey Road.

Sometimes you can only appreciate what's happened after the event. And in the history of the Beatles, there's no better example of this than the release of 'Paperback Writer' in June 1966. The single was the first new Beatles record for six months, which was virtually a lifetime in the ever-changing pop world of the mid-60s. Everyone expected the group to provide a new musical direction, but when 'Paperback Writer' was released, the overwhelming reaction was that people were disappointed. It still topped the charts around the world, but there was a sense among fans and critics alike that it wasn't quite up to scratch.

It took a while for people to realise that 'Paperback Writer' only seemed like a dis-appointment because it was so different to everything they had done before. When the *Revolver* album was released two months later, the single started to make a lot more sense. And these days, 'Paperback Writer' is renowned as one of the Beatles' finest works and the first evidence that the Fab Four were heading to places where pop music had never been before. Back in 1966, Paul explained that the song "came about because I love the word 'paperback'. When we did the song, we wrote the words down like we were writing a letter. That's it, really – there's no story behind it, and it wasn't inspired by any real-life characters." Looking back, though, it's easy to imagine that one of the inspirations for the song must have been the experiences of the Beatles' very own paperback writer: John Lennon.

John had caused a literary sensation with his first collection of poems, stories, jokes and doodles, *In His Own Write* (1964). It topped the best-seller lists and even provoked a debate in the House of Commons about the "declining standards of literacy among today's young people". But while he really enjoyed putting his first book together, he found his second volume, *A Spaniard In The Works* (1965), much more of a slog, admitting later that he'd written most of it in a single weekend under the influence of a bottle of brandy. In February 1966, just before the Beatles wrote and recorded 'Paperback Writer', John decided to break the contract he'd signed with publishers Jonathan Cape for a third book. He sent back the advance he'd been paid, filed away the manuscript of the only story he'd finished ('The Toy Boy') for safe keeping, and gave up all ideas of being a full-time author. As he told the press that month, "I should have finished a new book by now. It's supposed to be out this month. But I've only done one page. I thought, why should I break my back getting books out like records?" So the subject of books was definitely in the air when 'Paperback Writer' was composed. It's surely not a coincidence that one of the lines of the song, "It's based on a novel by a man named Lear", referred to the comic writer Edward Lear, who had been singled out by many critics as a major influence on *In His Own Write*.

As Paul explained, the actual writing of the song came very easily indeed: "I remember showing up at John's house with the idea. Because I had a long drive to get there, I would often start thinking away and writing on my way out, and I developed the whole idea in the car. I came in, had my bowl of cornflakes, and said, 'How's about if we write a letter, Dear Sir or Madam, next line, next paragraph, etc.?' I wrote it all out, and John said, 'Yeah, that's good'. It just flowed." 'Paperback Writer' duly went onto the list of possible album tracks when the Beatles arrived at Abbey Road studios on 6th April 1966, to begin their first recording sessions in five months.

That first session marked the end of the longest pause in the group's schedule to date, which had allowed them to take stock of their lives and their music for the first time since their dazzling rise to fame. While Ringo lazed around at home or abroad, George married his long-time girlfriend Pattie Boyd. Meanwhile, both John and Paul wanted to expand their horizons. Paul was in the process of buying a house in St. John's Wood, which is still his London residence today. Perhaps more importantly, he was enjoying all the attractions of London life. Through his girlfriend, Jane Asher, he had been introduced to many leading lights of the theatre and arts worlds. By the start of 1966, there was a growing underground scene as well. Paul bonded with these experimental painters, composers and writers, and during early 1966 he attended gallery openings, lectures, concerts, readings and exhibitions, often with his friends Barry Miles and Robert Fraser. He was soon helping them to open the Indica Gallery and its bookstore; placing adverts in underground magazines to find ideas for avant-garde movies; and messing around with the recording and film equipment in his home studio. Every so often he'd drive out to see John in Surrey, full of enthusiasm for his new projects.

John wanted to keep pace with his songwriting partner, so he too installed a home studio. "Paul and I are very keen on this electronic music," he said a few months later. "You make it clinking a couple of glasses together or with bleeps from the radio, then you loop the tape so it repeats the same noises at intervals. Some people build up whole symphonies from it." It was a bit early for the Beatles to be thinking in terms of symphonies, but their passion for experimentation was very evident when they began their April sessions by recording 'Tomorrow Never Knows' – by far the most outlandish and unconventional piece they'd ever created.

Over the next week, they kept up a busy schedule at Abbey Road, veering from that avant-garde beginning to the brassy soul sound of 'Got To Get You Into My Life' and then the Indian mysticism of George's 'Love You To'. It was already obvious that their next album would be very different to everything that had gone before.

On 13th April, it was the turn of 'Paperback Writer'. Paul arrived with the lyrics scribbled out on a sheet of paper, in the form of a letter, complete with an imaginary signature at the bottom. The Beatles made a first stab at the backing track, which broke down, and then nailed it second time around. Back in 1963, the record would have been at least half finished at that point, but by 1966 the fun was just beginning. Paul was very keen to improve the way that his bass guitar was heard on the Beatles' records: "I started changing style and became more melodic. The bass became more important. Also, we were listening to records that had more bass, in the discos. EMI had firm rules about that, which we always had to break. We were always forcing them to do things they didn't want to do."

As engineer Geoff Emerick explained: " 'Paperback Writer' was the first time the bass sound had been heard in all its excitement. For a start, Paul played a different bass, a Rickenbacker. Then we boosted it further by using a loudspeaker as a microphone." That was only the beginning of the sonic experimentation, as the Beatles and the EMI studio staff went through all the different gimmicks and tricks they'd learned at recent sessions. While Paul endlessly re-recorded the bass part, George Martin and his engineers ran the instrument through Leslie Speakers, echo units, compressors, limiters – anything that would give it an extra impact on the record. By the end, as Geoff Emerick recalled, there was concern that the bass had been recorded at such a high level that it would send the needle jumping off the record, and EMI's mastering department had to use their grandly titled Automatic Transient Overload Control to deal with the problem.

They started working on 'Paperback Writer' that evening. The Beatles went home early the following morning, but returned later to complete the mass of vocal and instrumental overdubs that the track required. George and John added their harmonies at the same time that George filled in with stabs of electric lead guitar. Even then, they weren't finished for the day: rather than being satisfied with completing one track, they immediately started work on the next – a John Lennon composition, written with a little help from Paul, called 'Rain'.

It was only a couple of weeks later, when EMI were nagging the Beatles and George Martin for a single, that they went back to

John working on the main guitar riff during the 'Paperback Writer' session.

about it. These are the songs of '66, looking at life instead of at dreams and heart-pangs." By 1966, the press were so bored with reporting success after success by the Beatles that they were delighted to find a reason for criticising them.

The fact that the single didn't immediately enter all the different UK charts at No. 1 in its week of release was greeted as a "shock". Ironically, the exception to the rule was the prestigious *Melody Maker* chart, where 'Paperback Writer' did go in at No. 1, while the group's previous single, 'Day Tripper' / 'We Can Work It Out', had only debuted in *MM* at No. 3. On the BBC charts, which were seen on *Top Of The Pops* and heard on radio's *Pick Of The Pops*, 'Paperback Writer' was stuck for a week behind the biggest-selling single of the summer – Frank Sinatra's 'Strangers In The Night'. In their second week, the Beatles took their rightful place at No. 1, but only for two weeks, and their chart run of 11 weeks was shorter than their previous hits. The papers soon boasted that this "flop" single (which had, after all, only reached No. 1) was the group's worst-selling release since 'Love Me Do'.

The Beatles must have been slightly worried by the feedback they were getting from their fans, who complained that they couldn't dance to 'Paperback Writer' the same way that they could to 'Day Tripper', and that the song wasn't suitable for a Fab Four single release. Yet the single had a different effect on people who hadn't been touched by Beatlemania. "I was in my early teens when 'Paperback Writer' came out," recalls music critic Adrian Gordon, "and at my school, lots of the boys preferred the Rolling Stones to the Beatles. We were convinced that the Beatles were only for girls. 'Paperback Writer' sounded so loud and exciting that it changed my mind overnight. It took that blast of 'Paperback Writer' on the radio to make me see sense." Indeed, the further away we get from the 60s, the better 'Paperback Writer' seems to sound.

That question from the *Daily Sketch* back in 1966 – "Are the Beatles on their way out now?" – seems ridiculously premature today. Nearly 40 years on, the Beatles are still the true kings of pop, and the rest of the world is still struggling to catch up. And the *Daily Sketch*? It went bust years ago!   (PD)

the songs they'd already recorded in search of the most commercial number. " 'Paperback Writer' was not specifically recorded as a single," George Martin explained. "We knew that we had to make an album and a single, and the single was more urgent, so we picked out 'Paperback Writer'." Ironically, nobody in the Beatles' camp seems to have felt very enthusiastic about the song. "As far as I'm concerned, there are other tracks I much prefer to it," admitted George Martin. "I'm sure any one of them would have done well." When the record was released, John was even more dismissive: "It's not one of our best songs, but it was the only one we had ready for the release date". That wasn't strictly true, but the Beatles realised that they couldn't possibly release 'Tomorrow Never Knows' as a single.

So 'Paperback Writer' was elected as the best available A-side, with 'Rain' as the equally punchy B-side. At the meetings the group had held with Brian Epstein the previous December, one of the subjects they'd discussed was how bored they were with having to traipse around TV studios all over the world, miming to their latest single. So director Michael Lindsay-Hogg was recruited to shoot two special films, which could be sent out to TV stations in place of the Beatles. Two days of filming took place

during mid-May 1966, the first at Studio One at Abbey Road, the second in the grounds of the minor stately home, Chiswick House. The two film clips were premiered on *Top Of The Pops* in June, and then shown around the rest of the globe. They were only just completed in time, as the release date for 'Paperback Writer'/'Rain' was set for 30th May in the USA, and 10th June in the UK and Europe. But on both sides of the Atlantic, its reception was rather lukewarm.

This was one of the richest musical periods in pop history. Among the songs in the charts alongside 'Paperback Writer' were the Rolling Stones' 'Paint It Black', Bob Dylan's 'Rainy Day Women', the Kinks' 'Sunny Afternoon', the Mamas & the Papas' 'Monday Monday', the Byrds' 'Eight Miles High', the Lovin' Spoonful's 'Daydream' and the Beach Boys' 'Sloop John B'. The general feeling was that 'Paperback Writer' was a bit of a letdown. *The Sunday Mirror* summed up the reaction: "They have, to put it bluntly, goofed. 'Paperback Writer' would have gone into my junk box had it been by another group." *The Daily Sketch* wondered, "Are the Beatles on their way out now?" And even the positive reviews, like the one in the *Daily Mirror*, sounded less than thrilled: "Neither side has any romance

Germany 1966

The group's last European tour included a nostalgic return visit to Hamburg

Every Beatles tour starts off with well organised precision. "The party will fly to Munich from London on Thursday June 23 via BEA flight number BE 502 departing London Airport at 11.05am", read the instructions given to everyone on the trip. But anyone who's been on a Beatles tour before knows that the plan can go awry. Every Beatle person in the country that the boys are visiting wants to meet and talk to the boys – who wouldn't? – and that can play havoc with the schedule. But there is always a big posse of police and guards equally determined to protect their charges, and Germany was no different.

The Beatles at a German press conference. Bravo magazine promoted the tour.

After a ninety-minute trip, the Beatles' Comet touched down at Munich Airport, and was immediately surrounded by a big crowd of aircrew, groundsmen and photographers. The boys emerged from the plane to a battery of clicking cameras, shouted questions, and hurried greetings from their press officer, Tony Barrow, who had flown to Germany before them to prepare for their visit. When everyone started to close in, Tony decided it was time to go, and whisked the boys and Brian Epstein into a white Mercedes, which took them to the Bayerischer Hof Hotel in Munich, where several hundred fans had gathered. Before anyone realised what was happening, the Beatles were inside and safely installed in their fifth-floor suite.

The boys had a bit of a problem on their hands. They had to do a bit of quick thinking, and come up with a good title for their new LP. After listening to the tracks on George's tape recorder, we all swopped suggestions and came up with names like *Magic Circle, Four Sides To The Circle, Beatles On Safari* and *After Geography* (a Ringo pun on the Stones' new album, *Aftermath*) – but still no luck.

Then it was time for the press conference. Everyone made for the lift, which was designed to take ten people. Fifteen crammed in, the door closed and the whole

(Right) John holds up a photo he'd been given of the group in Hamburg in 1961.

thing jammed between floors for ten minutes, whilst those downstairs waited and wondered, and everyone in the lift wondered and waited. The lift was repaired, the Beatles were freed and the press conference began. Photographs were followed by questions, followed by more photographs, and then a presentation of a trophy by *Bravo* magazine, the organisers of the tour. As soon as it finished, the boys returned to their suite to practice. They knew only too well that they were due on stage the following day to perform numbers they hadn't played for six months. The evening was spent quietly with just a quick dip in the hotel swimming pool.

The boys got up around midday on Friday, as they still weren't happy with their act. We left them to practice and made our way to the Circus Krone, where they would make two appearances. Cliff Bennett and the Rebel Rousers opened the show, followed by Germany's Rattles and then Peter & Gordon. As zero hour approached, the boys put on their new dark green suits with silk collars, underneath which they wore lime and yellow striped shirts with large collars and no tie. They dashed on stage to a terrific ovation and immediately launched into 'Rock'n'Roll Music', followed by 'She's A Woman'.

The boys had obviously decided that they were going to give their audience the old favourites they all knew. The rest of the act went as follows: 'If I Needed Someone', 'Day Tripper', 'Baby's In Black', 'I Feel

Fine', 'Yesterday', 'I Wanna Be Your Man', 'Nowhere Man', 'Paperback Writer' and 'I'm Down'. Although the Beatles' performance was as good as ever, we did hear a few duff notes being played, especially from John. Their second show was much better, once the cobwebs had been blown away, and everyone felt it was one of the most exciting shows they'd ever seen the boys give. The Beatles were certainly very happy and elated when they returned to their hotel to talk the night away.

After a very late night everyone stumbled into the garage under the Bayerischer Hof the following morning, where a fleet of seven white Mercedes awaited to take us to the station where we would board the train to Hamburg, stopping en route at Essen. The boys emerged through the garage door looking surprisingly awake, with the exception of John who tripped over the step – which

made him all the more unsociable. The police motorcade that escorted us was quite unnecessary at this unearthly hour of the morning, because there were only a handful of onlookers at the station. The special train that carried the Beatles' entourage was the same one the Queen used the previous year. The Beatles, together with Brian Epstein (who just only made the train!), Tony Barrow, Neil, Mal and Alf had their own suite of rooms, which consisted of a large dining-room, a lounge and four bedrooms and bathrooms. Surprisingly enough, this was the first time Mal and Neil had set foot in Germany. Mal, of course, didn't join up with the Beatles until they were already topping the charts, but Neil has been with them for years. "I would like to have gone with the boys in 1960," he told me, "but I couldn't afford it. It was all John, Paul, George, Stu and Pete could do to pay their own fare across. I used to stay at home and starve while they were in Germany, because I'd already left home and didn't have a job."

Breakfast was served about ten o'clock and consisted of fruit juice, cornflakes (the Beatles' favourite), bacon and eggs, rolls, tea and coffee. After breakfast the boys retired to their compartments to catch some sleep, which was interrupted by lunch about halfway through. After the meal, they went back to sleep again until about three o'clock, when they came through to the other compartments to chat with everyone and have a few photographs taken. Paul was wearing a beige suit with a cream shirt and a red, yellow and brown striped tie, plus his yellow-tinted specs. Ringo was dressed in black slacks and a polo-necked sweater with a brown suede jacket. George wore a self-

striped maroon velvet jacket, and John had put on his London Airport departure ensemble – red and white striped trousers with a white jacket.

The train pulled into Essen around four-thirty. As we stepped off the train there were about a dozen policemen making a big fuss as they held back about half-a-dozen people on the platform – quite laughable! Further down the platform, three men dressed as barbers in white smocks and bald-topped wigs, carried giant-sized combs. As we mounted the stairs it was obvious that the police had underestimated the crowd out-side, for suddenly there was a big swoop and everyone started running, including the Beatles. John thought it would be better to run the other way, in the direction of the train, but as the rest of us were being hurled into cars, Alf grabbed John and threw him in on top of everyone else.

Again it was the white Mercedes plus police motorcade that took us on a very slow drive to the Grugehalle in Essen. The reason for driving at a funeral march pace was to make sure that we'd arrive after the audience had gone to their seats. There were two dressing-rooms set aside for the Beatles – one for the boys to change in, the other to tune their instruments and make all the usual last-minute checks before they went on stage. Essen proved to be the wildest concert. John worked the audience into a frenzy by getting down on his knees and shouting "Meine Kindern" with arms outstretched. But the biggest ovation of all was when Paul announced Ringo. After the first show, everyone had a meal in the dressing-room. The huge crowd outside wouldn't move, but kept chanting "we want the Beatles". Then it was time for a press conference, no better than the others, with the same daft questions being asked again.

Before going on stage, John, George and Paul had another practice run through 'Paperback Writer'. But Paul was still very far from satisfied. The difficulty was that on record they sing a four-part harmony, yet on stage they only have three voices, and the fact that John's voice was cracking up didn't help matters. After the second show, which was even wilder than the first, we waited for the crowd to disperse before leaving the theatre to catch the train to the next venue.

George in the Beatles' dressing-room at the Merck Halle in Hamburg.

old days. But the boys barely had time to say hello before we were whisked off in a fleet of black Mercedes, which took us to the beautiful Schloss Hotel in Tremsbuttel, about thirty miles outside Hamburg. As soon as we arrived at the Schloss, everyone just flopped into bed and slept until about one-thirty, to allow plenty of time to get ready to leave by quarter-to-three. Even by two o'clock the crowd outside the hotel had grown from a mere thirty to about two hundred, and to make sure they weren't disappointed the boys stepped out onto the balcony, looking very fresh and wide awake.

Backstage at the Merck Halle in Hamburg, it was just like a reunion. Bettina was there, and so was another old girlfriend of Paul's named Katya. Gibson Kemp arrived with Astrid Kirchherr, Stu Sutcliffe's girlfriend before he died, of course. She was greeted by all four Beatles with great warmth and affection. Bert Kaempfert, who produced the boys' earliest recordings in Hamburg, popped in, and John greeted him with the opening line of his hit song, 'Strangers In The Night'. Hamburg held an extra something for both the Beatles and the people who came to see them, and as usual they went down fantastically, with just that extra something. After two very exhausting shows and a press conference, it was back to the hotel for a quiet evening with just a couple of friends – and not, as lots of people had anticipated, an evening at the Star-Club. So the Beatles' return to Germany came to an end, and they started preparing for the next leg of their 1966 world tour.   (FJ)

Paul putting everything into the final song of the night, 'I'm Down'.

It was about twelve-thirty when we arrived at the station. A very late dinner was served about one o'clock. Everyone was in excellent spirits – apart from poor old John, whose throat was getting steadily worse, so his evening was spent drinking lemon teas and sucking lozenges. Everyone else sat round the table playing cards and trying to think up LP titles – again! This time Paul fancied the word Pendulum. The night passed so quickly that before you could say 'Beatles' we had arrived in Hamburg – at six o'clock in the morning. The boys were very surprised to see so many people at the station, especially Bettina, a friend from the

The German security guards and medics removing an over-excited fan.

Far East tour

Their 1966 world tour was a mixture of triumph and trauma, as Tony Barrow reports

"Right, it's my turn to think of a word now" declared Paul. So Ringo passed him the dictionary and he began to hunt for an obscure sort of word that he hoped the rest of the Beatles had never heard of. It was Monday, June 27th, 1966 and we were flying high somewhere over the Atlantic in a 707 jet, on our way to Japan via the polar route. The Beatles had commandeered the lounge area of the aircraft and were playing a time-passing game they called 'Dictionary'. Each player

childish but, believe me, it could be quite good fun on a long haul, particularly once the airline's booze was flowing freely!

Then came the news that disgruntled all of us. The pilot explained that we could not fly on to Tokyo just yet, because Typhoon Kit was blowing up a mega-storm across the China Sea and all local aircraft were grounded. "What do we do, then?" asked Ringo, "Do we fly round and round the North Pole or what?" The pilot grinned: "We

Anchorage possessed to a luxury hotel. The Beatles wanted their beds and planned to sleep right through the stopover. But the local media very quickly became wise to what was going on under their noses. The Beatles dismissed the possibility of sleeping for the duration of their Anchorage experience when the radio station set up a mobile transmitting trailer beneath our hotel windows and told every teenager in town exactly where John, Paul, George and Ringo were located. "Come right on down, folks!" urged

in turn chose an unlikely word and everyone would write down his idea of what it meant. The dafter the definition, the funnier the whole affair became. In this case it was Paul's turn to read out what the others put down, slipping in the word's real meaning somewhere along the way. Points went to the players who could pick the correct definition, and bonus points were awarded for a player's made-up meaning if it fooled any of the others. Yes, I know it all sounds a bit

land in Alaska. We make an unscheduled stopover at Anchorage until the weather changes." And so we did. For the residents of Anchorage's suburbs, the sight of four Beatles cruising down the main street in an airport bus was something of a shock.

For us, the nine-hour stopover proved to be a drag. The airline people did the best they could. We were installed for the day in the bridal suite of the nearest thing

Brian, Paul, Rumi Hoshika, Tony, Ringo and Japanese promoter Tats Nagashima.

the deejay, "The Beatles are waiting to meet each and every one of you and we'll be on the spot to lead the screaming!" By now Brian Epstein had decided to hide himself away and phone everyone he could think of on the other side of the world just for the sheer hell of it. When the radio producer asked if the Beatles would come down to the mobile studio outside, I told them there was no chance but the boys had agreed to wave to their fans from the windows. Not satisfied, the radio crew gave their deejay a roving mike and sent him up to the suite. He came stalking into our midst, broadcasting 'live' and pushing his mike up each Beatle's nose in turn. "You'd know this was a bit of America", muttered George, as he disappeared into a bathroom.

Before dawn on Wednesday morning, we made it to Tokyo. Although the city's Hilton Hotel was a lot more plush than our makeshift accommodation in Alaska, the Beatles again found themselves spending most of the stay in Japan in their suite. We had an entire floor to ourselves, the group occupying the Presidential Suite, while each alternate room all down the corridor was used to house security guards. At first we could not understand why the police presence was so heavy. Then we discovered that the Beatles were being threatened with assassination by an extremist student faction whose members said that the city's Nippon Budokan Hall should not be used to stage rock'n'roll shows. A few days later, the boys faced an organised mob of angry and violent troublemakers at Manila International Airport. It was part of a hate campaign stirred up by a claim that they had snubbed the First Lady of the Philippines, Mrs Imelda Marcos, by not taking lunch with her and several hundred children of the local aristocracy. It was no wonder that a half-serious, half-joking George told reporters soon after that: "We're going to have a couple of weeks to recuperate before we go and get beaten up by the Americans".

The sensational nature of the news stories that emerged from Japan and the Philippines during the Beatles' last world tour in the summer of 1966 tended to overshadow other aspects of this visit to Asia. For example, a record-breaking number of fans, around 80,000 in all, watched John, Paul, George and Ringo at their pair of open-air performances in Manila, more than on any other single day throughout the group's career. But the figure remained an unofficial one because of the restricted communication we were able to have with the local concert promoter afterwards. An English-language newspaper in Tokyo, the Japan Times, reported that the first of five sell-out appearances by the Beatles seen by almost 10,000 fans at the Budokan was a "howling, screaming success". Policemen wearing white hats sat in the aisles while "the kiddies

screamed and waved their hankies, many with tears streaming down their faces". The reporter called John, Paul, George and Ringo "bushy-haired heroes". It was all over, he said, in 30 minutes: "The only time in the whole half-hour the crowd quietened down enough to hear was when Paul sang 'Yesterday' ".

Police set up a temporary Operation Beatles headquarters to co-ordinate every last detail of their master plan, mobilising an astonishing total of 35,000 officers, includ-

The Beatles climbing the steps to the stage of the Budokan arena in Tokyo.

ing unarmed riot policemen, plain-clothes men and women. The airport was closed to the public and guarded by 3000 officers for several hours in preparation for the arrival. Although our eventual flight arrival time was 3.40am, some 1500 fans turned out at the airport in the middle of the night to greet John, Paul, George and Ringo. It was one of the warmest and least scary airport welcomes we experienced anywhere in the world. Roadblocks were set up at intersections on almost a dozen main-roads between the airport and our hotel. A further 2000 security people stood by at the Tokyo Hilton Hotel.

It didn't dawn on us that there was anything sinister about the enormous police operation until a bunch of local fans in the lobby of our hotel read a story to us from the front page of a newspaper. Elsewhere in the world, particularly across Europe, some of us had at least a smattering of the local language and could read the papers, but not one of us spoke Japanese, so we discovered only what our hosts wanted us to learn during our stay in Tokyo. What the fans at the Tokyo Hilton told us left us open-mouthed. A small

Paul and George on stage at the Budokan Hall in Tokyo on 1st July 1966.

group of intensely dangerous students had promised that the Beatles would not leave Japan alive if they played at the Budokan. The venue, said this violent faction of zealots, was for top sporting tournaments, specifically Japanese martial arts events. Even judo matches were frowned upon in that setting.

From here on the otherwise incredible levels of security made more sense to us. The armed cops on bridges above the road between the Hilton and the Budokan were not there to hold back eager young fans but to spot suspect snipers. Similarly, the majority of the security forces stationed within the concert hall were not briefed to hold back fans but to spot potential killers lurking in the crowd. Apart from the gun-toting cops who were part of the security contingent, there seemed to be far too many press pho-

tographers all around the auditorium, pointing their huge lenses at sections of the audience on the far side. No, they weren't taking publicity shots for the fan magazines, and I guess most of them didn't even need to have film loaded in their cameras unless it was to photograph possible criminals. Their sole job was to keep their eyes open for gunmen, using the powerful cameras to pick out faces – and, perhaps deadly weapons – at long range. At one point, Mike Nakamura said to me: "Don't worry. We will not allow your Beatles to die here."

I formed the impression that all this meticulous activity was to preserve Japanese reputations. Patriotism and a national love of law and good order at all costs was at stake, not love for the Beatles and any real wish to stop them getting hurt!

The Beatles wore dark suits for the first Budokan show on 30th June 1966.

At the hotel we were under a sort of unspoken house arrest. The Beatles were made to stay on one floor and if any of them emerged from the Presidential Suite, guards instantly consulted their identification photographs of the Fab Four and hurried forward to usher him back into the room. Hotel lifts were fixed so that they would not come up to our floor until a guard put in the correct key. At one stage Paul even put on a makeshift disguise in an attempt to escape and do a little clubbing. I ordered one of our limousines to the hotel entrance, saying I wanted to go sightseeing, and Paul joined me in the lift, coat buttoned high around his neck to avoid easy recognition by the guards. But they spotted the trick and a pair of armed men turned us back as soon as we reached the main foyer, escorting us all the way back to the 18th floor. Towards the end of our stay, John and Neil succeeded where Paul and I had failed – as security slackened off a little, they managed to sneak out on an early morning shopping spree without being spotted or hauled back like naughty truants! The Beatles were bored stiff with their free

time in Tokyo, doing their gift-buying by summoning merchants and souvenir vendors to bring samples of their merchandise to the suite for their inspection. They looked at photographic equipment, silk kimonos, some remarkable sunglasses and painting sets. Otherwise they lazed around on their beds draped in colourful traditional 'happi coats', all the rage locally, or sat at little tables in their rooms and painted simple watercolours – Japanese brush painting, it was called – beneath the inadequate light of low-watt reading lamps. Between them, they painted one huge sheet of paper which was presented to the Tokyo fan club branch as a souvenir of the Fab Four's visit.

In Manila, although the media spotlight was thrown solely upon the so-called snubbing of President Ferdinand Marcos' wife by the Fab Four and the hard time we were given on our departure, the actual concerts were well-received by fans. Small groups of Beatles supporters gathered at our hotel and we were able to talk to them. One asked if the boys watched movies on their long-haul flights around the world. Paul said: "There's nothing like seeing the same in-flight movie for the third time round – we've done a lot

of flying recently!" Ringo took a mini-recorder with him and taped a sort of personal audio diary of the group's visit to Asia. The Manila Chronicle reported that the furore over the snubbing of the First Lady had put a damper on the day. It added: "An estimated crowd of 50,000 teenagers screamed, cried and moaned as the Beatles let out a succession of ten hit tunes during their matinee performance at the Rizal Football Stadium. Every number was accompanied by screams and shrieks from Beatlemaniacs, so much so that people could hardly hear the songs above the din. But most of them didn't mind at all." Another report opened: "The sound was terrible but the Beatles were terrific". By the time we left amidst a campaign of hatred inspired by the president's henchmen, even the kinder local headlines had turned sour. "Beatles Leave With A Kick And A Whimper" and "Beatles Booed, Roughed Up On Departure" were two examples. At the shows, 750 uniformed Manila policemen were on duty along with 200 armed forces and 300 other security guards. One of the gun-carrying troops said: "Security is so tight here today that it's like getting in a shipment of gold bars to Fort Knox"! (TB)

Candlestick Park

Tony Barrow remembers the end of the touring era in August 1966

People still ask me what it was like to be present at the very last public concert performance the Beatles ever gave. Some expect to hear a spectacular tale of a grand farewell gala show, loaded with mass emotion and public excitement. In fact, it wasn't like that at all. I'd say it turned out to be a very ordinary evening, neither hallmarked by any unusually fine performance from the boys, nor memorable for any dreadful disaster. There had been no announcement that San Francisco was to be

they didn't need to. Shortly before we left our hotel to drive to Candlestick Park, Paul asked me if I had my portable Philips cassette recorder with me. I had used it throughout the tour for taping press conferences and interviews, so that I could relay accurate details to journalists in London when we got home. "Make me a recording of tonight's final concert, will you", said Paul. Final concert? Of the summer series? Final concert for ever more? Paul knew as well as I did that at least two Beatles had

also been listening to what the Beatles were saying themselves when Brian wasn't about and that was a very different story. John and George clearly wanted to concentrate exclusively on recordings and films in future, ruling out concerts totally. Neither Paul nor any of the others had asked me to make a private souvenir recording of previous concerts, even to mark the end of the group's biggest tours. Was it really just a sentimental little 'end of term' impulse on Paul's part – or was he beginning to believe that the views of

the scene of the group's final show and the local deejays on KYA Radio just promoted it as the last of the Beatles' series of summer gigs in America.

The boys flew into San Francisco from Los Angeles on Monday August 29th 1966, after an incredibly wild Sunday concert for 46,000 fans in LA's famous Dodgers Stadium. The group had no plans to rehearse in San Francisco. At this stage of the tour

been pushing Brian Epstein to put an end to touring altogether, but Brian was sure he could convince John and George to change their minds. In America during the past fortnight, 'Eppy' had actually told me: "Wait until they're back home, back with their families, and I'll persuade them to forget this nonsense of packing in 'live' shows. Don't be silly, Tony. Certainly there'll be more tours. I've told you there'll be one in Britain before Christmas, haven't I!" But I'd

Candlestick Park – home of baseball and, for one night in 1966, the Beatles.

John and George might well prevail and all Epstein's tour plans for the rest of 1966 and beyond would go out of the window?

Although the standard Philips cassette recorders of the Sixties were by no means hi-fi jobs, I did carry a decent Beyer microphone with me. Apart from the excellent

160

quality of the mike, I had one other factor in my favour at the Candlestick Park concert. Because the audience were so far away from the stage, I'd be able to stand out on the field during the performance and record the sound from the giant loudspeakers, without picking up too much audience reaction to drown out the music or singing. The last gig of the 1965 US tour had been at an indoor venue in the same city, the world-famous San Francisco Cow Palace. At an indoor venue, it would have been far more difficult for me to collect stage sound without also getting more screaming, which would spoil the singing and playing. As the stands filled up with people, I wandered from one bank of loudspeakers to another, deciding upon my best position – noticing, incidentally, that 'Eppy' wasn't about, and thinking to myself how sad it would be if he missed what could turn out to be their farewell concert.

Tickets (costing under six dollars, or under £3!) were still selling to late-comers at the gate even after the supporting show started at eight, but the weather had turned colder and casual last-minute customers were not as plentiful as the organisers had hoped. The appearance of the Beatles, running out across the grass just a few minutes before half past nine, brought a roar of relief from the crowd. I switched on my cassette recorder, watched the level indicator soar as it picked up the continuous screaming, then turned the microphone away from the stands and towards the loudspeakers. There was feedback through the public address system as the boys tried out their guitars. A single yell of "Hello!" from the stage drove the level of screams from the stands higher than ever.

John, Paul and George tried a few more chords, striving to get a reasonable balance between their instruments. Then John was into Chuck Berry's 'Rock And Roll Music' and the fans went really wild. At the end of the first number, without any announcement, Paul counted the group straight into 'She's A Woman'. By now the group was reacting to the warmth of the crowd's reception rather than the chill of the Californian evening. Forgetting how fatigued they were feeling, the Beatles began to get into the spirit of the gig. Whatever their mood beforehand, the Fab Four could always be relied upon to give a professional performance once they were in front of their fans!

After 'She's A Woman', Paul spoke: "Thank you very much everybody and hello, good evening. We'd like to carry on with a song, not surprisingly, written by George, and this was on our *Rubber Soul* LP and the song is called 'If I Needed Someone'." For the first and only time that evening, George took over the role of lead vocalist. John did the next linking announcement: "Thank you everybody. We'd like to carry on now, carry on together, one together and all for one, with another number which used to be a single record back in, er, (he filled in here by playing a few guitar notes), er, a long time ago and this one's about the naughty lady called 'Day Tripper'." Paul moved forward to join John at the vocal microphones and they were off. At the end, while crowd applause and yelling grew to a new peak, the two stayed together, bowed and waved, and then went straight on into 'Baby's In Black'. "Thank you, thank you," cried George, on behalf of John and Paul when that one was over. "We'd like to carry on with something very old indeed. This one was recorded about 1959! It's called 'I Feel Fine'." Because of the way the sound from the stage was balanced, my recorder picked up the voices of both John and Paul more or less equally on 'I Feel Fine'.

George did the next introduction: "Thank you. Like to carry on with a song from *Yesterday And Today*, and this one was a single as well, and it features Paul singing a very nice song called 'Yesterday'." Of all the concert numbers, I think this one came out best on my cassette recording for Paul. Both his vocal and the accompaniment were clearly defined well above the sound of the audience. This was the closest the Candlestick Park crowd came to actually listening to one of the Beatles' songs that evening! As the song ended and the screams of appreciation swelled up, Paul warned Ringo to be ready for his solo number next. Then he thanked the fans for his own applause, adding: "It's a bit chilly. We'd like to do the next number now which is a request for all the wonderful backroom boys on this tour. The song is called 'I Wanna Be Your Man', to sing it . . . RINGO!"

The screams from the stands threatened to blow the level indicator off my recorder. Ringo was very popular in America by 1966! The special welcome he got brought a chuckle of delight from the drummer before he launched into the number, his head shaking happily from side to side, his entire drum rostrum rocking visibly in time to the beat. Above the tumultuous applause at the end of this one, John, Paul and George went into a verbal slapstick routine of repeatedly thanking Ringo and he returned each remark with another 'Thank You' in reply. "Lovely working with you, Ringo!", screeched John from above the noise. Then he went on: "We'd like to do another song from our BBC (??!!) album, and this one's called 'He's A Real Nowhere Man, Sitting In His Nowhere Land', oh yes!"

After this, Paul spotted a fan racing out across the field towards the stage. Briefly, the Beatles broke off to cheer her on. Then Paul said: "We'd like to carry on, certainly, definitely, but shall we just watch this for a bit. Just watch." Finally the cops near the stage caught the brave girl who had dodged the security in front of the stand to make her bid for fame and Paul was ready to continue: "The next song is called 'Paperback Writer'." Thanking the crowd afterwards, Paul added: "We'd like to say it's been wonderful being here in this wonderful sea air! Sorry about the weather, and we'd like to ask you to join in and clap, sing, talk, do anything. Anyway, the song is…" Here

his voice trailed off into a muttered "Good ni . . . ", not actually completing the word 'night', as he launched into a wild 'Long Tall Sally', which we all knew was the boys' final number.

The Beatles never announced that they were going into the last song of the show. It was a slip on Paul's part to even start wishing his audience "good night" as he did at Candlestick Park. Maybe the incomplete

message didn't get through to 25,000 fans in the stands. In any event, we didn't have any extraordinary problems in making our getaway. When we were back on board our plane, waiting for the rest of the entourage to join us for a midnight flight down the California coast to Los Angeles, Paul checked with me: "Did you get anything?" I told him: "I got the lot, except that you must have run just over thirty minutes on stage tonight. I had a C-60 cassette in the machine.

Side One of the tape ran out during 'Long Tall Sally'. The rest is OK!" Paul said: "Did you keep running between each number? Did you get all our announcements and stuff?" I assured him I had the lot, from the guitar feedback before the first number onwards. As soon as we were back home, I copied the original Philips C-60 cassette, giving Paul the second one and keeping the first one for myself. Almost precisely twenty years later to the day, at the end of August 1986, I reminded Paul about the souvenir cassettes, which only the pair of us possessed. This prompted him to hunt for his copy – only to find he'd lost it!

I dug out the precious original cassette from my own collection and made a new copy for Paul. While I was at it, I couldn't resist playing the whole thing through and reliving my personal memories of Candlestick Park. The strange thing is that it was not really an evening of outstanding significance at the time. From the extra bits of patter the boys did, like the send-up thanks to the back-room boys, Candlestick Park was clearly a special occasion in their eyes. But, because neither the Beatles nor 'Eppy' was prepared to make a public announcement that the touring era was over, there was no 'on-stage' reference to the fact that the Four Mop Tops would never tour together again.   (TB)

1966

COWBOYS ARE OUT
The Beatles are now quite definitely against the idea of playing the parts of cowboys in their next movie so, at the time of going to press, they are not going to do *A Kind Of Loving* for their next film. Producer Walter Shenson is now busy script hunting. In their two previous movies the boys tended to play themselves, but in their next film they want to develop the parts they play so that they'll be different to anything they've done before. (February 1966)

NO BUTTIES FOR GEORGE
By this time, every Beatle person knows that a jam buttie is Liverpoolese for a sandwich but recently anyone who has been having tea with George has invariably been asked to have a sarnie, which is now his term for a sandwich. A quick check with a genuine Liverpudlian lass revealed that sandwiches are commonly known as butties or sarnies on Merseyside, but the most popular term has always been buttie. (February 1966)

AWARDS PROTEST
The Beatles were nominated for ten awards at the Grammies in New York – but failed to win a single one! Now Capitol Records boss Alan Livingston has launched an official protest. The chief cause of his complaint is that 'Yesterday' failed to win the Song Of The Year prize. "It makes a mockery of the whole event", Livingston says. (March 1966)

NEW SINGLE SENSATION!
The boys may fly to Memphis on April 11 to record their new single. The reason for this is that they've heard so much about the American technicians and sound engineers that they want to see for themselves whether it makes any difference. George

Martin will be accompanying them, and they will rehearse their material at EMI Studios prior to their visit. (April 1966)

BACK ON STAGE
The boys have made their first live appearance for almost six months at the *NME* Pollwinners Concert at Wembley. Their full-power five-song set included 'I Feel Fine', 'Nowhere Man', 'Day Tripper', 'If I Needed Someone' and 'I'm Down'. (May 1966)

THE NUMBER 13 IS LUCKY FOR THE BEATLES
Thirteen may be an unlucky number for some, but it seems to keep on cropping up in a very fortunate way for the Beatles. George Martin had been with EMI for 13 years when he first met the boys, which certainly wasn't a bad thing for anyone. And the Fan Club is housed at 13 Monmouth Street.

Now, once again, the same number comes into the picture because the Beatles new single, 'Paperback Writer', was recorded on Wednesday April 13. Actually the boys recorded the basic track – meaning guitars, drums and vocal – on the Wednesday and returned the next day to add those special Beatle extras, which mean so much in their songs. But, all the same, "that number" has turned up once again.
(Johnny Dean's editorial, May 1966)

BEATLES HAVE TO BE CAREFUL WHAT THEY SAY
Most people can say what they like, how they like, when they like. But a Beatle has to remember that everything he says is liable to be taken literally. A joke can turn into a serious statement, an opinion into a fact, and as we have seen so clearly over the last month, the whole meaning can change if taken out of context.

It's ridiculous to suggest that John deliberately went out of his way to offend millions of people all over the world, by attacking their beliefs about Christianity with his "more popular than Jesus" remarks. In fact,

anyone who knows him well would say that he is much more likely to stand up for everyone's right to believe in what they want to, than most other people.
(Johnny Dean's editorial, July 1966)

KLEIN MOVES IN
American manager Allen Klein has made a bold prediction – he says he will be the Beatles' manager by the end of 1966! He has recently taken over management duties for the Rolling Stones, and now the confident New Yorker has his eyes firmly fixed on another of Britain's great treasures. But we reckon that there is a little obstacle – name of Brian Epstein – between Mr Klein and his ambition. (July 1966)

HONOURABLE JAPANESE
The Beatles experienced a completely different set-up in Japan from any other country they have visited. In the first place, the Japanese authorities considered it their responsibility to look after the boys, and if anything had gone wrong, they would have considered it a great dishonour to themselves. Also the Beatles had heard that Japanese audiences were much wilder but, in actual fact, they were more restrained, especially while the boys were singing. This might have been due to the fact that the 9000 audience in the Budokan had 3000 police to look after them! (July 1966)

INDIAN SOUNDS
The Beatles were one of the first groups to use Indian instruments on their records, when a sitar turned up on 'Norwegian Wood' last year. Now George has gone all the way on the boys' new LP, *Revolver*. 'Love You Too', one of his three compositions on the album, has a backing entirely made by Indian instruments. Can we expect to see the boys surrounded by sitar and tabla players the next time they appear on a British stage? (July 1966)

POLICE HELP OUT
When the Beatles departed from London Airport on their way to America, there was a delay for about ninety minutes before their plane took off. Instead of waiting in the VIP lounge, which would soon have become bedlam, the Beatles drove straight to the police building at the north side of the airport. There they met Chief Inspector Campbell, who showed them round the gymnasium and the pressing room (where the 'bobbies' press their trousers) and then into the canteen for a 'cuppa'. (August 1966)

JOHN'S FILM DEBUT

As you know, John is abandoning the other three Beatles (temporarily) to appear under the directorship of Dick Lester in a comedy called *How I Won the War*. He will fly out to Germany as soon as their American tour comes to an end. Most of the location work in Germany will be at night in pine-forests hundreds of miles from anywhere, so they can be sure of getting no fan invasion. After Germany they move on to Spain for more location work, this time in a desert – so unless fans bring their own water supply, they'll have no chance of surviving! (September 1966)

GEORGE IN INDIA

For a time it looked as though George and Pattie had managed the impossible. They hopped on a plane and flew off to India without anyone knowing. But a Beatle finds it hard to keep his movements secret for very long, and shortly after he booked into the Taj Mahal Hotel in Bombay, the news broke that George was paying a long visit to India, in order to study the sitar properly under the master of the instrument, Ravi Shankar. Anyone who thinks that George is not serious about Indian music is making a big mistake, and what he sees, hears and learns in India will undoubtedly influence future Beatle songs. In this issue we have an exclusive interview with George in India, plus one of the very few photos of George and Pattie in Indian dress.
(Johnny Dean's editorial, September 1966)

WEDDING HOAX

Everything was set, so the story said, and the invitations had been sent out. Journalists around the country received the official word that Paul and Jane Asher would be getting married in Liverpool on December 17th. There was only one problem – none of it was true!

A practical joker in Yorkshire went to a lot of trouble to convince the press that Paul and Jane were ready to tie the knot. But the entire thing was found to be a hoax, and millions of McCartney fans around the world breathed a sigh of relief. The wedding celebrations will obviously have to wait a little longer. (September 1966)

FOUR WAY SPLIT!

The Beatles are splitting up! But don't worry, it's only on film. The latest plan for the boys' third movie is that the four

Beatles will play four different aspects of the same character. One of the boys will play the main role, and he will then imagine himself as three other people – the other three Beatles, of course.

One of the results of the film is that it is very likely the Beatles will not be playing themselves in this film – and indeed there will be very few opportunities for more than one of them to appear on screen at the same time. A final script has not yet been approved, but filming is expected to begin in January 1967. (October 1966)

MIKE'S PRESENT FOR PAUL

Mike McCartney has given his famous brother lots of small "Alice in Wonderland" figures for his garden. Paul has dotted them all over the place and they certainly give it a very unusual atmosphere. Incidentally, Paul also has a sheepdog puppy, which he calls Martha. Its coat is black and white and it's got no tail. (October 1966)

PAUL WRITES FILM SCORE

As expected for a long time, Paul is to write a film score. He has been commissioned to write the theme music for *All In Good Time* – a Boulting Brothers production to be released by British Lion starring Hayley Mills, John Mills, Hywel Bennett and Liz Frazer. As yet, there is no release date, but it is expected to be released long before *How I Won The War*. It is now quite obvious that all four Beatles will diversify in different spheres – so hurry up George and Ringo! (November 1966)

MOPED JOHN

As most Beatle people know, John and Ringo are close neighbours in Weybridge, Surrey, so naturally, they pop across to see each other very frequently. John usually travels to Ringo's house on a motor-bicycle. It's quite a sight to see him tearing along the country lanes on his moped. (December 1966)

NO SPLIT

Both Ringo and Paul have been at pains to make it clear that the Beatles are NOT splitting up. There has been a shoal of rumours in recent weeks, most of which have been started by the fact that no Beatles concerts have been scheduled for the foreseeable future. But Paul insists: "We're all great friends and we don't want to split up. There's never been any talk or sign of it, except in other people's minds."

Asked about the lack of concert appearances, Paul explained: "Our stage act hasn't improved one bit since we started touring four years ago. The days when three guitarists and a drummer can stand up and sing and do nothing else on stage are over. Many of our tracks these days have big backings. We couldn't produce the sound on stage without an orchestra. We feel that people only really listen to us through our recordings, so that is our most important form of communication now." To that end, they have apparently recorded two four-minute songs which are being considered for their next single. (December 1966)

Roy Kinnear and John in a scene from 'How I Won the War'.

George at home

The first of four exclusive Beatles Book visits by Johnny Dean to their private houses

Long before the others got down to searching for that very special permanent pad, George bought himself a house near Esher in Surrey. It's not so much a house, in fact, as a long rambling, white-walled bungalow and an exclusive way of life. From it George regularly commutes along the A3, to recording sessions, London Airport, and all the other favourite Harrison haunts. You drive to Esher, turn off at the crossroads and after a few lefts and rights you end up in a private road. Half a mile along is George's house.

You enter through the massive wooden gate in one corner, and find yourself enclosed by a gigantic square, made up on three sides by a 12-foot-high brick wall and on the fourth by a massive hedge of fir trees. You turn right once you're inside and drive along the gravel path, passing the flower bed on the right until you reach the opposite corner, where George and Pattie park their cars in front of the double garage. The house stands in the centre of the plot and is mostly surrounded by cool green grass. I imagine that the high brick wall originally surrounded the kitchen garden of the big old house nearby, where Queen

Victoria is reputed to have stayed. It really is massive and seems to be a couple of feet thick in places. It's got alcoves, odd doors and lots of other mysterious ins and outs. The surface is pitted with nail holes, where many gardeners have tied up climbing plants over the centuries. If ever there was a war, I'm sure George could hold out for at least three weeks inside his fortress – that is, as long as nobody comes in from the South because, as I said before, that fence just consists of a very thick row of fir trees. Behind the house is George's swimming pool which George told me he designed himself. It's got everything, including changing rooms just in front of the fir tree hedge, and a reproduction of one of John's drawings in marble mosaic. George likes popping in and out of the water whenever he feels hot and he told me that if the weather's nice, he'll go in several times a day. There are stone pathways completely surrounding the pool and it's George's favourite place for eating tea and sandwiches.

In one corner is a massive weeping willow. You will remember that one of the photographs taken recently of George and Pattie together for a national magazine showed them under a willow tree. Well, that's where it was taken. Next to it is an old apple tree, which actually produces some apples, and near the apple tree are several spiky sisal plants. George very kindly gave us tea on the stone terrace by the swimming pool and afterwards we went into the house. As you come in from the swimming pool, you pass through the kitchen, which really is something else. It's beautifully modern, with every single convenience imaginable to ease the work of the housewife. It really is the kitchen that everyone's mum ever dreamt of having. The drawing room is dominated by a big black leather couch, while the walls are white and there is a beautiful wall unit taking up one complete corner, with books, magazines and all sorts of knick-knacks.

(Right) George on the sofa which was his favourite place for songwriting at home.

George and Pattie are obviously not afraid to mix the old with the new, and they have many Georgian bits and pieces, as well as plenty of modern furniture. Apart from that massive, black sofa in the drawing room, there's also a bowl-type wickerwork chair and a very attractive Minster stone fireplace, with a small clock and hourglass perched on the top. We've already showed you a picture of George's miniature record player – an old-type one with a big horn, like you see on old 'His Master's Voice' record labels. And perched on top of the coffee table is a miniature white piano. In the corner, opposite the wall unit, is an old wooden rocking chair. The room is obviously George's favourite 'sitting and thinking place' and I got the impression that he sits on that sofa and works out his songs whenever he has an hour to spare. George took us through the rest of the house, and showed us the dining room, where he and Pattie entertain their friends; and then his music room, which has one wall covered with the famous Harrison guitars, his collection of Indian instruments and a small jukebox standing just by the door. I looked at the titles on the jukebox and there were very few Beatle songs amongst them. The Beach Boys, Mamas and Papas, Lovin' Spoonful and the Stones were all well represented. The main bedroom is a very lovely room, facing the East, which means that the sun's rays pour in during the morning. There's a delightful brass bedstead and white lace cover on the bed.

The Beatles don't collect pin-up photographs of themselves, but they love anything a bit offbeat. In the spare bedroom, next to George and Pattie's, there's a massive six-foot high photograph of George, propped up against a wall, looking as though he's about to hit somebody. George thinks he's getting a bit tired of it, though, and might throw it out. George's home is not a mansion, but it fills all of his needs. He has always shown that he has a mind of his own, which can be made up quickly and decisively, and he's absolutely certain of what he wants. In 1964 he wanted this house and, having seen it, I know why!   (JD)

John at home

A private glimpse inside the Lennon mansion in Weybridge

John's house is situated in the same wooded stockbroker belt, near Weybridge in Surrey, as Ringo's and George's, but George's home is several miles away, while Ringo's is only a couple of hundred yards down the hill. The entrance to John's estate is marked by a pair of huge wooden gates. My first impression was of a large mock Tudor mansion, lots of red brick, white walls and an iron-studded, oak door. But this door was slightly different. It had been sprayed with paint aerosols in many colours. Over the large knocker was the crest of the Lennon clan. John opened the door himself, and led the way into the house. I was completely overwhelmed with the fantastic collection of instruments, pictures, furniture, antiques, flowers, stickers, models and books that met my gaze. I can honestly say I have never seen so many different things gathered under one roof. The result is extraordinary, because it all fits. I don't know whether John or Cyn is the genius, but rooms have two pianos in them, or a statue with a gorilla mask and a pipe stuck in its mouth, and still seem right.

On the ground floor there is a large, entrance hall, lined with shelves of books stretching from floor to ceiling. To the right it leads to the kitchen, which is situated in the centre of the house, and to the left to two rooms, one very large, one small. As soon as we entered the house Julian appeared. He is a fascinating boy, solemn-faced with sharp brown eyes, very like his father's. He obviously gets on tremendously well with Dad, who lets him work out his own small problems in his own way. After studying us for a minute or two, he very quickly made up his mind that, if his father was going to be photographed that day, then so would he.

The smaller room contained two pianos, one Broadwood, one Bechstein. The mahogany case of the Bechstein, however, was fast disappearing under a psychedelic design, which was being painted on by two Dutch artists, Simon and Marijke. The right-hand wall was covered with a bookcase. In the middle of the room was a television set covered with stickers, with upside-down phrases on them, like "Quiet Please, Explosion Nearby", and "This Cemetery Welcomes Dangerous Drivers". The next room was very large with three beautiful, soft sofas in it. In one corner was an extraordinary Chinese screen cutting, and next to it the brass statue with the gorilla's mask on it. On one side of the fireplace were three turntables. John is very fond of putting on LPs of noises these days, and one played constantly while I was there, broken only by bursts of 'All You Need Is Love'. On the shelves near the record player several of John's gold discs were displayed. In the centre of the fireplace was a huge colour television. John was one of the first people in the country to buy one.

Next John took us upstairs to see his music studio. This is only a small room, right at the top of the house. The cook probably slept there, before the Lennons moved in, but it's certainly different now. There's a battery of tape-recorders along one wall; an organ and piano along another, and on the third is a Mellotron. It looks like an organ, including the keyboard in front, but lodged in its inside are loads of tapes on which have been recorded actual sounds, like drums, horns, etc. When you press one section of the keyboard, and pull out the right knobs above it, you can get almost any rhythm background you like, and you can also play a tune on the other keys. In other words, you can produce the effect of a small orchestra all by yourself. John's always been one for unusual noises, and when it produced some really strange rhythms, a typical grin spread over his face. He picked all the guitars up, gave us a few demonstration twangs, and ran his fingers up and down all the other keyboards in the room.

John poses with his young son Julian in front of his psychedelic Rolls-Royce.

John in the garden of his Weybridge estate, overlooking the swimming pool.

Then it was downstairs again to the main lounge, where John flipped a new sound effects LP onto one of the turntables, through the dining room and into a small room overlooking the garden terrace. Every bit of space was covered with odd caricatures of John and the Beatles, faded Victorian photos, crosses, statuesfoot – you name it, John has already stuck it on a hook on his wall.

Then he led us into the garden. The back of the house looks down the hill, and the terrace immediately behind it is edged by a stone wall, over six feet high in places. John told us he likes to sit on this wall and meditate. It's his favourite 'thinking place'. The view was magnificent. You could see very few signs of humans, just glimpses of houses and a lot of trees near at hand, including a big silver birch, which John said was his favourite, stretching away into faint misty green distance. If you turn left, you go round to the front of the house again; turn right and you come to the Lennons' swimming pool. It's no fishpond either, but big enough to have to swim if you want to get to the other side.

John's garden is smaller than Ringo's but quite a bit larger than George's. Like Ringo's it drops away from you. There are lots of trees, a pool, paths, rose bushes, and at the bottom, a large greenhouse, which had recently been repainted. John told me that he still gets about fifteen people every weekend, charging across his grounds. Uninvited guests have broken most of the windows in his greenhouse over the past few months. But he didn't seem that worried about it. Few things upset the Beatles these days.

We wandered around the grounds, taking photographs, and eventually we ended back at the swimming pool. John came and sat down next to his pool in a cane chair. And that's where we left him, to think and dream. Over the past five years, through all the incredible hubbub of Beatlemania, John has always seemed to have a mind full of thoughts. That lightning brain of his can produce a quip about almost anything. His house mirrors his personality, and every room in his remarkable – and remarkably cluttered! – house reveals a different side of the man who can safely claim to be the most complex Beatle of them all.   (JD)

Paul at home

Unlike the other Beatles, Paul chose to make his home in the heart of London

The McCartney residence took a lot of finding. Long after George, John and Ringo had all settled for the Surrey stockbroker belt, Paul was still looking. For months, rumours flashed around the estate agents. "He's looking in Chelsea, in Belgravia, in Camden Town". Finally, news leaked out that Paul had bought a Georgian residence in St. John's Wood. For those who don't know London, St. John's Wood is not a heavily-treed estate, but a very exclusive residential area, a couple of miles north of Piccadilly Circus. The road is one of those odd avenues, which you don't realise is there until somebody points it out. It is only a few minutes from *The Beatles Book* offices, as I found when I visited Paul. After a brief push on the bell, the soft Irish voice of Paul's housekeeper, Mr. Kelly, asked for my name. A minute later I was shaking hands with Paul himself. "Come in and have a warm by the fire," he said, and led the way into the large drawing-room at the rear of the house.

Paul and his famous sheepdog Martha in the dome at the back of his London home.

Although Paul had the whole place completely redone, he made sure that it was restored in the same style as it was originally built, even preserving the carved cornice around the edges of the ceiling. My first impression was of flowered, rather Victorian-type wallpaper, huge tiers of shelves opposite the fireplace, a real coke fire burning in a small, old-fashioned grate, and, alongside the fire, an old, black, lacquered, coal-box plus loads of antiquey-type things all around the room.

How much do you think Paul spent on actually furnishing the room? £5000? £10000? Well, you're wrong! He told me that he picked up most of the stuff for just a few pounds. He pops into various auction rooms, especially one in Brompton Road, and when he sees something he likes, he asks them to bid for him. The very ornate metal clock on the mantelpiece only cost £7; the massive three-piece suite, which he has had re-covered in green velvet, cost £20; and the old mahogany antique table only £10. Paul

moved around the room restlessly, chatting about various pieces and where he had picked them up. He has obviously developed into quite a collector; but he only buys stuff that he likes, and doesn't seem to care whether it's worth anything or not.

Next door to the drawing room is the kitchen, which leads directly into the dining room. It'd be a pleasure, I'm sure, for any girl to cook in the kitchen of a Beatle house, even if she weren't a fan, because they are always so beautifully designed, modern and up-to-date and with all the latest equipment. Not that it was fully stocked when I saw it. Paul opened one of the cupboards and disclosed a salt cellar, a bottle of salad oil and a pot of marmalade. We walked into the dining room. Nothing lavish, just a table, chairs and an enormous clock, set into one wall, which Paul had bought ("I just liked it, so I bought it"), and an unframed painting of Highland cattle over the fireplace. It is a three-storied house, and the main staircase spirals up through the centre.

Every room has thick, luxurious, wall-to-wall carpeting, and the mahogany rail, which you cling onto as you climb the stairs, is highly polished. The first floor just consists of two massive bedrooms, each with its own bathroom and a loo. The front bedroom, which is Paul's, has a double bed and a long, long polished-pine, built-in dressing-table, which stretches all the way down one side of the room. It must be over twenty feet long. Underneath are loads and loads of drawers. Paul's bathroom consists of a washstand, sunken bath and shower, all completely tiled in blue and white. The guest bedroom is smaller, again containing a double bed, with lots of black and purple around. The guest bathroom is similar to Paul's, but tiled with a red and white pattern, with coloured towels draped over the rails.

On the top floor is Paul's music room. One wall is completely fitted out with shelves to hold tape-recorders, loudspeakers, LPs, singles, and Paul's other musical odds and ends. In the middle of the room sits a mini-piano. Paul got three of his friends to paint it with a fantastic pop-art design, which contains every colour of the rainbow. Paul sat down at the piano and played his theme music from the new Hayley Mills film, *The Family Way*. Facing him was a piece of metal sculpture called 'Solo'. It looks like a giant letter H, about five feet high, mounted on a metal base. The top of each upright ends with what looks like a motorcycle engine, and the open valves, two to each engine, stare at Paul like four eyes. But he and 'Solo' obviously get on very well together. In a small cupboard nearby were some of Paul's instruments. Leaning against the wall, on Paul's right as he plays the piano, is a massive, six-foot-high, triple portrait of a girl with red hair. No prizes for guessing who!

Paul's house has been beautifully designed to fill his every need and I am sure that his music room will give birth to many great tunes. Some of them will be on the LP which the boys are working on right now. If he wants to record one straightaway, his house is only a short Mini-Cooper drive away from EMI's Studios. But home is one place that Paul wants to keep private. It's a place he can retire to away from the tremendous pressures of the outside world. So if you know exactly where it is, Paul would appreciate it if you would keep the secret all to yourself! (JD)

Ringo at home

The Beatles' drummer bought a mansion close to John's Weybridge home

If there were no telephones and John had a bow and arrow — a powerful one, that is — he might just be able to send a message to Ringo, tied to an arrow, they live so close to one another. Once you've negotiated the paths through the rhododendrons, which grow all over the estate in which they live, you arrive at the big wooden gates which mark the entrance to Ringo's Weybridge mansion. There's a courtyard in front with garages for his cars, facing the massive Tudor-style house. A short walk across and you're at the front door. Ringo opened the door himself and after exchanging quick greetings, led us round to the back of the house, past Bricky Builders who are busy on alterations to the garden at the rear. The red, brick-built house has two storeys, but several of the walls have been painted white. At the back of the house is a massive balcony.

Ringo's estate occupies the northern side of a valley. On the other side is a golf course — the one they won't let him join immediately, but told him he had to go on a waiting list. Ringo has spent thousands on laying out his garden. As his garden runs down the side of a hill, all the grounds originally sloped downwards, but it has been completely redesigned so that there are a series of level lawns and terraces, which are connected by paths and steps. Immediately at the rear of the house is a terrace, the back entrance to the house being guarded by two massive stone lions. It's a fantastic place to explore because there are so many things to see. Steps lead down from the terrace to the first lawn. All round this lawn are rockeries and flowerbeds and loads and loads of rose bushes. This is where Maureen wanders to find flowers for the house. Below this first lawn is another one, but to reach it you have to walk down a series of steps, then past an ornamental pool surrounded by trees and shrubs, until you come to the lower lawn, which must be at least a hundred yards long, with fruit trees dotted all over it. When Ringo takes his dogs for a walk, this is where he likes to go. He has got three dogs, two Airedales, Daisy and Donovan, and Tiger the little white poodle, who is anything but fierce. While Daisy and Donovan go loping around the lawn, Tiger tears after them, yapping like mad.

Don't stop walking yet, though, because beyond this lawn to the right is the kitchen garden, and that must be a good 75 yards long. There are all sorts of sheds for the gardeners around the sides, and in the corner farthest from the house is a huge tree. Perched in its branches, about 25 feet from the ground, is a tree house. Ringo told us that the previous owner of the house was the chairman of some rubber company, Dunlop or Firestone, and that he built the tree house for his children. I didn't believe that Ringo had ever been up there. So he promptly climbed up the rope and through the branches to reach the tree house, while I watched. I think if Eppy, George Martin, or Walter Shenson, the Beatles' film producer, had been there, they would have had a heart-attack at the thought of him falling and breaking an arm, which would have put one-quarter of the Beatles out of action for quite a considerable time. But he didn't, and as soon as he had reached the house and proved his point, he slid down the rope and was once more beside us.

After wandering around the grounds we walked back up to the house and Ringo showed us his wood. It's a corner of the grounds that has just been left in its original

This is just one of many shots we took of Ringo in his garden at Weybridge.

Ringo's favourite seat on his back terrace.

state, with fir trees and bushes growing wild. The original owner used to keep a pack of Doberman Pinschers as guard dogs, in a compound in one corner. Ringo showed us the massive kennels where they used to sleep. He got an outside contractor to land-scape his garden, but the house was com-pletely refurbished by his own building company. They made all sorts of changes and the two most outstanding rooms in the house are the main living room, and his own private bar.

The main room of the house is really fan-tastic. It must be over 60 feet long and 40 feet wide. Bricky Builders completely re-built the fireplace, which is made of natural stone, topped by a tremendous log, about 15 feet long, which has been squared off and made

into a mantelpiece. An old flintlock rifle hangs on this. Ringo is very interested in 18th century arms and uniforms. He has several old guns and swords and he's obviously quite keen to add to his collection. Also on the mantelpiece is one of those little black boxes with red lights that go on and off all the time. Ringo told us that it was there to collect the electricity in the atmosphere, but then he and John are always thinking up odd reasons for their boxes. Opposite the massive fireplace is a door leading to the rest of the house, and on either side of the door are shelves filled with gold discs, trophies and other awards that the Beatles have been given. Ringo also had a fantastic loudspeaker system built all around the room, so that when he plays a record, the sound is really terrific. He usually offers vis-itors a drink in his bar. This is a little private room which he has had built just like a small pub. The walls are completely panelled.

There's a real bar along one wall with a prop-er counter, handles for pulling beer, and even a cash register, plus mirrors and rows of glasses behind the bar. It's called the 'Flying Cow'. There's a sign up on the wall to tell you what pub you're in and the name is also on the ashtrays and other items.

It's the room that Ringo and the other Beatles retire to when they call, so that they can sit and talk. It has a tremendously inti-mate atmosphere, just like a friendly pub, and from the windows there's a marvellous view over the garden and golf course. Ringo's house is really fantastic. It's big with beautiful rooms and tremendous grounds, but the master of the house is never satisfied, and right now Bricky Builders are busy building a cinema onto the Starkey mansion!   (JD)

With a Little Help From My Friends

Ringo's vocal became one of the most popular songs on the *Sgt. Pepper* album

ew Beatles recordings have ever been documented in such detail as Ringo's showcase on the *Sgt. Pepper* album, 'With A Little Help From My Friends'. Official Beatles biographer Hunter Davies spent the day with John and Paul while they were writing the song at Paul's house, and he described the process in a fascinating section of his book, *The Beatles*. Then, when the song was recorded, *The Beatles Book* team was there at No. 2 Studio, Abbey Road, to take some remarkable photos.

As Mal Evans told *The Beatles Book* readers before the *Pepper* album was released, 'With A Little Help From My Friends' began life under the working title of 'Badfinger Boogie'. That was the name which Paul wrote at the top of his original handwritten set of

lyrics for the song, and which he and John used as they were adding and changing the words. From the start, the song was intended for Ringo to sing, and at Abbey Road Paul sat down behind the piano and demonstrated how they wanted it to go.

During the session, Paul took the time to tell *The Beatles Book*'s editor, Johnny Dean, that he had been receiving lots of letters from their American fans, telling the boys how upset they were that the Beatles had broken up. "I can't understand where they got it all from," Paul said, "but I keep getting long letters which either say, 'Thanks for all the fun you've given us, we're sorry to hear you're

John and George recording harmonica tracks during the session.

Above: a view of the Beatles at work on 'With A Little Help From My Friends', taken from the stairs up to the studio control-room.

no longer together', or 'Why are you and the other Beatles no longer friends?'. It's all a bit of a mystery, but they must have got it from somewhere. The trouble is, our interviews never get printed the way we actually say things, and so people get the wrong idea. None of us has ever said that we're never going to record together again, or anything like that. But we have told reporters that we don't want to tour any more, or do dozens of TV spots every month. We've also said that we're unhappy with some of the recordings we've made in previous years, but what artist isn't unhappy with some of his earlier work?

"As for breaking up, we're here together now, aren't we? And, in fact, we've been here every week night for months now, all working together. The whole thing is a break down in communication, particularly as far as America is concerned. We could have done a special tape recording and sent it to all the radio stations in the States, but it didn't occur to us, because we knew the rumours weren't true. Sometimes people say we're impossible to get hold of, or talk to, but it's not true. I mean, I'm talking to you now, aren't I? And the people from *Life* magazine were in a couple of nights ago. In fact, people seem to be here most nights."

And with that, he went back to work on a song that has become a virtual anthem for Ringo, and which remains one of the most popular tracks on the *Sgt. Pepper* album.   (PD)

Left: Paul runs through the song for Ringo for the very first time.

Sgt. Pepper Pt 1: The Album

The Beatles' most famous album marked a revolution in the recording studio

Just for once, John and Paul were in total agreement. Lennon put it like this: "*Sgt. Pepper* was a real peak. The whole concept of the album took the Beatles onto a new level so far as recording was concerned." Paul added: "It was a goodie. We knew that as we were recording it." The Beatles, plus those of us who worked closely with them, knew from the start that *Sgt. Pepper* had a special significance in their career. It was their first major project since their retirement from touring, and a real milestone in their musical progress.

In the first few weeks of 1967, I remember John confessing to me that he thought half the world would pounce on the Beatles if the new album turned out to be anything less than sensational. He admitted: "Making an album used to be just another job for the Beatles. Now it's our main work and much more is expected of us in the studio." In 1967, the Beatles paved the way for other bands to devote far greater chunks of their working year to making records. After *Sgt. Pepper*, other bands did their best to emulate the Beatles by spending months on end in the recording studios, but very few came anywhere near *Sgt. Pepper* standards. Over a period of almost four months, the Beatles spent more than 700 hours in the EMI Studios at Abbey Road, mostly working through the night and knocking off when the rest of us were having our breakfast. The days when they could put down several new titles at a single session were long gone. Work on a song often began one night and was then continued a week or even a fortnight later, when John or Paul came up with new ideas for the arrangement.

At different times, both John and Paul claimed that it was their idea to link up the *Sgt. Pepper* tracks instead of leaving a gap between each song. John's explanation to me at the time went like this: "It makes the whole album sound more like a continuous show. We've put everything in a sequence that is balanced just like a set-list for a concert. It should be listened to all the way

A typical scene from the long Sgt. Pepper sessions, working on a backing track.

through, so there's no point in having a silence every few minutes. There was never any silence at our stage shows." This was a point which the Beatles and Brian Epstein failed to agree on. 'Eppy' told me: "People still want to drop the needle onto a favourite bit and play it more often than the rest of the record. It's more difficult to do that if the whole side is almost continuous instead of being punctuated by breaks."

Although Lennon's magnificently ingenious words play such a substantial part in *Sgt. Pepper*, it was Paul McCartney who dominated the actual sessions and controlled the production. He worked with George

All four of the Beatles wore flower-power clothes during the Sgt. Pepper sessions.

Martin in the studio, or with engineer Geoff Emerick behind the console upstairs in the control room. It was Paul who briefed most of the session musicians when they arrived, explaining their roles and putting their instrumental contributions into the context of the song – which was not strictly necessary but which the players appreciated. As many as forty musicians filled the EMI studio, and a four-track machine was in regular use – breathtakingly advanced by 1967 technological standards so far as rock'n'roll was concerned! The group also brought in

Mellotrons and a wide range of conventional instruments to augment their guitars.

But if Paul was the chief organiser, the one supervising each session, it was John who shone through as a composer and lyricist of absolute genius. Neither before nor since has his ingenuity been matched in the rock world: nobody has managed to create another 'Lucy In The Sky With Diamonds' or 'A Day In The Life'. John was never too interested in taking a high profile during recording sessions. He let others set everything up and then he'd do his stuff straight into the microphone. He wasn't in the least bit envious of Paul's powerful presence, or the way he took charge of the whole business. That didn't bother John at all. I think he knew the new strength of his writing and was content to let the material speak for itself. One morning, as he left Abbey Road, John told me: "That was the happiest I've ever been at a recording session. I could go back and do it again now if they wanted me to." And this was just after finishing a fourteen-hour stint!

Although Paul has since told the world that *Sgt. Pepper* was always built around the album's title track, I remember hearing other ideas at the time. At one point, Paul fancied making 'When I'm Sixty-Four' the centrepiece for a 'concept' programme which would showcase aspects of life in general and Liverpool life in particular. I seem to remember 'A Day In The Life' starting out as an extension of Paul's concept, but by the time this epic piece was completed, it was far larger than a reflection of day-to-day Merseyside existence. Whatever Paul has said since, we should not undervalue the importance of George Martin at the *Sgt. Pepper* sessions, and at those for 'A Day In The Life' in particular. His advice was sought on musical matters where John, Paul, George and Ringo still lacked the necessary expertise. In addition, he put forward his own ideas about accompaniments. The producer's enormous knowledge and experience proved of crucial value in the making of this entire album.

Not only was *Sgt. Pepper* the Beatles' first big venture after they gave up concert work, it was also one of the last where John and Paul collaborated harmoniously on the penning of new songs. After 1967, each would admit that most of his composing was done solo; but Lennon and McCartney clearly worked more closely than they had ever done before on some of the *Sgt. Pepper* titles.

As if to stress that this was a time of musical change and progression, the Beatles started to alter their physical appearance while the Sgt. Pepper tracks were being laid down. Their hair was allowed to grow longer, moustaches sprouted above their lips, and their clothing became much more flamboyant. The smart suits and crisp white shirts which Mal had carted round the world for their touring appearances were put away. In their place came the type of bright, outrageously-styled gear which the Fool would eventually retail on the Beatles' behalf at the Apple boutique in Baker Street. Scarves hung loose around the boys' necks, hats were worn at a rakish angle, and boots became more ornate.

Brian Epstein would probably never have approved of this clothing, despite his desire to look fashionable, but it all went perfectly with the photographs on the *Sgt. Pepper* sleeve – and with the garish clothes that were now beginning to be sported by young people on the streets of London. It was all part of their new 'natural' image, which the boys decided to adopt as part of their 1967 lifestyle. It was all a million miles away from the touring days of the Beatlemania period.

On the evening of Friday May 12th 1967, the pirate station Radio London claimed a world exclusive when it broadcast several *Sgt. Pepper* tracks for the first time. The following week, the Beeb took the decision to ban the song 'A Day In The Life' because, they said, they didn't like the drug references in the lyrics. On June 1st, the LP came out in Britain. On June 2nd, it was issued in America. And on June 3rd, it was at the top of the *Melody Maker* charts.   (TB)

Sgt. Pepper Pt 2: The Session

A day in the life of the Beatles at Abbey Road in February 1967

When the Beatles arrived at Abbey Road on the early evening of 24th November 1966, it was their first time in the studio for over five months. They'd spent that time completing their final world tour, and then taking an unprecedented break from each other's company, so that John and Paul could begin solo projects, George could take sitar lessons from Ravi Shankar, and Ringo could spend time at home with his family. The separation gave each of the Beatles the chance to reconsider the future direction of the group. For the first time, the ferocious pace of their career had slowed down, and the pause for breath set John, Paul, George and Ringo thinking – and not always about the same things! By November, John and George were convinced that they wouldn't agree to any more exhausting world tours. John had tasted the outside world by taking a part in Richard Lester's film *How I Won The War*; Paul had begun work on the score for another movie, *The Family Way*; and George had received a full-scale baptism into Indian culture at the hands of Ravi Shankar. So it was a very different group that began to work on the *Sgt. Pepper* album.

EMI's Abbey Road Studios became their home for the next seven months, as there was only one week during that period when the Beatles didn't spend at least one day recording or remixing. With few exceptions, they kept strictly to a normal working week, booking the studios from Monday to Friday, and only rarely requiring engineers to turn up at the weekend. But their hours weren't nine-to-five, as Beatles sessions began regularly at seven in the evening, and continued into the early hours. For the most part, there was a strict veil of secrecy over the *Pepper* sessions. EMI engineers working on other artists' recordings might pop their heads round the corner of the studio to see what was going on; sometimes the artists themselves would be invited to watch proceedings. But usually it was only the Beatles themselves, close aides like Mal and Neil,

By the time they came to record their Sgt. Pepper album, Paul had really mastered the art of mixing soundtracks to produce wonderful and unusual results.

and the EMI producers and engineers actually working on the sessions who were allowed to glimpse the Beatles at work. The exception was *The Beatles Book*, which was given exclusive access to some of the most important sessions that spring. Our team was there, for instance, on the night when they finally completed 'A Day In The Life'.

Though the group block-booked Studio Two for months at a time, that didn't mean they were there five nights a week, every week. They tended to record between Wednesday and Friday, while John and Paul assembled ideas for songs at Paul's home over the weekends or on Mondays and Tuesdays. This week, however, the Beatles

had been there every day. Their first two months of sessions had produced just three songs: 'Strawberry Fields Forever', 'When I'm 64' and 'Penny Lane'. Now the group were put under pressure to work a little faster. During the week in question, they'd been concentrating on four numbers: 'A Day In The Life', 'Being For The Benefit Of Mr Kite', 'Lovely Rita' and 'Fixing A Hole'. It had already been decided that the Wednesday session would be devoted to completing 'A Day In The Life', and then thinking about the songs which were due to be recorded next. So although the studio was set up for recording, there was no need for Mal Evans and Neil Aspinall to mike up all the instruments the Beatles had been using

in recent weeks – the fourteen or so guitars, Indian instruments like the sitar and the tamboura, different drums from around the world, and their dual-keyboard Vox electronic organ.

The enormous success of every record the Beatles had made for EMI won them complete freedom to do what they wanted, and spend as much as they liked. EMI and the Beatles both knew that whatever the studio sessions cost, the record sales would more than cover them, although EMI and Brian Epstein had managed to persuade the Beatles to release the first two songs they finished as a single in February. The recording studio had become the place where the songs and arrangements were actually written. When this kind of absolute freedom became the norm, almost every recording artist in rock wasted thousands of pounds experimenting with half-formed ideas. The difference with the Beatles was that their ideas worked. At this session, for example,

the boys had set themselves the task of manufacturing a definite ending for 'A Day In The Life'. Two weeks earlier, after the madcap recording session that produced the song's orchestral passages, the Beatles had multi-dubbed a long vocal hum, which they had placed after the final orchestral rush up the scale at the end of the song. Listening back to a rough mix, however, they had decided the hum wasn't strong enough. So Paul came up with the idea of using a piano chord, left to resound until every trace had vanished into the air. To get the desired effect, John, Paul, Ringo and Mal positioned themselves at three of the studio pianos, and made nine separate attempts to synchronise a simultaneous four-piece piano chord down to a hundredth of a second. When they found a take which they liked, and which lasted almost a minute from striking the pianos to the sound finally dying away, they doubled, trebled and finally quadrupled the sound – all to build up that magnificent finale.

When the final playbacks had been okayed, the session developed into playtime. Several visitors had arrived by this point, proving that the Beatles weren't planning any major recording for the rest of the night. They included Judith Sims, editor of the influential American pop magazine, *Teenset*; Alastair Taylor and Peter Brown from Brian Epstein's office at NEMS; folksinger Shawn Phillips; George's wife, model Pattie Boyd, sporting the latest Carnaby Street fashions and a stunning new hairdo; and David Crosby of the American group the Byrds, who were on a promotional tour of Europe. To this day, Crosby still recalls his excitement when the Beatles played him the finished mix of 'A Day In The Life' for the first time. As the visitors chatted to George, John and Paul ran through rough versions of a couple of songs they were working on. John performed 'Lucy In The Sky With Diamonds', while Ringo looked on approvingly and then dabbled at the EMI grand piano they'd used for the 'A Day In The Life' ending. Then Paul took over at the piano for a rendition of 'Lovely Rita', which the Beatles planned to record at their next session. As he ran through the song, Mal Evans and Neil Aspinall noted down the changes he made to the lyrics, and after a while they all suggested some alterations – some serious, others more lighthearted.

Now the stage was set for what was becoming something of a middle-of-the-night tradition in 1967: the end-of-session experiment. The Beatles produced a number of long, rambling recordings that year, almost always at the end of all-night work in Studio Two. On February 22nd, Paul spent a few minutes keeping up his skills as a drummer, before Ringo took over behind the drumkit, and began to hammer out a steady beat. The other Beatles joined in on congas and tambourine, and filled three tracks of a four-track tape for more than twenty minutes. There the experiment ended, and to this day the tape remains in EMI's vaults, waiting for the Beatles to decide what to do with it next! After that the session finally broke up, nearly nine hours after it had begun. The Beatles and their aides vanished quietly into the night, after talking briefly to a couple of stalwart fans who had waited throughout the evening for a glimpse of the boys. After a good day's sleep, it was time for the Beatles to prepare themselves for another night's work, this time to start recording 'Lovely Rita' – another step on the way to completing their masterpiece, *Sgt. Pepper.*   (PD)

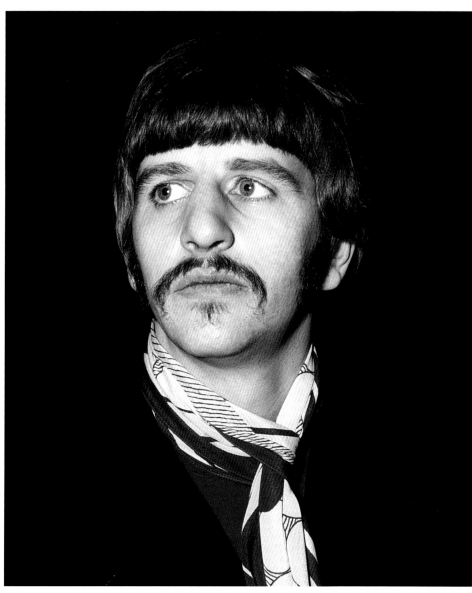

Sgt. Pepper Pt 3: Launch Party

Brian Epstein staged a series of elaborate events to launch the album

The release of the *Sgt. Pepper* album was surrounded by a whole summer of celebration. I had never seen the Beatles so excited about a new record coming out since their first single, 'Love Me Do'. Over the years, I saw them showing increasingly less surprise and joy when their records went racing to the top of the charts as soon as they were issued. The whole business had become routine for them. We knew they still cared about having hits, but some of the thrill had gone out of the climb to Number One when they no longer had to fight for each new success.

With *Pepper*, it was back to square one. John, Paul, George and Ringo knew they had pinned their future on a set of revolutionary new songs. Musically, most of the material on the new collection was light years ahead of anything they had done before, even further ahead of other bands in Britain and America during that era. But would fans appreciate the change of style? To most of us in Brian Epstein's office, it was soon clear just how keen the boys were to do everything possible to publicise the new album. John and Paul were never off the phone, asking if the special sleeve was ready, when radio stations would get finished records, and whether a particular reviewer could have a copy yet. Clearly they found the delay between the final recording sessions and the album's release date totally frustrating. They were very anxious that everything should be exactly right, with nothing left to chance.

They even came up with a series of outrageous publicity stunts to make sure the press and public knew about *Sgt. Pepper*. One idea was that they should dress up in the military gear they'd worn for the cover shoot, disguise their faces with extra large whiskers, and march through central London with a brass band behind them. They wanted to go all the way to Buckingham Palace, where we'd reveal to Fleet Street cameramen that it really was the Beatles! But stunts like this were simply not necessary and I remember explaining to them that their music was stunning enough to create headlines by itself. Instead, there was a series of very special parties to celebrate the arrival of *Sgt. Pepper*.

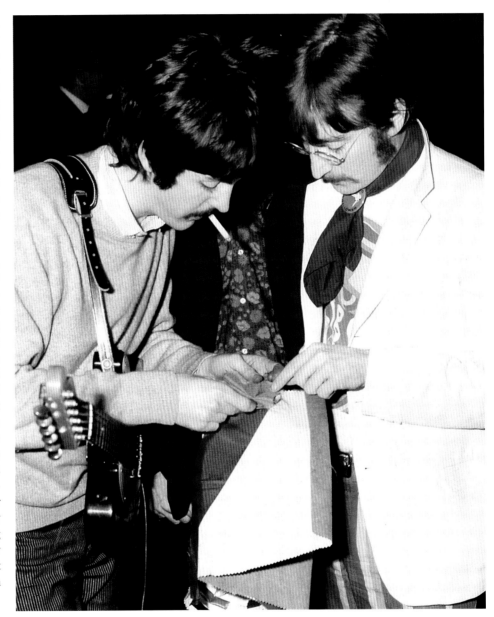

These were not enormous shindigs but private celebrations or house parties held at Eppy's place, where a few close pals, like 'pirate' Radio London deejay Kenny Everett, were invited down for evenings or long weekends. Most of the so-called Beautiful People in contemporary London seemed to make it to the well-guarded Epstein home at Kingsley Hill for one of Brian's glittery *Pepper* parties. They became the hottest ticket in town that summer – although the actual invitation was a personal phone call from Brian or a Beatle, not a printed card. There were few negative responses, even from the biggest stars. I was only involved with one launch party, held for the press at Brian Epstein's London house

The boys decided they wanted to choose the materials for their Sgt. Pepper uniforms themselves.

just a fortnight before the record's release date. For this occasion, the Beatles suggested that very splendid invitations should be printed. The group used to have a uniformed courier from Asprey's, the world-famous jewellers, deliver their personal Christmas presents each year. John or Paul suggested to me that we should get the same man, in his usual immaculate livery and white gloves, to deliver each of the Chapel Street party invitations to a dozen or so respected journalists. In the end, though, people were telephoned very

183

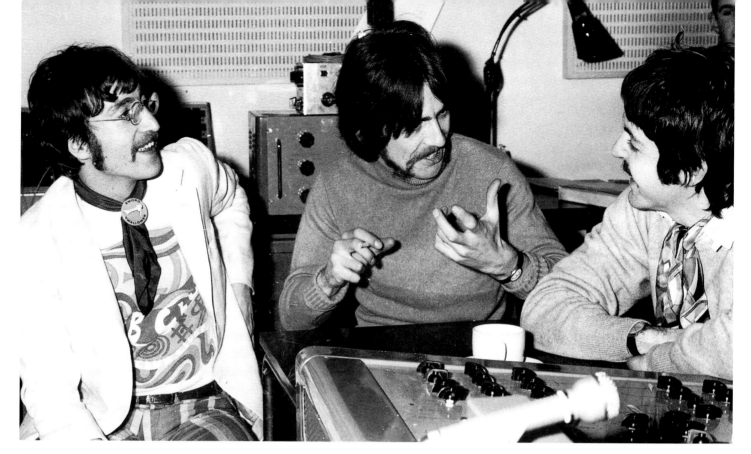

Whatever George said at this moment in the control room at Abbey Road studios, it certainly made John and Paul smile.

discreetly, not from the NEMS press office, but by Brian's personal assistant, Wendy Hanson.

Journalist Ray Coleman told me what he remembered about the *Sgt. Pepper* press party from a guest's viewpoint. Ray was at Chapel Street as *Melody Maker*'s man. He heard about the 'do' only a few days beforehand: "It was a telephone call from Wendy. She certainly didn't call it a launch party for the album. It was a matter of 'Brian would like you to come round for a few drinks', that was the tone of it. In fact there was a typical Epstein array of gourmet foods and fine wines. The glazed poached salmon, the caviar, the vintage champagne, all told us we were in for an event with a capital 'E'! I remember having a conversation there with Paul about 'A Day In The Life'. Paul said there was a problem with the BBC regarding the words. He thought it was ridiculous. It was about one line. Paul said 'went upstairs and had a smoke' could mean anything, just going up on the top deck of a double-decker bus for a ciggie."

Ray remembers getting a strong impression that the Beatles felt that every aspect of *Sgt. Pepper* was critically important to the next phase of the group's career: "They fussed around us that night, hoping we'd like what we heard on Brian's hi-fi system. I have this vivid memory of George telling me he felt they'd

broken through a real barrier with the album. He said, 'We've really jumped up onto a new layer with this one,' but the funny thing is that for the people hearing these tracks for the first time, it wasn't immediately apparent. I defy anyone on the first play of *Sgt. Pepper* in 1967 to say that here was an epoch-making album. It just wasn't like that at all. It was something like you'd never heard before, and it was unexpected from the Beatles, but you couldn't say this was going to be the most important album for the next twenty years. You'd need several plays at least to convince you it was of such lasting significance."

Ray also remembers what happened when he started to talk to John Lennon that night: "I took out my notebook to do a short interview with John. The notebook was frowned upon because Brian wanted to keep this a semi-social occasion." He recalls that Brian always seemed to be wary of notes being taken when John spoke to a journalist. This time there was an additional reason for Epstein's anxiety: "John was stoned, there's absolutely no question in my own mind about that. I said something intentionally challenging to John like, 'Aren't you worried about the popularity of the Monkees?', because some reporters were calling the American TV group 'the New Beatles' and they seemed to be heading that way as far as the fans were concerned. John really went for me. How dare I compare the groups! If the Monkees wanted all that Monkeemania crap, they were welcome to it. The Beatles had been through that for three years and packed it in last summer. John said: 'Tell the Monkees to get

stuffed!' His real point was that the Beatles had moved forward, and progressed into the album market, and that *Pepper* would prove it. It was quite a significant point." Ray Coleman's recollection of Brian Epstein's mood at the Chapel Street party is that the man was unusually subdued. In fact, even if journalists became exceptionally close to the Beatles, they tended to know very little about Brian's private life. The truth is that 'Eppy' was very ill. Until almost the eve of the big event, Brian was under close medical care at a private clinic, called the Priory. Amongst other things, the place specialised in treating drug and alcohol patients. Ray Coleman recalled: "We knew nothing of his illness. It was a beautifully kept secret. Fleet Street would have jumped upon it." But the last thing any of us wanted was adverse publicity just when the most important album in the Beatles' career was being released. The very fact that the party was held at Chapel Street was a crucial element of our PR cover-up. After all, surely 'Eppy' wouldn't be inviting pressmen into his living quarters if he was not well!

As it turned out, all of the Beatles' fears about the reception *Sgt. Pepper* would receive proved to be groundless. Almost without exception, the press reviews of the album were very favourable, and the record went on to become one of the biggest-selling albums of all time. But the way in which the album was launched shows how much the boys cared about this project, and how relieved they were that it had all worked out so well. (TB)

Sgt. Pepper Pt 4: The Fans

Beatles Book readers share their initial reactions to the Beatles' classic LP

My desk is buried beneath a mountain of mail about *Sgt. Pepper's Lonely Hearts Club Band*. Beatle People from all over Britain have written to tell me what they think of the LP, which took six months to produce. But is *Sgt. Pepper* too advanced for the average pop fan to appreciate? Here's a cross-section of your opinions. "I really enjoyed everything The Beatles recorded before *Revolver*," writes Karen Baird of Long Eaton, "but it's impossible to understand half the stuff they do today." "I'm not a true pop fan," begins Peggy Franklin of Loughton, Essex, "and I never used to collect Top 20 records. A year ago The Beatles became part of my life. They are the greatest talent the music world has ever known. *Sgt. Pepper* contains words and ideas which are far above anything anyone else is capable of creating. 'A Day In The Life' is the most moving pop song I've ever heard." Those very different comments represent two extremes: one fan who has been frightened off by the deepening complexity, of recent Beatles work, and another who can't find sufficient superlatives to use about the 1967 stuff they've put into *Sgt. Pepper*.

" 'All My Loving' was my favourite until I heard 'She's Leaving Home'," declares Marsha Newell of Nelson. "It's uncanny how John and Paul can think up such original stories for their songs. They get better and better all the time." "I was one of the first Beatle People in my neighbourhood to buy the new LP," says Joanne Tremlett of Welling, "but I can't tell you how disappointed I was. Only 'When I'm 64' and 'Sgt. Pepper' itself come up to standard. Everything else is over our heads and the Beatles ought to stop being so clever and give us tunes we can enjoy." "The first time I heard the LP, I was brought down," writes Valerie Samuel of Chertsey. "Then I listened again and again. Finally I was overwhelmed by what I heard. Not just impressed but overpowered. It's all marvellous, particularly 'A Day In The Life' and 'Lucy In The Sky With Diamonds'. But it's no good just half-listening. You've got to concentrate hard and let the Beatles hypnotise you. Then you're under the spell of *Sgt. Pepper* and a splendid time IS guaranteed for all!"

Now here's a very important point raised by Jackie Smith of Chesterfield, who writes: "I don't know what all the quarrel is about. If you want simple, catchy little numbers like the Beatles used to do, you've got 'When I'm 64', Ringo's terrific 'Little Help From My Friends' and Paul's happy 'Fixing A Hole'. If you want something more advanced, there's plenty of other numbers to choose from on the new LP." Wendy East of Ealing joins in: "How can people accuse the Beatles of progressing too far. That's what their talent is all about. I, for one, wouldn't want to hear 'Please Please Me' rehashed a hundred times. The Beatles mix new compositions, which are just as catchy as their old hits with more mature ballads, which make you think."

Of course it's impossible to please everybody: for instance, take George's number, 'Within You Without You'. "It's dreadful, just a crazy lot of noises with no tune at all," claims Jean Crosley of Stockwell. "It makes me dream beautiful dreams," says Pat Price of Mill Hill. "I wish the LP was 'banded' so that I could miss out that track," writes Maureen Burbeck of Preston. "Atrocious! Horrid! I can't hear the words and there isn't a tune at all. Let George make an album on his own instead of wasting five minutes of Beatle Time!" screams Claire Bennett of Bebbington. "It's the most beautiful music George has ever made and I can't get it out of my mind," is the reaction of Brenda Hampton of Morecambe. "Of all the new LP songs, I love George's best, because it's haunting," writes Marianne Sinclair of Edinburgh.

Nancy Ryan of Cheshunt writes: "I was just 15 when the Beatles started recording. Now I am nearly 20 and I expect to be married before Christmas. I've become bored with much of the music that makes the Top 20 but I've grown up with the Beatles and the Beatles' music has grown up with me. So we're still together, with the Beatles getting just a bit ahead now and again. It's fun trying to keep up with them. Of course, they record some things I don't like but it wouldn't be natural if everything they did pleased me. I can't wait to hear the fantastic songs they'll be coming up with by 1970!"

Of course, the Beatles have lost some fans along the way. I don't think Judy Conn of Leytonstone can be bothered trying to keep up with *Sgt. Pepper*: "The records I used to play most were *Help!*, *A Hard Day's Night* and *With The Beatles*. Now I've put them away and I love the Monkees." The same goes for Chrissie Wright of Tunbridge Wells: "It's a fat lot of good putting things like 'Being For The Benefit Of Mr. Kite' and 'Good Morning, Good Morning' on a record and pretending they're good music. In future, I'll stick to the Who, the Hollies and the Four Tops, thank you very much." Then there's Ann Turnbull of Bognor Regis, who feels very cheated: "I spent £2 (including the train fare) to buy *Sgt. Pepper* and there are only three songs on it worth hearing." So does Jan Williams of Caernarvon in North Wales: "I was looking forward to *Sgt. Pepper* but the title song is the only one I really like. It's the Beatles we used to know before they went stark raving mad and started to write rubbish."

Well, you can't hope to please everybody. Very little of the mail which reached *The Beatles Book* offices condemned *Sgt. Pepper* as nothing better than rubbish. Most of you admitted you liked certain parts of the programme, even if there were songs you couldn't understand or didn't find entertaining. And, of course, the vast majority of readers said everything on the LP was fantastic, fabulous, groovy, etc.

So the answer to my original question is that some of you feel quite happy about keeping up with *Sgt. Pepper*, while a lot more of you are prepared to make an effort to find out what the Beatles' 1967 music is all about, because you admire the group and you want them to stay an important part of your lives. Let me finish by quoting one final letter. It came in from Mary Noble of Luton: "If the Beatles stuck with the style they had in 1963, we would all accuse them of having nothing new to offer. Because they have so much new material and so many new ideas, some of us accuse them of being unfaithful to us and going off in their own directions. Now, let's be honest! WHO is being unfaithful to WHOM?" (TB)

BEATLE NEWS

1967

DRIVE MY CAR?

Stories about the Beatles are always flying around Fleet Street. The 7th January was very icy, with dangerous conditions on the M1 motorway, linking London with the Midlands. Towards the end of the day, a rumour swept London that Paul McCartney had been killed in a car crash on the M1. Of course, there was absolutely no truth in it at all – as the Beatles' Press Officer found out when he telephoned Paul's St. John's Wood home and was answered by Paul himself, who had been at home all day with his black Mini Cooper safely locked up in the garage.

Ironically, it was John who had a narrow escape this month, emerging unscathed but slightly shocked from a minor car accident in London. (January 1967)

MOUSTACHES ALL ROUND

All the boys have decided that a stiff upper lip is an absolute must for the New Year. Paul's moustache is growing long and black, John's is not so black but longer, George's you have already seen in photographs, and Ringo's is similar to Paul's. The biggest surprise of all, though, was that Mal Evans and Neil Aspinall have also decided to follow the Beatles and grow moustaches. Neil's is a truly magnificent growth – in fact, I didn't recognise him at first the last time we met! (January 1967)

STRAWBERRY FIELDS/PENNY LANE

Trust John and Paul to do the most unexpected thing! Just when so many people have been saying that the boys have completely forgotten the city where they were brought up, they produce two songs about places in Liverpool that they know well. John used to live very close to Strawberry Fields in Woolton, and Paul often used to go through Penny Lane on his way into town. The result is two great Beatle songs, which are already capturing a large percentage of the airwaves on all stations.
(Johnny Dean's editorial, February 1967)

NOT NO. 1 PENNY LANE!

The boys' latest single hasn't reached the top of any of the charts published by the UK music papers. This is the first time they haven't made number one in the week of release since 'Please Please Me' was released four years ago. At the moment, 'Penny Lane' is being outsold by Petula Clark's 'This Is My Song' and 'Release Me' by new boy Engelbert Humperdinck. (February 1967)

TV FILM OF LATEST SESSIONS

The boys' latest recording sessions are being filmed for a new documentary showing the Beatles at work. The idea is that a TV special will be shown, probably by the BBC, at the same time as the new album is released, either in May or June.
(February 1967)

FILMS DELAYED

In the struggle to meet the May release date, the Beatles have been forced to scrap all their filming plans. Instead, they will work on a TV special as soon as the album, which will be called *Sgt. Pepper's Lonely Hearts Club Band*, has been released. Later this year, the boys should also begin work on their long-delayed third feature film, which the United Artists producer still hopes will be in the cinemas before Christmas.
(March 1967)

BIG STEAL

More than three weeks before it is due to be released, "fans" stole two copies of their new *Sgt. Pepper* LP from Paul's home in St. John's Wood, North London. They broke in while Paul was out. (May 1967)

SPLIT DENIED

The Beatles' latest burst of activity has put paid to all the rumours of a few months back that the group were falling apart. "We have never thought of splitting up," Paul says. "We want to go on recording together. The Beatles live!" (May 1967)

GREEK GETAWAY

All four Beatles have just completed a week-long holiday on a Greek island – a chance to get away from it all after the intense period of work which led up to the *Sgt. Pepper*

The Byrds turned up during one of the 'Sgt. Pepper' sessions. Here's David Crosby greeting George.

album. A journalist got hold of the story that the Beatles were planning to leave Britain for good and move to Greece, and that their trip wasn't a holiday at all but a business assignment to look for a suitable island on which they could set up shop. The truth is that the Beatles did briefly toy with buying a small Mediterranean island as a getaway for themselves and their friends, but they have now decided against the idea. (July 1967)

TWO CLOSE SHAVES!

Keen observers will have noticed that two of the Beatles have now shaved off their moustaches. Although George and Ringo are still sporting hairy upper lips, John and Paul are clean-shaven again. (July 1967)

TRIBUTES TO BRIAN

The death of Brian Epstein has shocked everyone in the pop world – the Beatles most of all. John said: "I just can't find words to pay tribute to him. He was lovable, and it is those lovable things we think about now." Paul could only say: "This is a great shock. I am terribly upset." George added: "He dedicated so much of his life to the Beatles. We liked and loved him. He was one of us." The final word was left to Ringo: "We loved Brian. He was a generous man. We owe so much to him. We have come a long way with Brian." (August 1967)

WHAT IS APPLE?

When the word 'Apple' first appeared in connection with the Beatles, letters started arriving at the Fan Club and *The Beatles Book* offices asking what it meant. A brief and simple answer is impossible, because it may develop into many things, but the Beatles *do* have a direct interest in it. Apple has taken over a large building in Baker Street (of Sherlock Holmes fame) and very shortly it will start operating as the Apple music publishing office. (September 1967)

NO MEAT, PLEASE

As George becomes more and more interested in all things Indian, so his life is continuing to change. He has already found great comfort from reading the works of Indian mystics and gurus, and he has now become a vegetarian, as a result of his study of Indian religion. (September 1967)

PSYCHEDELIC PAINTERS

After John's Rolls and Julian's caravan, now it's John's Bechstein piano. The two Dutch masters of psychedelic painting, Simon Posthuma and Marijke (pronounced Mareshka) Koger, have been working on the

piano at John's Weybridge home. They started by painting the piano white all over, then drew the designs in pencil on the white background, and finally got down to the actual painting. (September 1967)

PAUL WANTS NEW MUSIC

Paul says that the Beatles have no definite schedule for the future. "We are not going to turn out records or films just for the sake of it," he explains. "We don't want to talk unless we have something to say. We enjoy recording, but we want to go even further. I would like to come up with a completely new form of music, and invent new sounds. But at the moment I'm thinking things out. There seems to be a pause in my life right now – a time for reassessment." (September 1967)

DAFT BAN

The Beatles have gone back to their famous collarless suits, designed by Pierre Cardin in 1963 – but you won't be able to see them on British TV! That's the ridiculous situation surrounding the special films the Beatles have made to publicise their new single, 'Hello Goodbye'. The clips showed them

John's piano being given a psychedelic update by the members of the Fool team.

posing in their old suits, and then miming to the song. But the Musicians Union have complained that it is too obvious that they are miming, which is one of the things you just aren't allowed to do on TV. Why? The rules were made to stop musicians being put out of work by artists miming, rather than having to actually play. But what harm can a film clip do to the nation's struggling musicians? (November 1967)

AFTER BRIAN EPSTEIN'S DEATH

Everyone in show-business wondered what John, Paul, George and Ringo would do when Brian Epstein died. Who would take over? Now, several months later, the answer is clear: no-one could, so no-one has.

Who makes all the arrangements, then? Again, the answer is simple, the Beatles and their road managers do. Most of the organisation for their *Magical Mystery Tour* was done by the boys themselves. If ever something can be said to have been written, directed, acted and produced by one team, then the Beatles deserve this credit.

The Beatles in clubland

Tony Barrow reveals how they socialised with the London 'in-crowd'

Even now, whenever I hear a 'golden oldies' DJ playing Procol Harum's haunting hit, 'A Whiter Shade Of Pale', I think of the Speakeasy, the all-night disco rendezvous in the centre of London where the Beatles and the Beautiful People of the Swinging Sixties used to gather after dark. It seemed to us at the time that they put on 'A Whiter Shade Of Pale' at least once an hour all through the night and even after dawn. And whenever they did, the dance floor filled up with famous faces, because it was THE record of 1967, a No. 1 hit with the 'in' crowd of London throughout that happy, hazy summer.

The Speakeasy club, at 48 Margaret Street, was a Rolling Stone's throw north of Oxford Circus. There, in an underground suite of flatteringly lit rooms, the likes of Mick Jagger and Marianne Faithfull or Paul McCartney and Jane Asher could be seen most nights of a typical week, rubbing

Kinks guitarist and playboy Dave Davies.

shoulders and exchanging chit-chat with Jimi Hendrix or Eric Clapton. All the best-known rock stars went down to 'the Speak' to drink, dine, and dance the night away with their dolly birds. The way into 'the Speak' was down a flight of steps and past a big, highly polished black coffin, where you signed the membership book if you were an unfamiliar face to Roy Flynn or one of his men on the door. If you were John, Paul, George or Ringo, you walked straight through and into the bar area. Everything there was American-style, from the bourbon and Southern Comfort on the shelves to the tall glasses packed with ice.

Eric Burdon of the Animals was a regular in the clubs.

Early in the evening the girls outnumbered the boys by a good five to one. They got down there early to stake their claim to a good place at the bar and the best of the available males as they began to arrive. Scores of girls used the Speakeasy without spending any cash. You'd hear them say to the bar staff: "Put it on John Lennon's bill. John said it was OK – ask 'Nel' over there if you don't believe me." And, of course, nobody ever bothered to ask. Frankly, the Speakeasy staff didn't care who paid up, as long as the money was right. So Lennon, McCartney, Hendrix and the rest finished up forking out, usually via a cash-carrying roadie, for dozens of double bourbons they'd never had. But it didn't matter. This was the summer of '67, the best time of all to be alive, and a few hundred quid spent on yet another good night on the town was all part of the game of being part of the 'in crowd'. Here comes 'A Whiter Shade Of Pale' for the umpteenth time – shall we dance?

Mick Jagger, the only pop star of the 60s who could rival the Beatles' star status.

During the memorable summer of '67, the Beatles watched a host of bands in live performance at the Speakeasy, from Procol Harum to Marmalade. One of the most memorable nights there was July 3rd, when just about anyone who was anyone on the pop scene attended the star-stacked party we put on in honour of the Monkees. Fanzine rumours had spread the word that the Monkees and the Beatles were deadly enemies. Of course they weren't. What's more, it was Brian Epstein's associate Vic Lewis who'd brought the Monkees into town for a series of concerts put on by NEMS at Wembley. The Speakeasy shindig was designed to prove that all the boys got on well together. The glass-walled VIP restaurant, where the stars ate in peace and could watch what was happening on stage without being in the crush, was closed for the evening for our party.

Amongst the first to arrive were the Who and Kenny Everett. Then came Cream, led by Eric Clapton, Manfred Mann (both the man and his band!), Peter Tork and Paul

with Jane Asher. Soon Monkees Micky Dolenz and Mike Nesmith and their women arrived. Keith Moon and John Lennon sang along loudly to 'A Whiter Shade Of Pale' as Procol Harum arrived in force. They didn't usually herald the arrival of a star by playing his hit record – that would have been a bit naff at a place like 'the Speak'. But Harum were everyone's heroes of the moment and the record was due to be played again anyway, not having been on for at least half-an-hour! The place was ablaze with colourful high-fashion clothes and high-flying musicians inhaling sweet substances in the musky, smoke-filled atmosphere.

Brian Epstein wasn't about, but he seldom joined the Speakeasy crowd, as clubbing of that sort wasn't his scene. Monkee Davy Jones and Beatle Ringo Starr were missing too, each for their own personal reasons. Klaus Voormann, another London 'in crowd' man of the moment since he'd designed *Revolver* for the Beatles, was deep in conversation with diminutive Scottish

Georgie Fame, who was playing at the Bag O'Nails the night Paul met Linda.

songstress Lulu, whose shrill laughter rang round the room. Dolenz's date Samantha Juste, a television pop show hostess of the era, was in a corner of the restaurant comparing notes with Dusty Springfield. George Harrison, standing beside members of the Fool, was discussing *Sgt. Pepper* with a model friend of Pattie's. It was just another starry, starry night at the Speakeasy. Before the partying was over, most of the biggest

Other key nightspots for the in crowd included the slightly folksy Cromwellian and the leathery Saddle Room, close to where the Hard Rock Cafe stands today at the west end of Piccadilly; the Pickwick club where Peter (Asher) and Gordon (Waller) used to play in a jazz group, watched by Paul and Jane; the thriving Soho R&B club, run by the Gunnell brothers who managed some of London's top R&B acts; and the Bag O'Nails in Kingley Street, close to Carnaby Street, where Paul saw Georgie Fame's act and got together with Linda over a drink with Chas Chandler, all on one fabulous evening; the Revolution club, in Bruton Place, in the heart of Mayfair, where the live shows ranged from Ike & Tina Turner to the Edwin Hawkins Singers; and the Scotch of St. James, in Mason's Yard, very near the site where Tramp would open some years later, which was a favourite haunt of Eric Burdon's Animals, the Stones and the Beatles. These last two places enjoyed almost the same degree of popularity as 'the Speak'.

The folksinger Donovan became one of the Beatles' best friends.

Although the Speakeasy remained London's most fashionable niterie for longer than the other best-known Sixties spots, a host of other clubs came and went and were just as popular for short periods at a time. Among the first was the Ad Lib club, just off Leicester Square, where P.J. Proby, Marianne Faithfull and Sandie Shaw were regulars, along with the Animals and the Rolling Stones. A bit later, there was a terribly high society place called Sybilla's, named after one of Richard

names there were often persuaded to take the stage for a fabulous jam session, featuring a multi-million-dollar international superband. There wasn't a single concert promoter in the world who could possibly have afforded to assemble a group like that, even if it was just for a one-night stand!

Burton's wives, located in Swallow Street, off Regent Street at the Piccadilly Circus end, which opened in June 1966 with all the Beatles there as guests of honour. George and his buddies often visited Sybilla's in the months afterwards (not least because he had invested a substantial amount of money in the place!).

The Miranda Club in London - better known in the 60s as the Bag O'Nails.

(Above) Top DJ and Beatles friend Kenny Everett. (Right) The legendary Yardbirds.

It was in places like the Speakeasy and the Scotch that I really got to know each of the Beatles in my early days of working with the group. In the heady atmosphere of these places, everybody let their hair down and spoke freely. One made friends – or enemies – very easily under such conditions. For example, in the Speakeasy one night, John decided to buy the place. Well, that's what he told me, anyway. We'd been having an in-depth discussion about property prices and, when Cynthia slipped away at one point, John said: "How much do you reckon it would cost me to close this place down and re-open it as a really different club just for musicians?" I told him I reckoned it was a bit like that now. John replied: "There are too many posers and gold-diggers getting in now. This place is changing. And I wouldn't like it to be like George's Sybilla's because there's a snobby crowd in there nowadays. If we owned somewhere like the Speakeasy ourselves, we could hand-pick who got membership cards, not just the right musicians but the right birds as well." Cyn rejoined us, and John joked: "I'm buying this place for my birthday." She ignored the remark: she'd learnt to do that! John went on to say the Beatles would love to play late-night sessions, unannounced and unpublicised, just for friends. Of course, it sounded great, but it was just the drink talking. He never did make a real attempt to purchase the place, although, like the rest of us, he remained a regular visitor for the rest of the swinging decade. (TB)

Cilla Black became a close friend of the boys during their Cavern days.

All You Need Is Love

The day they faced an audience of millions all round the world

Brian Epstein addressed us in his usual pompous style on these sort of occasions: "It's all absolutely confidential and not one of us must utter a single word outside these four walls, but the Beatles are going to give a most important live performance next month." It was the second week of May 1967 – I remember the date because it was my birthday. 'Eppy' had gathered together a handful of his executives who worked closely with the Fab Four in the largest office at NEMS Enterprises for what we were told would be "a significant announcement". After eight months of unsuccessful effort, had he persuaded John, Paul, George and Ringo to do their first concert since the previous year's farewell gig at San Francisco's Candlestick Park? This would have surprised us, because Brian no longer seemed at all close to the Beatles. He was spending most of his time hidden away from us in his country home, seldom coming into the office and seldom meeting even his favourite artists, Cilla Black and the Beatles. What was this highly secret live performance that Eppy had to tell us about? We wondered why the Beatles were letting Brian handle such an announcement when we knew the group was about to go public with the launch of its own new Apple companies, which would relieve NEMS of almost all future management responsibilities. We guessed it must be a Royal Command. But we were wrong.

The Beatles' manager continued grandly: "At the invitation of the BBC and the European Broadcasting Union, the boys are going to sing their latest song for a global audience of hundreds of millions, the largest number of viewers in television history, and it'll be a live broadcast from Abbey Road. They're to represent Britain in the first worldwide satellite link-up." Sharp intakes of breath all round on our part! Someone asked what the new song was called and Brian replied tersely: "I haven't the least idea. They haven't written it yet, as far as I know." As details of the hush-hush project emerged, we learnt that the Beatles would be half of the BBC's British contribution to a two-hour programme entitled *Our World*. Viewers would get the impression they were witnessing the actual recording of a new Lennon/McCartney composition in the

---

The Beatles outside Abbey Road with the 'Our World' director Derek Burrell-Davis.

EMI Studios, although to make the affair visually spectacular, it would be anything but a routine session. One week after our meeting with Brian, news of the unique event was made public by the BBC. In the intervening days, John and Paul went on network television in America to announce the launch of the group's company, Apple Corps. This was a bitter blow for Brian, who was finally forced to accept that his protegés were not offering him any role in the operation of their new companies.

For John and Paul, the extraordinary challenge of *Our World* was to come up with an exceptionally good new song in a very short period of time. It would have to be something that easily crossed language barriers, so the maximum number of viewers around the world could understand it. The BBC's co-ordinator for the show was director Derek Burrell-Davis, via whom the initial invitation for the boys to participate in *Our World* had been received. He stressed to John and Paul that simple lyrics and a catchy, straightforward tune were essential to the success of their segment of this historic show. The Beatles' producer, George Martin, remained unconvinced that the group were taking the project seriously enough. He was concerned that they would not prepare themselves sufficiently and explained patiently that while the BBC wanted their appearance to depict an ordinary session with the boys at work on their next record release, they couldn't possibly rely on an off-the-cuff situation. Not only did a new song have to be ready in good time, but backing tracks would need to be laid down in advance. In effect, said George, this would be a fully rehearsed and totally professional public premiere of a completely produced new recording. In fact, he added, this was the most valuable television 'plug' in the history of pop music, like doing hundreds of *Top Of The Pops* appearances all in one go!

The truth was that John and Paul were taking the task seriously but so far they hadn't been able to agree on an approach for the new song. As a result, they went their separate ways, each writing a new composition without collaborating with the other. The race was on: two reputations were at stake! It was quite a shock to us when John came bounding home with the more suitable song. There was no fight about it, as the two agreed on their choice without any argument. We expected John to write something

Paul, John and George recording 'All You Need Is Love' at Abbey Road.

too obscure and complicated for this very specific purpose and we were sure Paul would win hands down by creating another of his catchy and infectious songs. 'All You Need Is Love' was one of John's earliest so-called 'anthems', made in the mould he was to use again for 'Give Peace A Chance' and 'Power To The People'. John called them his slogan songs.

In its theme, the central message of 'All You Need Is Love' was a natural progression from some of the earliest Lennon/McCartney successes that had also contained key references to love – such as 'Love Me Do', 'She Loves You' and 'All My Loving'. Eventually, as if to underline this intentionally backwards glance, the final recorded version of 'All You Need Is Love' had the boys chanting 'She Loves You' at the end.

If the new song was also intended by John to be part of the Californian make-love-not-war and wear-a-flower-in-your-hair movement of that summer, it arrived a little late in the day, following a well-established inter-national pop trend of 1967 rather than setting a fresh one. But this did not reduce the strength and instant impact of the piece. It had a persistent, persuasive, repetitious and mildly revolutionary quality that made it ideal for the boys to perform on *Our World*. George Martin was growing increasingly anxious that everything should be ready on schedule, as he knew the programme's producers were looking to him to co-ordinate all the musical details with the Beatles. It was his professionalism, not the group's reputation, that was on the line as far as the BBC was concerned. By hook or by crook, he had to deliver!

The prestigious satellite broadcast was set for Sunday June 25th 1967. On the night of June 14th, at around 10 o'clock, the boys went to work on 'All You Need Is Love' – not at the famous Abbey Road, but behind locked doors in the privacy of Olympic Sound Studios in Barnes, south-west

Paul demonstrating how he wanted the trombone part played on the song.

London. The first task George set them was to get the basic rhythm track on tape. This took over four hours, and during the night Paul played double bass, John moved onto harpsichord, George (Harrison) tried out a violin part that George (Martin) quickly deleted, and Ringo played drums. More than 30 complete recordings of these backing tracks were made before George (Martin) was satisfied. One was selected and five nights later, this time at EMI's studios, the boys added vocals.

George Martin was taking no chances. If the Beatles were not in top form on the day of the televison broadcast, he had back-up tapes to help out. He told the Beatles that he would have a four-track tape machine standing by in the studio. He said: "When we go on the air, I'll play you the rhythm track, which you'll pretend to be playing. But your voices and the orchestra will really be live, and we'll mix the whole thing together and transmit it to the

waiting world like that." Before a full orchestra was brought into Abbey Road, the unfinished recording was given to Derek Burrell-Davis on an acetate and he conveyed his approval to George Martin. Then, with only 48 hours to go, more than a dozen musicians and their musical director came to Abbey Road to add an expansive orchestral backing to the recording.

At this stage, although the Beatles and those who worked with them were fully prepared for an announcement that 'All You Need Is Love' would become the next Parlophone single to be released by the group, this remained unpublicised until the last minute. The BBC was against the use of *Our World* as a vehicle to plug a new record on such a grand global scale. As far as they were concerned, the priority was to present a specially written number, prepared and produced for the show. There is a difference of opinion over the origin of the recording's ending, which featured snatches of other tunes played over and over. George Martin wrote in his book, *All You Need Is Love*: "I

did a score for the song, a fairly arbitrary arrangement since it was at such short notice. When it came to the end of their fade-away as the song closed, I asked them: 'How do you want to get out of it?', and they said, 'Write absolutely anything you like, George, put together any tunes you fancy, and just play it out like that.' The mixture I came up with was culled from the Marseillaise, a Bach two-part inventio, 'Greensleeves' and a little lick from 'In The Mood'. I wove them all together at slightly different tempos so that they still worked as separate entities."

Paul's version was that the Beatles thought up not only the idea of putting in the French national anthem at the beginning (to stress from the outset the international theme of the song and the entire project) but also the bits at the end. Paul said: "We said to George, there's the end, we want it to go on and on. We thought of all the great cliches because they're a bit random. Actually, what he (George) wrote was more disjointed, so when we put all the bits together we asked if

his back-up tapes, co-ordinating the audio output from Studio One to the BBC mobile control unit outside the building. The single was issued two weeks later and, in July, it went to the top of the charts on both sides of the Atlantic. Ironically, after several weeks at No. 1 in Britain, it was knocked from the top spot by Scott McKenzie's flower-power anthem, 'San Francisco'. There was one small hiccup over copyright concerning the end of 'All You Need Is Love' – a sting in the tail as George Martin called it. He wrote later: "I had chosen the tunes (for the bits at the end) in the belief that they were all out of copyright. It turned out that although 'In The Mood' was out of copyright, the Glenn Miller arrangement of it was not." As a result, EMI were asked by its owners for a royalty and had to settle with the publishers. Nearly 40 years on, when the words of other pop hits from the brief flower power-era sound amusingly dated, 'All You Need Is Love' lives on as a timeless piece of writing, a John Lennon anthem as memorable now as it was in 1967. (TB)

The scenes at Abbey Road studios as the Beatles rehearsed for their record-breaking TV appearance.

we could have 'Greensleeves' right on the top of that little Bach thing and on top of that we had the 'In The Mood' bit.

National broadcasters in 26 countries in five continents came together to take the live transmission of *Our World* and the eventual audience was put at between 400 and 500 million, more than twice the forecast. The appearance of the Beatles, with well-known jazz presenter Steve Race acting as the segment's anchorman at Abbey Road, was made to look like an outrageous Swinging Sixties London party, with a host of the group's famous friends singing along with them in a streamer-strewn Studio One. They included Mick Jagger, Keith Richard, Keith Moon, Eric Clapton, Jane Asher, Pattie Boyd (Harrison), Marianne Faithfull, Graham Nash, Gary Leeds and Paul's brother, Mike McCartney. People danced the conga round the studio and roadie Mal Evans collected up the tea cups. Mike Vickers of Manfred Mann conducted the orchestra for George Martin, who stayed in the control room with

Magical Mystery Tour

Their road managers Mal and Neil reveal the background to the Beatles' TV film

Magical Mystery Tour marks the beginning of a very important new stage in the Beatles' career. For the first time they have created their own show for television. They have worked out the scenes, hired the cast, written the basic script, composed the songs and incidental soundtrack music, directed the actual shooting and edited the finished film. And, of course, they have taken part in the show, playing the parts of four *Magical Mystery Tour* coach passengers plus a number of other roles.

If everyone likes the show, and if the Beatles themselves are satisfied with the finished result, then it is pretty certain that they will make their next full-length cinema film the same way. That is one of the first major projects they will be discussing in the New Year. So if it all goes well, their long-delayed third motion picture will now be something really special.

At the start of 1967, the Beatles realised that there was no point in giving any more concerts, since they'd have to rely on using old and out-of-date material, that would not be representative of their current style. The obvious alternative to touring was to produce their own TV shows, which could be seen all over the world, in countries they had never visited for concert tours. So the decision to make television films dates back almost twelve months. Early in April, Mal Evans was with Paul in Denver, Colorado, for Jane's 21st birthday. During that trip, Paul thought of building a TV show around the idea of a coach tour. In Mal's diary for April 7 he wrote: "Getting quite excited about planning the television film. Idea going at the moment is to make it about some sort of Mystery Tour (Roll Up! Roll Up!). Paul is getting lots of ideas and we're jotting them down as we go." The same week, his diary had an entry reading: "Took charge of Hertz rented car. Drove Paul and Jane up into the Rockies for what I can only describe as a real Magical Mystery Trip." Flying home to London on Tuesday, April 11, Paul worked on the first words for a 'Magical Mystery Tour' song. On the plane he borrowed a pad of paper from the stewardess and drew a big circle, dividing it up

One of the surreal scenes dreamed up by the Beatles for their 1967 film.

into sections. The circle represented 60 minutes, and the sections were marked off into bits for songs and sketches. When we got home Paul used this sheet of paper to describe to the others what he had in mind. Lots of sections of the circle were left blank, but the others threw in extra ideas and, one by one, the blank sections were filled until the Beatles decided they had the makings of a 60-minute TV programme.

In The Bag O'Nails discotheque club one night towards the end of April, we were brought into the group's discussions on possible items for the 'Coach Show'. Basically it was agreed that the plan should be "all-inclusive, non-exclusive". This meant trying to fit something for everyone into the show, as wide a variety as possible.

We jump forward to the second half of August to find the next bit of *Magical Mystery Tour* activity. On Thursday August 24th, only a few days before he died, Brian Epstein had a long chat with John, Paul, George and Ringo and everybody talked about things to be done for the rest of the year. Brian was very enthusiastic about *Magical Mystery Tour* and wanted us to get going right away with filming the show. It goes without saying that Brian's death provoked much soul-searching amongst all of us. At first, the majority agreed that it would be best to take a good long break, accept the Maharishi's invitation to spend two or three months with him in India and shelve all other plans until afterwards. But, as the days went by, everyone began to realise that it made much more sense to go ahead with *Magical Mystery Tour* and then take a break after the production was completed.

On Friday September 1st, there was a general get-together at Paul's house. While everyone added ideas, Paul sat at his typewriter and with one over-worked finger put down a list headed 'Main Points'. Underneath he typed: "Coach Tour (Three Days) with people on board. Week beginning Sept 4. Cameraman, Sound, Cast, Driver. Hotels to be arranged for 2 nights. Magical Mystery Tour Emblem to be designed. Yellow coach to be hired (Sept 4 to Sept 9). Microphone system in coach. Must be good all-round vision. Tour staff – Driver, Courier, Hostess. Three staff uniforms required. Coach destination – Cornwall??? After coach - Shepperton Studios (One Week)." On another sheet he typed out a sequence of arrangements to be made: "Write outline script. Decide cast.

Paul dressed up in one of the magicians' costumes specially designed for the boys.

Engage cast. Decide when shooting starts. Sets for studios. Fix completion date." In fact, shooting could not start until Monday September 11th, a week later than Paul's proposed starting date. Even then we had one of the most hectic weeks of our lives, preparing everything in time! The coach tour took five days to film (in Devon and Cornwall) and it was far too late to book space at Shepperton Film Studios for the following seven days. So we hired a couple of disused aircraft hangars at West Malling RAF station just outside Maidstone in Kent. By September 11th, the Beatles had a big sheaf of papers filled with outline scripts to describe the scenes they wanted to film. In total there were 43 people on the big yellow and blue bus. This included a full technical crew (cameramen and soundmen).

The rest? Most of them were cast as 'ordinary passengers', a cross-section of types you'd find on any average Mystery Tour bus. We had an elderly couple, a mother and her little daughter named Nicola, a bunch of teenage girls (including Freda Kelly and three Fan Club Area Secretaries) and other assorted people. In addition we had the key characters, played by actors, actresses and

so forth. The part of the Courier went to Derek Royle, the Tour Hostess was played by Mandy Weet, Scottish comedian Ivor Cutler was a strange bloke who thought he was the Tour Courier, actress Jessie Robins was Ringo's Auntie Jessie, Maggie Wright was cast as Paul's friend 'Maggie, The Lovely Starlet', Little George Claydon was the Amateur Photographer and veteran music hall comic Nat Jackley was Happy Nat the Rubber Man. Who is missing? Well, Alf Manders, the bus driver, played himself, and so did Shirley Evans, who is a professional accordion player.

Originally the Beatles reckoned it wouldn't take more than a week or so to edit all the film and make up a 60-minute programme. In fact the job took more than six weeks. Each day you'd find two or more Beatles busy in a tiny editing room in Old Compton Street, Soho. The work began around ten in the morning and they very seldom knocked off before six or seven in the evening. The editing could have been left to other people, but the Beatles wanted to

get everything exactly the way it should be, and they knew it was well worth spending all that time looking at strips of films and joining up all the scenes. All told there must have been 20 or 30 hours of colour film to plough through!

Most evenings, after working all day on editing, the Beatles gathered at the EMI studios, to put together all the songs for the soundtrack. The big problem was how to present these recordings to the public. There was too much music to fit on an EP disc but not enough to fill a full-length 12-inch LP. At one stage the proposal was to use a 7-inch record at LP speed, rather like the special discs the Beatles have made for Fan Club distribution each Christmas. But there was a technical problem here, as George Martin advised us that there would be a loss of volume on a 7-inch LP record. It was not until the beginning of November that everything was solved. There would be a set of two EP records inside a special book, plus a single, 'Hello Goodbye'. (ME/NA)

ON THE BUS!
Two of the group's Fan Club secretaries report on their week on the Magical Mystery Tour

The Wednesday before the lads started to film *MMT*, I was up in Liverpool sorting through the latest mountain of mail from club members when Tony Barrow, the Press Officer at NEMS, telephoned me. He said the lads wanted to know if I'd like to join them on their special bus that was going off filming in Devon and Cornwall. Would I *like* to? *Like* was an understatement! It was a marvellous surprise. Tony said there were four bus seats reserved for Fan Club girls and we discussed how to fill the other three spaces. What a difficult job – 40,000 Beatle People on our membership lists and only three places to be filled! Eventually I decided to send out telegrams to Area Secretaries based not too far from London. The first three girls to telephone and say they could get the week off would be the three *MMT* passengers. Sylvia from Sussex, Barbara from Essex and Jeni from London were the lucky girls.

We all met up at 10.30am the following Monday in Allsop Place, just beside the London Planetarium. A man approached me on the pavement and said, "I'm sure I've seen your skull before"! That was an offbeat introduction to Scotsman Ivor Cutler, the comedian who had been booked to take part

in the show. We were all there on time, but the bus wasn't, as it was being decorated with colourful 'Mystery Tour' signs. So Paul and the rest of the cast filled in the spare hour drinking tea in a London Transport staff canteen and the hospitality was very welcome.

At last we got underway, with a crowd of press photographers watching our departure and then hurrying to their cars to follow. At Virginia Water, not too far from Weybridge, we picked up George, Ringo and John, which completed the party. Before we started to film, the boys moved people around and asked us to keep our new seats all the time so that whenever we happened to be in camera range we'd be in the same part of the

bus. What's more, we had to wear the same clothes all week, which created a hygiene problem as the days went by!

Paul came over to chat. "Have these for a slim figure like yours", he said, handing me a box of Maltesers! We stopped at a restaurant called the Pied Piper for lunch. The staff were overwhelmed to find such distinguished customers arriving unexpectedly, and gave the boys whatever they wanted very promptly. I sat at a table with Sylvia, Jeni and Barbara and we still hadn't got our orders when the lads were onto their second course. George looked over and asked why

(Left) One of Paul's disguises in the film.
(Below) Ringo with Ivor Cutler on the bus.

The Beatles in their full psychedelic garb. Note that John isn't wearing his glasses!

we were still waiting. Then he went straight into the kitchen and emerged again a moment later with my lunch. "The others are coming right away", he told the girls.

We filmed in all kinds of places: little wayside pubs, a chip shop in Taunton, and a tent in a field near Newquay. It really was a Mystery Tour. We didn't know where we were going from day to day. Eventually we spent three nights in Newquay instead of just the one that was planned, because the lads found such a wealth of locations in that area that there seemed no point in moving on. Sometimes the team would split up so that two lots of filming could be done at once. One day Paul and Ringo took us girls off with them to film bits of dialogue between Jessie Robins and Ivor Cutler. Meanwhile John and George stayed behind at the Atlantic Hotel, Newquay, to film with comedian Nat Jackley, who had this very funny sequence with a lot of girls around the hotel's outdoor pool. And I nearly forgot the day we lunched in Plymouth in a big restaurant just a few yards from the famous Hoe. More than forty of us poured into the place and took the staff by surprise. They thought they'd finished serving lunch for the day! During the meal John started singing "Freda Kelly is a Nelly" at the top of his voice. Paul added "And she has pimples on her knees!"

It was a marvellous week, one I wouldn't have missed for anything. To make it even better, all the people on the tour were good friends by the end of the week. The professional actors and actresses mixed in with all us 'amateur' passengers and we had a great time. I can't wait to see the finished television film, as I know it's going to be unlike anything ever seen on telly before!

Freda Kelly

I remember sitting alone in the coach on Monday thinking, "What have I let myself in for?". On the train coming into London that morning I'd been saying to myself, "I might even meet them". Little did I dream that I would finish up spending most of those five days with the Beatles, getting to know them well. People have asked me what they are really like. I reply that they are four very nice people, but just ordinary, like you and me. But I'm sure people don't believe me.

When Paul got out of his car in Allsop Place I just couldn't believe my eyes. I remember very clearly that the bus drove through pouring rain and that it stopped near Virginia Water to pick up the other Beatles. John clambered aboard and said "Hello happy everybody!", and I felt my pulse to see if it was still there. The next day, Freda, Jeni, Sylvia and I sat at a table next to John, Paul, George and Ringo for lunch in

Plymouth. I remember how rude people were, persistently bothering the four lads while they were trying to eat. On Wednesday morning in Newquay, Sylvia and I went for a walk while we were waiting for the coach to leave the hotel. In a sweet shop, one woman said something about the Beatles having left. Sylvia turned round and said: "They can't go without us!" The woman looked at her and must have thought, "Who the hell does she think she is!" On Thursday morning I decided to do a bit of local window shopping because it didn't look as though we'd be taking off for a while. When I got back to the bus, the Beatles and all the other forty passengers were waiting for me. "We nearly went without you, Barbara," said Paul as I climbed onto the coach. He gave me such a warm smile that it cheered me up tremendously.

Suddenly it was Friday. We all felt a big sinking feeling because it would soon be over, and we'd be back to reality. No more magic, no more mystery, no more dreamy Beatles. We all sang and drank beer from bottles as the bus rolled along towards London. Some of us tried to get the boys to sing their songs but they stuck to the old-timers. I had the experience of my life. It was a week I'll never forget. I'd like to thank Freda, the Beatles and everybody for a wonderful time. I'm just beginning to believe it really happened to me!

Barbara King

Victor Spinetti

An interview with the Beatles' favourite actor, who appeared in three of their films

Sprightly Victor Spinetti bounds into the restaurant, hand outstretched, sporting a black peaked cap that could have easily come from John Lennon's wardrobe circa 1965. Sitting next to him, you are instantly drawn to his eyes – those warm, slightly worried orbs that so memorably enhanced his role as the harassed TV director in *A Hard Day's Night*, all those years ago.

Grabbing a brief respite between shows at Eastbourne's Devonshire Park Theatre, Victor recounted some choice anecdotes about his association with the boys – a relationship that has now entered its fifth decade, and which he defines as "real love". They, in return, christened Victor "The man who makes the clouds disappear". Originally it was John and George (not known for their love of musicals) who spotted Spinetti in *Oh! What a Lovely War* during its West End run in 1963. Victor says the

pair collared him in his dressing room and hastily recruited him for their first movie: "When we met we talked as though we really knew each other. They'd seen the show and they wanted me in the film. George said, 'You've gotta be in all our films, because my mum fancies you!' " When the film was released in July 1964, Victor was appearing on stage on Broadway. "I was accessible and playing in New York at the same time that *A Hard Day's Night* was showing around the corner," he recalls. "I was the nearest person in the film that people could come and talk to. They really loved the Beatles. I loved them too, that's why I could understand it, and anything I could do to fulfil that love, or satisfy it a little, I would."

In fact, it wasn't unusual for gaggles of uncontrollable fans to regularly attend Victor's performances and bring the show to a halt with their screaming the moment he appeared on stage. As a result, a Beatles

'question-and-answer' session was hastily organised at the end of each performance to satisfy the insatiable desire for news of anything Beatles related, and to allow the shows to continue unimpeded. Given the boys' admiration for Victor, he was naturally asked back to appear in *Help!*, the band's second, glossy travelogue movie.

After the glorious spontaneity of *A Hard Day's Night*, there was a definite sense that a lot had changed when the production crew reconvened in the spring of 1965. "*Help!* didn't connect in the same way as their first film," Victor recalls. "There was far too much distance between the director, cast, and fans. It was all summed up by the first shot we did in the Bahamas. We came out into the ocean on a yacht because the fans were screaming at us on the shore, and the director had to come out on a pontoon to film us, shouting directions through a megaphone. Dick had become a genius, and a genius does a lot of thinking, and so there was a lot of silence. We met up and chatted whenever we could, but it was all very distant. Suddenly everyone was writing to me saying, 'get me this or get me that', even asking for some of George's hair or one of his cigarette stubs or candles from the birthday cake. It was unbelievable. There wasn't enough direct contact between the producers, the writers, the actors, the cast, and the Beatles."

At this point, the boys had started indulging heavily in their preferred relaxant, marijuana. According to Victor, in the scene in *Help!* where his Mad Professor attempts to remove Ringo's ring in a laboratory, you can see the boys are much the worse for wear after a heavy session. Luckily, their delinquency somehow escaped the eagle eye of the director. "They were stoned in that one scene in *Help!* and Dick didn't know," says Victor. "In fact, they were so stoned that they had to concentrate on me for the close-ups. They were just laughing and falling about. I was never involved in that. I didn't even smoke cigarettes at that point. I was super cool. I remember John giving me two joints, and saying: 'Smoke these one day when you grow up'!".

A Hard Day's Night: Victor Spinetti looks on as John Junkin and Ringo play cards.

Victor played a cameo role as a recruiting sergeant in Magical Mystery Tour.

Victor was especially keen to talk about his brief but fascinating time working on the band's audacious *Magical Mystery Tour*. The picture will undoubtedly enjoy a renaissance of sorts fairly soon, as a DVD release is currently being compiled by Apple, with Victor acting as commentator on some of the sequences. Contrary to the received wisdom that Paul had an overbearing presence on the entire production of the movie, it was John who recruited Victor to play the Sergeant Major from Hell in one of the cameo sequences. "John called and said 'You've gotta be in it'," Victor recalls. "They wanted me to be on the bus as the courier, but I couldn't do that because I was doing a show in London at night, so I couldn't join them. So John said: 'Why don't you do that thing that you do in the show *Oh What a Lovely War* – the drill sergeant's scene? Just come in and do that for us'. I said: 'Yeah okay', and John said: 'I'll send you what we've got of the script to have a look at, but you might as well do your own thing'. He wrote on the script as a joke: 'Got any uppers?'!"

Victor filmed all his scenes for the picture in just one day in September 1967 at a cavernous aerodrome in West Malling, Kent. There was an air of improvised immediacy on the set. John hastily recruited a stuffed cow that just happened to be lying around, so Victor's character could bellow at it. In contrast to the press speculation about the group's use of narcotics, Victor never witnessed anything of the sort on the set of *Magical Mystery Tour*. In fact, he was incredibly impressed with the professionalism the boys exuded. "John was directing

that day and Paul was acting. There was no public display of 'now let's get stoned and shoot the movie'. They kept regular hours and they did all the proper things. It was a straightforward job. I was very impressed by the way it was done. Strict, no nonsense, no hanging around, no waiting, except after lunch, when there was a pause for meditation when everyone had to lie down for a quarter of an hour".

Magical Mystery Tour was premiered for an unsuspecting nation caught between their turkey sandwiches and mince pies on Boxing Night 1967. The press were clearly just gagging for an opportunity to trash the boys, as Victor observes: "Everything they did before was amazing, they were loved – and then they began to do things like drop acid and freak out. I think they were expecting it. 'We're going to be kicked up the arse', they told me. Before then they were the 'Mop-Tops' and now they were having a voice of their own; they were speaking in many tongues." Once filming was completed, Victor had the impressive distinction of being one of the few outsiders who was invited to appear on a Beatles' recording session – in this case a cameo on the band's 1967 Christmas Fan Club recording. "John said, 'Come up to the studios when we're recording', and I said, 'I don't want to bother you', and he said, 'Vic, only the fucking bores turn up!'"

During the early part of 1968, the boys seriously considered attempting the mammoth task of adapting J.R.R. Tolkien's trilogy of fantasy novels, *The Lord Of The Rings*, to the screen. Reportedly, Patrick McGoohan, hot from his cult success with *The Prisoner*, was earmarked as director,

with Victor naturally incorporated in the boys' proposed plans. "They sent me all the Tolkien books. John said, 'Read these, Vic, we're going to do it. You're going to be Gandalf. It's all cast.' And then I read them and thought, 'Do I want to do this?' "

In the event, it didn't happen, but Victor did work with John on another project before the end of the 60s, when he collaborated on the stage version of John's literary works. Contrary to Peter Brown's assertion in his book *The Love You Make* that John handed the entire project over to Spinetti, the reality was that John attended many of the play's rehearsals during the summer of 1968 and appeared on BBC TV's *Release* programme to promote the show. He also had a rather special surprise waiting for Victor at the stage door on the show's opening night: "There was a great huge rubber elephant swaying at the door with a card around its neck reading: 'I'll never forget Victor Spinetti', says John Lennon'."

Victor always did his best to keep up with the boys individually after the Beatles split up and he spoke to John shortly before his death in 1980 (John informed Victor that he would be coming to Britain and would "see you at Christmas"). Paul also popped over to Victor's flat in Brighton recently and spent an emotional few hours discussing John, Linda and other friends who have passed on. Victor feels the presence of John's spirit guiding him whenever he gets involved in Beatles' projects. His place in the Beatles' history is assured as the only actor to appear in all the group's small canon of scripted films. He jokes that "Yoko played my part in *Let It Be*"! (SW)

India

Mal Evans reports on his trip with the Beatles to Maharishi's Academy of Meditation

For me the trip began early. On Wednesday, February 14th 1968, I picked up bundles of advance luggage from Weybridge and Esher – suitcases, guitars and trunks belonging to George and Pattie, her sister Jenny, and John and Cyn. Then I caught Qantas flight 754 for Delhi, leaving London at 3.30 in the afternoon. The idea was for me to arrive a day ahead so that I could organise transport at the other end from Delhi to Rishikesh. At London Airport I had to pay £195 19s. 6d. in excess baggage charges, so you can tell how much stuff I was taking out on behalf of the Lennons and Harrisons!

In Delhi, one of my first jobs was to buy George a new sitar. I knew where to go – the same shop George had been on his previous visits. The whole window was full of photographs of George – pictures of him with the shop-owner, showing the type of sitar he'd bought there last time. At 8.15am on Friday morning, George, John, Pattie, Cyn and Jenny flew in. There to meet them and say "Hello" was Mia Farrow. I'd already introduced myself to her back at the hotel and found out that her brother, Johnny, was due to fly in about the same time as the two Beatles.

The country is very flat between Delhi and Rishikesh, which is about 150 miles. We stopped at a Western-style hotel/restaurant situated in the middle of nowhere known as Polaris, where we had a lunch of egg and chips. There were very few Europeans there so we caused quite a stir! Our arrival in Rishikesh was perfect, with the Maharishi there to greet us with kind words and a most welcome cup of tea.

Maharishi's Academy of Transcendental Meditation is situated on a big flat ledge, like a giant shelf, 150 feet above the River Ganges. The views are wonderful. You look out over the river, across to the town of Rishikesh and the plains beyond. There are mountains on the other three sides and jungle all around. Colourful peacocks strut about, and you can see a monkey or two in

Maureen and Ringo lead the Beatles' party across the bridge to the Maharishi's camp.

every glance, staring down at you from almost every branch of the trees whenever you go outside.

Having heard a mixture of strange stories about the place, I think we all half-expected to find ourselves living in tents with cardboard boxes for seats and tables. So we had a very pleasant surprise when we saw the high standard of accommodation. We lived in one of six little cottages. It had been luxuriously done out. Each of our rooms was neatly furnished, with twin beds, new rugs on walls and floors, dressing-tables, shelves and cupboards, and a bathroom with toilet and shower facilities. The water supply broke down from time to time, but when there was water, we had a choice of hot or cold. And there wasn't a single creepy-crawly thing in sight!

Our days at the Maharishi's ashram began early. As a rule, John was first out of bed. He'd spend a while meditating and then I would accompany him to breakfast around seven o'clock. We would leave the little row of cottages, and walk down towards the Ganges, past the lecture hall and towards one of two dining halls. They're building a new swimming pool alongside the lecture building. We went past the kitchens on the edge of the Ganges and, if it wasn't too chilly, we'd usually eat in the uncovered dining hall – no roof, just huge glass walls. The alternative was a covered and fully heated hall to have meals in if the weather was cold. Breakfast would start with cornflakes, puffed wheat or porridge. The porridge was to be avoided because it tended to be a bit lumpy! To drink, there was fruit juice, tea and coffee. With it there was toast and marmalade or jam. Everything was made locally. I remember how odd it seemed to find jars and bottles with labels that looked identical in every detail to a top British brand, except for the maker's name, a local Indian company. After breakfast we'd meditate for as long as we wanted. There were no hard and fast rules, and everything was free and easy, with no schedule or timetable to stick to. Anyone who just wanted to sleep round the clock could do so!

For lunch and dinner we'd get soup and then a vegetarian main course, with plenty of tomato and lettuce salads, turnips, carrots, and rice and potatoes to accompany it. The vegetarian diet satisfied John and George, who gave up eating meat a long time ago. Although I'm fond of my meat I found the Maharishi's menu a pleasant change. When Ringo arrived later he found some of the curry dishes a bit hot, with too many spices. When I went into Delhi again, I collected a good supply of eggs so that we would have plenty of alternatives – fried, boiled or poached!

The second Beatles arrival, bringing Ringo, Maureen, Paul and Jane, drew a lot of press attention. Everyone was filmed as they came off the plane. Raghvendra, one of the Maharishi's disciples, and I placed garlands of red and yellow flowers around the necks of the newcomers, a traditional token of greeting and welcome. When he got the chance Ringo told me he needed a doctor. It wasn't anything serious but his injections were giving him trouble, his arm was swollen and painful and he thought it best to see if any treatment was required. Our driver lost his way and led us to a dead-end in the middle of a field. The press came to our rescue – a whole stream of cars had been following us! In the end we accepted directions from some helpful reporters and found a hospital. The doctor assured Ringo all would be well without treatment, and it was.

He felt fine again after his first night's sleep in Rishikesh. Birthday celebrations in Rishikesh were made into big ceremonial occasions. There were three which involved the Beatles during their stay: George's 25th on 25th February, Pattie's 23rd on 17th March and a 21st party for a bloke named Mike. I arranged a special cake for George, with white icing and pink flowers and an Indian greeting, "Jai Guru Deva", written in gold letters. Then I bought a bundle of fireworks and some streamers and balloons. Earlier I'd bought an Indian banjo as a gift to George.

The weather was good on the day so we had an outdoor party. Pattie wore a lovely yellow sari for the occasion. We put decorations in the trees and everyone put garlands of flowers round George's neck, till he disappeared beneath a colourful and flowery mountain of garlands before we'd finished! Then there was the special surprise of the evening. At the suggestion of the others, I'd organised a band of local Indian musicians and a singer to perform at the party. The Maharishi made a nice little speech about George, presented his gift and then we got down to letting off the fireworks and listen-

A group photo in Rishikesh: (left to right) Pattie Harrison, John, Mike Love, the Maharishi Mahesh Yogi, George, actress Mia Farrow, Donovan, Paul, Jane Asher and Cynthia Lennon.

ing to the music. Pattie's birthday was just as much of a fun occasion. Everyone was only too willing to join in a bit of a party. Pattie had another huge cake with nine or ten candles. Again there were dozens of beautiful garlands of red and orange flowers for everybody and Pattie played a new dilruba, her favourite instrument these days.

The third party was a key-of-the-door affair for this Lancashire boy named Mike, who had hitchhiked to India with a mate named Paul. They were on their way to Australia but had stopped off at Rishikesh, got themselves initiated as meditating students of the academy and were paying for their keep by working in Maharishi's kitchens! Mike and Paul had been fans of the Beatles for years, having attended a 1962 ballroom appearance in Southport.

Beach Boys singer Mike Love joined the Beatles at the Maharishi's camp.

but they declined because George had agreed to appear in a semi-documentary film in Madras with his friend Ravi Shankar, and John and Cyn were eager to get back home!

We had a lot of good times to look back on. Quite apart from the serious side of the meditation, there had been plenty of opportunity for sightseeing. On sunny afternoons we strolled along the pebble-covered banks of the Ganges, taking roll upon roll of film as we walked. The little town of Rishikesh was fascinating. Most of the buildings were covered with holy sayings from the Gita (the Indian bible). There was a bridge across the Ganges with a big notice saying "No Camels or Elephants"! One night we all went in torchlight procession down to the river and into a couple of boats. On the way back, we cut the boat's engines and just drifted silently under a clear, starry sky. It was magnificent. Then Mike Love got out a set of pipes, Paul fetched his guitar, and everyone had a sing-song before we got back to Rishikesh.

I imagine most of you are wondering what difference those weeks in India have made to the Beatles, both as a group and as individual people. The change, the rest and the entirely different atmosphere did everyone concerned a lot of good. I know the fellows felt really great afterwards. Meditation has helped them to look at their own lives in a clearer way, to see what is important and what is not, to sort out their problems and to decide what things are worth worrying over. In a nutshell, it has helped them to be calmer, more tolerant people and it has cleared their mind for new work. It's left their heads open for a rush of fresh ideas which they'll make use of, not only for recording and other Beatles group activity, but for working out the future of their Apple companies.

Now the Beatles are ready to get going on more recordings and to start on their much-delayed film. Although they are keeping up their meditation in the privacy of their homes, they believe that they've given enough time to learning the Maharishi's philosophy for the time being. Right now they are concentrating on catching up with Beatles projects, and they're all in a great frame of mind, and raring to go!   (ME)

After the first couple of weeks the long flat roof above the main lecture hall was used as a sun balcony where we would all gather for music sessions after our meditation periods were over. The Beatles had their guitars, George used his sitar and folk like Mike Love and Donovan would join in. In no time, the fellows were singing away together and new tunes were being made up all the time! In fact, John wrote fifteen new songs while he was at Rishikesh, and Paul came up with a similar number. George also penned several new things, and even Ringo wrote a new song. When the Beatles started their new series of recording sessions, it was this material that they began to put on tape for their new LP – "son of *Sgt. Pepper*", as John put it!

The Maharishi's students gradually built up their periods of meditation, with the Maharishi explaining at discussion sessions what our various experiences meant and how we might progress from there to the next stage of the course. John and George were meditating for anything up to eight or nine hours each day. The record for the course was a non-stop 42 hours! Then, as the course drew towards its end, the idea was to decrease the length of time spent in deep meditation so that everyone would come out of India ready to return to normal life at home. Ringo and then Paul left for home first, followed at Easter by John and George. They were invited to spend an extra fortnight with the Maharishi on a houseboat,

Apple

The Beatles' corporation began with great expectations, but it soon began to decay

In the late Sixties, the Beatles launched their own group of companies, under the collective title of Apple Corps. Besides the obvious Apple Records division, there was also Apple Films, Apple Tailoring, Apple Retail, Apple Electronics, Apple Music and much more besides. Financially, it made good sense for the Beatles to pour money into a fresh business venture in 1967. Their accountants were quite rightly telling them that millions of pounds would go to the Treasury in taxation payments unless a hefty chunk of the group's accumulated fortune was spent very soon on new forms of investment.

The boys played down the money angle. As John Lennon said, "The aim of the company isn't a stack of gold teeth in the bank. We've done that bit." On an artistic and creative level, the Beatles were very attracted to the idea of opening up their own recording facilities, not only for their own personal use but also to provide an opportunity to develop young musical talent. They were very aware of their own good fortune in having been discovered by Brian Epstein six years earlier, which gave them the chance to prove themselves beyond the boundaries of Merseyside, and they were keen to offer similar chances to other artists. They liked the thought of producing an increasing number of records with new bands and singers. Lennon and McCartney saw such activities as an additional outlet for their songs. Paul put it like this: "We want to help other people, but without doing it like charity and without seeming to be stuck-up patrons of the Arts. We always had to go to the Big Man on our knees, touch our forelocks and plead for the freedom to try new things for ourselves. We don't want people to say 'Yes Sir, No Sir'. Apple is not our ego trip."

George said he knew several bands that deserved a break, and Apple could give them a decent start. Privately, it was also quite clear that George reckoned he might claim an increasing share of the songwriting cake for himself if he gave original Harrison compositions to unknown or rising recording acts under his wing. By taking them into the studios himself and acting as both songwriter and record producer, George could maintain total control over the final product,

an artistic luxury the Beatles had seldom afforded him in the past. Financial and musical considerations were not the only fundamental factors that contributed to the creation of Apple. The Beatles acted as a magnet for all sorts of weird characters, inventors, boffins and designers looking for sponsors with cash to hand out. Unfortunately, some of these hangers-on were simply poseurs, people seeking a place in the limelight where the money was easy and the publicity plentiful.

As a result of their 'open door' policy to anyone who sounded as if he had a novel idea, the Beatles found themselves being conned by unscrupulous and untalented folk, who gained their patronage and robbed them of major sums of money. Paul had said very openly: "If you come to see me at Apple and tell me you have a dream, I'll give you some money to send you off to do it, do whatever it is that's in your dream, We've already bought our dreams. We want to share that possibility through Apple." How did Brian Epstein fit into all this? I remember him bringing up Apple with me at one of the regular meetings he and I had to discuss upcoming press and publicity plans not only for the Beatles, but also for other NEMS artists and for 'Eppy' personally. I can't put a precise date on it, but I know he mentioned Apple long before any of the

The famous design painted by the Fool on the side of the Apple shop in Baker Street.

Beatles had started to discuss the idea with outsiders. Brian's initial expectation was that he would be directly involved with Apple at the highest level. But I recall he climbed down a bit in our later conversations, saying he'd still be a part of Apple's executive structure but he might not have a boardroom vote. He told me he wanted the Beatles to run things for themselves without his intervention, but he'd be there to give advice.

Within days of his death, the Beatles took their first concrete step towards the launch of an Apple boutique in London. They were shocked and saddened by the loss of their friend and adviser, but they needed to show the business world that they were firmly in control of their financial operations. They handed over £100,000 to Simon and Marijke, a couple from Amsterdam, who were part of an outrageous design group calling themselves the Fool. They would use the cash to put together a fine collection of colourful clothes and fashion accessories, all reflecting the very latest trends in psychedelic gear for London's so-called Beautiful People. Premises in Baker Street, on the corner of Paddington Street, were acquired and painted on the outside with enormous mural designs. George Harrison's very pretty sister-in-law, Jenny Boyd, was brought in to make sure the shop would be just right for the high-spending 'in-crowd'. John fetched in his old mate, Pete Shotton, who had supermarket management experience. Shotton wrote later: "I tried to persuade John that Apple, and the boutique in particular, was in desperate need of competent, trained professionals. There's a lot more to running a shop than shoving a jacket on a hanger and taking the money."

Alexis 'Magic Alex' Mardas was the next beneficiary, with the creation of Apple Electronics in October 1967. The young Greek boffin was handed sufficient capital to set up an expensive research laboratory, so he could invent and manufacture a series of fantastic new gadgets and 'executive toys', and design recording studio equipment for the Beatles' own future use. By now, the Beatles were getting really carried away with the far-flung possibilities of Apple. There was talk of a mail order men's tailoring business, Apple Limousines, Apple Cinemas and a string of shops selling nothing but greetings cards (a new idea at the time). There might even be an Apple School, where the groovy kids of London's Most Beautiful People could be educated in an atmosphere of revolutionary new enlightenment! Like the West End stores and chain of provincial boutiques, these plans were shelved indefinitely. But the Baker Street shop was open in time to catch the pre-Christmas trade, and a barrage of publicity

helped to pull in the crowds when John and George performed the official ceremony at a lavish opening reception in the first week of December.

Although many of the boys' plans seemed extravagant and over-ambitious, the establishment of an Apple music publishing firm and an Apple Films outfit made relative sense. A man from the motor trade, George's close pal Terry Doran, was handed responsibility for heading up the publishing business. Doran had been a partner of Brian Epstein in a firm called Brydor Cars. Tony Bramwell, once an office boy at NEMS, was named as the first boss of Apple Films. It

was only a matter of time before Apple Records would be in position alongside the rest. Meanwhile, the Beatles took their pick of other personal mates and former employees of NEMS Enterprises to provide their Apple personnel. These ranged from NEMS general manager Alistair Taylor to telephone switchboard supervisor Laurie McCaffrey, both associated with the Four Mop Tops since early Liverpool days. Apple's top executives included the group's former roadie, Neil Aspinall; ex-journalist and PR man Derek Taylor, who was brought home from

John in front of their Apple Tailoring shop in 1968.

George and John with a heavily disguised John Crittle, the boss of Apple Tailoring.

America's West Coast to take charge of the Press Office and run Apple Publicity Limited; and Peter Brown, once a Liverpool record assistant and, more recently, Brian Epstein's closest aide at NEMS.

In the earliest weeks of 1968 various administrative and investment companies which existed to hold and move around the Beatles' income underwent name changes which allied them directly to Apple. On January 22, new Apple Corps headquarters opened formally for business at 94 Wigmore Street, a stone's throw away from EMI Records in Manchester Square. The Managing Director was Neil Aspinall, who remains the key figure at Apple to this day. On the board of directors were Peter Brown and accountant Harry Pinsker, who had acted for Brian Epstein and a number of NEMS stars in the past. Paul was pleased to be able to bring in Jane Asher's brother, Peter, as recording manager at Apple Records. Several other specialists were recruited, including Dennis O'Dell to head up the Apple Films operation, and American record executive Ron Kass to be Peter Asher's boss.

Apple's flagship effort, the Baker Street boutique, was the first division of the Beatles' amazing new business empire to fail. After the initial yuletide rush, it didn't attract regular customers in sufficient numbers to cover huge overheads or offset large-scale thieving. But this was viewed as only a minor mistake by the Beatles, who refused to get upset about the failure. By now they were even prepared to play the game of being office workers with a bit of a daily business routine. They rose early – well, relatively early for Mop Tops – and attended executive meetings of all Apple's various divisions. "Everything is possible", Paul said at the time. "Why not Apple motorbikes, Apple discotheques and Apple electric shavers?" And he wouldn't even draw the line at Apple washing-up liquid!

Naturally enough, however, the music side of Apple remained closest to the hearts of all four individual Beatles. George began to take specific steps to expand his record production interests, working with his old Liverpool friend Jackie Lomax, while Alistair Taylor posed for photographs used in press adverts to seek demo tapes from unknown writers and bands. Meanwhile, Paul signed up Mary Hopkin, a shy little 18-year-old Welsh songstress he'd seen on telly in Hughie Green's *Opportunity Knocks* show. By the time the spring blossoms were coming out, 1968 looked like being a glorious year for all concerned.

But the rest of the year proved to be a particularly stormy period in the Beatles' lives, both personally and professionally. In July, Jane Asher publicised the end of her long love affair with Paul. In August, Cynthia Lennon sued John for divorce. In the autumn, George – having discovered that his deal with Northern Songs was not about to be renewed – was forced to set up a music publishing company of his own. In November, Yoko Ono lost John's baby by miscarriage. In December, George filled all the unoccupied rooms at Apple HQ in Savile Row with visiting Hell's Angels from California, who dossed down and settled in for a long spell of yuletide hospitality at the Beatles' (substantial) expense.

Of course, the Apple era coincided with the slow disintegration of the Beatles, which ended in the decision of John to leave the group at the end of 1969, and Paul (the first to make the split public) to follow the next spring. The boys had spent the best part of a decade living in each other's pockets, spending a remarkable amount of time together. With no touring commitments, and plenty of attractive solo projects on the horizon, it is not surprising that the idea of a total split began to seem attractive. The problems they were encountering at Apple only added to the tension.

After a power struggle between competing sets of lawyers, the American entrepreneur Allen Klein, who had made his fortune fixing huge new deals for top rock stars, was brought in by John to try and put Apple right. Klein promised to clear out the 'parasites' who he thought were at the heart of the company's problems, and to restore Apple's profitability overnight. His method was to fire most of Apple's staff, including some utterly loyal employees who had served the Beatles well over the years. Some deserved to go; others went because Klein didn't bother to sort out the goodies from the baddies. Klein's actions certainly cut down on Apple's costs, but they also marked the end of the Apple dream. The company reverted back to what it should have been in the first place, a record label for the Beatles and their pet projects. And in that form it was very successful. Apple can't really take credit for the huge sales of the Beatles' records during this period, both as a group and as four solo artists, because John, Paul, George and Ringo would have been successful on any label in the late Sixties. But Apple did certainly produce a series of big worldwide hits for other artists as well.

Remarkably, Neil Aspinall still runs Apple today, more than 37 years after the company was launched, from behind the closed doors of a small London office. His functions include looking after every part of the

Beatles' empire, and liaising regularly with its four directors: Paul, Ringo, Yoko (on behalf of John's estate) and Olivia (who now acts in lieu of George). His job could easily last a lifetime – or longer! One of Neil's ongoing tasks is to buy back bits of the Beatles' heritage, the truly unique pieces of memorabilia that have passed into the hands

of third parties and that regularly crop up at auctions around the world. He also tackles the complex legal problems raised by the tremendous success of the Beatles, and the vast amount of money involved in every aspect of their career. Neil remains an absolutely vital part of the Beatles' team after forty years. (TB)

The launch of Apple Tailoring seemed to predict a great future for the company.

Hey Jude and Revolution

The first single on the Apple label in 1968 was a landmark in their career

George and Paul during the very tense recording session for 'Revolution'.

recording. It's not exactly a protest song but John's lyrics try to take a look at the world's problems and put some of them over in very, very simplified form. It's a hopeful sort of song with a reassuring chorus line saying that everything's going to be all right.

Three further versions of 'Revolution' were recorded before the Beatles were thoroughly happy with the finished production. Work was started on Version Number Three on Tuesday, July 9. That night Ringo arrived at EMI earlier than the others. So he dropped in on a session in one of the other studios and did a bit of handclapping on a record Solomon King was making! As usual the first job was to lay down on tape the backing tracks. Nothing extraordinary was used in the way of instrumentation, just the normal line-up of three guitars and drums. Then, when there was a break, Paul, Ringo and I trotted off to a nearby pub for toasted cheese sandwiches. Before the end of the month there were four completed variations of 'Revolution' to choose from, and it's the fourth and final one which is set to go onto the B-side of their next single.   (ME)

MAKING HEY JUDE

By the end of July, a total of seven recordings had been completed for the next Beatles LP. In addition the boys had been getting pretty involved with some of the other Apple singles. George had been supervising the recording of Jackie Lomax's 'Sour Milk Sea'. Paul had been producing the Mary Hopkin single, 'Those Were The Days'. And there had been the first sessions with yet another Apple discovery, James Taylor. All this work had been done at Trident Studios, in Wardour Street, which they had never used before. The basement studio there is just great – large enough to give plenty of scope, but small enough to be comfortable and informal.

On Friday, July 26, John and Paul spent most of the day at Paul's house putting the final touches to their latest composition, 'Hey Jude'. The following Monday evening at EMI they began to rehearse it with

MAKING REVOLUTION

The Beatles will be in the recording studios more or less continuously from now until the middle of August, working on the new songs written by John and Paul while they were in India between February and April. The title that took up most of the time throughout the first week of recording was 'Revolution', something John wrote in India. The Beatles have changed their habits a bit as far as the timing of sessions is concerned. Until now they have preferred night-long sessions beginning around eight in the evening. But 'Revolution' was started very promptly at two-thirty in the afternoon, and each day's sessions after that took the form of a three-hour afternoon stint and then a second long spell in the studio from half-

seven until well after midnight. There were visitors a-plenty, with Lulu, Davy Jones and Twiggy amongst the celebrity droppers-in.

'Revolution' was more than ten minutes long in its original form, though it's unfinished as I write. It might be issued as the Beatles' longest-ever track, but it depends what the boys decide to add to the existing tape. So far they have guitars, drums and Paul's organ and piano playing. As it stands, the arrangement drags a bit in the middle. There are two alternatives: either the whole middle chunk will be scrapped and the finished version of 'Revolution' you hear will be four or five minutes shorter; or John and Paul will get together with George Martin to think up extra ideas to add to the centre part of the

George and Ringo. The next night we had a load of film people in to take movies of the 'Hey Jude' session at EMI for a 50-minute feature about Britain's national music scene. Then, on the Wednesday, we moved from EMI to Trident, which is where the rest of the work was done on 'Hey Jude'. In fact a fresh version of the number was started from scratch with George on electric guitar, Paul on piano and Ringo playing the tambourine. On top of the first backing tracks, Paul added his solo vocal and then the others joined him to put on the harmony stuff.

On Thursday, August 1, we imported a 40-piece orchestra, the largest group of musicians we'd used since the Beatles did 'A Day In The Life' for *Sgt. Pepper* well over a year ago. 'Hey Jude' starts out as a plaintive ballad with Paul's voice well up in front of a fairly simple backing. Then the arrangement begins to build up towards an exciting climax. That's where the big orchestra came in. Mostly they just held single notes for long periods to underline and emphasise the

whole atmosphere of the recording. Towards the end of the evening, we decided we'd make double use of the 40 musicians by asking them if they'd like to do a bit of singing and clap their hands. They were quite pleased to oblige, and the entire orchestra stood up, clapped and sang their parts under Paul's close supervision!

So 'Hey Jude' was finished that night at the end of a highly spectacular session. The next day we went back to Trident to do the final remix job on the tapes and by Friday afternoon we had the first test discs, or acetates as they are called, back at the Apple offices for everyone to hear. I can't go into great detail about most of the other July and August sessions just yet because they were all for the next LP and the titles are still 'hush-hush' until a bit nearer the release date. All I can say is that there's some terrific material on tape, more than half the LP is ready and the rest of the tracks are being done this month. Ringo has recorded two titles, one he wrote himself and another that

Soon after this shot was taken, the Beatles ordered the studio to be cleared of guests.

John and Paul did for him, which has a 30-piece orchestra, a choir and even a harp on it! One of the new numbers Paul wrote turned into a 24-minute recording, a right old jam session, with John playing bass guitar just for a change. It's handy having Paul's house so near the EMI studios. Sometimes if we're feeling a bit peckish by midnight or thereabouts, we troop round to his place for a nosh break. George is getting great at cooking fry-up suppers and his speciality in the kitchen line is a hearty blend of eggs, bacon, tomatoes and fried bread, which stimulates everyone in readiness for the rest of the night's recording!   (ME)

HOW PAUL UPSTAGED MICK JAGGER TO LAUNCH HEY JUDE

The Vesuvio Club in London's Tottenham Court Road was never destined to become one of the Beatles' regular late-night haunts, but a bunch of friends and I went along to

Paul was the only Beatle to keep his cool during the 'Revolution' session.

the star-studded opening party one evening early in August 1968. Located just north of Oxford Street and a few doors down from Tottenham Court Road police station, this fragrantly smoke-filled basement club was co-owned by Mick Jagger, fellow Rolling Stone Keith Richards and the band's entrepreneurial assistant, Spaniard Tony Sanchez, who managed the place. On opening night they welcomed many famous faces, including Beatles John and Paul. Mick flew home from California especially for the occasion using the club's inaugural bash to mark his 25th birthday. He also had an extra motive for making sure he made it to the Vesuvio that night. He had brought with him one of the first advance pressings of *Beggar's Banquet*, the long-awaited and lavishly produced new album which the Stones looked upon as a "make or break" affair so far as their musical future was concerned.

However, to Mick's surprise and shock, he wasn't the only one ready to show off some new music that night. Paul had brought along a hastily pressed version of the brand-new single by the Beatles, pairing up 'Hey Jude' and 'Revolution'. Nobody outside the Beatles' small inner circle had heard 'Hey Jude' until Paul passed it to Tony Sanchez inviting him to play it for the celebrity crowd saying "See what you think of it, Tony, it's our new one". When John heard the song ringing round the club, he was astonished. He turned to a group of us and shouted angrily through the thick haze of smoke and above the barrage of sound: "We shouldn't be playing this in public, it's not ready for outsiders to hear!"

The two Beatles had spent many hours during the past week at Paul's house in Cavendish Avenue, St John's Wood, discussing what to do about the extraordinary length of 'Hey Jude', which ran for over seven minutes, almost three times longer than the average single of the day. Only hours before going to the Vesuvio, they had left the group's producer, George Martin, at Abbey Road, where he was remixing 'Hey Jude'. John was not certain that the acetate Paul had brought away with him from the EMI studios represented the final version. At the time, I remember feeling that John's abrasive reaction was not because Paul had

organised this unexpected and premature premiere for the track without telling anyone, but because he was pushing his own song in preference to John's 'Revolution'! I had watched an increasingly hostile, behind-the-scenes power struggle being waged between Lennon and McCartney, as each one in turn tried hard to convince George Martin that his song should be the A-side – the one given top priority when the time came to plug the new release on radio and television. It was very clear to all of us that 'Hey Jude' was by far the more commercial side, but as a compromise, the Beatles made promotional films for both 'Hey Jude' and 'Revolution'. This worked out very well and gained a whole lot of television exposure for both songs, particularly on provincial programmes around the regions.

Under the circumstances, I thought Mick and the Stones remained remarkably calm about having the debut of *Beggar's Banquet* all but overshadowed by 'Hey Jude'. It virtually brought the house down and had to be played over and over again. Eventually, possibly prompted by the sight of John's stony face, Paul asked Sanchez to turn the disc over and give 'Revolution' a spin. At a party hosted and paid for by the Stones in their own club, Paul had managed to steal the spotlight and turn it on to the Beatles. It was a brilliant and wicked piece of promotional one-upmanship, by the one member of the Fab Four with an outstanding flair for PR. Tony Sanchez confirmed afterwards that when he stuck the record on the sound system at Paul's request, "the slow thundering build-up of 'Hey Jude' shook the club". When it was over, he "noticed that Mick looked peeved" because "the Beatles had upstaged him". Paul remembers a benign Mick coming up to him and without a hint of jealousy or irritation saying: "That's something else, innit?" So many influential people from the London music scene were totally impressed by the debut of 'Hey Jude' at the Vesuvio, that word spread through the business like wild fire. The unanimous verdict was: "It's another instant world-beater".

Paul created 'Hey Jude' as a solo project. He says he thought it up as he drove out to Surrey to visit Cynthia at the Lennon family home. Cynthia was touched by Paul's concern and even more moved by his thoughtfulness when he handed her a single red rose and told her about the new ballad he had come up with, dedicated to Julian. She said: "I will never forget Paul's gesture. It made me feel important and loved, as opposed to

discarded and obsolete." Paul and Cynthia, and five-year-old Julian, nicknamed Jules, had been very good friends "for a million years", and he wanted to show them that the end of her marriage to John didn't change anything for him. As he drove, Paul came up with: "Hey Jules, don't make it bad, take a sad song and make it better". Paul told biographer Barry Miles: "I knew it was not going to be easy for him. I always feel sorry for kids in divorces. I relate to their little brains spinning round in confusion, going 'Did I do this? Was it me?' Guilt is such a terrible thing and I know it affects a lot of people. That was the reason I went there."

The first people to hear 'Hey Jude' were Cynthia and Julian. Back in London after the trip, Paul started to hone the tune and complete the lyrics in his music room at Cavendish Avenue. At one point John and Yoko came up behind him just as he was doing the line: "The movement you need is on your shoulder." Embarrassed, because he expected John to pick holes in the wording, Paul said hastily that he was going to change this bit because "it sounded like a parrot or something". He said to John: "I'll fix that later." "You won't, you know!", John said firmly. "That's the best bit of the song, it's the best line in it! Leave it in. I know what it means." Whether this remark was sincere or cloaked in typically Lennonesque sarcasm isn't clear but this was the total extent of the Lennon & McCartney collaboration on the song!

When I played one of the first test pressings of 'Hey Jude' in my office a few days later, a colleague declared that the grand final section must be part of an entirely separate song, which Paul had stuck on the end of 'Jude' as an after-thought. This was also Mick Jagger's first reaction at the Vesuvio, when he said to Paul: "It sounds like two songs." Paul explained that it wasn't intended to go on quite that long at the end but everybody was having such a fun time in the studio that he let it run on.

John admitted in one of his more generous moments that in his opinion 'Hey Jude' was the finest song Paul had ever done and also one of the best recordings the Beatles had ever produced. But there was growing tension and a fair amount of in-fighting among the Fab Four during their prolonged all-night studio sessions. There were petty but stressful arguments over trivial points and more serious quarrelling over how some songs should be interpreted. Paul's way of establishing his superior strength at sessions was to openly force through little points of musical policy. During the making of 'Hey Jude', this attitude led to some unpleasantness between Paul and George, when the pair disagreed over where and how often George should come in with repetitive guitar phrases each time Paul sang the title. George didn't take Paul's emphatic direction too well, as he resented the way Paul sat down to show him how his guitar licks should sound. Paul confessed afterwards that George "was pretty offended" by his approach, adding: "It was bossy of me, but it was also ballsy, because I could have bowed to the pressure".

In later years, I was surprised to see John putting a completely different spin on 'Hey Jude', claiming that in his view it wasn't simply about Julian, but had a deeper secondary message. John said: "If you think about it, Yoko's just come into the picture. When Paul first played and sang it for me, I heard 'Hey Jude' as a song to me about Yoko and me, our relationship and also about my songwriting partnership with Paul in the Beatles. He's saying 'Hey John, go out and get her (Yoko)' – subconsciously he was saying, 'Go ahead, leave me'. The angel in him was saying 'Bless you'. The devil in him didn't like it at all, because he didn't want to lose his partner in the group. I thought of it as having that double meaning if you read between the lines."

I often wonder why John waited so long to bring forward this interpretation of Paul's lyrics. Why didn't he talk to any of us about it at the time it was released? Neither I, nor any of my former colleagues from those days at Apple or NEMS, remember him saying anything about 'Hey Jude', other than to praise it as one of the group's best-ever singles – which indeed it was. (TB)

1968

MAGICAL MYSTERY TOUR

Perhaps you have to be a Beatles' addict to appreciate everything the boys do, but all the attacks on their *Magical Mystery Tour* seem to go right over the top. The really silly thing was the way EVERYTHING about the show was torn to pieces. And yet only a couple of weeks later the *MMT* EP shot to the top of the charts with sales zooming up towards the million mark in this country alone. No one is trying to say that the Beatles' very first production was a complete masterpiece – considering that the boys did everything themselves, it would have been amazing if it had been – but as the EP sales have shown, it wasn't ALL bad either. We've had loads of letters about the television show and I am very happy to say that 99% of you said that you disagreed with the critics.
(Johnny Dean's editorial, January 1968)

SINGING FANS JOIN BEATLES

The recording session for 'Across The Universe' was well underway when John and Paul decided at the last moment that they needed girls to sing a particularly high falsetto section of the song. So Paul walked out and started talking to the crowd of Beatle people outside the recording studio gates. Eventually, he invited two girls to come in for a try-out take: Lizzie Bravo of London NW6, and Gayleen Pease of London N16. The Beatles were delighted with the girls' voices and so Lizzie and Gayleen were suddenly transported from being Beatle fans to actually recording with them. Said Lizzie: "I still don't believe it happened!" Added Gayleen: "It was like a dream. The Beatles are so easy to get on with." And from producer George Martin: "Considering the girls had never done any recording before, I think they were really great." (February 1968)

LADY MADONNA

'Lady Madonna' is a classic example of perfect Beatle timing. It's no secret that the song is mainly Paul's creation and he obviously sensed that the mood was changing and that the record buyers wanted something tougher, simpler and wilder. He's certainly given it to them! But the great thing about the new Beatles' single is that it is not just a rehash of the old rock style. The sound is very original and Beatleistic. And no doubt hundreds of groups will be trying to develop it for their own use over the next few months!
(Johnny Dean's editorial, March 1968)

APPLE ADS

Strange adverts have been appearing in the music press recently, featuring a picture – and the solitary word 'Apple'. As you might have guessed, the ads have been placed by the Beatles' new company. As yet, the label has no artists or records to promote, so all they are trying to do is publicise their name. The first advert featured a laughing baby holding an apple. The second one was more cryptic, with what looked like a very worried Chinese mandarin sitting on a chair. What do they have to do with Apple Records? Only the Beatles know the answer! (March 1968)

PACKAGE TO INDIA

No sooner had Ringo arrived back from India than he parcelled up some emergency supplies to send to the three Beatles still there – not food rations, but a box of 16mm cine-film! (March 1968)

INDIA - LINKING IT TO THE WEST

Now the Beatles have crossed the previously almost impenetrable barrier between the backward East and the modern West and formed a link with the teeming millions of India. Just think, if all their new Indian fans could afford to buy each new Beatles' single, their world sales would probably double

overnight. But, unfortunately, most of them are far too poor. If the Beatles can help to improve the lot of just a few, then their new interest in Indian mysticism will have been very worthwhile indeed.
(Johnny Dean's editorial, April 1968)

NO TOUR PLANS

The boys have now returned home from India, and do not plan to take part in any more activities with the Maharishi. As a result, plans for a possible concert tour linking the Beatles with their guru – as the Beach Boys are now doing in the States – have now been abandoned. (May 1968)

TRIPLE LP NEXT?

At the special party held to celebrate the opening of Apple Tailoring in the Kings Road, George spoke about the Beatles' plans for the future. "We're involved in a hectic recording scene at the moment. There's about 35 songs we've got already, and a few of them are mine. God knows which one will be the next single. You never know till you've recorded all of them. We could do a double album – or maybe a triple album, as there's enough stuff here!" (May 1968)

APPLE

What do you think of those record labels on the first Apple release? What do the boys intend to do with them with later releases? Are they going to let the Apple ripen? Who knows. But it certainly must be the most unusual label in the world.
(Johnny Dean's editorial, August 1968)

MORE APPLE RECORDS

The new and luxuriously equipped recording studios built into the basement of 3, Savile Row, the Beatles' new Apple headquarters in London's West End, are almost operational and ready to cope with the first flood of sessions. The studios will be used not only by the Beatles, who plan to complete their own LP recordings there, but by other artists who will be on the Apple label and by outsiders who will be able to hire studio space from time to time.

Meanwhile the list of Apple Records artists has already started to grow. In most cases one or more of the Beatles will be closely involved in the production of other artists' records for the Apple label. Paul is said to be particularly enthusiastic about Drew & Dye and a group to be called the Iveys. Peter Asher has produced two sides for a single with an American artist, James Taylor. In addition Apple Records are scheduling for October release an LP album by the Modern Jazz Quartet. (September 1968)

MORE LIVE TV

After performing 'Hey Jude' and 'Revolution' in front of Videocolour cameras at Twickenham film studios, the Beatles are keen on the idea of filming or videotaping a full-length television show. Unlike *Magical Mystery Tour*, the type of TV show the boys have in mind would involve the filming of actual live performances given in front of an invited audience. As with the 'Hey Jude' videotapes, there could be plenty of audience participation. In other words the aim would be to present a Beatles concert, but instead of the audience being limited to several thousand at a single theatre or stadium, the TV programme would be made available to millions throughout the world.

Beatles' Press Representative Tony Barrow comments: "This new line of thinking proves once more that the boys are not against the idea of giving stage performances as such. It doesn't mean they are going to start touring again, but I can see them playing somewhere like the Royal Albert Hall and other major venues where they can install really good sound systems." (September 1968)

BACK ON STAGE!

The Beatles have booked the Royal Albert Hall in London for a live concert in December! That's the amazing news coming out of Apple this week, and it is likely to bring a flood of ticket enquiries from all over the world. The Beatles will be joined in the concert by fellow Apple artists Jackie Lomax and Mary Hopkin. (September 1968)

BEATLES BOX

The boys' new album will last at least 90 minutes – spread across two discs, of course. The double set is due for release in November, probably in a special presentation cardboard box, which will also include a booklet featuring all the lyrics. The title of the set has yet to be confirmed, but it is expected to retail for between £3 and £4. (October 1968)

JUDE RECORD

The boys' recent 'Hey Jude' single has now amassed six million sales around the world, making it easily the group's biggest seller. And Mary Hopkin's 'Those Were The Days' is nearing four million sales worldwide. It adds up to ten million sales in all – and an amazing start for the Beatles' new record label. (November 1968)

AMAZINGLY POPULAR

This Christmas there can be very few people in the world who have not heard of the Beatles. And it is an extraordinary fact that a Beatles' song is now being played somewhere in the world almost every single minute of every day and night. (Johnny Dean's editorial, December 1968)

RECORD SALES

Despite the double price tag on this two-LP set, *The Beatles* has been setting sales records in the States. Capitol have announced that it is now the biggest-selling LP in the company's history. The album is still No. 1 in the British charts, and in Sweden it has done even better – turning up at No. 7 in the Top 40 of the singles chart! For a set that costs eight times the price of a single, that's an incredible achievement. (December 1968)

BEATLES BOOK EXCLUSIVE!
50 Pairs of Beatle People will see the 'Live' Performances!

The Beatles will shortly be preparing the world's biggest concert. They'll be rehearsing and recording an hour-long show that will be seen on a hundred million television screens all around the world. Through *The Beatles Book*, 50 pairs of Beatle People will have the opportunity of watching John, Paul, George and Ringo in action, making an historic TV programme. What's more, the one hundred lucky winners won't have to solve puzzles or answer competition questions. This is an open-to-all, costs-nothing-to-enter, BEATLES LUCKY DIP!

At press time it is not possible to tell you the exact dates of the performances, which will be videotaped in colour in the New Year. Neither the Beatles themselves nor their Apple helpers have sorted that out. But the dates will be sometime during January and the 100 special free seats reserved for *Beatles Monthly Book* readers will be allocated by Apple for one or more of the shows as soon as possible. On January 1st 1969 all your applications will go into a drum. The first 50 pulled out will get A PAIR OF TICKETS! (December 1968)

George at one of the celebrations to mark the emergence of the Apple empire.

The White Album

It took six months to record the legendary double album they issued in 1968

How do you follow up a masterpiece? That was the problem facing the Beatles in 1968 when they started work on a new set of songs for the album to follow their enormously successful *Sgt. Pepper*. But before the group went into Abbey Road to start recording, there was something else on the agenda. At the end of February, the four Beatles and their partners flew out from London Airport to Rishikesh, India, to study Transcendental Meditation under the Maharishi Mahesh Yogi. The trip had been postponed after the tragic death of manager Brian Epstein the previous August. They took their acoustic guitars with them, and John, Paul and George all found that by meditating and enjoying the relaxing atmosphere of the school, they were able to produce a steady flow of new songs. Ringo, too, started to write his first 'proper' song, although he and his wife Maureen spent only a week-and-a-half in India, before leaving because Ringo discovered he was allergic to the exotic food.

Although the trip ended with some bad feeling towards the Maharishi, the Beatles returned home with a bumper crop of new material. They reconvened at George's house in Esher in late May to record demos of 23 songs. Four of the songs they taped there were never officially released by the Beatles. 'Child Of Nature' was John's song about India, which was later issued with different lyrics as 'Jealous Guy' on his 1971 solo album, *Imagine*. 'Sour Milk Sea' and 'Circles' were both written by George: the first was given to his new Apple discovery, Jackie Lomax, while the second was only recorded by George in 1978, and then finally released on his *Gone Troppo* album in 1982. Finally, Paul's 'Junk' (then known as 'Jubilee'), was an early sketch of a song that eventually appeared on his debut LP, *McCartney*, in 1970.

Two other numbers, 'Polythene Pam' and 'Mean Mr. Mustard', were held over until the *Abbey Road* album was completed the following year. The remaining songs, the ones that actually made it onto the new album, demonstrated that the foreign atmosphere of India had encouraged the Beatles to look back to their childhoods and their early musical influences. For example, 'Back In The USSR' was a classic Chuck Berry-style rock'n'roll number with Beach Boy backing vocals thrown in for good measure. 'Honey Pie' and 'Good Night' evoked memories of Hollywood musicals. 'Rocky Raccoon' was the stuff of Saturday morning picture show Westerns. And 'Julia' was John's touching tribute to his mother, who died when he was a teenager. India did leave its mark, though. 'The Continuing Story Of Bungalow Bill' was written about another pupil at the Maharishi's school, who was on his way to bag a few tigers on safari after finishing his lessons. 'Dear Prudence' was written about Prudence Farrow, the sister of movie star Mia, who spent all her time studying indoors, away from the glorious Indian weather. 'Everybody's Got Something To Hide Except Me And My Monkey' was taken directly from the Maharishi's teachings. The most bitter of the new songs was 'Sexy Sadie', originally an attack on the morality of the Indian holy man until John changed the lyrics to avoid offence.

Inspiration also came from the group's immediate environment at home. 'Cry Baby Cry' started life as a TV advertisement ("Make your mother buy"), while 'Glass Onion' was John's good-natured swipe at those fans who claimed to have discovered hidden meanings in Beatles songs. Paul wrote 'Mother Nature's Son' at his father's house in Liverpool, using the old standard 'Nature Boy' as his starting point. 'Martha My Dear' was a simple love song, although the title was taken from the name of Paul's Old English sheepdog. "Our relationship was platonic, believe me," Paul has since reassured us! George was given an unprecedented four songs on the album. 'Savoy Truffle' described his guitar-hero friend Eric

John in December 1968, the month The White Album hit No. 1 around the world.

Clapton's liking for the Good News chocolate assortment. 'Piggies' was a "social comment" at the expense of the press who hounded the Beatles. 'Long Long Long' tenderly described his search for God; and 'While My Guitar Gently Weeps' started life as a challenge George set himself while he was visiting his parents. "I decided to write a song based on the first thing I saw upon opening any book," he remembered in 1980. "I picked up a book at random – opened it – saw 'Gently weeps', then laid the book down again and started the song." Finally, Ringo made his songwriting debut with 'Don't Pass Me By', a number that he had apparently been working on since 1963.

Recording sessions got underway with John's politically charged song 'Revolution'. The session was notable for the presence in the studio of his new love, Japanese avant-garde artist Yoko Ono. The final take of the song lasted a staggering ten minutes, with John repeatedly screaming "all right" and Yoko contributing words and phrases. It was clear that the song would have to be edited for release, so the last six minutes were chopped off and taken away by John and Yoko, who used them to created a terrifying eight-minute collage of sound, noise, spoken word and snippets of music entitled 'Revolution 9'. "It has the basic rhythm of the original 'Revolution', with some twenty loops put on," remembered John in 1980. "We were cutting up classical music and I got a tape on which some test engineer was saying 'Number nine, number nine, number nine'." Both Paul and George Martin were shocked by the finished number and tried to persuade John to delete the track from the album. But John was adamant: 'Revolution 9' would be included on the new LP, while 'Revolution 1' (as it was now known) would be the next single. When the others complained that the track wasn't upbeat enough to be a 45, John called their bluff and led the others into a speeded-up, distorted stomp through the song.

This type of petty disagreement became increasingly frequent as the sessions went on through the summer. With each Beatle taking care of his own songs, many tracks were recorded without all the others taking part. 'Mother Nature's Son', 'Blackbird', 'Martha My Dear' and 'Wild Honey Pie' were McCartney solo performances, with Paul playing all the instruments himself to get the sound he wanted. 'Why Don't We Do It In The Road' featured just Paul and Ringo, which annoyed John, who wanted to be part

of such a risqué number. George took care of his own songs, even bringing in Eric Clapton to play the guitar solo on 'While My Guitar Gently Weeps'. George Martin thought that the album was becoming too unwieldy and suggested that the group drop some of the songs to produce one brilliant single album, but nobody was prepared to compromise. Unfortunately, the atmosphere in the studio began to deteriorate as the weeks went by, and the four began to argue openly in front of Abbey Road staff. The constant presence and involvement of Yoko Ono, and Paul's assumption of the 'leadership' of the group after Brian Epstein's death, don't seem to have helped matters. The feeling became so bad that Geoff Emerick, their engineer since 1966, quit in mid-July. Even more dramatic was Ringo's sudden announcement that he was leaving the band during a session for 'Back In The USSR' on 22nd August. He declared

George really came into his own as a songwriter during the 1968 sessions.

himself to be "unloved and unappreciated". Recording continued unabated with Paul on drums, until Ringo returned two weeks later, to find his drum kit covered in flowers. Even George Martin felt the strain and went on holiday in September, leaving his deputy Chris Thomas in charge.

Occasionally the four Beatles managed to forget their differences and produce some of their best work. 'Happiness Is A Warm Gun' showed how well the four could work with each other. 'Yer Blues' was recorded live in a tiny room next to the studio, the boys enjoying the thrill of performing together as a group again. "Small stages push you together as a band, when you're shoulder-to-shoulder," Paul told Barry Miles for his book *Many Years From Now*. "Ringo came

Paul pictured during the six-month-long sessions for the group's double album.

in with his drum kit and I had the bass, and we just played as a band." 'Helter Skelter' was similar, with the Beatles recording a 27-minute version of the song before ditching the original bluesy idea in favour of a more uptempo, heavy rock style inspired by the Who. 'Birthday' was virtually improvised on the spot. Chris Thomas remembered: "Paul was the first one in and he was playing the 'Birthday' riff. Eventually the others arrived, by which time Paul had literally written the song, right there in the studio."

However, some songs were not so spontaneous. 'Ob-La-Di, Ob-La-Da' went through dozens of takes, none of which came up to Paul's high standards. He employed session musicians to provide horns on one version, before completely scrapping it. While Paul, George and Ringo were struggling with another attempt at the song, John arrived, sat down at the piano and pounded out the version that was eventually issued. "We were very pleased with his fresh attitude," Paul recalled. "It turned us on and

turned the song around." Paul garbled the lyrics in the final verse ("Desmond stays at home and does his pretty face"), but the others quickly convinced him that there was no need to perform the vocals again. Two songs recorded during these sessions never made it onto the album. 'What's The New Mary Jane' was a bizarre, rambling Lennon song with a long instrumental break that included swanee whistles, ringing bells and yelping from Yoko. John later tried to release the song as a Plastic Ono Band single, but to no avail. 'Not Guilty' was a George song that stalled after an enervating 102 takes. In the end, it didn't see the light of day until he re-recorded it for his *George Harrison* album.

After a mammoth 24-hour mixing session, the Beatles finally had a running order for the finished album. George had one song on each side, and no writer had two songs in a row. Paul's 'Wild Honey Pie' was included because George's wife Pattie liked it, and a snatch of a song improvised during the sessions for 'I Will' ("Can you take me back where I came from?") was sandwiched between 'Cry Baby Cry' and 'Revolution 9'. John's lullaby for his son Julian, 'Good

Night', naturally closed the album. Many fans found the diversity of the material hard to accept, but both John and Paul liked the finished set, as they felt that each of the four Beatles had more opportunity to shine. George, however, was of the opinion that this was the album where "the rot began to set in".

Nevertheless, the name given to the LP continued to reflect the notion that the group was still a fully-functioning unit. An early proposal was *Doll's House*, which was based on the idea that the songs could form the score to a fictional musical set in a house of pleasure run by a woman named Doll, where the characters in the songs would congregate. This idea was rejected, though, after the group Family released an LP with a similar title LP in July. Instead, the double-LP was called simply *The Beatles*.

This was the first Beatles album to be released on their newly formed Apple Records label, and as such deserved a special package to carry the records. Paul commissioned several designers to produce ideas, one of which was a transparent wallet with a colour photograph that was revealed once the discs were removed. He eventually chose Pop artist Richard Hamilton, who came up with the exact opposite of the complicated *Sgt. Pepper* cover: a plain white sleeve, with the name of the group subtly embossed onto the cardboard.

The project was co-ordinated by Jeremy Banks from the Apple office, and a designer called Gordon Howes was enlisted to produce a finished prototype of the sleeve. They wanted to do something original, so they decided to give each copy in the first run its own unique number, like a limited edition art print. Paul apparently wanted to stage a lottery using the numbers, giving away a fabulous prize to the owner of the 'winning' album. When someone pointed out that surely the Beatles didn't need such cheap stunts, the idea was dropped. It was always assumed that the four Beatles were given the copies numbered 1 to 4, but that theory collapsed when No. 2 was sold in the early 90s. It had apparently belonged to a businessman who had been John Lennon's landlord in 1968. The landlord recalled visiting Lennon one day, and noticing a large white pile of the unreleased albums on a table. When he asked what they were, Lennon apparently said, "Help yourself to a copy, but don't take No. 1", so he took No. 2 instead!

White Album No. 1, autographed by Ringo, was later sold at auction in 1985 for £550. Meanwhile, No. 6 is owned by Neil Aspinall, the managing director of Apple, though apparently it was damaged by flooding in his basement. Peter Shotton, Lennon's long-standing friend and the manager of the Apple boutique, was the proud owner of No. 8, while Beatles press officer Derek Taylor received No. 9.

Richard Hamilton also designed a poster, which carried the album's lyrics on one side and a collage of photos on the other. Many of the pictures came from the Beatles' own collections, while some were the work of Paul's new partner, Linda Eastman. To finish off the package, there were four glossy portraits of the boys by John Kelly. The Beatles also thought of promoting the album with several TV adverts to coincide with the record's release on Friday, November 22nd 1968 – a concept unheard of in the 1960s. It was planned that Ringo would appear on screen and introduce brief snippets of the songs. Also proposed were white double-decker buses in London and a giant windsock flying from the GPO Tower, but both ideas were eventually ruled to be too expensive. Paul also planned a Beatles concert at the Roundhouse in London, which would see their return to the stage after more than two years, but was unable to persuade the others to take part. Of course, the album didn't need any of these gimmicks to become a best-seller. *The Guinness Book Of Records* says that it sold "nearly two million" units in its first week of release in the US. 'The White Album' (as it soon came to be known) has turned out to have a lasting influence on pop music to the present day, showing just how versatile it is possible for one group to be. It contains an astonishing range of styles, taking in reggae, heavy metal, blues, folk, rock'n'roll and experimental noise in the space of a mere 90 minutes.

Even the snippets of chat and music between tracks add to the enjoyment. Even more than *Sgt. Pepper, The Beatles* showed that a pop LP could be much more than simply a collection of singles. Despite it being a time when their working relationship had become more difficult than ever before, the Beatles were still able to produce another undoubted masterpiece. (MOG)

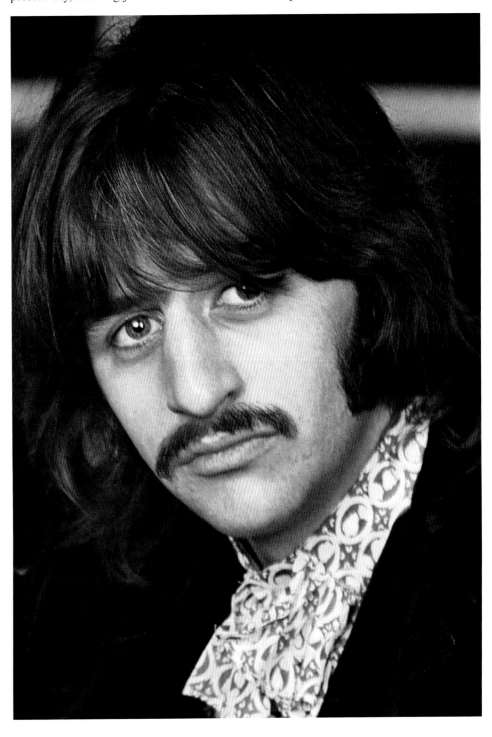

The photo of Ringo that was given away with original copies of the White Album.

The Yellow Submarine premiere

The Beatles' cartoon film was launched at the London Pavilion cinema in July 1968

Four years and eleven days after the opening of *A Hard Day's Night*, the London Pavilion cinema was under siege again from thousands of Beatles fans. Nobody expected to see another outbreak of Beatlemania in 1968. The boys hadn't been touring for two years and it seemed as if the wild crowds that used to halt traffic and close whole streets around concert venues in the mid-Sixties were now part of pop history. But on July 17, 1968, renewed scenes of Beatlemania filled Piccadilly Circus with the happy sound of youthful screams, yells and chants of adoration aimed at the Fab Four.

The occasion was the world premiere of *Yellow Submarine*. This feature-length cartoon film was a bit of an oddity. After *A Hard Day's Night* and *Help!*, the Beatles had agreed to make a third movie for cinema release. In the event, a number of scripts were rejected, either because of Brian Epstein's desire to avoid involving his group in controversial screen roles, or because the stories were simply not good enough. To prevent contractual problems, 'Eppy' agreed in 1966 to the making of a film that would involve little or no effort on the part of John, Paul, George and Ringo. This was *Yellow Submarine*, an animated feature with a

soundtrack carrying 'a dozen Beatle songs', albeit few new ones and no spectacular new ones. Brian Epstein led the Beatles to treat *Yellow Submarine* as little more than a business deal, a painless contractual obligation that was nothing they need worry about too much. After his death, when the cartoon was actually in production, the Beatles paid little attention to what was happening, apart from providing – under pressure and with little genuine enthusiasm – the four fresh numbers that Brian had promised the producers. These consisted of two titles left over from the previous year's sessions, Paul's 'All Together Now' and George's 'It's All Too Much', an extremely long number that was edited for the *Yellow Submarine* LP; plus John's 'Hey Bulldog' and another Harrison composition, 'Only A Northern Song'. John dashed off 'Hey Bulldog' at an Abbey Road recording session in February 1968. He said: "I had a few words at home so I brought them in and whipped off the song." The song wasn't included in the US copies of the film when it was originally released, though it did appear elsewhere in the world.

The second side of the *Yellow Submarine* album was filled with George Martin's original soundtrack score. Although it ended up selling over one million copies worldwide, this record failed to top the charts in Britain, where it was blocked from the No. 1 spot for a spell by the Beatles' own two-record set. When the Beatles actually saw *Yellow Submarine*, they were genuinely shocked that 'Eppy' had written off the entire project so casually. By this time it was difficult for them to start lavishing praise on the production in public, having paid so little personal attention to the making of it. But, in private, insiders heard them speak highly of the spectacular and innovative animation techniques. They hadn't expected to find the film so enjoyable. In separate conversations with me at the time, both John and Paul expressed belated disappointment that they hadn't got involved far more actively in the production, rather than leaving writers Lee Mintoff and Al Brodax to get on with it. John was particularly taken with Mintoff's

The Beatles examine the script for their cameo appearance at the end of the film.

original creation of 'Pepperland'. One could easily imagine Lennon himself creating belligerent 'blue meanies' and menacing 'apple bonkers'! The scenes inside and outside the London Pavilion cinema on premiere night were made all the more colourful because 1968 was the era of 'the beautiful people'. Most of the capital's 'in crowd' presented themselves in Piccadilly Circus that evening in their brightest new finery, many wearing brilliant shades of yellow for the occasion.

While lines of policemen held back the fans, celebrities were delivered to the Pavilion entrance by a constant stream of Rolls-Royce cars and sleek limousines. Both male and female guests offered a non-stop fashion parade of multi-coloured outfits, stunning hairstyles and sparkling accessories. A tall Blue Meanie greeted suitably startled new arrivals, who were handed apples by people swathed in yellow. One or more of the Beatles themselves might have missed the star-spangled premiere, but for

the fact that the group was in the middle of a marathon series of recording sessions, so everyone had to be in town. The Apple headquarters had just moved from Wigmore Street to Savile Row, another centre of much personal interest for John, Paul, George and Ringo.

Ringo and Maureen turned up soon after 8pm, claiming the instant attention of several dozen newspaper cameramen. Maureen wore a magnificent white lace top, buttoned to the neck. Ringo had a flamboyant bow tie inside his lavish suit. George and Patti wore yellow. Paul, John and Yoko Ono were the last to draw up outside the Pavilion. Paul had a flashy yellow tie and dark suit in contrast to John's dark shirt beneath a white suit. Together they made a colourful bunch. A supporting cartoon was already showing as the Beatles were led to their front row seats in the circle. The press and television newsmen crowded down the aisle after the Fab Four, flashing cameras and TV lights distracting the rest of the cinema audience –

The amazing scenes in Piccadilly Circus on the day of the film premiere.

most of whom didn't mind a bit, as it gave them their first chance to see what the VIPs were wearing. In celebration of the premiere, the Rank Organisation opened a small and exclusive new Yellow Submarine Disco under their Royal Lancaster Hotel at Bayswater. It was here that the Beatles and their many guests drove from the Pavilion. More than 200 people packed into the disco for a midnight party attended by hosts of familiar faces, from the Bee Gees to the Rolling Stones.

Champagne flowed freely and splashed generously over suits and gowns for the rest of the night, as the small room heaved with happy revellers. The Beatles came and went, while the rest of us stayed on to take full advantage of Rank's hospitality. John said to me as he struggled through the crowd towards the door: "I want to write the next Beatles cartoon film". But he never did.

Ringo and Maureen Starr arriving at the Yellow Submarine premiere.

Meanwhile, *Yellow Submarine* met with a mixed reaction from both the press and the public. Some hailed it as a great work of animated art. But many Beatles fans were put off by the fact that the voices of John, Paul, George and Ringo didn't speak the dialogue on the soundtrack. In fact, I think the use of actors for that job had its positive side. The Beatles were never good at reading lines from scripts. Actors, on the other hand, took on the task with enthusiasm, giving larger-than-life impressions of the Four Mop Tops which fitted the bill perfectly in the circumstances, and gave the film extra touches of humour that might otherwise have been lacking. There was also something else very special for fans of the Beatles in *Yellow Submarine*. The faces and figures of the four boys were preserved permanently as they'd looked at the height of *Sgt. Pepper*-era Beatlemania. Even now, many years after the premiere, *Yellow Submarine* shows four good-humoured, happy, youthful Beatles as they were in their heyday, with not a wrinkle in sight! Perhaps that's where the true magic of the movie lies – that, and the eternal attraction the film has for children.   (TB)

ONE BEATLES FAN MANAGED TO SNEAK INTO THE PREMIERE!

In 1968 David Stark was a fifteen-year-old schoolboy, who like countless other Beatles fans the world over was prepared to go to almost any lengths in order to meet his idols. During the next few years he achieved this aim on several occasions, but the first – and possibly the most daring – of his encounters occurred on the day of the *Yellow Submarine* world premiere in London. He arrived in Piccadilly Circus with a school chum in mid-afternoon, and spent several hours watching the gathering crowds from the roof of the cinema (thanks to an open door at the side and a conveniently placed elevator). Then the two lads managed to enter the theatre's 'dress circle', only to be stopped by an usher who demanded to see their tickets. "I told him that we'd left our tickets when we came in downstairs", recalls David. "When the manager arrived and asked us why we were there in the first place, I replied that we had been sent tickets by our 'good friend' Clive Epstein, whom I had in fact met while on holiday a few years earlier. Well, the manager wasn't too convinced by that explanation and took us to the

bar to find Clive – gulp! – but he was more impressed when I spotted Dick James and asked him if he had seen Clive. He told me that he had been held up in Liverpool, at which point the manager said, 'Okay, I can see you know people here. You can stay, but next time hold on to your tickets!' It was unbelievable luck!"

Even more incredibly lucky was David's choice of seats – immediately behind the Fab Four and their friends! "We just stood around as everyone came in", he recalls. "I remember seeing Status Quo, Grapefruit and some members of the Who. And then all of a sudden camera flashguns started going off everywhere, and the whole place buzzed as the Beatles arrived with their entourage. They went down to the front row of the 'dress circle', closely followed by the photographers, and as the photographers left I noticed two empty seats behind Paul! As we moved into the seats, I was really sweating, especially when I looked to my right and saw that I was sitting next to Keith Richards of the Rolling Stones! I thought we were going to be thrown out at any moment. Eventually I plucked up the courage to ask Keith if it was okay to sit there, and he said it was, as the seats were reserved for Mick Jagger and Marianne Faithfull, but they were still in the States. John Lennon then turned around and asked Keith Richards something like, 'So who are your friends?', and Keith said, 'Oh sorry, haven't I already introduced you to Mick and Marianne?'!

"It was quite amazing, sitting there behind the Beatles and watching the first screening of their new film! I remember during both 'Hey Bulldog' and 'All Together Now', Paul turned around and asked me what I thought of the new songs. Obviously I thought they were absolutely great, but I was hardly going to run them down even if I felt otherwise!" A better opportunity to speak to John, Paul, George and Ringo came after the feature-length cartoon finished and the audience were showing their appreciation. The Beatles stayed in the foyer, waiting for the pandemonium outside to subside a little and for their cars to arrive, and David took full advantage of the situation to talk to both John and George. "Everyone was really up", he recalls. "They were obviously pleased with what they had seen on the screen. John, with Yoko at his side, was telling me about the new Apple offices they had just moved

This shot gives a vivid impression of the crush as the Beatles arrived.

into in Savile Row, and when I asked him if the Beatles were recording any new songs he said he'd been working on one that was constructed around a children's nursery rhyme. I worked out later that he must have been talking about 'Cry Baby Cry'. George, meanwhile, in his yellow suit and hat, told me he hoped his soundtrack album for the *Wonderwall* film would be released sometime later in the year. Apart from meeting the Beatles, the most vivid memory I have of that night was the incredible sight of thousands and thousands of people outside the cinema, all struggling to get a glimpse of their idols and chanting the chorus to 'Yellow Submarine'. Incredible!" David did not attend the party held afterwards at the Royal Lancaster Hotel – after all, he had not been invited! – but at least he had seized what was probably the last ever opportunity to experience Beatlemania at first-hand.

LETTERS *from* BEATLE PEOPLE

1967-1969

PRAISING AUNT MIMI

Dear John,

I think you're one of the richest men in the world – because you have an Aunt Mimi! While visiting London in September, my girlfriend and I got permission to spend a few hours with her, and I have never, in my entire life, met a woman quite like her! Her heart must be made of pure gold, and her soul of sincerity. I really enjoyed the time we spent with her, discussing your music, your fans, and the world in general. She spoke freely, was honest, and warm hearted. We laughed, drank tea, and listened to Beatle records together. When it came time to say goodbye, I felt like I was leaving an old friend, someone I had known for years. I found her holding my hands tightly and wishing me a safe trip home. I had become a lot richer after just knowing her for a few hours, richer in thought, admiration, respect, and friendship! But you, John, are the richest of all: you have Aunt Mimi.

Sharon Goetzinger (19)
621 South 46th St.,
Baltimore. Md. 21224, USA

CHANGE IN ATTITUDE IN THE USA

Dear Beatles,

I have to tell you about the noticeable change in the attitude toward the Beatles here in America. Magazines, newspapers, TV, etc., are now spending generous amounts of time talking about you, and it's all in your favour. Just a few weeks ago *Time* magazine featured the most highly complimentary article I have ever read on you. It was unbelievable! *The New York Times* is paying a lot of attention to your songs in particular, and variety shows on TV such as *The Smothers Brothers* and *Hollywood Palace* are singing your songs, both the old and the new ones from *Sgt. Pepper.*

I can't account for the change, except that you have finally lost your mop-top image and have begun to be respected as men who aren't just making a noise and are popular with teenyboppers. Lately you've proven yourselves and have shown what great things you can do. And people are listening!

J. Moore,
Parmlee Hill Road, Newtown, Connecticut.

THANKING PAUL WHEN SHE MET HIM

Dear Paul,

The place was Bradford, on a sunny Sunday afternoon outside the Victoria Hotel.

The date was June 30. During the morning you had been conducting the Black Dyke Mills Band. Remember? My friends and I travelled from Barnsley, Yorkshire, in the hope of seeing you. We ended up sitting beside you and Martha (both of you are very cuddly) on the hotel steps during a television interview. I was terribly nervous and trembled at the thought of being only inches away from you. However, I built up my courage, and gave you the belated birthday present that my friend and I had bought for you. The moment our eyes met, torrents of tears trickled down my cheeks. I felt ashamed of myself for letting my emotions take over, but you wiped away a tear from my cheek and gave me a reassuring smile and suddenly, I felt so very happy. I really am grateful to you for making me the happiest person in the whole world. I've never met anyone as patient, generous, tender and kindhearted as you.

Jean,
82 Worsborough Road, Birdwell,
Barnsley, Yorkshire.

APPEALING TO ANTI-POP GRANDPARENTS

Dear Beatles,

You really are very catching. About a week or so ago I went to my Gran's. I get on well with both my grandparents except for one thing: they are sworn haters of pop music and its singers. I had taken my *Sgt. Pepper* LP with me and eventually persuaded my Grandad to play it. The scene was painful. We were all sat on hard-backed chairs waiting for the opening bars, the two of them all ready to be really stern critics. But something strange happened: nobody spoke. The music moved on to Ringo's song but still no-one said anything about long hair or moustaches. Then I noticed my Gran was sitting back beaming and really enjoying it, and my Grandad was slyly tapping his foot, hoping I wouldn't notice. At the end I said, "Well, did you like it?". The answer was, "It was alright". I was stunned. Secretly I knew they both had enjoyed your performance although they just couldn't bring themselves to say so!

Jill Hancock,
17 Hunter Court,
Hunter House Road, Sheffield.

The house near Poole that John bought for his Aunt Mimi.

HOW NOT TO MEET PAUL, BY AN OPTIMIST

If I go to Paul's house,
He'll either have come back from Greece
two hours after I've gone,
Or he'll just have left for India.
Whenever Paul goes to Regents Park or
Hyde Park
He makes sure I'm not there.
Whenever Paul takes Martha for a walk,
Before he does so, he
Makes sure Sheila Skillman isn't outside
And doesn't get a chance of seeing him.
When Paul records at the EMI studios
He makes sure I'm not hanging around;
When I phone up the EMI studios,
It's one of the secretary's unco-operative
days,
Or she doesn't know, or
She's got no idea, luv.
When Paul's at the Apple offices,
He makes sure I'm not going to be in the
vicinity,
And then decides it's safe to turn up.
When the Beatles, ages ago, went to
Sevenoaks,
They made sure that
When they were driving up Court Road
through Orpington,
S. Skillman wasn't taking her dog for a
walk
At the same time.
(Because she lives just off there).
In short, S. Skillman Has Many Ways Of
Not Meeting Paul
But don't worry, she'll do it one day.

Sheila Skillman,
134, Felstead Road, Orpington, Kent,
BRG AF9.

GETTING TO LIKE YELLOW SUBMARINE

Dear Johnny,
A few weeks ago I went to see the Beatles' film *Yellow Submarine*. I dragged my friend along too, but she only came under protest, and after much persuasion, because for some reason best known to herself, she is a confirmed Anti-Beatleist. I hauled her into the foyer, bought her ticket (a condition she imposed before agreeing to come) and propelled her into the forbidding gloom of the back stalls. As the signature tune resounded through the building, she made a last desperate bid for freedom; but I made a swift grab at her retreating form, and restored her posterior to its rightful position. She surrendered, but did not submit, and continued to mut-

ter under her breath, slandering with glorious abandon, me, the Beatles, *Sgt. Pepper* and anyone else that came to mind; addressing no one in particular, and everyone in general.

Then, suddenly, whilst drawing breath for another verbal assault, she happened to notice the film. Conversion wasn't in it! She gasped, in a manner in which goldfish have been known to gasp under similarly excruciating circumstances; and fell back with a cry of amazement. She didn't utter another word until the last bars of 'All Together Now' had finally died away. (RIP) Then she couldn't say enough, one word falling over the next, and the next, and the next, in an unceasing hymn of praise. I have never known anything like it. It's really awe-inspiring to see one's friend instantly converted from an absolutely confirmed Beatle-hater to a, well, "almost fan"!

Lots of luv and best wishes,

Maria Tindall,
Ivy Bank, Pool-in-Wharfdale, Yorkshire.

BEATLES GETTING SICK OF CONCERTS

Dear Beatles,
Hunter Davies's biography was fascinating. But there is one thing that bugs me, about your concert days. We went to see you

Most of their fans were very sad when the Beatles decided to stop touring in order to concentrate on recording.

because we loved you. You may have hated the concerts, as it was always the same old thing, but to us, it was something we looked forward to for months. We had a great time!

Dena Elmberg,
PO Box 9162, Seattle,
Washington 98109, USA

PAUL'S MARRIAGE

Dear Johnny Dean,
I don't think any fan will desert Paul for getting married. Not a genuine one, anyway. Meditation didn't really make him happy; but I'm certain family life is much more likely to do so. He has given his fans so much happiness that they will surely be glad that he now has the chance of happiness himself.

Anyway, what difference will his marriage make to us? Far from deserting us, he's working harder than ever on new records. He looks as appealing as ever and marriage won't alter his voice or gift of song. As for him now being finally out of reach, wasn't he always?

Anna Renton,
Galashiels, Selkirk.

Recording Abbey Road

Martin O'Gorman recalls the troubled background to their final album

Early 1969 saw the Beatles trapped in the project that eventually became known as *Let It Be*, but was then going under the title of *Get Back*. They were meant to be rehearsing at Twickenham Film Studios for a TV show, and the whole process was being documented by a film crew. But they were all in deep depression, brought low by a mixture of boredom, their hatred of being filmed, and the general sense that they didn't know where they were going. George had already walked out during the sessions because of John and Paul's insensitivity, and it appeared that John, who was focusing more attention on Yoko than the group, could easily be next. Meanwhile, Ringo seemed to prefer his burgeoning acting career to endless hours of drumming.

Once the rehearsals were over in late January, no one knew what to do next. Was that the end of the project, or were they still going to play a concert? Should they try and release an album from what they'd recorded, or simply leave everything in the can? Engineer Glyn Johns, was given the task of compiling an LP from the completed tapes, only to have his efforts rejected by the band.

During the summer, with the fate of *Get Back* becoming increasingly uncertain, the Beatles continued to work on fragments of songs that had first been aired during the January filming. John's ode to Yoko, 'I Want You (She's So Heavy)', was one of the songs they had rehearsed at Twickenham. But they only began to record the song properly a month after the Beatles' final 'rooftop concert'. The intensity of John and Yoko's relationship was illustrated by the song's lyrics, which some critics claimed were not up to his usual standard. John retorted: "This is about Yoko. There was nothing else I could say. When you're drowning, you don't say, 'I would be pleased if someone would have the foresight to notice me drowning and help me', you just scream."

'I Want You (She's So Heavy)' proved to be the first number recorded for *Abbey Road*, the last complete album made by the Beatles. The second song recorded during the *Abbey Road* sessions was George's love song for his wife Pattie, 'Something', which had been written the previous year and then offered to Joe Cocker. George told the *NME* in November 1969, "I got the bit about

'something in the way she moves' and the chord progression seemed to follow naturally. People tell me this is one of the best things I've ever written. It's very flattering."

The next 'new' song for the album was Paul's 'Oh! Darling', which had also been attempted earlier, during the *Get Back* sessions. Paul explained to Barry Miles in *Many Years From Now*, "I wanted to get the vocal right, and I ended up trying each morning as soon as I came in. It was unusual for me, I would normally try all the goes at a vocal in one day." Afterwards, John felt he could have done the job better: "It was more my style than his." Next on the list was Ringo's second composition to date, the charming 'Octopus's Garden', which was misreported in the press as being called either 'Octopussy's Garden' or 'I Should Like To Live Up A Tree'! Ringo wrote it after he stormed out of the 'White Album' sessions the previous summer. He and Maureen holidayed off Sardinia on Peter Sellers' yacht, where they were told how

George and Pattie sharing an intimate moment during the turbulent 1969 sessions

octopuses gather stones and 'arrange' them on the seabed. The song later became a children's favourite, but the lyrics betray its bitter genesis: "We would be so happy, you and me/No one there to tell us what to do".

Early in July, while on a driving trip to Scotland, John and Yoko were involved in a serious car crash, so the sessions resumed without them. When he returned, the Beatles decided to put all their bad feelings behind them by completing a new album. As George Martin recalled, "I was very surprised when Paul rang me up and said, 'We want to make another record, will you produce it for us?' I said, 'Yes, if I am really allowed to produce it'." Tensions remained, however, most notably when a bed for the recuperating Yoko arrived at the studio.

'You Never Give Me Your Money' was Paul's first new composition since the *Get Back* sessions, and he later explained that it was inspired by his feelings about the band's business and legal troubles. The opening lines mention the 'funny paper' that was the cause of their woes. "Soon we'll be away from here/Step on the gas and wipe that tear away", he sings later in the song, and that was exactly what Paul did in April 1969, disappearing with Linda to their Scottish farm. The song was left open-ended, so that it could open the 'long medley' of songs that took up most of side two of Abbey Road.

Two more McCartney songs, 'Golden Slumbers' and 'Carry That Weight', were recorded together as part of the medley. 'Slumbers' was inspired when Paul found a lullaby of that name, by the 16th-century writer Thomas Dekker, in a songbook at his father's house. Sitting at the piano, Paul tried to read the music, but failed, so he decided to make up his own melody. 'Her Majesty', which Paul had played at Twickenham with the other Beatles, was knocked off one morning before the others arrived at the studio. When the long medley was assembled, Paul wasn't happy with its

proposed position between 'Mean Mr. Mustard' and 'Polythene Pam', and ordered it to be scrapped. But engineer John Kurlander had been told never to throw anything away during Beatles sessions, so he cut the song from the master tape of the medley and tacked it onto the end. When Paul heard the short ditty coming out of nowhere after twenty seconds of silence, he was so pleased with the effect that the song remained on the album. The next song to be recorded for the medley was, surprisingly, 'The End', which was designed to follow on directly from 'Carry That Weight'. The track featured the only Ringo Starr drum solo ever recorded for a Beatles song, and a short segment of duelling guitars in which McCartney, Harrison and Lennon take it in turns to play a solo.

After that, the missing pieces of the medley were assembled. 'Sun King' was a brief Lennon tune that was eventually linked onto the end of 'You Never Give Me Your Money' by some exotic tape loops prepared by Paul. 'Sun King' was taped as one long recording with another John song called 'Mean Mr. Mustard'. The latter was inspired by a newspaper story concerning a man who went to extraordinary lengths to hoard money. Similarly, 'Polythene Pam' was recorded together with Paul's 'She Came In Through The Bathroom Window'. John wrote 'Polythene Pam' in Rishikesh about the girlfriend of Liverpool poet Royston Ellis, who actually dressed up in plastic. Paul composed 'Bathroom Window' in May 1968, while he was in New York to announce the formation of Apple Corps. It was loosely based on an incident when a fan had broken into Paul's house and had stolen clothes and photographs. Paul had done some detective work ("and so I joined the police department") to find the culprit.

Of the other Abbey Road songs, John wrote 'Because' after hearing Yoko playing Beethoven's Moonlight Sonata on the piano, reversing the melody to form a new tune. 'Maxwell's Silver Hammer' was one of Paul's songs that had come within a whisper of being recorded for the 'White Album'. "It was my analogy for when something goes wrong out of the blue," Paul told Barry Miles. "I wanted something

---

One of the last publicity photos of all four Beatles, taken in their Apple offices.

symbolic for that." The song originally featured roadie Mal Evans clanging a hammer on a genuine blacksmith's anvil – although *The Beatles Book* revealed in September 1969 that, since Mal was away when the final version of the song was recorded, the anvil was actually struck by Ringo! The second of George Harrison's songs for *Abbey Road* was another of his best-loved numbers. "I wrote 'Here Comes The Sun' in Eric Clapton's garden," he told the *NME* in November 1969. "It was done about the time we had all those business meetings and I had headaches. So one day I took the day off, and went to Eric's because it's nice, with trees and things. The song just came right out." 'Here Comes The Sun' was also notable as being one of the *Abbey Road* tracks that featured the group's new Moog synthesiser. According to Mal Evans, George Harrison had bought this electronic instrument for an incredible £10,000 in Hollywood in the autumn of 1968. The massive piece of equipment was used to colour the backing tracks for 'Here Comes The Sun' (where it can be heard echoing the riff, "Sun, sun, sun, here it comes"), 'Maxwell's Silver Hammer', 'Because', and 'I Want You'. The swirling white noise on that last track actually caused the engineers problems when they were remastering *Abbey Road* for release on CD.

John's most memorable song on the album was 'Come Together', which was originally written for self-styled 'acid guru' Timothy Leary's campaign for governor of California. The line "Here come old flat top" was taken from the Chuck Berry song, 'You Can't Catch Me', as Paul told Miles: "He originally brought it over as a very perky little song, and I pointed out to him that it was very similar to Chuck Berry's song." Paul recommended that they tried to get away from the sound of Berry's number: "I suggested we try it 'swampy'. I laid the bass line down, which very much makes the mood." Nevertheless, the similarities between 'Come Together' and 'You Can't Catch Me' would come back to haunt John, when Berry's publishers took legal action against him in the 70s.

With the addition of some overdubs – including a 30-piece orchestra playing for thirty seconds on 'The End' – the album was completed by the end of August 1969. John supervised the editing and mixing of 'I Want You (She's So Heavy)' (insisting on the brutal tape-cut that ends the song), and all four Beatles decided on the final running order of the album. Sadly, 20th August 1969 was the last day that John, Paul, George and Ringo were in the studio together at the same time.

John on slide guitar while George sings 'For You Blue' in January 1969.

The cover of the album is the subject of Beatles legend. According to one story, the four wanted to call the album *Everest* after the brand of cigarettes engineer Geoff Emerick smoked, but they couldn't be bothered to fly to the Himalayas for the photo shoot. Instead, they chose to be pictured outside the EMI studios in St. John's Wood. Taking the idea from Paul's quick sketches, photographer Iain Macmillan snapped the Beatles on the zebra crossing at 11.35am on 8th August. The shot immediately became one of the Beatles' most enduring images, and made Abbey Road famous around the world. Amazingly, Macmillan only snapped six quick shots to get the pose he wanted. These days, when committees of stylists and designers are in charge of album covers, the same thing would probably take weeks. As usual, the Beatles came up with the perfect image for their swansong and made it look easy. The cover was so memorable that it became the subject of numerous imitations. The Red Hot Chili Peppers, cartoon characters Ren and Stimpy, and comedian Benny Hill have all used the famous crossing for their own records. Eric Idle's spoof Beatles group, the Rutles, mimicked the sleeve for their *Shabby Road* album (although as an alternative to Paul's impromptu shedding of his sandals for the pictures, Rutle Stig was wearing no trousers). Soul group Booker T and the MG's didn't just copy the sleeve for their *McLemore Avenue* album; they covered most of the Abbey Road songs, too!

Abbey Road was released on 26th September 1969 (the record was delayed by two weeks because the sleeves were delivered late), which was only a month after the sessions had ended. What is most surprising about the record is that after the frustrating and drawn-out experience of *Get Back*, the group had reconvened to produce a professional, coherent album in a mere two months, including some of the finest recordings of their career. The pin-sharp sound heralded the take-over of hi-fi stereo – for the first time a Beatles album was not made available in mono. The record was previewed on a special edition of the BBC2 programme *Late Night Line Up* on 19th September. The Beatles themselves approached the BBC with the idea, as "they liked the manner in which the series dealt with pop subjects", according to the press. Sir George Martin has since gone on record as saying that *Abbey Road* is his favourite

Beatles album, although John later damned it as "something slick to preserve the myth". Whether or not you think the album is the Beatles' masterpiece mainly depends on your opinion of the 'long medley', and some commentators have been critical of how insubstantial it is. Lennon himself was scornful of the medley, even though he'd written much of it himself. At one point, he tried to insist that all of his songs should appear on one side of the album, with Paul's on the other. He then tried to flip the sides, putting the medley on side one, and finishing side two with the abrupt climax of 'I Want You' – which would have been a harsh ending to the group's recording career.

Nevertheless, the album contains some of the Beatles' finest songs, and was definitely a return to the glories of earlier years. But the magic had gone, with only the mopping-up exercise of *Get Back/Let It Be* left to be done. As Paul told the *Evening Standard* in 1970: "Things have changed. Even on *Abbey Road* we didn't do harmonies like we used to. I think it's sad. On 'Come Together', I would have liked to have sung harmony with John, but I was too embarrassed to ask him." The dream was over; and sure enough, on the cover of *Abbey Road*, the Beatles can be seen walking away from the studios where they made their name. (MOG)

1969

John and Yoko celebrated their marriage with a highly-publicised bed-in.

BEATLES AFFECTING IRON CURTAIN

Extraordinary, isn't it, the way the Beatles' songs and thoughts have crept into so many aspects of our lives. Two events towards the end of '68 showed just how true this is. The first concerned the hard-faced men in the Kremlin, who show no fear of the Western countries' rockets and bombs. Suddenly, they seem to be scared stiff that their iron grip on the youth of the Iron Curtain countries is slipping. And who do they blame? That's right – John, Paul, George and Ringo.

The other event is right at the opposite end of the scale. Just a small paragraph, which appeared in most national papers at the beginning of December, to the effect that the 'Old Groaner', Bing Crosby, has finally got round to recording a Lennon & McCartney song, 'Hey Jude'. It may be hard to realise it now but Bing, in his own way, was the Beatles of the late '30s and early '40s. He rang up the fantastic sale of 200,000,000 records. But he always seemed to ignore the Beatles' material, even when everyone around him was rushing to record their songs. Now, even he has finally capitulated.
(Johnny Dean's editorial, January 1969)

TV SHOW MYSTERY

After a magical mystery tour of on-and-off press stories, January 18 was finally cancelled as the date for the making of the Beatles' much-delayed TV show. The boys spent more than a fortnight from January 2 in Twickenham Film Studios preparing for the colour videotaping of what promised to be a 90-minute TV spectacular, in the form of a 'live' performance given to an invited audience. Within the first 12 days at Twickenham the group had written and rehearsed eight new songs for the show. An earlier plan to have a full-scale audience

of up to 1,500 people present during the making of the programme was scrapped.

During the first week of January, Paul was talking about the possibility of making the show on location in Africa or "somewhere just as sunny". Indeed, it was the Beatles' strong desire to make the show out of doors that led to the cancellation of the January 18 production date. Nowhere suitable could be found in good time. Various other possible locations abroad have been mentioned but *The Beatles Book* understands that there is NO likelihood of the performance and TV show being recorded in America, despite a wild spate of rumours to that effect.

Even after the January date had been put off, the Beatles went on working at Twickenham, getting eight new numbers and other material ready for the TV show. This suggests that whilst everything has been shelved as far as an immediate production is concerned, the group are still keen on the idea of making such a show. (January 1969)

INVISIBLE CONCERT

After a gap of more than two years, the boys finally performed together as a live group again this week. But you could only have seen the show if your rooftop overlooks the top of the Beatles' Apple building in Savile Row. (January 1969)

GEORGE'S EMPTY THROAT!

George left University College Hospital in London a fortnight ago, after an eight-day stay during which he lost his tonsils! He had been experiencing throat problems for some time and doctors decided that a tonsilectomy was the only answer. Within ten days of being released, however, George was feeling well enough to record some demos of his new songs. (February 1969)

WEDDING BELLS

After months of speculation, not one but two Beatles were married this month. First to tie the knot was the last Beatle bachelor,

Paul, who married American photographer Linda Eastman at Marylebone Register Office in London on March 12. Paul's brother Mike was best man, while Mal Evans and Peter Brown were also in attendance, as was Linda's daughter, Heather. The couple were blessed in a short ceremony at a church in St. John's Wood, before attending a reception at the Ritz. Paul and Linda haven't had a honeymoon, as such, but they did travel to the States three days after the wedding to stay with Linda's family.

Eight days after Paul and Linda were wed, John and Yoko became man and wife after a short ceremony in Gibraltar. They flew there from Paris, where they had spent several days campaigning for peace. After the ceremony, they moved on to Amsterdam, where they began a week-long bed-in at the Hilton Hotel. (March 1969)

HAPPY, RINGO?!

The 'Get Back' single is due to be released soon. Ringo says: "Paul takes lead vocal, and you can say it's a lovely little toe-tapper. If you can sit down when this one is on, then you're a stronger man than I am. Put that in. It will give me a smile when I read it. It'll make me happy!" (March 1969)

PRESS VIEWS ON BEATLES

The Beatles have been getting more coverage in the national press recently than at any time since Beatlemania was at its peak. The writers can be roughly divided into two camps. On one side are ranged the 'knockers' who think John and Yoko are crazy and that the Beatles are getting far too much publicity. On the other side are the 'leave the Beatles alone' group, who state that the boys should be allowed to do anything they want to do in their private lives and they wish everyone would just let them get on with it undisturbed. Both sets of writers take great columns of space to make their point and usually include a few choice pictures to illustrate their remarks. (Johnny Dean's editorial, April 1969)

OH NO, WINSTON!
He's John Winston Lennon no longer. In a short legal ceremony on the roof of London's Apple HQ, John has officially changed his name to John Ono Lennon. He explained that he had made the change as a gesture of love for Yoko, who became an 'Ono Lennon' herself when she married John, of course. (April 1969)

INSTANT FOLLOW-UP
The new Beatles single, 'Get Back', has just entered the charts. So what is the last news you would expect to hear? Another new Beatles single has been recorded, and may be issued within the next few days!

The new single is titled 'The Ballad Of John And Yoko', and it was recorded at a very unusual session indeed – featuring just two of the Beatles. As soon as the news broke that John and Paul had been working without George and Ringo, the press started printing stories that the Beatles had split up. (April 1969)

COVER UPDATE
The next Beatles album will have an updated version of the *Please Please Me* cover photo on its sleeve. "We had our picture taken in the same position as on that early album," John explains, "but looking like we do now. It looks great!" (June 1969)

PLASTIC ONO BAND
You are the Plastic Ono Band – that's the message behind John's first 'solo' single, 'Give Peace A Chance'. It was taped during John and Yoko's recent bed-in in Montreal, and it features a collection of friends and passers-by – anyone who was in the vicinity of their hotel room, in fact! (June 1969)

GET BACK POSTPONED
A last-minute decision by the Beatles has led to the postponement of their *Get Back* album, which was scheduled for release at the end of August. Instead, the Beatles launched themselves into a concentrated series of July recording sessions to complete another, entirely new LP for rush-release.

Explaining the switch of plan, Apple's Mal Evans told *The Beatles Book*: "The fellows listened together to the final tapes of all the *Get Back* LP recordings after they got back from their trips abroad. They realised that it would be much more appropriate to hold back these recordings so that they could put together an LP to go out when their documentary is shown. In the meantime they wanted to get their first 1969 LP out as soon as possible." (July 1969)

LENNON FOR FESTIVAL?
An all-star line-up has been prepared for next month's three-day rock festival in Woodstock, New York, and John and Yoko may be joining them. The Lennons plan to appear at Woodstock, unless the US embassy in London refuses to give John an American visa. If they do make the trip, then John and Yoko will take a batch of other Apple artists with them. (July 1969)

JOHN BACK ON STAGE
The Plastic Ono Band, featuring John and Yoko, have made their first ever live appearance, at the Toronto Rock'n'Roll Revival festival. The performance ended with a long number by Yoko. John explained that it "was half rock and half madness, which really freaked them out! After Yoko had been on about a quarter of an hour, we all left our amps going like the clappers and had a smoke on the stage. When they finally stopped, the whole crowd was chanting 'Give Peace A Chance'." (September 1969)

GEORGE SOLO
George has plans to record a solo album in the new year. "It's mainly to get rid of all the songs I've got stacked up," he says. "I've got such a backlog, and at the rate of two or three an album with the group, I'm not even going to get the ones I've already done released for three or four years. In future, the Beatles are going for an equal rights thing, so we'll all have as many songs as each other on the album." (October 1969)

JOHN LENNON EX-MBE
The weird and wonderful world of John Lennon has taken another strange turn, as he has announced that he is returning his MBE award to the Queen. But although John has sent the medal back, his title of MBE still remains, as it cannot be refused after it has already been awarded to someone. (November 1969)

JOHN'S 1984 MUSIC
John, Yoko and the Plastic Ono Band have made their UK debut at the Lyceum Ballroom in London. The all-star group of musicians, which included George and Eric Clapton, upset some of the audience by just playing two songs in their 40-minute set. "It is only to be expected that some people were disappointed," John says. "We play 1984 music. I'm trying to get it across that the Plastic Ono Band plays the unexpected. It could be anything – 'Blue Suede Shoes' or Beethoven's Ninth! People can expect something from the Beatles or the Stones, but with Plastic Ono, anything goes."

In other concert news, the Beatles have turned down a £2 million offer to play 13 concerts around the world next summer. Their decision has rekindled the rumours about a possible split in the group that have been filling the pages of the world's press in recent months. (December 1969)

END OF THE BEATLES BOOK
For six-and-a-half-years *The Beatles Book* has been the official link between the Beatles and hundreds of thousands of people all over the world. Now the link is about to be broken, as this must be the last issue.

The end of any magazine is a sad event, but especially so in the case of *The Beatles Book* because it has been the official publication of four individuals who have done a tremendous amount to shape the pattern of the decade which is now ending. I have always been impressed with the sort of person who is a Beatles fan. Although obviously biased in favour of everything Beatles, most of them still seem to retain a sense of proportion and, most important of all, a sense of humour about the world around them.
(Johnny Dean's editorial, December 1969)

Paul and Linda on their wedding day.

John's last UK concert

The Plastic Ono Band's sole appearance in England was a memorable event

At the Lyceum Ballroom on London's busy Strand, John Lennon, Yoko Ono and the Plastic Ono Band held their first official UK concert on Monday December 15th 1969. Bizarrely, it also turned out to be their last. John and Yoko had performed together before in Britain, notably at Cambridge earlier in 1969. But the Lyceum gig was the first show that was announced beforehand, rather than being a spur-of-the-moment decision. Just a few weeks earlier, the couple had appeared at the Toronto Rock'n'Roll Festival, a concert that was quickly immortalised on an Apple LP called *Live Peace In Toronto 1969*. The Lyceum appearance led many fans to hope that these concert appearances would become a regular occurrence, and that the Lennons might even launch the kind of British tour that the Beatles had avoided after 1965. Instead, John and Yoko spent most of 1970 out of the spotlight; and then in 1971 they moved to New York, where after a brief flurry of concert appearances they again went into virtual seclusion. 1981 was suppposed to have been the year that John and Yoko embarked on a world tour, but of course tragic events got in the way. So the Lyceum performance turned out to be an important milestone in John's career.

Typically, the build-up to the concert was confused and surrounded in rumour. John and Yoko had spent most of 1969 campaigning for peace, allowing the world's press scores of interviews and photo sessions, and scarcely managing a day's rest away from the hubbub of media attention. Throughout the year, they had been involved in so many bizarre and unusual events that their names soon began to be linked with almost every charitable cause imaginable. Every peace event anywhere in the world was rumoured to involve John and Yoko, and the couple soon found it impossible to keep up with the demands on their time. Their last-minute decision to attend the Toronto festival, where they played a mixture of rock'n'roll songs, new material by John and some of Yoko's avant-garde music, only helped to increase the speculation about their future activities.

John performs 'Cold Turkey' at the Lyceum, with Yoko in a white bag at his feet.

So it was no surprise when, early in December 1969, reports began to appear in the press that the Plastic Ono Band would be appearing at a UNICEF charity concert ("Peace For Christmas") at the Lyceum Ballroom. Also on the bill at this stage were the cast of the rock musical *Hair*, actor/singer Richard Harris, DJs Simon Dee and Tony Blackburn, musicians Jimmy Cliff, Blue Mink, Black Velvet and Ram Jam Holder and TV personality Hughie Green!

In fact, at this point John hadn't even received an invitation to appear, let alone accepted. "We got back from holiday", he said at the time, "and kept reading we'd agreed to do it. Anyway, because of the way the public was a bit conned about it, I knew we'd only get the finger pointed at us if we said no. So we've said we'll do it anyway, because it's a good thing and it's in aid of UNICEF." John began to assemble a massive group of superstar friends, who would make up the constantly changing Plastic Ono Band for the evening. Klaus Voormann, Alan White and Eric Clapton had played with him at Toronto; and Eric brought along the rest of the band he had just been touring with, Delaney & Bonnie and Friends. The 'Friends' included one very special guest, George Harrison – making his first live appearance with John since Candlestick Park three years earlier. Also along for the ride was the Who's drummer, Keith Moon, the Bonzos' Larry 'Legs' Smith, Billy Preston (who had been recording with the Beatles earlier in the year) and anyone else who could be persuaded to turn up.

After brief rehearsals, the band was ready to perform. As the photographs show, the concert had none of the modern stage technology or heavy security that you would expect at today's superstar gatherings. The Lyceum stage was crammed full with musicians – the horn players and guitarists on the left, John and Yoko and the drummers in the centre, and Billy Preston and Klaus Voormann on the right. Behind the group was a huge 'War Is Over' poster – like the ones that were displayed on city centre billboards around the world that Christmas, as part of a seasonal message from John and Yoko. The audience stood behind crash bar-

riers just a few feet from the musicians, surrounded by Christmas balloons and tinsel. And on both sides of the stage, behind the tiny (by today's standards) amplification, were hordes of reporters and photographers, anxious to capture the rare sight of two Beatles playing together again in public.

The Plastic Ono Band were the last act to perform that night, and the anticipation was tremendous. Press reports before the show had suggested that John would be singing his latest single, 'Cold Turkey', plus some of the rock'n'roll oldies he had showcased at the Toronto festival. But anyone who had experienced the Lennons' other artistic activities that year – like the *Life With The Lions* album or their Amsterdam bed-in - knew that they should expect the unexpected. As it turned out, the Plastic Ono Band performed just two songs – the A- and B-sides of their recent single. While the band plugged in and tuned up, John made a brief announcement: "We'd like to do a number. This song's about pain." What followed was a scorching version of 'Cold Turkey', with some ear-splitting Eric Clapton guitar cutting through the verses, and then the whole band turning the choruses into a rock'n'roll boogie. John, clad in an immaculate white suit, screamed his way through the number, while at his feet Yoko lay sprawled in a white bag, completely invisible to the audience. As the number reached its climax, Yoko emerged from the bag – dressed, like John, entirely in white. The concert was about to enter its second, and most bizarre, stage.

Yoko took the microphone and began to call out "John, I love you". Then she wailed: "Britain! You killed Hanratty, you murderers. You killed Hanratty!" (John and Yoko had been campaigning on behalf of the family of a convicted murderer who had been executed several years earlier – unjustly, as far as his relatives were concerned.) Then on a signal from John, the band launched into 'Don't Worry Kyoko'. For seventeen minutes, they powered through a succession of heavy rock riffs, while Yoko screamed and screeched her way through her message to her daughter. At first the band were clumsy, uncertain what to do. But after a few minutes they found a tight groove, and began to respond to Yoko's vocal noises rather than just playing over the top of them. Not everyone would describe it as music but it was certainly a powerful sound, and probably the best example ever of the fusion of Yoko's avant-garde approach and John's rock'n'roll. The piece climbed to a cacophonous climax, with the brass wailing, Yoko screaming and the guitars giving out piercing feedback. Just as at Toronto, the audience were stunned into silence, and it was only after the musicians had left the stage that they began to applaud and call for more. Not everyone was

impressed. The *NME*'s Alan Smith described how "this same piece of music kept going for a marathon 40 minutes or more, and I'm still not sure why. Without wishing to be offensive, the physical result was that it gave me one of the worst headaches I've suffered since I don't-know-when."

John, however, was ecstatic afterwards: "I thought it was fantastic", he said after the show, "I was really into it. We play 1984 music. The Plastic Ono Band plays the unexpected. It could be anything – it could be 'Blue Suede Shoes' or it could be Beethoven's Ninth. With Plastic Ono, anything goes." A year later, in his infamous *Rolling Stone* interview, John remarked that he had just been listening to the tapes of the show, and that it was the greatest music he had ever heard. In 1972, he gave the rest of

(Right) George soon followed John's example. Here he is in the studio recording 'Something' with soul singer Joe Cocker.

us the chance to judge by releasing the tapes on the 'Free Jam' record with the *Some Time In New York City* album. And in one of his final interviews in 1980, he looked back at the show as being a possible inspiration for the new wave musicians of the late 70s. Most Beatles fans would probably have preferred an evening of recognisable John Lennon songs – but that wasn't John's way. The Lyceum concert, for all its controversy and confusion, was one of the major events in his solo career - and, thanks to the music and the musicians, one of the most important rock concerts of the Sixties. John's last UK concert turned out to be as experimental and surprising as the man himself.   (PD)

The Plastic Ono Band at the Lyceum, with John and Yoko joined by friends such as George Harrison, Keith Moon, Billy Preston and Eric Clapton.

Wings

Peter Doggett asks: why don't they get credit for being one of the top acts of the 70s?

Imagine being a mountaineer. You start off with gentle climbs in Wales or Scotland, then try your hand at the Alps, and finally pluck up your courage and head for the Himalayas. In your mind is a single dream: to climb Mount Everest. And then one day you do exactly that. But there's a problem. You can't stay on the summit of Everest forever. So what do you do when you come down?

Paul McCartney and the other Beatles stayed on the top of Everest for longer than most, but when the group officially split up in 1970, they each had to decide what to do with the rest of their lives. Like John, George and Ringo, Paul set out on a solo career; also like John, he soon started making records with his wife. But being a master studio musician, a world-renowned composer and one of the richest and most famous men on the planet didn't satisfy all his creative urges. Ever since he was 15, Paul had been in a band – and when the band wasn't there anymore, he missed it in a way that none of the other Beatles seemed to do.

True, John had the Plastic Ono Band, but that was simply a convenient name for any musicians who happened to be in the vicinity. What Paul wanted was that all-for-one, one-for-all feeling that he'd enjoyed in the Quarry Men, and then the Beatles, almost up until the end. He wanted to jam, to play old rock'n'roll songs, to have fun, to go out on the road. He'd tried to persuade the Beatles to go back to the beginning and play small clubs, but none of the others went for the idea. So when he emerged from the sessions for his first two solo albums raring to make music with other people, he set about forming a group. "I didn't know how you got groups together," he said years later, "because in the past I'd always joined a ready-made one. So I just got together a bunch of mates."

The result was Wings, unveiled to the world in the final weeks of 1971. Over the next eight years (a recording career that lasted longer than the Beatles'), they made a stream of hit records, filled arenas and eventually stadiums all over the world, and went through a sometimes bewildering series of line-up changes. But the strange thing about Wings is that despite their enormous success, they haven't gone down into history as what they were – one of the three biggest-selling acts of the Seventies. As Paul discovered, it didn't matter how many platinum records they racked up and how many stadiums they filled to overflowing, Wings could never escape from the shadow of the Beatles. To some extent, everything that the solo Beatles did was compared to their achievements in the Sixties. But the problem was particularly intense for Paul. Because he was the most musically active ex-Beatle, and because he'd chosen to form another group, the critics were always waiting to dismiss his work as a poor copy of what he had done in the past. In fact, Wings came up with some of the most commercial and enjoyable pop music of the Seventies. They made irresistible hit singles such as 'Listen To What The Man Said', 'Jet', 'Band On

The original Wings line-up on BBC TV's Top Of The Pops in the early 70s.

The Run' and 'Let 'Em In', plus glorious album tracks like 'Bluebird', 'Let Me Roll It' and 'Tomorrow'. But quite simply, Paul was laying himself open to criticism whatever he did with Wings. If he asserted his rights as one of the most successful composers and performers in history, sang all the songs and laid down the musical law to the rest of the group, then he was accused of being heavy-handed and dictatorial. It was exactly that problem which led to the break-up of the original Wings line-up in 1973. So Paul decided on the *Venus And Mars* and *Wings At The Speed Of Sound* albums to spread the spotlight around, and let the other people in the group contribute songs and lead vocals. Then the critics accused him of letting his standards slip by recording mediocre material. So if he did it all himself, he was a bully; if he shared the load, he was avoiding his responsibilities. It's no wonder that when Paul put together another group in the late Eighties, he made no bones about the fact that it was *his* band, performing *his* songs. As his world tours proved, that was exactly what his fans wanted to see.

So where does that leave Wings? Well, they recorded a superb variety of McCartney music, and their *Wingspan* retrospective stands up against any other greatest hits album from the Seventies and early Eighties. Its range of styles and sounds is quite staggering, and its non-stop commercial appeal proves that Paul never lost the knack of making superb pop records. But Wings will probably end up in the history books as Paul McCartney's backing group, at least in the studio. There was one place, however, where Wings really did function as a group, and that was on stage. Anyone who was lucky enough to see them in concert can confirm that they were anything but a one-man band. They were ultra-tight, but with just enough rough edges to keep the music fresh and exciting. They could switch from a delicate ballad to a full-bore rocker at a moment's notice. And night after night, they brought out the best in Paul, who got all the pleasure from playing live that he and the rest of the Beatles started to lose when their music was drowned out by screams.

THE FIRST WINGS LIVE SHOWS

On the morning of Tuesday February 8th, 1972, Paul, Linda, Heather and Mary McCartney, Denny Laine, Denny Seiwell and Henry McCullough left London in a car and caravan, followed by a small truck full of instruments and amplifiers. Turning off the M1 at Hatherton – simply because it reminded Paul of his elder daughter's name – they made their way towards Nottingham. As they approached the city, with no firm destination in mind, guitarist Henry McCullough recalled that the previous year he had played a memorable show with the Grease Band at Nottingham University. So

Paul, Linda and Denny Laine were the core of Wings from beginning to end.

the entourage motored to the campus, where Paul collared the first two students he came across, and asked them: "How's about us giving you a concert here tomorrow?" And that's exactly what happened. At midday on the following day, Paul and his new band, Wings, took the stage in one of the college halls, and performed an impromptu one-hour concert which was Paul's first live show since Candlestick Park in August 1966.

The new five-piece Wings had gone into the studio together for the first time on 1 February 1972. They emerged with easily the most controversial song Paul has ever written: 'Give Ireland Back To The Irish'. Written in response to the 'Bloody Sunday' shootings in Northern Ireland, it succeeded in arousing a storm of protest when it was scheduled for immediate release as a single. Before they'd even heard the song, both the BBC and Radio Luxembourg banned it. When it eventually made the charts, DJ Alan Freeman was forced to ignore the title of the song in his weekly Top 30 run-down on Radio 1's *Pick Of The Pops*, and simply say, "A new entry at No. 21 is a record by Wings"!

Paul reckoned that the new line-up was good enough to take on the road, and he didn't want to spend months rehearsing till they

Wings launched their London Town LP with a fish-and-chip lunch on the Thames.

were completely tight. Instead, he revived the idea he'd first thought of when the Beatles were on the verge of collapsing at the end of 1968: taking his band out to play small, unannounced dates, where they'd be free of the microscopic attention of the London or New York press. A week after their first recording session, then, Wings set off in a northerly direction, assuming that someone somewhere would let them play. After the success of the initial show at Nottingham, where amazed students queued all morning to get into the concert hall, Wings went back on the road. The next day they turned up at York, then at Hull, Newcastle, Lancaster, Leeds (where they broke with tradition by playing at the Town Hall, rather than a college campus), Sheffield, Manchester, Birmingham, Swansea and finally Oxford, where they played their last British show of 1972.

At every venue, the response was ecstatic. University campuses were used to getting visits from top rock bands, who regularly included college shows on their tour schedules in the early Seventies. At Sheffield, for instance, the university newspaper noted that both Led Zeppelin and the Who had performed there in recent months, though neither had been such a hot attraction when it came to ticket sales. But the sheer surprise of one of the Beatles turning up unannounced, and the secrecy surrounding every one of the concerts, made sure that they were treated as very special events - with

no-one looking to criticise the band for their obvious lack of rehearsals. In some ways, that was just as well, for Paul and Wings had only had the bare minimum of rehearsals before the first show. They'd spent just a couple of days working up the skeleton of a live set. Their repertoire included a few classic rockers from the 50s (like 'Lucille', 'Long Tall Sally' and 'Blue Moon Of Kentucky'), some tracks from the *Wild Life* album, and a bunch of new numbers.

Several songs were unveiled for the first time during the university shows, including 'My Love', which became a hit single a year later; 'The Mess I'm In', which became the flipside to 'My Love'; 'Henry's Blues', a self-explanatory song by Mr McCullough; and 'Seaside Woman'", announced by Paul as Linda's first-ever composition. Linda was understandably very nervous at being onstage, and didn't really give her best during the early shows, but she grew in confidence as the tour progressed. Instrumentally, as well, there were plenty of rough edges. New songs like 'The Mess I'm In' and 'Seaside Woman' had obviously been worked out vaguely beforehand, but no-one had agreed on a definite ending or a structure for the solos. So those university shows were a bit ramshackle, rather like some of the rock'n'roll out-takes from the *Let It Be* sessions three years earlier. But these first Wings live shows were supposed to be spur-of-the-moment surprises, a bonus for those lucky enough to attend - and also a way for Paul to knock his band into shape before they went out on a proper, scheduled tour of Europe later in the year.

Certainly there were few complaints from the audiences at the time, even if the Sheffield University Students' Union paper did wonder whether 'Give Ireland Back To The Irish' had been banned by the Beeb on musical grounds, rather than because of its title! By contrast, the Newcastle University *Courier* raved about Wings' "brilliant impromptu concert", saying that "the crowd was almost ecstatic at the end". As the Birmingham University paper, *Redbrick*, explained in their report, "It took a moment before (the audience) realised it was really them. The McCartney aura filled the stage, with all eyes on him."

Most observers expected him to follow up this surprise tour of British universities by going straight into the studio and recording an album for summer release. Then, Paul and Wings would surely set out on a proper tour of Britain and elsewhere in the autumn of 1972. As we know now, things didn't go entirely to plan. The 'Give Ireland Back To The Irish' single didn't sell as well as might have been expected, although it obviously wasn't helped by the lack of airplay on radio and TV. A couple of months later, Wings produced another single. The contrast couldn't have been more obvious. The new release wasn't about politics; instead, it was simply the old children's nursery rhyme, 'Mary Had A Little Lamb', set to a beautiful new tune. Paul explained that he had written the song for his young daughter, Mary, but the press couldn't help wondering whether the whole episode was Paul's sarcastic response to the 'Give Ireland Back To The Irish' episode, even though Paul denied the idea.

As it turned out, there was no Wings album in 1972, even though the group spent quite a lot of time in the studio. Despite the musical talents of the group, Paul found it difficult to inspire them to produce the sound he knew they were capable of, and the initial results of the recording sessions were disappointing. As a result, all plans to rush-release an LP were cancelled, and instead, Paul focused his attention on a full-scale Wings tour. Forget Britain or America, though: Paul set off for France! It was only in 1973 that Wings scheduled an orthodox UK tour, while the rest of the planet had to wait until the world tour of 1975/76 – which turned out to be the most successful and lucrative set of concerts staged up to that time. Maybe Wings were never quite as big as the Beatles, but in their prime they broke records that the Fab Four had set a decade earlier!   (PD)

Tributes to John

Friends, family and fans pay tribute after John's tragic murder in December 1980

On Monday 8th December at 10.50pm, John Lennon and Yoko Ono returned from a recording session to their home in the Dakota Building apartment block in New York City. As they got out of their limousine, they were challenged by a man with a gun, who called out John's name. When John turned towards him, the man fired repeated shots at John, hitting him at least five times. Yoko and the doorman of the Dakota Building dashed to help him and called the police. As soon as officers arrived they rushed John to the city's Roosevelt Hospital, where every attempt was made to save his life. It soon became apparent that there was nothing doctors could do, and John's death was broken to Yoko, and then announced to the world.

Police arrested Mark David Chapman, a 25-year-old who had come to New York that week from Hawaii, and who had made no attempt to leave the scene of the murder. Chapman had apparently obtained John's autograph at 5.00pm that same evening and had then waited for John and Yoko to return. Police could find no immediate motive for the murder. In a statement issued hours after John's death, Yoko Ono said: "John loved and prayed for the human race. Please do the same for him." Besides Yoko, John leaves two sons, Julian (17) from his first marriage to Cynthia Powell, and Sean (5). (PD)

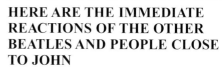

HERE ARE THE IMMEDIATE REACTIONS OF THE OTHER BEATLES AND PEOPLE CLOSE TO JOHN

PAUL McCARTNEY: "John was a great man. His death is a bitter, cruel blow – I loved the man. He will be sadly missed by the whole world. John will be remembered for his contribution to art, music and world peace. I can't tell you how much it hurts to lose him."

GEORGE HARRISON: "After all we went through together, I still have great love and respect for him. I am shocked and stunned. To rob life is the greatest robbery in life."

RINGO STARR: "I am extremely shocked and saddened."

CYNTHIA LENNON: "We are all terribly upset by John's tragic and sudden death. I have always held John in the deepest regard since our divorce and encouraged the relationship between him and Julian."

GEORGE MARTIN: "He was a true original. His zany sense of humour could elevate the meanest of spirits. He will be sadly missed."

JOHN'S AUNT, MIMI SMITH: "I still can't believe it. I keep saying to myself, 'He'll be over soon'. He seemed happier

One of our favourite shots of John, sitting by his pool at his Weybridge home.

John concentrating on a playback during the Sgt. Pepper sessions at Abbey Road.

other and lesser musicians incited hatred. He offered hope where they exploited despair. Until, for some crazed unreasoning reason, he was instantly destroyed. In the words of one of the Beatles' most beautiful songs: 'Yesterday came suddenly'."

DAILY EXPRESS: "John Lennon was in the line of great British eccentrics – at times engaged in the bizarre, at others in the downright potty. The ripples of the Beatles' musical genius, of their inimitable Liverpudlian sound, with its sometimes sensitive, sometimes surrealistic, sometimes satirical lyrics rush out – washing the shores of all continents, not just those who speak their language. In the minds of all of us, he will remain not just a nostalgic reminder of our lost times and selves but much much more – a living symbol of feelings that are forever real."

THE TIMES: "Lennon and McCartney were supremely gifted songwriters, among the most creative and versatile in the history of popular music. McCartney was the soft partner, the creator of lovely melodies. Lennon was the poet. His lyrics were witty, socially aware, incisive and often very beautiful and moving. The music of the Beatles became, and has remained, in a true sense, universal."

DAILY TELEGRAPH: "A man who lived with a philosophy of peace has perished by the gun. In the Sixties the Beatles were a symbol of the culture of the times. Lennon's death has some grim meaning, if we know where to look for it, in the Eighties."

THE GUARDIAN: "He will best be remembered both for his gutsy singing with the early Beatles and for the hopeful, dreamy and idealistic vision of his best-loved ballad, 'Imagine'. His death at 40 is even more untimely than that of Elvis Presley, for Lennon still had the capacity for producing the great and the unexpected."

DAILY MAIL: "For millions of us as we woke Tuesday morning, the news of John Lennon's death was like a door slamming with finality on our own youth. John was the troubadour of our times. His love songs tell of yesterday. His senseless death says more than enough about today."

DAILY STAR: "It is not just the world of

now than he had for a long time. I remember him as the little boy who was happy from morning to night and would sing himself to sleep. We did not have any children of our own. He was our son. He brought the greatest happiness to myself and my husband George that anyone could bring."

MICK JAGGER: "I was shattered when I heard the news. I have known and liked John for over eighteen years."

U.S. PRESIDENT JIMMY CARTER: "John Lennon helped to create the music and spirit of our time. In the songs he composed he leaves an extraordinary and permanent legacy. I know I speak for millions of Americans when I say I am saddened by his death and the senseless manner of it."

SIR HAROLD WILSON: "John Lennon's death will come as a great shock to countless young people and not so young in almost every continent of the world."

MIKE McCARTNEY: "John was a good man, a fine human being and, contrary to what most people believe, he did not become weird when he met Yoko. I met him in New York a few years ago and he was the same old John."

ALL OF THE BRITISH DAILY NEWSPAPERS CARRIED EXTENSIVE TRIBUTES TO JOHN

DAILY MIRROR: "Lennon reached out beyond entertainment to offer a gentle philosophy of life. He preached love where

John performing 'Instant Karma!' on Top Of The Pops on 19th February 1970.

pop that mourns John Lennon. His murder has left us all sickened and stunned. He was so much more than just a former Beatle. He was a vastly talented man whose music touched the heart of millions. Sadly, all we have left are the songs that have enlightened, entertained and enraged us for two decades."

THE SUN: "It was Lennon who provided the Beatles' unique bitter-sweet quality: the haunting irony and sad humour, the questioning and protest that lay beyond the jingles. He never lost his gentleness, his almost child-like faith in the power of love and goodness. It is the final, sad irony that such a man should fall victim to a mindless act of violence."

MANY READERS OF *THE BEATLES BOOK* ALSO SENT IN TRIBUTES

So John Lennon had faults – so what. He was the first to admit that he was only human. To millions like me, he was more a friend than a hero. We all want John to know that even though his life has been taken away, he will always be here, as absence makes the heart grow fonder. We love you, John Lennon, and always will.

Mandy Worthington, Doncaster.

I woke up that morning feeling quite happy. I'd started a training scheme the previous day, and it seemed that finally I was getting somewhere with my life. Then my mother told me the news. I sat down and had a cup of tea. It was strange. I seemed to accept it. Then I went upstairs and saw the posters on my wall. It was then that I began to feel the strangeness in my stomach that has been there ever since. I went to work, though I didn't feel like it, and I collected as many papers as I could with John's name on them. In the evening, I enjoyed the tributes, I laughed at the best bits in *Help!*, and by the time I went to bed I felt like crying.

What can you say? Just what can you say? How can I express what I feel? It may be wrong to say it, but John's passing has affected me in exactly the same way as my father's death. I've been a Beatles fan since I can remember, at least since the age of seven, ten years ago. Sometimes I wish I could have been born in the 50s, so I could have enjoyed them while they were still together. But what can you do? I'm resigned to the fact that my peers, some of them, think I'm soppy because I go all quiet when a Beatles track comes on the radio.

Everyone said that John was the leader, and now I tend to agree. I loved them together and I loved them apart. Now there are only three left, and I'm very unhappy. I just wish I had had the chance to see him live, but now that's gone for good. I try not to be too sentimental because John would have laughed at that. I just hope that people will

keep listening to him for a long time to come. He did everything for peace and there will never be another like him.

I loved the man. I loved the music. He had style.

Robert Cashin, Birmingham.

It's hard to believe that John is dead. I'm still stunned by what has happened. I don't know any Beatles or John Lennon fans where I live, so I hope you don't mind me pouring out my thoughts to you. I'm 19 years old and have been a Beatles fan since I was 14. It's such a tragic waste of life, just when John was making a return to the music world. I wish I could have been in New York with the thousands of people keeping a vigil outside his apartment, as it seems empty sitting here just listening to Beatles records. I still can't believe it has happened.

Vicki Hurst, Bournemouth, Dorset.

Poor, poor John. When I heard the tragic news, I could not believe it, yet I knew deep down it was true, and nothing could or would change events. Although I am 26, married and 'old enough to know better', I cried and cried uncontrollably. Being born and bred in Waterloo, Liverpool, and eight years old at the time of the Beatles' first single, I grew up with all the mounting excitement of Beatlemania. What a marvellous time!

John was a brilliant man in many ways. His ability and sheer knack for words was a joy in itself, and his unmistakeable and individual personality came through on every song he wrote. His basic, down-to-earth style was very moving – you only had to listen to a song like 'Jealous Guy' and a lump sticks right in your throat. I will miss him greatly. How tragic he never got round to writing and recording even one more time with Paul. Those two had a special chemistry and there will never be another partnership like them.

Poor John. Yoko must feel absolutely desolate without him. I will miss him. We all will.

Susan Moore, Port Talbot, Wales.

I know I will be just one of thousands of people who have written to you to express their feelings. However, I hope that you will print this, not because I want to express my grief and that of others, but mainly because I want to try and help, and give some consolation to those who have been hit hardest. For those who were terribly shocked by John's tragic death, I can only say that John may be gone, but our lives must continue. Of course, he gave us so much and everything he said will always be remembered – but also remember that he will never be dead in our hearts. I've seen people fall into despair and feel that after John's death life is no longer worth living. But, as John said, "you've just got to carry on". Millions of fans have endured the suffering, not to mention the personal agony of Yoko, Paul, Ringo and George.

Those who grieve deeply can be helped by those more able to cope, and I'd love to see as many Beatles People as possible getting together, as talking and seeing others in the same situation is a marvellous stimulant for reviving faith. We can carry on where he left off, and continue our search for peace. Although it's a tragic way to obtain his wish, there is a glimmer of light in the fact that John wanted peace and now he has it. May his soul rest in peace forever. We'll never forget him, but we must Let It Be.

Miss S. Solomons, London N3.

After having read the review of *Double Fantasy*, I finally decided to buy a copy of the album on Monday evening. I spent several hours carefully listening to all the tracks, and found it a great relief, as I was rather anxious that John might have lost his touch. Four of the compositions on the album are easily among the best he has ever done: 'Watching The Wheels', 'Woman', 'I'm Losing You' and 'Beautiful Boy'. It was truly heartwarming to see how much John was enjoying life with his wife and son. I went to bed feeling very happy for him.

So you can imagine how shocked I was on learning the tragic news the following morning. I will not drag on about my feelings about the senseless murder of a great man, but I would just like to say how sad the whole thing is. It's terrible that John's life should be ended at this particular time, when everything seemed to be starting up again. It is obvious that he had many more artistic years ahead of him. It is made all the worse by John's pure enjoyment of life recently. He finally appeared to be settling down to middle age quite happily, having turned his back on the normal pop star existence of wild parties and drugs.

I really do feel for Yoko and Sean. I hope now that all true Beatles fans will support her, having seen how much love, peace and happiness she gave John, rather than looking upon her as the one who broke up the Beatles, which just isn't true.

John in thoughtful mode during the recording of Sgt Pepper.

Looking on the positive side of all this is quite difficult, but I do think that in some ways it is a lot better for John to have met his end this way, rather than from a drug overdose like so many rock heroes. He will now be remembered in a much better light, almost as a martyr. It is easy to see how much the world loved and respected John, from the tributes given since he died, but it's a great shame we did not show more affection while he was still here to receive it. As George Martin said, it seems that nobody is interested in people being happy these days, which is what John's new album is about. We all feel robbed of a great man and his future music that we will now never hear. I am only glad that John chose to lead his life his way, as his last five years were surely his happiest.

David Costello, Ascot, Berkshire.

After reading the tributes to John Lennon sent in by other readers, I want to say that I am in the same state of mind, stunned and shocked by it all. What upsets me more, though, is the fact that on the song 'Beautiful Boy' on the *Double Fantasy* LP, he sings about his son Sean and says that he cannot wait to see him come of age. Now he will never be able to see that happen.

There is one consolation, however: John did see his son grow to the age of five. Sean too, will have memories of his dad. Later, when he is slightly older, Sean will remember his dad as a person, not a voice on a record. Those lyrics on 'Beautiful Boy' will touch my heart forever. God bless you, John.

Carol, London E17.

Tributes to Linda

Beatles Book readers remember a much-loved lady

News of Linda McCartney's death prompted an avalanche of post into *The Beatles Book* offices. It made a sad contrast with all the tears that were shed on the day in March 1969, when Linda Eastman married Paul at Marylebone Register Office, London. Back then, the news that Paul McCartney had finally been 'snapped up' prompted a sea of emotion, both from the Apple Scruffs who used to hang around outside his St. John's Wood home, and fans from Tokyo to Toronto. The fact that his wife was not a famous celebrity, like Julie Christie or Jane Asher, but a little-known photographer from America, seemed to make matters worse. There was something down-to-earth about Linda that every girl could relate to. Paul's wife could so easily have been one of them!

But the thing that originally worked against Linda McCartney turned out to be the reason why her death was greeted by such a genuine sense of sadness. She never played the part of a superstar's wife. Instead, her main priority was giving her children the most normal upbringing she could, despite the fact that their father was one of the most famous men in the world. When she did demand the public's attention, it was invariably to campaign on behalf of others. She was a vegetarian because she cared for animals (and the nation's health). If she sometimes came across as angry, then it was for all the right reasons. The world is a poorer place without Linda McCartney. That is the message many readers have sent us in the weeks since her death. (PD)

"Monday morning's news was such a shock. It took me back to a similar breakfast-time one Tuesday morning in December 1980. Every radio station, every television channel and every newspaper headline was eulogising Linda's achievements, her standpoint on animal rights, vegetarianism and the environment.

How ironic. Only thirty years ago, these same people in the media were vilifying both Linda and Yoko as the women who took 'our Beatles' from us. They were the Lennon-McCartney partnership who, it seemed, had broken up the band. Was the world really that naive? All that Linda, and Yoko too, was really guilty of was falling in love. She and Paul were not your typical, run-of-the-mill showbiz couple. She gave Paul stability, a solid base that most stars in the music industry never have. Theirs was a very private marriage, something that most of today's stars could learn a lot from.

Together, they brought up their children very sensibly – a very down-to-earth approach, with no airs and graces, and certainly not as spoilt brats like the offspring of some lesser stars. Linda has my admiration for the warmth and love she gave to her family. As a parent myself, these are values I hold dear to my own heart. It is so painful to see someone like Linda taken from her family so early in life. Fifty-six is still so young. After almost thirty years, Paul is now facing a future without her. I can't pretend to imagine what that must feel like. I can only offer my heartfelt sympathy to Paul and say that as fans of your music and what you achieved with the Beatles, we're all here for you in spirit. 'Time is a great healer'. What a useless cliche that is at a time like this. Maybe Paul could take some comfort from some of his lyrics as the years pass. Maybe, you can take your sad song and make it a little better?"

Terry Mann, Derby

"I cannot even begin to fully express in words my sadness at Linda's death. To me, Linda was and always will be an inspiration. Her strength and determination set her apart from the rest. She never gave up without a fight. Her battle with cancer is an example of to all of us; she fought to the end. I am glad that she proved her critics wrong in so

many things, particularly as far as her marriage to Paul was concerned. I hope with all my heart that she has found the peace and serenity she so rightfully deserves."

'Yellow Submarine', London

"I was so sorry to learn of Linda's death. Dear Paul, on behalf of your fans all over the world, please remember that our thoughts and prayers are with you and your family at this time. Linda was regarded so highly and respected so much by us. She was like a friend, so kind, so gentle, nice."

Phil Judd, Essex

"They Said":
They said you couldn't have him,
But you did us all proud.
You gave Paul all he needed,
Without being loud.
They said that you were hard,
But kindness was your creed.
Good children were your reward,
Devoid of any greed.
They said you were a crank,
When you told us meat was bad.
Now being veggie's alright,
And they're the ones that are mad."

Betty Fryer, Hampshire

"Dear Paul, I am shocked and deeply saddened that your beloved wife Linda has lost her fight against cancer. You must allow yourself time to grieve at this tragic news, and take support from your family and your many admirers. But you can draw strength from the many good things about Linda, that she leaves behind for others. Her sheer determination is a reminder to us all that, no matter how bad things get, there is always hope, and that it's always worth fighting for what you believe in.

The papers this morning are saying that Linda broke a thousand hearts when she married you; now her passing breaks many more because we all came to love and admire her, and we will continue to do so. Paul and Linda: the two are inseparable, both physically and mentally. I write just a month after losing my own father to cancer. My dad lives on, around me and in me. Linda likewise will do so, through her compassion for animals, her vegetarian beliefs (just think how many people have turned vegetarian because of her), and quite simply through her unwavering love for you all. I send my deepest condolences, and I know that the strength with which Linda fought for the past couple of years will now become your strength. You'll get through this because Linda would want you to. Your fans

will be hoping that you can find the strength to do so. You wrote 'Little Willow' for Ringo's first wife. Now, for many, that lovely song will also be for your beautiful wife. I am praying God will give you strength."

David L. Fairey, Sheffield

"On 9th March 1993, as a LIPA ticket-holder, I was very fortunate to be able to meet Linda, Paul and the band at the Melbourne leg of the New World Tour. I handed Linda some flowers; she in turn gave me a hug and a kiss, and requested that a photo was taken of the two of us together. I would just like to send my deepest sympathy at learning of Linda's passing, to Paul, Heather, Mary, Stella and James, and to other family members and close friends. I still have the two photos that LIPA sent me from New York. I cherish them with fond memories of a very special lady who not

only touched her husband and family in a special way, but others too. I will sadly miss Linda's influence in her loving and enduring marriage to Sir Paul."

Ed Story, Melton FM radio, Australia

"The thing that I'll always remember most about Linda is her courage – not just the way she handled her final illness, but her bravery in standing up to the appalling treatment she received from certain sections of the press. Many journalists could never resist the chance to take a potshot at Linda, her music, her passion for animals and vegetarianism, and even the way she brought up her family. Some of the stories must have been heart-breaking for her and the McCartney family to read, but through it all Linda retained her dignity. Good for you, Linda: you showed them what real courage was all about."

Susan Baylis, Southampton.

Tributes to George

Friends and fans remember the youngest Beatle

Both Ringo and Paul had an emotional last meeting with George in New York on 12 November 2001. Paul was in the city to promote his charity single 'Freedom', while Ringo was in the US to see his daughter Lee, who is suffering from a brain tumour (she was being treated in Boston for what is, sadly, her second tumour in six years). Paul and Ringo's reunion with their stricken comrade took place at the Staten Island University Hospital, where George was undergoing stereotactic radiosurgery. Paul was reported to have broken down in tears during the six-hour meeting, but was "amazed that George was able to sit up the whole time". George's cancer was now widespread and he fully understood the seriousness of the situation.

Three days later, he and his family flew to Los Angeles to stay at the private residence of long-time friend, Gavin De Becker, in Beverly Hills. George was due to undergo still more chemotherapy at the renowned UCLA Medical Centre, but this was cancelled as the doctors decided that that all they could do was to keep his pain under control. George died on Thursday 29th November, at 1.30pm (9.30pm GMT). Gavin De Becker said "He died with one thought in mind – love one another". George's wife Olivia and son Dhani were both with him when he died.

George's body was cremated in Los Angeles within nine hours of his death, before the news was released to any of the international media. George's family and friends were quick to pay tribute to the man they loved. In addition, Her Majesty The Queen issued an official statement in which she said she was "very sad" to hear the news. Prime Minister Tony Blair described George as not only a great musician and artist, but someone who did an immense amount for charity, and who would be greatly missed.

Although George's death wasn't as much of a shock as John's murder some 21 years earlier, the tragedy still inspired a wave of grief that swept around the world. Here's a selection of the other tributes paid to George by his relatives and friends.　　　　(PN)

OLIVIA HARRISON: "He often said, 'Everything else can wait but the search for God cannot wait'. He left this world as he lived in it, conscious of God, fearless of death, and at peace, surrounded by family and friends."

PATTIE BOYD: "I'm so sad. I just loved him so much. He has always been so important for me. He was my first love and my first husband, and I loved him until he died."

PAUL McCARTNEY: "George was a lovely guy and a very brave man with a won-derful sense of humour. We had so many beautiful times together. He was just my baby brother, and he will be sorely missed. His music will live on forever, as will his personality."

RINGO STARR: "I loved him very much and we will miss him greatly for his sense of love, his sense of music, and his laughter. He was a best friend of mine. Both Barbara and I send our love and light to Olivia and Dhani."

NEIL ASPINALL: "It was my privilege to have been his friend."

GEORGE MARTIN: "George was a marvellous bloke, intensely loyal, a very warm person, caring deeply for those he loved, and he inspired much love in return."

JULIAN LENNON: "George always offered sound advice and was very encouraging."

YOKO ONO: "Thank you, George. It was grand knowing you."

BOB DYLAN: "He was a giant, he was like the sun, the flowers and the moon, he was a lovely man, and it was my privilege to call him my friend. He will be sorely missed by a world already lacking craftsmen."

RAVI SHANKAR: "He was a friend, disciple and son to me. I was struck both by his sincerity and his deep humility. It was my sitar and Indian music which connected me to George in the beginning, but very soon our relationship went beyond that. We spent the day before he died with him, and even then he looked so peaceful. George was a brave and beautiful soul."

JOOLS HOLLAND: "We've lost one of the most important figures in popular music."

HERE ARE JUST A FEW OF THE HEARTFELT TRIBUTES SENT TO *THE BEATLES BOOK* BY GEORGE'S FANS

George Harrison wasn't just one of my musical heroes: with John, Paul and Ringo, he was a friend. Whenever things weren't going well in my life, I would put on one of their albums and my spirits would be lifted. They could make you smile and laugh, and today's news almost makes me want to cry. I still find it hard to accept, after 21 years, that John has gone. That phrase, "The three surviving Beatles", is difficult to get your head around. And now we all have to face the reality that we only have Paul and Ringo.

George's passing wasn't unexpected, but it was still a shock. I'm trying to look at all this in the way that I think George would have wanted. In a philosophical sense, George hasn't died, he has only left one room for another; and we all have to face the fact that we'll be going through the door to that room one day. My one comfort is that with his passing, his pain is now over, and he has now found the peace he deserves.

Like millions of other fans, I am going to miss him, but he'll always be alive in our hearts and on our stereos. Thank you George for all the love, peace and happiness you gave us, and for being one of "the four lads who shook the world". I'd like to end with something that I think would appeal to George's Pythonesque sense of humour: he is no more, he has ceased to be – now that's what I call an ex-Beatle!
Terry Mann, Allenton, Derby.

Words cannot really express how big a hole the death of George Harrison has left in all our lives. Right until the end he was speaking his words of love and peace and for that he will never be forgotten. Please accept my small tribute, because my thoughts come right from the heart. My love to Olivia and Dhani at this deeply emotional time.

Is this what it takes for people to realise
The amazing talent that is in you
All those beautiful words, thoughtful
*   melodies,*
Your songs bring peace where others will
*   never do*
Now you're at peace, no longer in pain
Just moving along in your life
Leaving the message 'love one another'
To the friends, fans, your son and your
*   wife*
Thank you George for caring
For helping all people big and small
The world will feel this loss forever
And your words will live on in us all.
Jenni Robinson, Welton, Lincoln.

I want to send my deepest sympathy to George's family and Paul and Ringo at this very sad time, as well as every Beatle fan around the world. I can't believe another of our heroes has gone. I know we expected it, but it is no easier to take. If ever the saying "only the good die young" was true, it certainly is now. George was one of the gentlest, most loving and caring men who ever lived. I hope he gets to heaven and meets the God he so obviously loved. I cried when I heard the news, but I won't cry anymore because he is in a far better place. John will look out for him as he always did. May God bless them both.
Gary, London.

Reading the newspaper reports, I was shocked to see so many people dismissing George as nothing more than "the guitarist of the Beatles" and "the third Beatle who failed to match up to Lennon and McCartney". As all true Beatles fans know, however, that is sheer nonsense. George was always a key factor in the 'Beatles dream' that brought so much magic to the world. His musical genius and witty yet moody character graced us all for many years, and brought joy to countless people.

In many ways, I thought that after the break-up of the group, George created the best music of the four individual Beatles. In particular, songs such as 'Beware Of Darkness', 'Run Of The Mill', 'Awaiting On You All', 'You', 'Blow Away', 'Faster', 'Life Itself', 'Just For Today' and 'Cheer Down'

George's final album

Peter Doggett reviews *Brainwashed*: a celebration of George's life and beliefs

It should have been a landmark in Beatles history, a source of excitement and joy for anyone who loves George's music. Instead, the release of *Brainwashed*, the album he was working on at the time of his death, is inevitably tinged with sadness. Anyone who plays the album, however, will quickly discover that gloom and doom were the last things on George's mind when he was making it. Most of the songs were written when George knew that he was facing a life and death struggle, that he was almost certainly going to lose. There are several places on the album where he talks about the harsh and sudden reality that he is having to face. But one emotion that is entirely missing from *Brainwashed* is despair.

Quite the opposite, in fact. Most of the songs on this beautiful record are very upbeat and surprisingly optimistic. They are the work of a man who had profound spiritual and religious beliefs, and who felt certain that death was not the end of the story, but a new beginning. In the hands of another artist, someone who was more bogged down in everyday life, *Brainwashed* could have made very traumatic listening. Coming from George, it's a real affirmation of joy, love and peace – a remarkable final statement from a man who stumbled across his spiritual home of India in the mid-60s, and stayed under that influence right until the end. It's almost impossible to listen to the record without a wide smile creeping across your face. I'd expected to feel immensely sad when I heard George's final recordings; instead, I was reminded exactly why I had always loved his music so much in the first place.

When George realised that he wouldn't be able to finish the project himself, he asked his son Dhani, and his old friend and fellow Traveling Wilbury Jeff Lynne, to see it through. "Before we started working on the album, George and Dhani had collaborated extensively on pre-production," Jeff Lynne recalls. "George would come round my house and he'd always have a new song with him, which he'd strum on a guitar or a ukelele. The songs just knocked me out. Then George said, 'I'd like you to finish them for me'. We talked about it, and he said

Above: The emotional tribute concert at the Albert Hall in 2002 in memory of George.
Left: In this shot Paul is joined by Eric Clapton and Dhani.

that he didn't want the album to be posh, but more like demos." Jeff admits that he didn't do entirely what he had been told: "The songs deserved more than that, because they were great. As far as I was concerned, if I left them as rough as he would have liked, they wouldn't have come over as well. I wanted to make them as good as they could be, and I think we struck a good balance. So, sorry, George, I made them a little bit posher than you may have wanted! But I felt I was only doing them justice."

Before his final illness, George had already worked out the full track listing for the album, and he left plenty of notes and instructions for Dhani and Jeff to follow. They set to work last spring, at Jeff's home studio. As Dhani admits, it was an eerie process at first: "I remember coming in from England and recording guitars with Jeff the first night. It was the most surreal thing ever. I kept turning around, looking for my dad – 'Er, is that all right?' But there was no one there to tell me." It helped, Dhani says, that they were doing what George had planned all along. "The album was always going to be finished this way, with Jeff helping my dad and me with the final production. We stuck to the plan, except that my dad died, which made our job more difficult."

The first thing you hear on the album is George's unmistakeable voice, telling the engineer, "Give me plenty of that guitar". Then we're into 'Any Road', a smooth rocker with a real mood of celebration. George's voice stands out, not showing the slightest hint of his illness, and so does his

George at the time of his Cloud Nine LP.

familiar slide guitar. Other highlights include the gorgeous 'Pisces Fish'. Obviously written when he knew the worst about his illness, it is a remarkably peaceful piece of work, with a chorus line that captures his vision of eternal life: "I'm a Pisces fish and the river runs through my soul". Like 'Pisces Fish', 'Rising Sun' gives the chance to transform his philosophy of life into a metaphor about the natural world, complete with another stunning melody. But they're just the tip of the proverbial iceberg. The entire album is an emotional and musical trip, which more than lives up to Jeff Lynne's hope that it will be "a celebration of George's life".

No doubt we'll hear more 'new' songs from George in the future, as he entrusted Dhani with plans for a long-term reissue programme of his albums, which will feature unreleased material. But *Brainwashed* is the last 'official' record from a complex, incredibly talented man, who had the ability to transmit his love of life, and his spiritual insights, to the rest of the world. This album does that with grace, style and enormous love. Thanks, George.   (PD)

Paul and Heather

The last Beatle wedding in June 2002 turned out to be the most spectacular

For some weeks, everyone thought the date would be June 6 and the ceremony would be held at a hideaway Long Island location in the Hamptons on America's east coast. But in a typically wily attempt to preserve the privacy of his multi-millionaire wedding plans until the very last moment, Macca beavered away in secret with his bride-to-be to finalise the real details, managing to keep both date and venue under wraps until days before the big event.

It was 87-year-old Sir Jack Leslie, owner of picturesque Castle Leslie at Glaslough in County Monaghan, who spilled the beans by leaking the news to reporters that his romantic 100-acre pile had been selected as the fairytale setting for Paul and Heather's marriage ceremony. He announced that the sumptuous shindig was scheduled to be held the following Tuesday, June 11, precisely one week before Paul's 60th birthday – adding that, of course, the information was all absolutely top secret! Paul's choice of Castle Leslie, located close to the Northern Irish border, was linked to the fact that his mother Mary, who died when Paul was a teenager, had family roots in nearly Castleblaney.

Once dear old 'Uncle Jack' had blown it, Paul's publicist put an official spin on the news, saying "It's a rock'n'roll wedding – no dress code" and "It's a proper Liverpool wedding, with beer on the piano to be taken in large measure". Indeed, we were able to watch one heavily-laden truck pass through the gates with a cargo of Guinness to augment a reported 300 bottles of vintage Cristal and Laurent Perrier champagne, worth around £54,000, plus 1000 bottles of beer and copious supplies of Merlot and Australian Chardonnay wines.

On the Monday, little more than 24 hours before they were due to exchange their vows, Paul and Heather broke off from a wedding rehearsal to come out and confront the hundreds of international media people and sightseeing locals gathered at the gates of Castle Leslie. Their appearance brought on a brief bout of Heathermania among the

media. Heather and Paul looked cool and comfortably casual. Both wore jumpers. With hers, Heather had a pair of tight-fitted faded blue jeans with wedge-heeled sandals, while Paul sported baggy old trousers and rubber clogs. Eyeing the battery of clicking cameras and hand-held microphones, Paul handed Heather a single red rose, and said: "We just want to have a quiet, private wedding. Lots of family and friends. There won't be more than ten people you'll have heard of." Paul admitted that he felt a bit nervous, and then in response to a hasty prompt from Heather, he added: "And excited, yeah, excited".

As assorted relatives, celebrities and hired help started to roll up by sleek limousine, ordinary taxi or crowded coach, Paul's squad of minders kept the castle gates completely uncrashable by denying entry to all but the authorised and chosen few, who had been allocated individually numbered and colour-coded security passes. During the morning, a jolly bunch of almost 100 relatives from the extended McCartney clan flew into Belfast by chartered aircraft from Liverpool's John Lennon Airport, arriving at Castle Leslie in boisterous, ready-to-party mood after lunching at a local hotel. Occasionally a minder would take a wary

Paul and Heather kiss for the world's press photographers before the wedding.

look at the sky above to check on the swooping helicopters hired by press and television people to survey the scene – the only intruders the security team could not control.

Family members and VIP buddies who had stayed in the castle's 14 bedrooms overnight made their way on foot from the main building to the estate's tiny church of St Salvator. The rest of the 300 guests came in either from the airport or local hotels. Paul's suggestion that only ten faces would be familiar to the press and general public turned out to be fairly accurate, as a short, star-studded procession of arrivals challenged the photographers to capture images of all the right people. Ringo was chauffeured to the castle in style from his private jet, which had landed at Belfast Airport. Other prominent arrivals included Sir George Martin, hot from his Royal Jubilee concert duties, Eric Clapton, Jools Holland, Twiggy accompanied by her actor husband Leigh Lawson, Mike Batt (the music man behind the Wombles) with his actress wife Julianne White, tennis ace Monica Seles, Pink Floyd's Dave Gilmour, lyricist Sir Tim Rice and Pretenders frontwoman Chrissie Hynde.

Wearing a floor-length gown of ecru (ivory and cream) coloured lace and carrying a bouquet of pink and red McCartney roses (named after Paul some nine years ago) augmented with several peonies, the bride came to church across a lake on a vintage 40-foot barge decked with white lilies – arriving a mere eight minutes late and only just escaping a sudden shower of rain. Waiting for her to land was Paul, in a dark brown three-piece suit spectacularly lined in deep purple with a rose in the buttonhole. The ceremony was delayed not only for the usual reason that the bride arrived suitably late, but because the engine noise from media helicopters overhead threatened to drown out what was happening. As Heather walked down the aisle, the bridal march was a version of Paul's new composition 'Heather'. The venerable Cecil Pringle, Archdeacon of Clogher, conducted the 30-minute service. Guests sitting close enough to the altar to see noted that Heather shed a few tears as she said "I do".

Hymns included 'Praise My Soul The King Of Heaven' and 'Lord Of All Hopefulness'. Paul's good friend, the poet Adrian Mitchell, read a piece he had written especially for the occasion, entitled 'Roses In The Summertime'. The half-hour ceremony, described by Paul's PR man as "joy-ful and moving", finished soon after five o'clock, and as the guests poured out of the church they were just in time to see a perfectly formed rainbow appear over the castle, as church bells began to peal. The rainbow was a magical touch. From the church, everyone made their way to the massive lakeside marquees where the evening reception was to be held.

Once they were inside, the new Lady McCartney (who has said that she dislikes the idea of using the title) had a chance to show off her splendid ring of white gold, inset with six yellow diamonds, to gasping admirers. In one area of the long tented structure, surrounded by all manner of appropriate decorations including Indian silks, an Indian-style buffet banquet was laid out, featuring various veggie-based curry dishes created for the occasion by the castle's in-house chef, Noel McNeel. Both the décor and the eats seemed to be Paul's way of paying homage to George, who would have been close to the top of the couple's guest list had he lived.

When the guests had eaten, Paul's tour band went into action on one stage, while a ten-piece Indo-Celtic group, the Celtic Ragas, performed elsewhere, playing violins, keyboards, penny whistles and an Indian harp, accompanied by a troupe of Indian dancers. An amusing ten-minute 'home movie' of Paul and Heather in a series of energetic snogging sequences shot in 20 different countries of the world was shown during a break in the live entertainment, and drew roars of laughter punctuated by wolf whistles and cries of encouragement! The wedding cake was a five-foot-high affair created by London specialists the Little Venice Cake Company, with four dark chocolate-based tiers topped with decorative white roses also made of chocolate.

Paul and his brother Mike made the customary speeches. Paul recalled (with deliberate exaggerations) the McCartney family's impoverished Liverpudlian lifestyle during his childhood: "My trousers were so thin that when I sat down on a penny coin, I could feel which way up it was, heads or tails." In those days of post-war food shortages he'd only have gone to a wedding to take home the rice! At one point Heather sang the Beach Boys' 'God Only Knows', Paul's favourite song, but she couldn't upstage Paul's own vocal offering, a splendid gangsta rap spoof in

The Beatles Book MONTHLY
JULY 2002
£3.00

FULL STORY OF THE WEDDING
The Beatles and 'The Lord Of The Rings'

How The Beatles Book celebrated Paul's marriage to Heather in 2002.

honour of his new wife, performed with support from Mike plus a group of professional rappers and dancers.

Eventually, at shortly before two in the morning, the bride and groom made a spectacular departure, standing on the deck of their flower-strewn boat and waving to everyone from beneath a colourful arc of roses. Meanwhile, an impressive firework display based on some floating pontoons began to light up the night sky, with a kaleidoscope of bright colours accompanied by loud explosions that caused Heather momentarily to cover her ears. A spotlight followed their progress as they sailed away to the estate's helicopter pad from where a waiting aircraft whisked the couple away to Belfast Airport. Here the final leg of their honeymoon journey began, as the newly-weds boarded Paul's privately chartered executive jet plane, which sped them across the Atlantic.

Soon after Paul and Heather left the party, fleets of cars and coaches ferried most of their happy but weary guests from the castle grounds, while a small convoy of stretch limousines collected a couple of dozen VIP passengers. Each guest clutched a silver ballpoint pen engraved "Love Paul and Heather" – a prized memento of an event to remember long after the ink runs out. (TB)

'Back in the USA' with Paul

Gillian Gaar reviews Paul's Driving USA tour and finds him in superb form

Throughout his amazing career, Paul McCartney has revealed time and again that he simply loves to perform before a live audience. In the late 60s, he tried hard to persuade the other Beatles to go back to playing concerts, even if that meant showing up unannounced at tiny halls – something he did himself a few years later when he launched his group, Wings. In between tours, he regularly turns up for one-off performances – anything from a Prince's Trust concert to

MTV's *Unplugged*. So it was no surprise to learn that a second US leg would follow last spring's 'Driving USA' tour, a very successful venture that saw all but three dates sell out.

His second tour, titled 'Back in the USA', featured 23 dates, plus a few surprises. The tour visited regions of America that Paul had missed the first time round, including the Pacific Northwest, where he played in Portland, Oregon (his first visit to the city

since the Beatles played there in 1965), and his first-ever appearance in Tacoma, Washington. It was evident that great attention had been paid to every detail of the evening from the moment the audience entered the halls. Apart from tour merchandise, tables had also been set up for people to promote two of Paul's pet causes: Adopt-a-Minefield and PETA (People for the Ethical Treatment of Animals). It meant that you were just as likely to see fans sporting 'No More Land Mines' t-shirts and 'Stop Eating Animals' badges as McCartney tour shirts.

The unusual pre-show entertainment enhanced the festive atmosphere. A hint was given in the programme that we were going to enjoy a "benignly-bewildering tour through the antiquity of entertainment". That translated into an assortment of characters – from Grecian statues, Harlequin clowns toting giant balloons and a contortionist displayed in a clear box, to Asian warriors who'd apparently escaped from *Crouching Tiger, Hidden Dragon* – traipsing through the audience to remixed versions of Paul's Fireman music. The trippy troupe assembled on stage, dancing faster and faster as the music built to a final, crashing chord, and a silhouette of Paul appeared on one of the stage's screens to ecstatic cheers from the crowd. The screen rose to reveal Paul (dressed in a blue suit with a Nehru-style jacket in Portland and a black suit in Tacoma) and his famous Hofner bass guitar.

The band included longtime McCartney keyboard player – and music director for the tour – Paul 'Wix' Wickens, guitarist Rusty Anderson and drummer Abe Laboriel, Jr., both of whom played on *Driving Rain*; and guitarist/bassist Brian Ray, who joined the band when they played the Super Bowl last February). They launched into 'Hello Goodbye', a song making its live debut on this tour. It was a choice that set the mood for the evening: of the 35-song set, 21 numbers came from the Beatles era, with the rest featuring six Wings classics, and eight solo McCartney numbers. One of the complaints from otherwise happy concertgoers was the absence of more Wings material and latter-era McCartney music, such as songs from *Flaming Pie*, an album that reached No. 2 in

America. But Wings fans were undoubtedly satisfied by the next song, 'Jet', which had the audience pumping their fists in the air as they joined in the rousing chorus. It was back to the Beatles era for an equally lively 'All My Loving', and then came another surprise – 'Getting Better', another song never done in concert before. It underscored one of the tour's greatest pleasures; though it's fun seeing Paul doing his familiar hits, it's extra-special to see numbers you've only heard on record (or CD) finally come to vibrant life on stage. In Tacoma, Paul acknowledged the song's reception by holding his guitar aloft and saying, "Good to be here. I must say, nice place".

Next was 'Coming Up', a harder-edged version of a song that's been a live favorite since its concert debut in 1979. 'Let Me Roll It,' one of *Band On The Run*'s highlights that was a concert staple during the Wings years, and reappeared on the setlist of Paul's 1993 world tour, was another welcome return. Following the song, Paul removed his jacket to reveal a long-sleeved red T-shirt, as the band chimed in with a short snippet of 'The Stripper'. Then came a trio of tracks from *Driving Rain*. Oddly, for a tour ostensibly promoting it, Paul performed few songs from the album. For some in the audience it was undoubtedly the first time they had heard the heartfelt 'Lonely Road', the lively 'Driving Rain' (inspired by a drive up the California coast), and a moving 'Your Loving Flame', dedicated to "someone special in the audience tonight" – a reference to Paul's new wife, Heather Mills. One of the best aspects of the show's production was its use of screens. Banks of small screens hung in a semi-circle over the stage, flanked by larger ones on the sides. The total "acreage" of the screens was 120 feet by 20 feet, according to set designer Roy Bennett.

They not only offered close-ups of the action on stage, but they also displayed carefully chosen images for each song – frantic scenes of Beatlemania accompanying 'All My Loving' for example. During 'Lonely Road', footage from the video, which recast the song's lyrics as street signs, was shown, while the numbers shouted out during the chorus of 'Driving Rain' danced across the screens during that song. Then came what for many would be the show's highlight: the acoustic set. Paul has featured these sets in his tours before, but rarely has he done so many songs on his own, with the band sent offstage. A delicate 'Blackbird', with Paul

playing acoustic guitar, set the appropriate mood (and received a standing ovation at both shows), followed by 'Every Night', a *McCartney* track that Paul has regularly performed live. 'We Can Work It Out' was next, and was similar to its *Unplugged* arrangement. Paul's psychedelic piano was then rolled out on stage by two of the pre-show characters, including a strong man, prompting Paul to joke, "I warned him about using steroids!" He then played another song not previously performed live, a medley of 'You Never Give Me Your Money'/'Carry That Weight' (though 'Weight' was featured in the closing medley of the 1989-90 tour). Much has been made about Paul apparently flubbing the lyrics of 'Money' – a presumed "mistake" that was mentioned in many reviews – but anyone who saw more than one show (or heard a tour bootleg) would realise it is just a well-rehearsed deliberate "pastiche" that's done every night!

Before the next number, Paul related a few amusing stories about "massages I have known" on tours around the world. Mention of a massage in Japan drew some response from the crowd, prompting Paul to say "No, not that time!" – another regular bit of business that drew laughter. Wix then joined Paul for 'Fool On The Hill', while clips from, naturally enough, *Magical Mystery Tour* played on the screen.

Then Paul returned to centre-stage alone with an acoustic guitar, to pay an emotional tribute to two departed friends. After asking the crowd, "Let's hear it for John!", Paul performed 'Here Today,' his eloquent love song to his songwriting partner. Then came the only non-McCartney song of the night, George Harrison's 'Something'. In a neat twist, Paul accompanied himself on a ukulele that George had given him, no less. The performances of both songs clearly tugged at everyone's heartstrings, and drew a great response. The whole band returned for 'Eleanor Rigby', apart from Ray Laboriel, who came down front to sing harmonies on the song. But he was back behind his kit again for another number drenched in harmonies, 'Here, There And Everywhere'. Wix took up the accordion for a wonderfully atmospheric 'Michelle', while typically Parisian scenes were projected on the screens.

But the crowd was soon on its feet again as the group stormed back with 'Band On The Run', accompanied by footage from one of Paul's most notable swings through the Northwest, when he set an indoor attendance record with Wings at the Seattle Kingdome in June 1976. 'Back In The USSR', was another crowd-pleaser, the Tacoma crowd being especially receptive to Paul's uptempo numbers, pounding the stalls with their feet enthusiastically after the song. Paul moved to a grand piano for the next three songs, beginning with the highly emotive 'Maybe I'm Amazed'. Then came 'Let 'Em In', newly added to this leg of the tour, followed by 'My Love', which Paul explained was written for his first wife, Linda, and which he dedicated to "all the lovers in the house". When it ended, he made a heart symbol over his head with his arms. The next song was not only new to this tour leg, it had also never been performed live before – a beautiful rendition of 'She's Leaving Home', which again had Laboriel coming down front to provide harmonies (threatening to drown out Paul at times). The energy soared once again when the band charged into 'Can't Buy Me Love', accompanied by *A Hard Day's Night* footage. Then came 'Freedom', the song Paul wrote for the US in the wake of the 9/11 tragedy (though he simply introduced it as a song he'd written for last year's "Concert for New York City"). A banner

The promo handbill printed to promote Paul's US tour in 2002.

with the Statue of Liberty was unfurled and, urged on by the band, the crowd clapped along and waved small American flags (though a few Canadian flags were also spotted in the audience). But that was nothing compared to the reception for 'Live And Let Die' (with Paul back on the grand piano), which featured explosions, fireworks, and flame jets, and had the Tacoma crowd excitedly pounding the bleachers again. "I gotta tell you, Tacoma rocks!", Ray enthused afterwards. "You guys are crazy!"

Both nights, the halls were lit up with lighters held on high during 'Let It Be', mirrored by footage of flickering candles on the screens. The psychedelic piano was rolled out on stage again for a number Paul told the audience they "might want to sing along to". What else could it be but 'Hey Jude', which, as usual, ended in a mass audience singalong led by Paul, who at one point had the men and women singing separately to see who could perform best. It was apparently a draw, as Paul pointed to different members of the audience afterwards and exclaimed, "You were great...and you were great...and you...!". That brought the main set to a close. But there was still more to come. For the first encore, the band returned to the stage carrying an American flag, along with the appropriate state flag (and Paul in a "No More Land Mines" T-shirt). Paul returned to the piano for another of his trademark ballads, 'The Long And Winding Road'.

Then it was back to the high-energy end of the spectrum, with a pulse-pounding 'Lady Madonna', as the screen flashed shots of notable women, from cartoon character Betty Boop to artist Frida Kahlo to Princess Diana. 'I Saw Her Standing There' kept the crowd dancing – including Heather, who came into the photo pit for the number, bopping along as Paul pointed to her and her image appeared on the screens. Afterwards, he probably made a few hearts stop by casually tossing his legendary Hofner across the stage to his personal assistant, John Hammel. Once again, the band left the stage. But how could Paul leave without performing his most famous song of all? He couldn't, of course, and so he returned to the stage, acoustic guitar in hand (informing the audience it was the one he'd used on *The Ed Sullivan Show*) to perform 'Yesterday'. Then the full band joined him once again for a medley that neatly bookended the 'Hello Goodbye' beginning: 'Sgt. Pepper's Lonely Hearts Club Band (reprise)' coupled with

'The End'. During the final curtain call, confetti exploded from above to cover the band and the now delirious audience. Though Paul has toured the US as a solo act in 1989-90, 1993, and this year, and has toured America previously with the Beatles and Wings, he still brings new fans to his show. A number of concertgoers *The Beatles Book* spoke to had never seen Paul in concert before.

Overall, it proved to be an exhilarating trip through the past, and a reminder of just how extensive Macca's back catalogue is. Amazingly, there are songs in the setlist Paul first played live almost 40 years ago, and to see them still giving such enjoyment to people must be a performer's dream. Paul clearly prides himself on his ability to please an audience, as he says in one of the programme's revealing interviews: "[The show's] what I think an audience would basically want – an average audience; not a Wings audience and not my *Flaming Pie*

audience, or a Beatles audience." Although hardcore fans may have wanted a set with a broader range of material, he clearly wanted to satisfy as many people as possible. Judging by the reactions I saw, this tour is an overwhelming success (although complaints were made about the ticket prices, which went as high as $250 and drew criticism in the Seattle press – not surprising as Washington state currently has the nation's highest unemployment rate). But it was undeniably a show of consummate professionalism, well paced and visually exciting. In general, the band provided solid backing for Paul (though Laboriel tended to be too heavy-handed on drums). Paul's voice did show some strain in the upper register, but it never dampened his enthusiasm, and he displayed all the energy of a man half his age. Flyers on seats throughout the halls may have been promoting Paul's upcoming live CD and DVD, but when the man says "See you next time!" at the end of each show, you can be sure he means it.   (GG)

Beatles memorabilia

Rare personal Beatles items and even cheap novelties have become very collectable

S ince the early 80s, pop and rock memorabilia has become one of the fastest-growing and most profitable areas of collecting around the world. All the top auction-houses in London, Liverpool, New York and California hold regular sales, while hundreds of thousands of private collectors enjoy buying and selling rare and desirable items. But one group dominates the field completely. Usually, Beatles items make up more than half of every major auction, and prices for their memorabilia, autographs and rare records easily outstrip their rivals'. The sales potential of items connected with other acts has fluctuated greatly down the years, but one thing has remained constant: the Beatles are easily the most collectable act in rock and pop history.

Much of the collecting market is devoted to novelty items issued at the height of Beatlemania, which most people treated like throwaways. Nobody imagined that 40 years on, collectors would be competing with their chequebooks to buy items that sold for just a few pence or cents back in 1964.

These ephemeral items were originally issued as a blatant cash-in on the group's popularity. No sooner had the Beatles achieved fame in Britain, than the manufacturers of everything from bubblegum to bed linen realised that there was a chance to make some easy money. In the summer of 1963, the boys' names and faces began to appear on all manner of unusual objects, most of which they never saw or were even informed about before they went on sale. The great Beatles merchandising explosion had begun.

Then, in 1964, the Beatles broke big in America – bigger, in fact, than any artist before or since. And as you would probably expect, the Americans set about producing Beatles memorabilia in a much bigger way than the British. Almost overnight, stores in the USA were awash with Fab Four items, most of them issued without the approval of the group or Brian Epstein. Eventually, the

A bass guitar autographed by several top stars, including Paul, John and George.

A very rare acetate copy of the Beatles' second single from January 1963.

group's lawyers managed to assert some kind of control, and unauthorised items were withdrawn from sale. But by then the financial damage had already been done. It's been called one of the great scandals in pop history, as the Beatles received only a tiny fraction of the money they should have earned from all this merchandising. Brian Epstein eventually appointed people to look after the Beatles' merchandising rights in the States, but even then the proceeds were a fraction of what they would have received if the same situation occurred today.

As the first excitement of Beatlemania died away, so did the tide of Beatles memorabilia. There was a brief resurgence of activity when the *Yellow Submarine* film was released in 1968, and the group's Apple organisation issued some tie-in promotional items of its own at the same time. But far fewer things were available in the stores around the world at the end of the 60s than had been on sale five years earlier. That might well have been the end of the story, if the Beatles had faded from memory like most 60s bands. But instead, the group's popularity kept on growing, and as a result fans have been prepared to pay huge sums of money for rare collectables ever since.

Basically, Beatles memorabilia falls into two main categories: mass-produced items, and one-offs. In both cases, it's vital to be able to tell an original from a later copy, or even a fake. Many of the Beatles novelties that have been sold in the shops over the last thirty years look very much like the original items from 1963 and 1964, but are worth only a fraction as much. And in the field of one-off items like autographs, experts can easily distinguish real Beatles signatures from those written by other people. The key word here is 'authentication'. It is not enough to have the name of a Beatle scrawled on a piece of paper, as anyone could have written it. Before you buy an autograph, you need some proof that it was actually signed by a Beatle.

That's where problems can arise. In the early years of Beatlemania, printed versions of the boys' signatures were included on all kinds of novelty items, from curtains to travel bags. So anyone who wanted to copy John's signature, or Paul's, or add the names of all four to a favourite Beatles photo, had plenty of material to copy. Given some artistic flair and a lot of practice, almost anyone could duplicate the Beatles' signatures. In fact, many people who worked for the group in the 60s specialised in doing exactly that. At the height of their fame, the Beatles were far too busy to fulfil every request for their autographs. It wasn't unusual for hundreds of fans to hand in their autograph books at a Beatles concert, and if the boys had signed them all, they would never have had time to

This brief McCartney lyric sheet for an unpublished song was sold at auction.

sing. So instead, close Beatles aides such as Neil Aspinall and Mal Evans learned how to fake a very convincing set of Fab Four signatures. The fans went home happy, thinking that John, Paul, George and Ringo themselves had signed their book. It can come as quite a shock to discover 40 years later that it was actually Mal or Neil who had written their cherished Beatles autographs. Experts at the main auction houses in London and elsewhere around the world can now distinguish between a real and a 'roadie' set of autographs, and the difference in value can be hundreds or even thousands of pounds. Bizarrely, George Harrison was also quite capable of knocking off a very realistic looking set of Beatles autographs – something that he used to do as a party trick to impress journalists in later years!

In many cases, a fan was lucky enough to have their photo taken while their favourite Beatle was signing their book; or else they can prove that they were present on a particular occasion and met one or more of the group. It is always much easier to authenticate signatures

A page of John's Daily Howl artwork from the 50s

that come with inscriptions – with an extra message, in other words, from one or more of the Beatles. Fraudsters can easily fake a John Lennon signature by copying it from a book or magazine, but it's much more difficult to copy John's handwriting exactly on a longer message. Other signed items authenticate themselves, of course, like contracts, letters or even cheques which were signed by one of the Beatles. The really exclusive items, like handwritten sets of lyrics for the group's songs, can sell for almost unbelievable prices – as much as $400,000 for a manuscript of 'Nowhere Man', for example.

Being able to prove where an item comes from is just as important if you are hoping to buy or sell an instrument or other object once used or owned by one of the Beatles. The guitars, drums and keyboards that the group used in the 60s were first listed in detail in *Beat Monthly* (later *Beat Instrumental*) magazine. More recently, Andy Babiuk's book *Beatles Gear* drew on this information and other sources to compile a comprehensive list of the Beatles equipment. The boys held on to most of the instruments that they played on their records, but a few have come up for auction, complete with legal documentation to confirm their origins. These are probably the ultimate Beatles collectables.

Only a handful of people around the world have been lucky enough to own a Beatles

One of the strangest items of Beatles memorabilia ever sold: John's bed!

guitar or piano, of course. 99% of collectors are happy to make do with mass-produced items – some of which can be surprisingly rare in their own right. Almost every record the Beatles released in the 60s was a million-seller, but that hasn't prevented a very healthy trade in Beatles discs. The rarest examples are one-offs, such as the acetates which were cut in EMI or Apple studios so the boys or their management could listen to what they had just recorded

In later years, unreleased tracks would have been passed around on cassette, or later CD, or these days sent as MP3s via e-mail. But in the 60s, individual acetates – much thicker and less breakable than normal vinyl singles and LPs – were used. Many of these have survived, and some of them document work-in-progress rather than finished songs. For example, one fascinating acetate was sold in London at the start of this decade, featuring the boys' original instrumental backing track for 'All You Need Is Love'. It sounded nothing like the completed record, and it was probably the only remaining copy of this early version of the song.

Despite the heavy sales of Beatles releases in the 60s, original first pressings of many of their records can still fetch very good prices – as long as they're in perfect condition. Items that are particularly sought-after include the original red-label Parlophone releases of the 'Love Me Do' and 'Please Please Me' singles from 1962/63; the first gold-and-black label edition of the *Please Please Me* LP; and the version of the *Let It Be* LP that was released in 1970 in a special package with a photo book called *The Beatles Get Back*.

There are plenty of rare solo items as well, such as John and George's early LPs on the Apple label; Paul's instrumental album under the pseudonym of Percy 'Thrills' Thrillington; and Ringo's collection of children's songs, *Scouse The Mouse*. And that's just records issued in the UK. America produced dozens of rarities of its own, and the same is true for many other countries around the world. Many encyclopaedic volumes have been published down the years, to document all the potential Beatles rarities.

In recent years, a whole new range of Beatles memorabilia has been produced.

When it comes to Beatles memorabilia collecting, though, there is nothing quite like the merchandising that was sold in the mid-60s. It's true that much of it was of quite poor quality, and that almost all of it was done as a blatant cash-in on the boys' success. But over the years, these rather cheap and nasty items have taken on a real air of nostalgia, because they conjure up the authentic spirit of the first wave of Beatlemania. The Fab Four weren't the first pop stars to become the targets of the merchandising men; Elvis Presley and Cliff Richard had already been commemorated in the same way. But nothing in pop history has ever come close to matching the impact and extent of the Beatles merchandising phenomenon.

It all began slowly enough. As the Beatles racked up their second No. 1 hit with 'From Me To You', the people who sold stars' photos in the UK music press – firms like Starpics, Topstar, Starfotos and Pop Portraits – began to add the Beatles to their portfolios. The manufacturers all claimed their photos were 'exclusive', but most of them were familiar copies of the Dezo Hoffmann shots taken around the time of their first album. Then, in October 1963, came the start of a new form of cash-ins – in the form of the first Beatles-style clothing. The group's French collarless jackets had caused quite a stir, and soon one firm was advertising 'Beatles jackets' at just under £6 – not cheap for 1963! Other companies quickly followed suit. Besides the jackets, there were 'Beatle boots', of the Cuban-heeled variety that the boys had helped to

popularise. By Christmas, you could buy a Beatles head scarf, a jewellery set featuring the Fab Four, and a comb bearing the message "I like the Beatles". It wasn't all clothes and accessories: there was also Beatle-headed notepaper, Beatles Christmas cards, a Beatles calendar, a mirror with glass on one side and a picture of the Fab Four on the other, and a Beatles travelling bag, with one of Dezo's famous pics on the side. One dealer even offered full-sized photographs of each of the group, measuring six feet high by two feet across.

Christmas 1963 was just the first high-water-mark for memorabilia; it was also the moment when Brian Epstein clamped down on unauthorised memorabilia. From now on, manufacturers had to show that their goods were officially approved by the group. Everything else, even the pens and notepaper, simply disappeared overnight. The first item to bear the official stamp of approval was a set of four Beatles lapel badges, most of which were soon attached to clothing or

school satchels. Next came a variety of plastic figures of the group – which are worth much more today if they come complete with their original cardboard boxes. Most people immediately threw all the packaging away, of course, which is why the boxes are so rare. Beatles instruments were the next

craze, ranging from plastic guitars to a Ringo Starr drumkit for kids, and even a John Lennon harmonica. But the biggest selling item of 1964, especially in America, was the Beatles wig. Top politicians and showbiz stars posed for publicity pictures wearing pretty horrible Beatle moptops, as Beatlemania swept across North America with even more speed and force than in Britain the previous year.

February 1964 marked the beginning of the second great wave of Beatles merchandising. The Beatles completely dominated the US charts over the next few months – at one point they had the two best-selling LPs in the States, plus the top FIVE singles in the chart. Meanwhile, manufacturers set to work, to satisfy the incredible demand for anything bearing the Beatles' name. The sheer variety of US memorabilia made in 1964 is quite staggering: records made out of liquorice, cookies, cereal bowls, drinking glasses, mugs, coasters, cake decorations, panties, stockings, sweatshirts, aprons, sunglasses, caps, hats, tennis shoes, leather belts, combs, ties, talcum powder, towels, bubble bath, blankets, bedspreads, curtains, lampshades, colouring books, paperweights, pencil cases, ash-trays, medallions, thermos flasks, wallpaper . . . the list goes on and on. Among the most sought-after items among collectors today are the Flip Your Wig board game; the Bobb'N'Head Beatle dolls; and, bizarrely, the Beatles banjo – an instrument that the group never actually played! (PD)

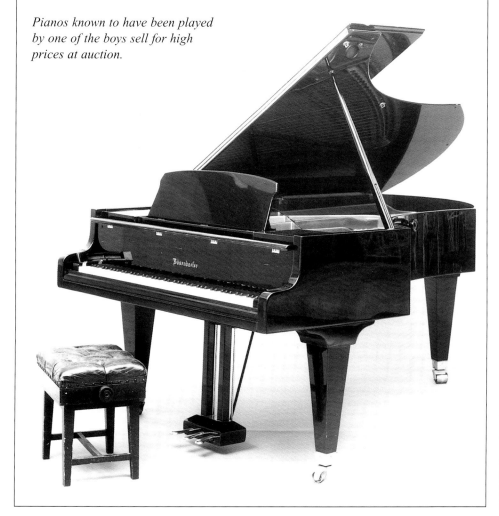

Pianos known to have been played by one of the boys sell for high prices at auction.

> We haven't listed values for most of the items mentioned in this feature because they are constantly changing.

Rare Beatles posters

Pete Nash produces the documents that chart their early rise to fame

Concert posters are designed to be slapped on a wall or a hoarding for a few weeks, and then torn down and thrown away. But as anyone who has been following the trends at London's pop and rock memorabilia auctions knows, vintage Beatles posters from the early 1960s are now very valuable collector's items, changing hands for hundreds or even thousands of pounds. Besides their financial value, these posters offer a fascinating glimpse of a world in which the Beatles were minor celebrities in Liverpool, but virtually unknown everywhere else in the world. You can trace their progress from second on the bill at the Kaiserkeller in Hamburg, to becoming "the North's top group" in 1962. It's amazing to think back to a time when you could see the Beatles – and four other Merseybeat bands, one of them destined to follow the Beatles to the top of the charts – for just 25p (or five bob, as it was back then).

It's amazing to look back at a time when promoters were quite incapable of spelling the Beatles' name correctly; when the boys were being billed as "Stars of Polydor Records", thanks to their 'My Bonnie' single with Tony Sheridan; and when John, Paul and George had to play second fiddle behind Ringo's group, Rory Storm & the Hurricanes.

Some posters from the pre-fame era of the Beatles' career have been reproduced in recent years, sometimes on paper as facsimiles of the originals, and sometimes in completely different formats. Souvenir stalls around Britain sell metal copies of these posters, designed to be screwed to walls or doors. But the authentic posters from the 1960s are always easy to spot. They always show signs of their age, and are often torn or damaged. But in anything like good condition, items like the ones illustrated here can be worth a small fortune. (PN/PD)

They were paid £20 to do this 1961 show.

The Beatles took second billing behind Ringo's group on this 1960 poster.

You can just read the Beatles name in the small print at the bottom of this poster from April 1962.

They didn't even spell the Beatles' name correctly on this 1962 poster for 'The North's No. 1 Combo'!

A special concert for the promoter's engagement party!

One of their last 'local' gigs on Merseyside.

This gig was the day after the group sacked Pete Best.

Even in March 1961, the Beatles were 'sensational'.

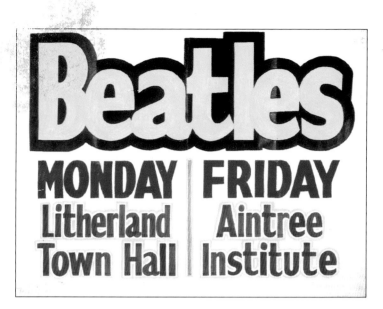

As the Beatles appeared regularly at Litherland Town Hall and Aintree Institute, the promoter put out this double poster in 1961.

In August 1961 they played second fiddle to Acker Bilk on this poster advertising a riverboat shuffle.

Five top beat bands for five shillings made this gig a real bargain night out in 1961.

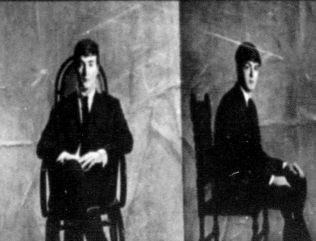

Lots of Paris hoardings carried this poster to promote the Beatles' concerts in January 1964.

Beatles London tour

Simon Wells takes you on a guided trip around the capital city's famous Beatles sites

Paul drops in to say hello to Richard Porter on one of his Beatles tours.

It's now more forty years since the Beatles' first professional engagement in the capital required them to make the 200-odd-mile trip down to London for their ill-fated Decca audition on New Year's Day 1962. The group's time in the capital was as important – indeed, some would say more so – as their gestation period in Liverpool. They recorded, wrote, rehearsed, filmed, played businessmen and lived in the metropolis for the majority of their recording years. One person who has been something of a flagwaver for the Beatles' London has been Richard Porter, a likeable thirty-something, whose passion and knowledge of the group is apparent from the moment you meet him. Four times a week he traipses the streets of a bygone Beatles London, leading parties of anything up to eighty people around the sights and sounds of the group's Metropolis, opening up each building's Beatles connection and history with vivid detail and anecdotal information.

One thing that becomes immediately apparent during Richard's tour is how much the Beatles moved around London during the 1960s, leaving their mark on some of the city's otherwise

The gents' toilets in Broadwick Street where John appeared in a 1966 TV show.

innocuous buildings. A gentlemen's toilet in Broadwick Street W1, for instance, where John Lennon spent a morning in 1966 acting as a commissionaire for Peter Cook and Dudley Moore's *Not Only But Also*, is one such establishment that will forever be stamped with the word 'Beatles' on it. To the bewilderment of passers-by, unfamiliar to

such a gathering outside a public toilet, Richard points out that this is where John first publicly displayed his trademark 'Granny' spectacles to the press, which immediately entered the fashion consciousness of the world. The sleazy environs of Soho, presumably familiar territory to the boys after their Hamburg stints, formed the backdrop to many a Dezo Hoffmann photo shoot, as his studios were housed in Old Compton Street.

A short walk away, in the Dickensian quarters of 17 St. Anne's Court (in reality, nothing more than a narrow alleyway), lies the site of Trident Studios. It came as a surprise to many on the tour that the Beatles briefly abandoned Abbey Road studios in favour of this minuscule Soho basement to record a handful of songs around the period of the 'White Album', not least the anthemic 'Hey Jude'. Today the building is known as The Sound Studio and it is principally the film and television industry that utilises the deceptively expansive studio below street

The famous Palladium theatre, where the Beatles appeared several times.

level. The recording area has undergone extensive renovation since 1968, and recently the owners sold the piano which the boys played for the recording of 'Hey Jude' (Queen used the same studio piano for 'Bohemian Rhapsody' in 1975). When you look at the tiny doorway, you wonder how they got the instrument out of there! The ostentatious exterior of the London Palladium at 7-8 Argyll Street W1 was the next major location on the itinerary. As far as the press were concerned, 'Beatlemania' started here on the night of 22nd October 1963, when the boys performed on the huge-

ly popular *Sunday Night At The London Palladium*. Having completely failed to report the amazing scenes that had surrounded the Beatles wherever they went in the British Isles for many months, the journalists finally woke up when they saw the group run out of the front entrance of the theatre into a phalanx of rabid fans. At long last the scales dropped from Fleet Street's eyes and they immediately rushed back to their typewriters to announce that "Beatlemania has been born!".

The fact that the group's waiting car was nowhere to be seen gave the photographers a marvellous extended opportunity to record the chaotic moment for posterity.

The entrance to Sutherland House – the base for Brian Epstein's organisation.

Carnaby Street was the centre of the Swinging London scene in the 60s.

Brian Epstein must have enjoyed the close proximity to the Palladium, as he relocated his entire NEMS Enterprises organisation next door to the fifth floor of Sutherland House in March 1964. One interesting fact is that John Lennon held his ill-fated "more popular than Jesus" interview with *Evening Standard* journalist Maureen Cleeve within the walls of this building. A stone's throw away, at 9 Kingly Street, lies the location for the Bag O'Nails club, a popular meeting point for the 60s rock illuminati. The boys often repaired here to relax after the madness of a stressful day's work, and the club is probably best known for Paul's first meeting with Linda Eastman in May 1967, while they were both checking out Georgie Fame.

Above left: 3 Savile Row, Apple's head-quarters from 1968 onwards. Above right: The former site of the Indica Gallery.

Today, the establishment is known as The Miranda, a popular gentleman's club. Around the corner lies the now infamous Carnaby Street. It is probable that the Beatles came here on a few occasions dur-ing the 1960s, if only to pass through it, although to be fair their sartorial tastes were far more exclusive than the tacky imitations the street had to offer. Today the street still trades off its glory days of the 60s and is always busy, but it is best avoided.

Next to Abbey Road, 3 Savile Row – the legendary one-time Apple HQ – is London's most memorable Beatles site. With the ever-present cacophony of traffic from nearby Regent Street, and the occasional waft of music, it isn't that difficult to conjure up the sort of landscape that back-dropped Thursday January 30th, 1969; the day the

The Playhouse Theatre, where Johnny Dean first met the Beatles in 1963.

The Directors Lodge Club – better known to the Beatles as The Scotch of St. James.

13 was another popular nightclub for the groups to repair to. The Beatles adored the club, and had a table set aside for them in a prime position, reportedly with a brass plaque secured to its top to confirm its permanent reservation for rock's royalty. Like the Bag O'Nails, this venue is still a club but it is now called The Director's Lodge Club, yet another gentleman's establishment.

On entering and leaving the 'Scotch' (as it was affectionately known), John Lennon wouldn't have taken much notice of the building opposite at number 6 Mason's Yard, which was then the Indica Bookshop. But Paul McCartney popped in a few times as he was a co-investor in Indica during 1966-7. However, during the night of November 9, 1966, an event occurred in the building that

boys assembled on the roof to record the finale to *Let It Be*. Watching from outside, your eyes are magnetically drawn to the rooftop, and you get the feeling that at any moment a Beatle might pop his head out of one of the windows, or walk out of the door onto the pavement and into a waiting car. Savile Row left the boys' ownership in 1974, although it has changed little from outside. Inside is a different matter, though! In keeping with the group's haphazard and cavalier approach to running their utopian Apple empire, the building soon fell into dereliction. The principal culprit was 'Magic' Alex, whose designs for their state-of-the-art recording studio made the building unsafe after the supporting walls of the building were removed to accommodate his electronic pipedreams. As a result, the building took years to restore back to its former glory. As with Abbey Road, a steady stream of Beatles fans daily pay homage to the building, which is now in the ownership of the Building Society Association. Due to safety restrictions they forbid anyone to visit the hallowed roof, although an exception was made to commemorate the 30th anniversary of the Beatles' last live appearance when, in 1999, the Bootleg Beatles were allowed onto the roof to play a replica set. The narrow and affluent streets of the St James' district of Piccadilly can occasionally offer up a few unusual surprises, not least Mason's Yard, a well-hidden West End backlot. Like the Bag O'Nails, The Scotch of St. James at number

Brian Epstein eventually moved his HQ to this building, Hille House.

Abbey Road studios, where the Beatles recorded most of their hits.

would change the 26-year-old Lennon's life forever. At a loose end between acting in Dick Lester's movie *How I Won The War* and the sessions for what ultimately became *Sgt Pepper*, John had been invited by close confidant John Dunbar to a gallery night at Indica. Lennon had thought what was described as a 'happening' event might involve a drug-based orgy or something similar, befitting the swinging London scene of the time. He was apparently mildly miffed to find it was a conceptual art exhibition entitled *Unfinished Paintings and Objects*, by 33-year-old Japanese artist Yoko Ono. It would be pointless to repeat yet again the details of John and Yoko's first ever meeting. But this otherwise nondescript building was the scene for the beginning of one of the most famous romances of the twentieth century, and as such it is an important stop-off for any Beatles tour. Although both Indica and the Scotch have long since gone, Mason's Yard still offers a pleasant retreat from the chaos of nearby Piccadilly.

There's something quite unusual about St John's Wood from the moment you step out of the tube station. Maybe it's the sight of the palm trees battling against the chill that does it. It certainly has a feel that definitely isn't quite London. As you cross over the busy main thoroughfare and down the stuccoed affluence of Grove End Road, the traffic mysteriously becomes silent. A little farther along, you approach a junction and

spy across the road what to all intents and purposes looks like a large Victorian doctor's surgery. The white wall outside is covered in a mess of graffiti although, defying the usual rules of the 'artform', the majority of the messages convey love and devotion. The graffiti is so prolific that the owners have to re-paint it every three months (although they photograph some of the more inventive and memorable inscriptions). Welcome to Abbey Road, now much more than an album sleeve or a recording studio. It's a living shrine to the Beatles' golden legacy and those incredible moments within its walls. Of all the places of Beatles worship, Abbey Road is the primary spot for all Fabs devotion. The signals that were sent to all four corners of the globe from here still resonate in the walls of the building.

The almost rural feel generated by the album sleeve is somewhat different 30-plus years on, as traffic has increased tenfold. Many fans have been injured by straying obliviously onto the busy road, camera in hand, and into the oncoming traffic, in pursuit of their own *Abbey Road* sleeve. The zebra crossing itself is probably the most heavily used piece of living Beatles memorabilia in the world today and its 12 black and white panels make up some of the most heavily trodden tarmac in the western world. The sad and untimely death of George Harrison brought hordes of film crews and reporters to the gates of the building as the natural place to draw opinion and meet Beatles fans who flocked from all over the globe there to pay their respects. Touchingly, the studios blasted out George's *All Things Must Pass* album from the steps of the building in their own tribute to one of their favourite sons. The present Abbey Road staff appear to be a very pleasant bunch, and will happily accommodate anyone who wishes to have their photographs taken on the steps leading up to the studios, although for obvious reasons, no-one other than bona fide visitors is allowed to actually enter the premises. It is here that Richard concludes the tour to loud applause. I was impressed that he wisely steered the group away from Paul McCartney's nearby town house, especially as Paul spends a lot more time in London since Linda's death. Nonetheless, Paul still regularly records at Abbey Road. Occasionally Paul bumps into Richard's tour and he always has time to stop and greet the fans and pose for pictures.   (SW)

A mass re-creation of the famous Abbey Road cover shot by a party of fans.

The Cartoon Beatles

Some of illustrator Bob Gibson's memorable drawings for The Beatles Book in the 60s

The Beatles' Liverpool

A tourist's guide to Fab Four-related sites in the boys' hometown

Each August there is a six-day programme of special events for devotees of the Beatles in Liverpool, culminating during Bank Holiday weekend with the annual Beatles convention and the Mathew Street festival. For visitors who want to make the most of their stay in the Beatles' hometown, here is a guide to sightseeing and fact-finding that's custom-tailored for serious fans of the Fab Four and is available throughout the year.

The magic begins at Liverpool's Albert Dock on the banks of the river, not far from the Pier Head where the famous Mersey ferries sail. Here, in the basement setting of Britannia Vaults, part of an extensive dockland redevelopment, The Beatles Story is a good place for any fan of the Fab Four to start a memorable three-part experience, involving a visit to the best Beatles exhibition and museum in the world. Then you can take a two-hour sightseeing trip on a vintage Magical Mystery Tour bus and, finally, a stroll around the city's famous Cavern Quarter.

THE BEATLES STORY
Exhibition and Museum
Britannia Vaults, Albert Dock,
Liverpool L3 4AA
Open 7 days a week throughout the year
(except Christmas)
Ring 0151 709 1963 to check
opening times

Located a stone's throw from King's Dock, where Paul has given two open-air concerts for 100,000 people, both in 1990 and 2003, The Beatles Story is housed in underground vaults beneath one of the Mersey waterfront's many historic warehouse buildings. There is no admission charge to the foyer souvenir shop which not only sells books, T-shirts, CDs plus a range of other Beatles-associated souvenirs but also boasts a fascinating new George Harrison Tribute Wall, launched on what would have been George's 59th birthday. The wall gives visitors the chance to add their own personal messages, memories, poems, pictures or computer designs to the colourful array already on show. This is one of several new interactive features and

exhibits introduced by The Beatles Story's innovative director, Mike Byrne. Highlights of the walk-round exhibition include a pair of pianos, one an original and the other a replica, each evoking vivid memories of John's early relationship with Yoko and the period when he wrote and recorded 'Imagine' shortly before they left England to live in New York. One is the Steinway Model Z upright piano on which John composed 'Imagine', loaned to The Beatles Story by its present owner, George Michael, who reportedly paid around one and a half million pounds to buy it at auction. The other is a replica of John's famous white grand piano.

When John and Yoko bought Tittenhurst Park, a vast Georgian mansion set in 72 acres of rural Berkshire at Sunningdale in 1969, they used John's share of recent Lennon & McCartney composer royalty payments to make some major alterations to the property.

They tore down a number of internal walls which had divided up the ground floor, to create a massive minimally-furnished living area at the front of the house which they decorated entirely in white. One corner of the famous Tittenhurst white room, including as its centrepiece a replica of the white

grand piano at which the couple were photographed and videoed in the summer of 1971, is reproduced in one of The Beatles Story's most memorable and moving exhibits. On the piano is a distinctive pair of sunglasses, along with a portrait of John at the keyboard. Nearby on the floor lies one of his guitars. The whole scene is framed in a dramatic white-walled setting draped with long, white, window curtains that waft in a realistic breeze. For the record, the original white piano from Tittenhurst was moved to New York where it became a central feature of the Lennons' lounge in their apartment in the Dakota building.

At each twist and turn, the exhibition brings fresh surprises, ranging from displays of photographs, stage outfits, posters, instruments and other unique pieces of memorabilia, to a wall of video screens pumping out the hits and set pieces depicting some key landmarks in the history of the Beatles. You can stare at an impressive display of vintage guitars and amplifiers ("available on 24 monthly payments") through the mock-up windows of Frank Hessy's music shop where most of the Merseybeat groups bought their instru-

The Beatles Story exhibition is housed in a former waterfront warehouse.

ments on hire purchase agreements. Hessy's used to be located in Whitechapel, the city-centre shopping street where Brian Epstein had one of his most profitable branches of NEMS, the records and electrical goods outlet. Young musicians who bought their guitars at Hessy's were offered free tuition at evening sessions often attended by up to 70 people, all eager to learn the basic chords. George and John were good customers of Frank Hessy, calling in regularly to see what new gear had been delivered on their way to the Cavern, which was just a few minutes' walk away.

Turn another corner and you find yourself apparently in the middle of Bill Harry's cluttered editorial office in the heady days when he ran *Mersey Beat*, the local music paper that reported the pop news for musicians and fans alike. Bill persuaded John to do a series of "wacky writings" for *Mersey Beat* under the heading 'Beatcomber' and he likes to think that this and other early mentions in his paper helped to make the Beatles more popular with Merseyside fans until they topped his readers' poll in 1962.

Most people agree that the Casbah Club was "The Birthplace of The Beatles", as Ringo's predecessor, drummer Pete Best, calls his mother's spacious basement coffee bar, which Pete's mate, Neil Aspinall, who was studying to become an accountant, helped to run. Opened in 1959 below their

large old house at 8 Hayman's Green in the Liverpool suburb of West Derby, the Casbah allowed kids to dance to jukebox sounds during the week and watch the resident group, John's Quarry Men, playing live on Saturday nights. During their opening gig there, Paul sang 'Long Tall Sally' and John did 'Three Cool Cats'. Under their new name of The Beatles, the group continued to play the Casbah regularly in 1960 for up to 300 over-heated fans, until an increasing number of bookings at the Cavern lured them away to Liverpool's city centre and another sweaty basement where audiences were more than twice the size and the pay was much better. Dominated by a waxwork image of Pete surrounded by flashing neon signs, the Casbah exhibit is too small to really convey the exciting atmosphere that must have been created whenever the Quarry Men got up to play.

Just as the Beatles moved on from West Derby to Mathew Street, so visitors to The Beatles Story can walk down a dimly lit alleyway (made to look longer with

mirrors). There they'll find a Cavern Club sign that leads to an exhibit depicting one section of the famous cellar, including the stage where the Beatles' gear is set up, and the Cavern Snack Bar, where Cilla Black occasionally served Coca-Cola and hot dogs so she could see her favourite bands without having to pay. Exhibition visitors can get up on the stage, dress up as their favourite Beatle, belt out one of the Fab Four's hits, and have their performance recorded as a personal souvenir!

Other impressive areas range from EMI's Abbey Road studios, complete with wax-work figures of the Fab Four in action wearing white shirts and dark waistcoats, to a large and colourfully lit walk-in Yellow Submarine Play Area which re-creates the film's spirit of zany fun and adventure. Most youngsters find this part of The Beatles Story the one that holds their interest the longest!

THE BEATLES' MAGICAL MYSTERY TOUR

The sightseeing coach tour of city and suburban Beatles' landmarks departs from The Beatles Story and from Queen Square Tourist Information Centre. It terminates at The Cavern Club, Mathew Street.
Tickets must be purchased before boarding. For tour times and booking information, ring 0151 236 9091/0151 709 3285.

After you've spent an hour or two wandering through The Beatles Story exhibition and browsing among the adjoining shop's tempting treasury of souvenirs, a trip on the Magical Mystery Tour bus provides an ideal way to relax in comfort and take in the sights of Liverpool from the luxury of a coach seat. Apart from the Albert Dock, there is another departure point at Mersey Tourism's Information Centre in Queen

The Magical Mystery Tour bus that takes fans round the sites of Liverpool.

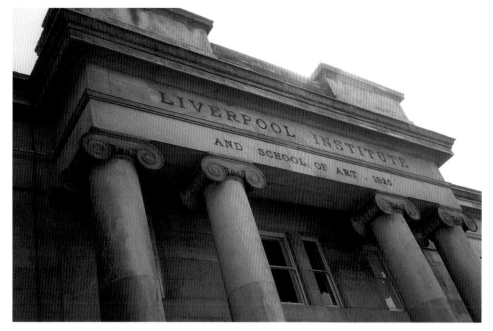

Square, which is conveniently close to Lime Street train station, Liverpool's main rail terminal, and a cluster of the city centre's most popular hotels. The vintage vehicles used by tour operator Cavern City Tours are almost perfect replicas of the bus we used back in September 1967 to make The Beatles' *MMT* film on location in the West Country and Kent. An eerie feeling of *deja vu* swept over me as I climbed aboard the bus at Albert Dock. I couldn't help seeing mental pictures of Ringo sitting in the window seat of one of the front rows beside larger-than-life Auntie Jessie (the one John smothered in spaghetti in the film) and of John sitting a couple of rows further back with a little girl named Nicola perched on his knee.

In the film we had The Delightful Wendy Winters as Tour Hostess and Jolly Jimmy Johnson serving as the Courier, but on the real-life 2002 version of the tour both jobs are combined in one MMT guide. Ours was Edwina, one of a well-trained team who are required to pass a stringent Beatleology exam before qualifying for their jobs on the buses. Edwina not only had a mountain of useful facts, statistics and anecdotes about the Beatles and their hometown haunts to tell us, but she is also a first-rate entertainer with a typically sharp Liverpudlian sense of humour. Her 'audience' of passengers included American, Japanese, Australian, German and Dutch tourists of all ages, from teenagers to pensioners. They included many who were born long after the Beatles

The gate to the children's home that inspired a famous Beatles song.

disbanded, and others who must have been full-grown adults during the Beatlemania years of the middle Sixties. For some the tour would be a first-time learning curve to colour in their sketchy second-hand knowledge of the Beatles' early history. For others it would revive personal feelings of nostalgia.

I won't attempt to trace the tour's route in sequence — indeed it's possible that prevailing city traffic conditions can cause changes to the running order — but one early landmark on our particular journey was a glimpse of Rosebery Street, where John's Quarry Men performed Lonnie Donegan's 'Putting On The Style' and similar skiffle numbers, on the back of a coal delivery lorry in the middle of the road for a street party on June 22, 1957, to celebrate 750

years of Liverpool's Royal Charter from King John. Girls screamed at John and his five sidemen, provoking boyfriends to threaten the group with a beating-up, so John ordered a hasty getaway, and the Quarry Men took refuge in a friend's house at 84 Rosebery Street until the antagonists dispersed. A mere fortnight later, on July 6 1957, John met Paul for the first time when the Quarry Men played in Church Road, Woolton village, at St Peter's Church Fete. Our MMT bus paused outside the front gates so that we could see the field beside the Victorian Gothic sandstone church where the group played that afternoon some 45 years ago. In the evening they crossed to the church hall on the other side of the road and played again, this time for dancing.

For most passengers, the houses in which the youthful Beatles were raised proved to be one of the highlights of the tour. Everyone poured off the bus to take snapshots of 12 Arnold Grove, George's terraced home for the first seven years of his life. The present owners have hung a basket of flowers beside the front door of the tiny red-painted house, while their neighbours, obviously keen to preserve their privacy, have installed mirror glass so people can't peer in through their windows In Beaconsfield Road, Liverpool L25, we saw the familiar red-painted wrought-iron gates and old stone pillars at the entrance to Strawberry Field, the wooded grassland where John took his first girlfriends and realised that "nothing is real". The original Victorian children's home of John's day has

been replaced with a smartly modern and far more inviting building to which Yoko brought young Sean when they visited Liverpool after John's death.

Situated just round the corner from Strawberry Field and almost opposite picturesque Calderstones Park is the Woolton house where John lived with his Aunt Mimi between 1946 and 1963. As our bus drew up briefly outside 251 Menlove Avenue with its circular blue celebrity plaque on the front, Edwina reminded us of Mimi's immortal words: "The guitar is all very well, John, but you'll never make a living out of it!"

The house in Menlove Avenue where John lived with his Aunt Mimi.

Paul's terraced home, at 20 Forthlin Road in the suburb of Allerton, looks only slightly less impressive than John's place and has a low privet hedge. There's a polite little notice saying "Private" across the path to the front door. The McCartney family moved in there only a year before Paul's mother died and the house later became a favourite rehearsal spot for the embryo group, largely because of his father's leniency. The National Trust bought the property in 1995 and by prior arrangement a curator now shows small parties of about a dozen visitors around the house at a time.

Penny Lane is one of the most eagerly anticipated stops on the tour. The bus arrives at the leafy-green end of the Lane, close to Liverpool College, one of various private schools where the Beatles' manager Brian Epstein was educated. On the stone wall beneath shady trees there is a painted street sign, put there because every conventional metal sign nailed onto the wall in the past was quickly "acquired" by souvenir hunters. In ones and twos our tour passengers posed in front of the wall and pointed at the words 'Penny Lane' while friends took their pictures. The sights that Paul referred to in his lyrics are at the other end of the Lane, where the bus only pauses briefly. The shelter in the middle of the roundabout still has public toilets to the rear of it, but the front part now houses Sgt. Pepper's Bistro And Licensed Restaurant – though somehow I doubt that fish and fingerpie is on the menu! In Penny Lane there is still a barber, Tony Slavin, with just a photograph of the Beatles in his window.

20 Forthlin Road, the former McCartney home now owned by the National Trust.

longer relevant or visually attractive. We did see Ringo's old school, St Silas C of E in Dingle, where Billy Fury was a fellow class-mate, and we had a distant view of Sefton Park's renowned Palm House, recently refurbished with a £100,000 donation from keen gardener George. We didn't see the Jacaranda in Slater Street or the Blue Angel in Seel Street, late night haunts of the Beatles run by Allan Williams, nor the sites of the Iron Door and Odd Spot clubs where the group occasionally performed. The tour terminates in the Cavern quarter within easy walking distance of various other city-centre sites associated with the Beatles in their early days. The Beatles' Magical Mystery Tour bus trips operate throughout the year (except over the Christmas and New Year holidays) and there are extra tours laid on at peak periods such as convention time. Whichever departure point you choose it's important to buy your ticket to ride before getting on the buses.

On the drive back into the city the bus went through the university district and we caught a quick glimpse of the Ye Cracke pub halfway down a narrow alley known as Rice Street. Frequented by Art College students and tutors, this is where John and Cyn spent many evenings downing beer and eating pork pies. In Mount Street, we passed the old Liverpool Institute building, where Paul and George went to school. It's now Paul's LIPA (Liverpool Institute For Performing Arts) with a bright new annexe added to one side. A number of well-known Beatles-related sights both in the city centre and the suburbs are not on the Magical Mystery Tour schedule, either because they are in geographically inconvenient areas too diffi-cult to visit on a two-hour timetable, or because their appearance has changed so much since the Sixties that they are no

THE CAVERN QUARTER
Mathew Street, Liverpool L2 6RE
Re-built Cavern Club, various pubs, Cavern Walks (souvenir shops, cafes, boutiques)
Various opening times, and most places do not charge for admission.

The Cavern Club which can be seen today at 10 Mathew Street is only 18 years old and forms part of a tall, modern office and shop complex, including Cavern Walks, devel-oped by Royal Life Insurance. Still situated deep down in the ground, the Cavern was rebuilt to the original dimensions using 50% of the original bricks and now operates as a thriving music venue for the 21st century.

Mathew Street is at the centre of August's annual International Beatle Week and boasts a host of interesting places to visit ranging from the pubs (the Grapes, the Cavern Pub, Lennon's Bar) to the shops, cafes and sever-al remarkable statues of the Beatles. In the Grapes, the favourite watering hole for musicians appearing at the (unlicensed) Cavern in the Sixties, you may well encounter one of the Beatles' old cronies, who will exchange an anecdote or two for a pint or three if they're in the mood for a chat.

12 Arnold Grove, Wavertree, where George was born and lived until he was six.

The 21st century replica of the Cavern stands close to the site of the original club.

Within easy reach on foot are Whitechapel, where Rushworths music shop used to provide John and George with imported Gibson guitars, and the site of the NEMS record shop, which is now bizarrely an Ann Summers sex aid outlet; and also Stanley Street, where Fifties singer Tommy Steele's Eleanor Rigby statue can be seen and where Hessy's used to sell music instruments to most of the top Merseybeat bands in the 60s. Unfortunately, some other nostalgic city-centre places which played a

The Beatle Week festival brings thousands to the streets of Liverpool.

part in the hometown history of the Fab Four are long gone, including Blacklers departmental store where George worked briefly as an apprentice electrician and Reece's Restaurant in Clayton Square where John and Cyn went for lunch on their wedding day. But there is still more than enough of interest to captivate any Beatles fan. (TB)

A recreation of the original Cavern Wall, with an authentic set of Beatles equipment.

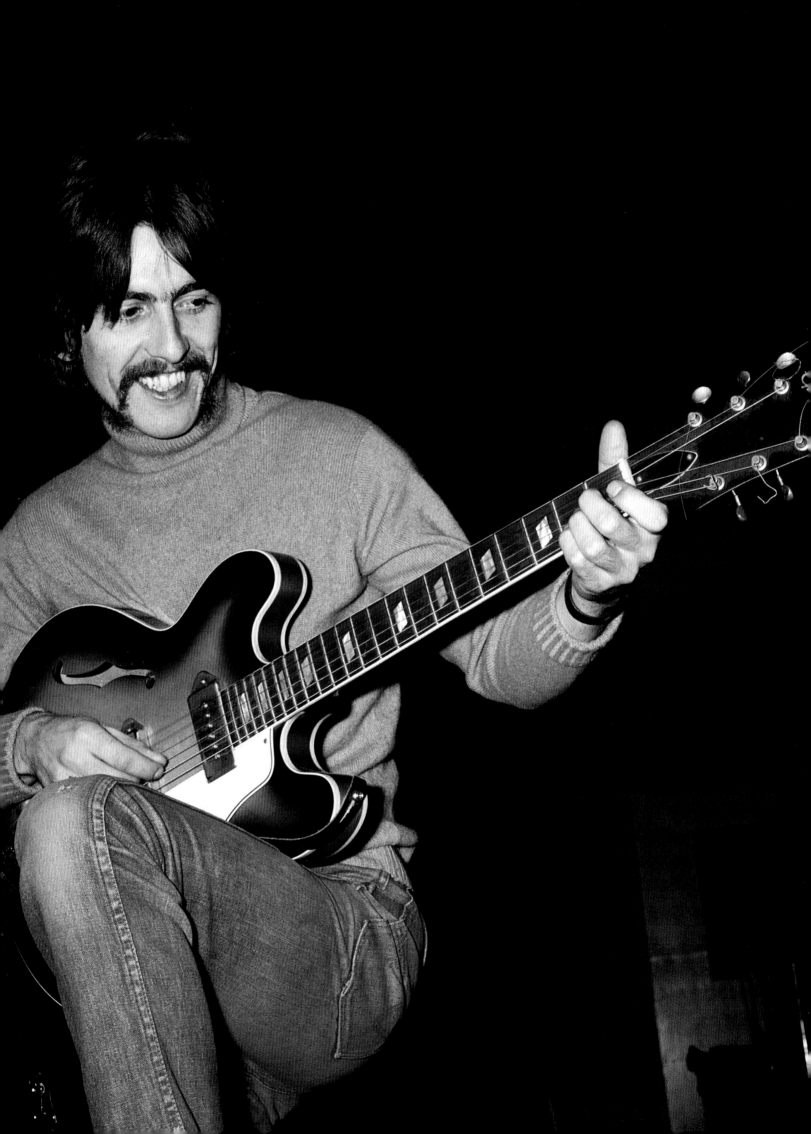

George: the complex Beatle

The Beatle who was always a more talented character than he seemed

George always got along well with the ladies. He was known for it within the Beatles' circle. When the group did a TV show involving dancers, George would steam in there like a shot, to chat up the best-looking showgirls, two or three at a time. They said he was cheeky, had a smashing smile, and stared deep into their eyes. Other people had very different views. Some thought George was the shy Beatle, the one who said very little. He frowned a lot on stage, giving fans a false impression that he was being temperamental. He wasn't really in a bad mood – just trying hard to hear if his guitar sounded right through the loudspeakers.

Not only was George the Beatle who changed most during the lifespan of the group, he was the one who was seen very differently by different people. To some he was serious, studious and sometimes sulky. Others saw him as a pleasant, chummy and cheerful lad. Others would say he was far too deep for them. In a way, everyone was right, and he was all of these things and more. George wasn't a simple person to assess, even once you got to know him, but the one characteristic that never changed was his fundamental sincerity. George genuinely believed in what he said and did.

It wasn't a simple task to point the spotlight at George, even after the press became keen to interview the Beatles on a daily basis when Beatlemania developed into Fleet Street's latest fad. Feature writers always wanted to interview John or Paul first. Some would go for Ringo because he was the cute one with the nose and he was expected to make the occasional hilariously funny remark. But few journalists picked George as the Beatle they most wanted to talk to. In their eyes, he took himself too seriously and didn't mix easily. George was the straight-faced fellow who stood in the background and didn't go out of his way to be at the centre of a conversation – at least, that's how the press saw him. George was certainly more at home and most at ease with specialist music writers, the magazine people who were aware of his studious approach to playing and would get a good story from

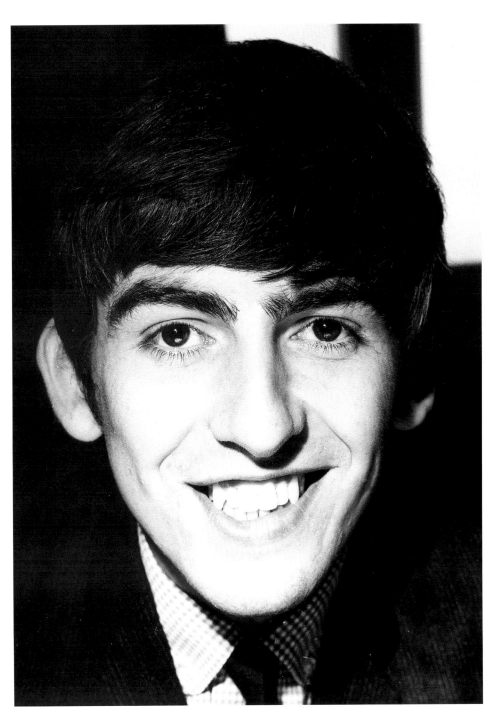

him on that level. Otherwise I had to sell him pretty hard to persuade journalists to interview George. Just when I thought that the situation was getting very difficult, a golden opportunity turned up. A national newspaper rang me to say that they wanted to run a regular column by a Beatle for a while. George was ideal for the job, because he got on well with *Daily Express* man Derek Taylor, the guy chosen to ghost

the articles. Their friendship grew, and survived until Derek's death in the late 90s.

But George didn't always get a good press for himself. In Paris, just as the Beatles were becoming famous, George threw a glass of fruit juice over a PR aide at breakfast in a fit of temper. It wasn't a crucial incident by any means, but it blew up into a big story because the Beatles had such a clean-cut

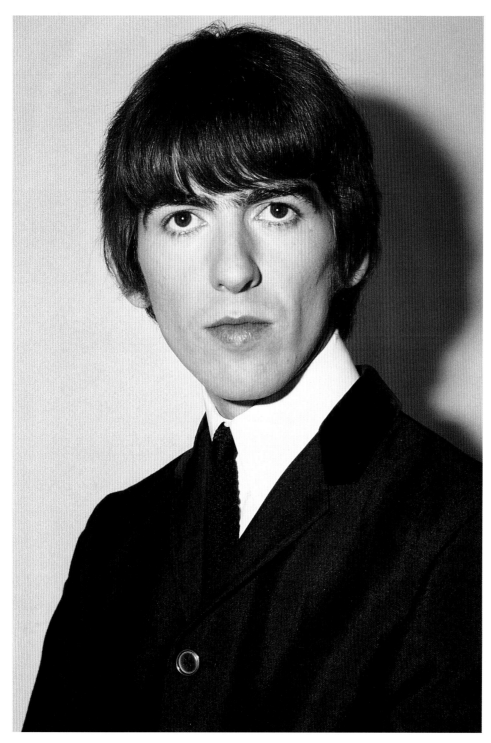

It is well-known that George was the first to crack under the pressures of excessive popularity, affected mentally if not physically by the unique battering the Beatles withstood when Beatlemania was reaching a peak. Insiders watched a former chum change into an individual from whom hostility rather than friendliness flowed only too readily. Some couldn't understand it at all. He'd been such an easy-going Beatle before. Now the calmness and contentment were all gone, along with his sense of humour. Of course, the truth is that George was still the same chap underneath. But he wore this heavy armour of belligerence in the hope that it might frighten Beatlemania away. In August 1966, on our chartered jet plane after the Beatles' very last concert, George sighed and declared it was all over: "That's it. I'm not a Beatle anymore."

We knew what he meant. Without the touring, the uncomfortable trappings of Beatlemania would become obsolete, and George would be able to get back to making music in the relative peace of a recording studio instead of on the battlefield of a concert stage. Well, that's how it seemed to George, and who can blame him? No serious musician could enjoy those last massive stadium concerts where an inadequate sound system fought for supremacy with 60,000 screaming fans.

In the post-touring era, George resumed much of his placid approach to life, finding considerable mental tranquility in Transcendental Meditation and the musical heritage of the East. By 1967 he was chatty and cheerful again, smiling more or less as he'd done in the old days. His main happiness came from India, from his mantras and sitars. His only remaining unhappiness was that the Beatles did not record more of his compositions, and that his personal chart successes were few and far between. George's near-obsessive interest in Eastern cultures brought with it a number of eccentricities which onlookers couldn't understand. Yet they made much more good sense than drugs and set a better example. I confess that I felt a little out of my depth with Transcendental Meditation but I made an effort to find out more about it so that I could appear more knowledgeable when the media asked me about George's new craze. When I questioned George, he misunder-

image for being four good-humoured, fun-loving rock'n'rollers. A single example of bad manners stood out, even if it took place within the privacy of the group's hotel suite. I met George soon after 'Love Me Do' was released and I got to know him in 1963. Someone warned me he could be snappy. Not only that, he'd apparently lash out with his fists if he felt cornered. At school it was said that he'd been in more than his fair share of punch-ups.

All this surprised me. He seemed such a mild bloke, not at all aggressive and only too ready to make new friends and share a joke. He had this curious but harmless habit of bringing his face within an inch of the per-

son he was speaking to, male or female, giving the impression that what he was about to say must be highly confidential and well worth hearing. Then he'd ask how you were, where you'd been or what time it was.

He seemed a little out of his depth in the company of John and Paul. At a party he'd brighten up visibly when he spotted a familiar face. Within the Beatles, he was not a dominant personality, not a party to the policy-making machinery that traditionally involved John, Paul and Brian Epstein. On the whole, he let them take care of business, although he did concern himself quite closely with financial affairs. He was far more careful with his money than the other three.

Four intimate shots of George off-duty in the early-to-mid 60s. Though he sometimes seemed serious to outsiders, he could be a very witty and humorous companion.

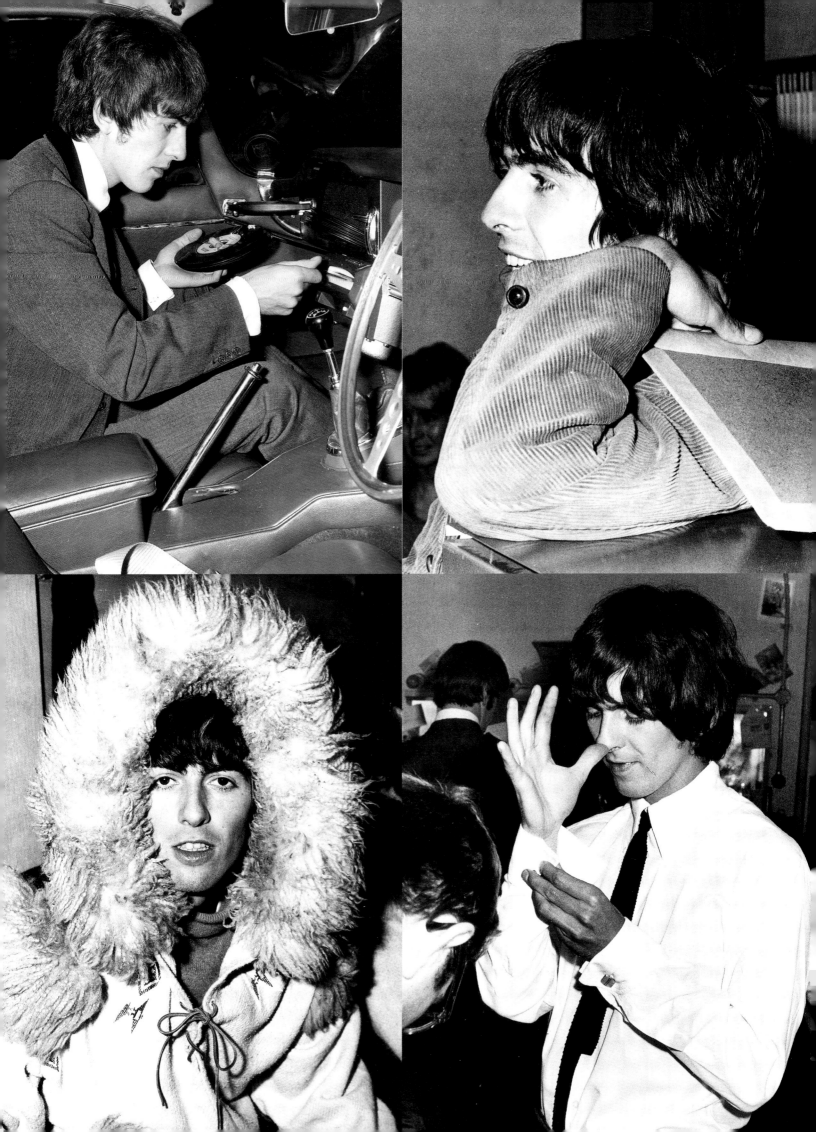

George was an excellent guitarist. Here he is playing his Rickenbacker 12-string.

stood my motive and thought I was taking a personal interest – with the result that he brought me a great pile of books on the teachings of the gurus. "Please keep them after you've read them," he told me. "Maybe you can pass them on to friends." I didn't like to explain that all I needed was a sketchy outline of what was involved rather than these thick volumes of heavy reading.

During the early and middle Sixties, when the Beatles were churning out so many hit singles, George kept hoping that one of his compositions would be used on the next one. For some time he didn't realise that his songs simply weren't in the running. The competition was between John and Paul, with one getting the A-side and the other the B-side, and George had to be content with an occasional album track. When the truth dawned on George, he became a little bitter, because he believed that the stuff he was writing was just

as worthy as Lennon & McCartney material, and he wanted to prove the point by scoring a No. 1 chart hit off his own bat.

I believe that George would have enjoyed massive success as a songwriter much earlier in his career if he had not been working under the shadow of John and Paul, a pair of world champions when it came to creating catchy hits. It's no coincidence that George came bursting out of the Beatles when the group disbanded and almost immediately had his own international No. 1 with the single 'My Sweet Lord', and the brilliant *All Things Must Pass* – the pop scene's first triple album, which is still admired and acclaimed today and is hailed in many quarters as the best solo work recorded by any Beatle.

Although George kept his hand in during later years with an occasional concert appearance and a controlled flow of new recordings, he backed away more and more from the public spotlight into the sanctuary of home life

with his second wife, Olivia, and their son Dhani. He took up gardening, and as usual, he became avidly keen on the subject. He tended his plants personally and with pride, giving them the same loving care he once used to lavish on his cherished guitars. He was quite literally going back to his roots.

I believe that George's reclusive lifestyle in later years was a consequence of the mental bashing he had endured as he battled his way through Beatlemania. The Quiet One's craving for peace and quiet had its origins in the noisy and uncomfortable times of the touring era. George never did get his head round Beatlemania, but he made up for it by the wonderful performances he gave in the recording studio and the outstanding songs he created, especially in the post-Beatles period. Having achieved so much, who could begrudge him his final spell of privacy and calm, spiritual well-being when he eventually put the rest of the world at arm's length towards the end of his colourful life? (TB)

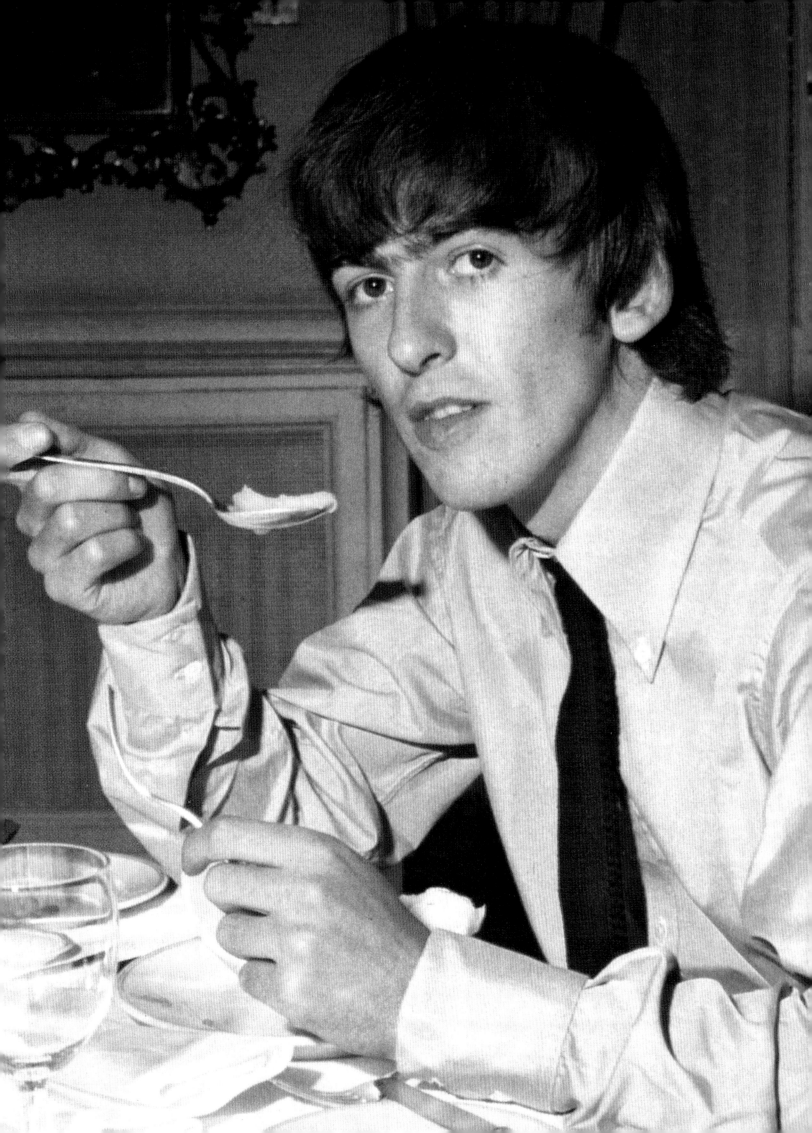

John: the original Beatle

The founder of the group, and its most controversial and outspoken member

John Lennon once said to me: "If the Beatles hadn't happened, I'd have spent my life being a professional shirker". Before becoming a musician, John had never concentrated long enough on any other activity to make a living from it. He could have been a commercial artist, but he liked to doodle daft cartoon characters and sketch fictional monsters, rather than apply himself to drawing straight lines and getting designs precisely to scale. He said: "I don't like drawing for art's sake. I do it to get ideas out of my head and down onto paper. Drawings come easier than doing it with spoken words. Show people one drawing, and it gets your point of view across. I can draw just as well in Chinese or Russian, you know!" He could have become a writer, but his concentration ran out too quickly. Many times as a young man he started novels which seldom lasted beyond the first few chapters. He said: "I got bored and killed off all the characters. They weren't interesting enough to keep alive."

The thing I liked best about John was his total honesty. He never adopted a pose and refused to be moulded into the traditional image of the Sixties pop star. He was a rebel but never a pretender for the sake of making a good impression. Although he claimed to fancy himself as a shirker, he was a thoroughly industrious guy, not lazy until he was really very tired. He never actually shirked hard work so long as it achieved a purpose that interested him. Nor would he ever back away from a battle if he thought the cause was worthwhile. Usually it involved a war of words and wits, and occasionally a physical fight with his fists, but I don't believe he weighed up the strength of his opponent before charging in there. He didn't have to believe he could win, he went for it anyway.

Many times he could have made life much more easy for himself if he'd lied. Instead, he preferred to stand his ground, state his case and let fate take its course. Very often, in public life and in private, his simple honesty got Lennon into hot water. But he never learnt his lesson and always came back for more. He'd say: "If you go turning the other cheek, some idiot will punch it in for you". Lennon was the most misunderstood Beatle, the one people saw as a bit of an ogre. I think John liked having that reputation. Of all four Beatles, John was the most complex as a person. His friends knew a very different Lennon to the one who was supposed to be the most outspoken member of the world's biggest pop supergroup. A lot of Lennon's public shouting was down to bravado, an attempt to conceal uncertainty, nervousness or real fear behind a bold façade of arrogance. More has been written about John than any of the other Beatles, partly because he was murdered, and partly because writers look upon him as the most outrageous and, therefore, the most fascinating of the four.

Unfortunately, a lot of it has been appalling rubbish. Take, for example, the totally ridiculous fiction that John had a

Although most of his sexual adventures remained secret until long after John's marriage with Cynthia was over, Lennon made big news headlines in other ways, particularly the much debated "We're more popular than Jesus" controversy. He also played a key role in the affair of the so-called 'butcher' pictures of the Beatles. To John, those celebrated photos of the boys, posing with joints of meat and broken dolls, was an act of defiance. He thought it was a giggle to challenge the establishment and get the pictures published before Brian Epstein could stop them. By 1966 the highly polished public image of good-humoured decency that Epstein had fought to build for the Beatles in earlier days was on the brink of disappearing forever. Lennon was reponsible for hurrying along the era of change, in which the publication of those crude 'butcher' photos played a part. Quite often, John was accused of bragging and boasting just to draw attention to himself in public. It's true that he could turn into an incorrigible show-off when he felt prevailing conditions demanded such a stance. But he wouldn't bother playing the big bad bully unless he had an audience to see it happening.

Once, when he'd been roaring away at Brian Epstein over some relatively trivial management matter, earning the obvious approval of the other three Beatles in the process, I remember him changing completely when he and I left the room together and were on our own. In private, when the rest were not around, I confessed to John that I thought he was in the wrong and Eppy was right. John grinned and agreed: "Of course he was right, but we're not going to let him know he was, are we?!" I can't remember a single occasion throughout the many years I knew John in the Sixties when he and I had a downright quarrel when we were on our own. If there were spectators to witness the verbal brawl, John would often let fly with a load of abuse, but 90% of it was just for effect, to startle and shock assembled observers. At the end of the day, his bark was worse than his bite. Though seldom given credit for it, he could be generous, appreciative and gentle – though this didn't always fit in with the way that the media liked to portray John to the world.

Four different faces of John: in their 1964 Christmas show, playing Ringo's drumkit in Abbey Road studios, giving a signature to a fan club secretary and with Julian at home in Weybridge.

long homosexual relationship with Brian Epstein. The plain truth is that he did not. But I do believe that Epstein boasted to his own circle of gay acquaintances that he was having an affair with John when he wasn't. Amongst those who shared the same sexual preferences, rumours of a fiery relationship with Lennon would have done wonders for Epstein's reputation. But it was no more than wishful thinking on Epstein's part, pretending his dream fantasies had actually taken place, when in reality they were simply vivid pictures in his terribly troubled mind. Let's face it, gay men lie about their sexual conquests from time to time, just like everyone else. And Eppy was well-known for his love of name-dropping. Paul has said: "With the exception of his close relatives, I knew John longer than anyone. In all that time there was never the slightest hint of homosexuality. In fact, quite the opposite – John was very attracted to women." Having worked with the Beatles myself all the way from 'Love Me Do' to Magical Mystery Tour and beyond, I can echo Paul's remarks. When we toured, I watched many new partners disappear into John's bedroom for the night, including more than a few famous faces – an English actress, an American folksinger – but every one was female!

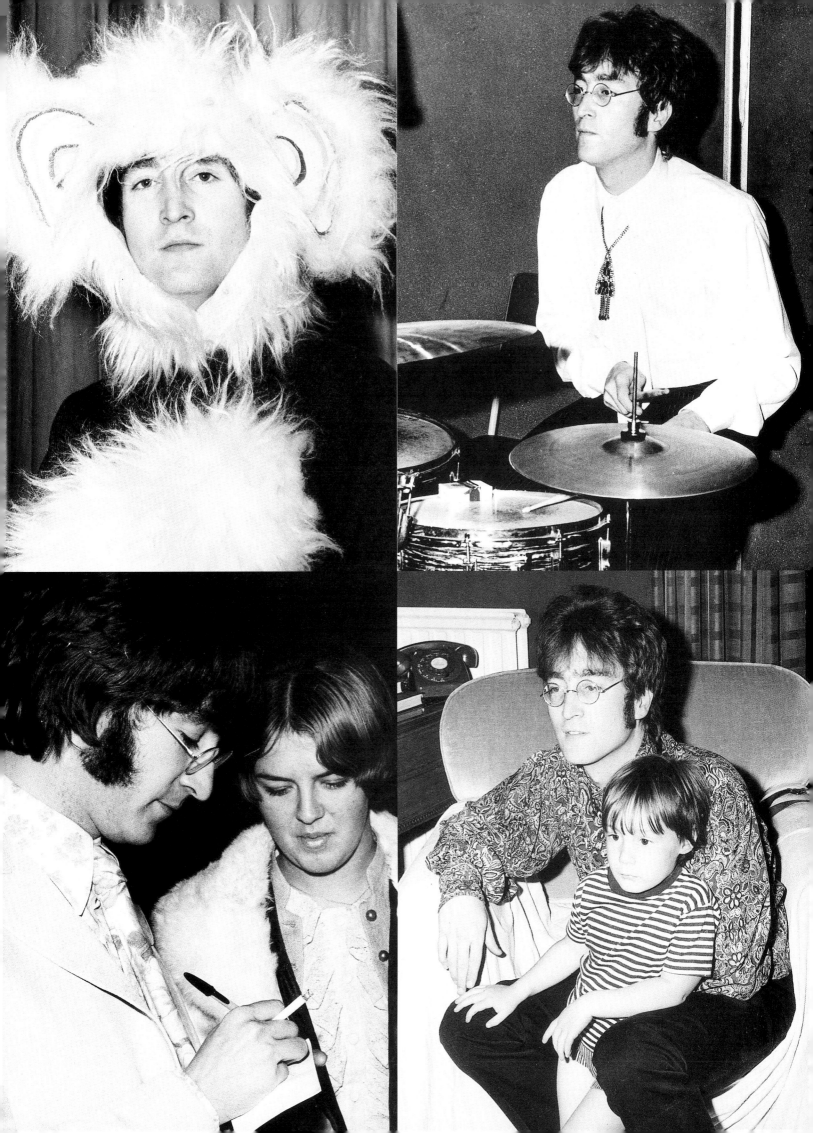

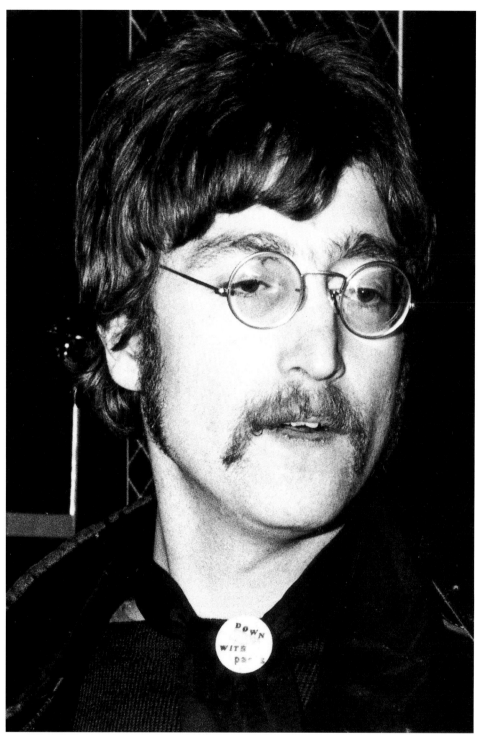

Lennon wanted people to take him for what he was worth, no more than that. While McCartney was planning his future career with some care, doing things exactly right – at least as far as he could within the limitations of being a Beatle – John was just enjoying himself, getting his kicks by shunning the conventions of showbusiness.

To say that John lived life to the full is a massive understatement. He was constantly keen to dare himself to do new things, to experiment, to stretch the range of his conscious experience to the limit – and a wee bit beyond. This applied to his music, his lyric writing and all other sectors of his life. He wanted to try every possible new way of finding fresh joy, whether this involved taking new drugs he hadn't tried or adding to his wide range of experiences with women. He was faithful to his own liberal ideas, but not to any traditional rules of the game. At close quarters, some females were afraid of him, but they needn't have been. But John was not a passive person and looked for an equal measure of experimentation in the women he went with.

His lusty adventures with women when he was far from home had nothing to do with true love. In his own way, he felt he was faithful to his first wife, Cynthia. John and I had a long conversation late one night about marital fidelity, each of us having fairly recently got married at the time, and each to a lady from Liverpool. He asked me: "Should we have waited, do you reckon? If Cyn hadn't been pregnant, would I have married her? If the Beatles get really big, maybe I could have a Hollywood film star for a wife!" I said I thought one famous person in a family was enough. He grinned wickedly: "We can always have a film star or two as well, can't we?"

Fans watching a stage performance by the Beatles often saw John as a poker-faced and humourless individual. He didn't smile a lot when he was playing, and he told most of his outrageous jokes without changing the expressionless look on his face. Indeed, he kept all his deepest emotions to himself.

In reality, John enjoyed performing far more than his fans knew. He liked being in front of a screaming crowd, he was at his happiest when he was singing a fast-rocking song, and he looked forward to big live appearances. To him, a concert was an occasion to relieve the tension of being a famous celebrity. He could let off steam in the best way he knew how, via his voice and guitar, and nobody was going to get offended or hurt. He said to me once when we were on the road: "This is the life. Do we have to go home next week?" On the other hand, I don't believe his love of stage performances was connected with any form of professional ambition. He didn't really enjoy being a star. He was in it all for the fun. He wasn't any sort of businessman, leaving that to George Harrison. He certainly didn't have the flair that Paul developed for turning on the charm with everyone he met.

Then he became serious, and confessed how much he relied on Cynthia in many ways. He added: "I'd hate to come home to an empty place. I couldn't live on my own." This sounded odd, coming from a man who so often craved solitude and would close himself off from all around him not just for hours but sometimes days at a time. I told him: "You know you love your own company. Even Cyn says you can go for days without speaking to her. She feels a million miles away from you." As ever, John had the final word. He replied: "Ah, but she's not, is she? She's in the kitchen, putting the kettle on." (TB)

Paul: the extraordinary Beatle

The group's greatest performer who has never stopped writing, recording and touring

The private personality of Paul McCartney has always been poles apart from the public image he has chosen to project when he's been playing his role as a Beatle. One of the most memorable McCartney gatherings I attended was to mark the wedding of Paul's brother Mike in June 1968. Paul's relatives knew how to put on a good 'do' and they never missed an opportunity for a family get-together. The 'McCartney Mafia' consisted of a large and friendly bunch of Merseysiders, whose warmly informal functions were big, boisterous and enjoyable occasions, with the food provided in generous portions and the booze laid on in sufficient quantity to flow freely until the following morning!

Paul was still with his actress girlfriend Jane Asher at the time, and he brought her up from London with him for the wedding. Before the private family celebrations began in earnest, there was one essential bit of showbusiness to get out of the way. I'd been doing my usual PR job. In such circumstances the trick was to 'leak' information about the gathering to the papers at the very last minute. This had kept things as quiet as possible at the church, but brought a swarm of photographers and national newspaper reporters to Jim McCartney's house.

Paul could be relied upon to cope professionally with the inevitable questioning over the absence of the other Beatles. He told them: "It's Mike's big day, this one. Remember I haven't been invited here as a member of the Beatles. I'm not here to represent the group. I'm here as my brother Mike's best man, and I wouldn't have missed it for anything." He explained that John, George and Ringo had sent telegrams. George and Ringo were on their way to America, with Patti and Maureen. Paul didn't add that John was with Yoko, although the pair had appeared together, without Cynthia, at an Apple boutique opening in Chelsea a fortnight earlier.

Then Paul and Jane stood behind Mike and Angi, all broad smiles and cuddles, and we satisfied the demands of the media by doing a quick photo session on the lawn. For the rest of the day – and most of the night, as

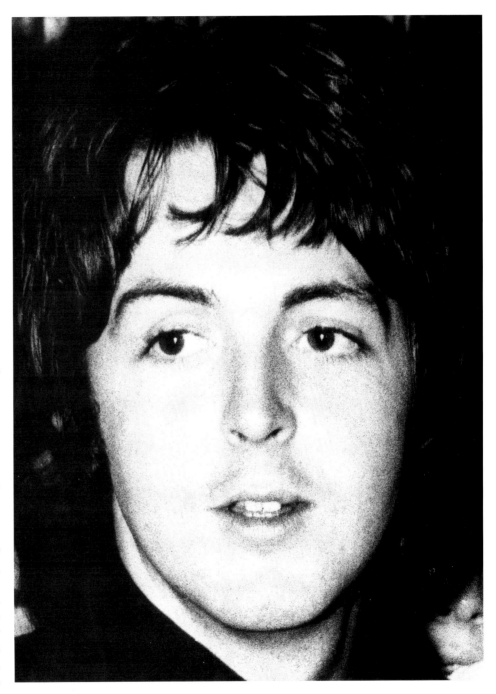

far as I remember – Paul let his hair down, and had a good time. It was still a showbiz affair, as some of Mike's guests had well-known faces, but Paul was relaxed, very contented, obviously off duty, knowing he was among trusted friends and there was no need for poses of any kind. Later, seated at the family's grand piano, Paul led a typical McCartney 'knees up' sing-song. Seldom before or since, have I seen Paul in such totally happy mood. Such occasions only

cropped up rarely. This one was so successful, partly because Paul was away from the rest of the group and acting so naturally, partly because we were far from London's sophisticated social circle where Paul would have behaved more formally, and partly because his whole family surrounded him.

The penalty of being a Beatle was that there were very few chances to let your hair down so completely, knowing that you could

his list of life's great priorities. With Paul, his music is a means to an end. He's good at playing the guitar or the piano, good as a singer, and outstanding as a songwriter. But he's not a motivated student of these activities. He's not an obsessive musician or a devoted composer. He makes the clear distinction that these are not pastimes, but jobs that need attending to if the name of Paul McCartney is to remain highly regarded.

Don't let me give an inadequate impression of Paul's happiness in the songwriting sector of his life. He couldn't possibly turn out such masterpieces if he wasn't interested in what he was doing. Undoubtedly he enjoys songwriting, but it's the end product, the No. 1 hit record and the platinum album, which is his chief goal. He has to believe that every project he tackles will be another world-beater – another feather in the McCartney cap. I don't think he'd ever sit down and spend time developing a new song, a movie script or any other sort of artistic creation, just for the sheer fun of it or to prove to himself that his powers were still there. Paul derives his greatest pleasures, his true job satisfaction, from visible success and public recognition, not from the actual process of preparing and manufacturing a fresh piece of work in the first place.

Of all the tasks he takes on, Paul clearly loves performing best of all. He does it all the time, in private conversations and business meetings, but most effectively, of course, in an auditorium or stadium, into a microphone or a camera, when the lights are up and a hushed audience is ready to respond to his artistry. He certainly doesn't need the money when he gives a performance today, whether it's in a studio or on a stage. But he needs the reassurance that someone wants him to perform, wants to watch him play, hear him sing, and see him smile that baby-faced smile which won him his very first wide-eyed young female fans in the Cavern Club. Until Linda came on the scene so forcefully, Paul was probably a relatively selfish partner, insisting that the women he went out with adapted to his moods, plans and desires. Any sensible girl

do so in safety. For once there was no danger of someone taking down everything you said and putting it on the gossip page of the paper next day! Some people scoffed when they heard talk of a multi-millionaire superstar like McCartney trying to be an 'ordinary' person and bring up his kids as non-celebrities, with as little publicity and fuss as possible.

But the truth is that this was no new policy for Paul. For as long as I've known him, he's worn a number of different faces according to the occasion, and the one his fans have seen when he's on display and in the spotlight is far removed from those he's shown to insiders, family and friends. I noticed the big difference even in the early days of our association, soon after I went to work with the Beatles on a full-time basis in 1963. In front of any third party, another Beatle, Brian Epstein, a member of the NEMS staff, a record company representative or whoever, Paul put on his official ambassadorial attitude. He had to look right and behave as he felt a proper star should. Long before the outbreak of Beatlemania, Paul had obviously taken the trouble to prepare himself for the big time, and he organ-

ised his mind to cope with being an exceedingly famous person in the public eye. When he found himself in a one-to-one situation, Paul changed dramatically and behaved as he might have done if the Beatles had never existed. He was less brittle, less concerned about how he looked, less careful to say exactly the right things, more honest in the opinions he gave, more direct and sincere in his opinions, and much more relaxed, mentally as well as physically. Even then, though, I'm sure his defences were never entirely down. I don't think he ever lowered those all the way to the ground, because he wasn't the type of man to let a fellow human being too close to his soul, in case a few frayed edges might be seen and show him up.

Paul was and is his own best advisor. He's the one he turns to for ultimate help when he's cornered, privately or in public. He's the one he relies upon for professional advice; nobody else comes up to scratch when it's a matter of serious career decisions. His second best friend is not his guitar, although he's kept one or two pretty close at (left) hand ever since he started writing songs as a teenager. But Paul's guitar comes well down

who wanted to stay on his arm and in his affections longer than 24 hours made sure that she fitted into Paul's existing schedule as surreptitiously as she could. She needed special abilities, particularly a flair for looking stunning day and night. Paul never minded being the envy of every full-blooded male around, provided his very tasty-looking partner performed precisely according to plan, which meant she'd step one pace back into the shadows whenever the plan called for Paul to shine and sparkle. I've indicated earlier that Paul acted differently in private and in public. He also chose to be with different ladies for different purposes.

The ones he liked to flash in public – and there weren't really too many of those – were stylish, well-bred, intelligent, accustomed to handling public attention. In private sometimes, he'd choose the company of other types. Associates were surprised at some of his choices, but the simple fact was that he liked to enjoy a change, and looked forward to being surprised in new ways by

the relatively few women he let into his life for any length of time. In Paul's youthful heyday as a charming ladykiller, he must have broken more than a few Liverpudlian hearts, but beneath the swashbuckling image of the conquering rock'n'roll hero, there was a dormant layer of romantic sentimentality in the make-up of Paul's innermost personality. You only have to listen to the man's lyrics to be convinced of that.

It doesn't amaze insiders who know him well, that Paul turned into a conventional family man, father and husband, who displayed many traditional, even old-fashioned, traits, as soon as he married Linda. Paul had enormous respect for his dad, Jim McCartney, and such instinctive admiration led him to adopt many of the same standards. Jim didn't allow the fame and fortune of his two sons, Paul and Mike, to disturb his way of life too dramatically. He was a man who had his own very sharply defined set of values, and who stuck meticulously to his personal moral code. Much of this

rubbed off on Paul, which goes a long way towards explaining his protective attitude towards his closest family. Jim tried to show his sons that transitory good luck and the resulting wealth it might bring should never overthrow a man's real aims, or be permitted to destroy his established lifestyle for too long. Now that the Beatlemania period is long gone, and Paul has time and space to consider his personal position outside the unrealistic realms of showbusiness, he chooses to go back to McCartney family roots, to the extent that he follows many of the traditions his father taught him.

He doesn't appear with the poseurs on the in-crowd West End club circuit very often, and he doesn't party with today's rock'n'roll stars unless he's promoting one of his own ventures. It's not easy to stick to those old family guidelines when you're as wealthy, popular and world-famous as Paul McCartney, but he has proved that it can be done, and he has always felt that he and his family have been better off that way.   (TB)

Ringo: the swinging Beatle

Although he joined the group long after the others, he soon came into his own

John once quipped: "Ringo doesn't know the meaning of fear – or any other word of more than three letters!" It became fashionable within the Fab Four to make jokes at Ringo's expense. They weren't intended to be hurtful. John, Paul and George were always fond of schoolboy humour among themselves, and Ringo, as the last to join, came in for plenty of jesting and hoaxes. It was a way of relieving the tension when Beatlemania was tightening all around them.

At first, Ringo took it all without fighting back. After all, he was the new boy, who'd been brought in to play the drums, so he reckoned that he didn't have too many rights. Eventually he did start to speak up for himself within the privacy of the group. This only made matters worse, because John laughed it all off and just went on making the same barbed remarks. Ringo was on the receiving end of Lennon's wickedly pointed wisecracks throughout his early months with the Beatles. Most of the joking went on in the presence of insiders, but sometimes it would spill over into press conferences, with the result that fans felt sorry for Ringo and took him to their hearts. When I got to know him, however, Ringo turned out to be an unassuming, shy and quietly spoken guy with a lot of sensible things to say on non-showbiz topics.

Like John, Ringo was forced to hide his love away in the early days of Beatlemania. Maureen was kept out of the spotlight, spending most of her time in Liverpool. He talked about her a lot. In fact, he mentioned her name so often that it was clear he was very much in love with Maureen. I don't think he'd had any previous girlfriends for whom he'd felt that strongly, but this didn't stop Ringo taking a close and active interest in all the available new talent on offer to him in London.

He had a healthy and voluminous appetite for adventure, swinging along with the Sixties as if the era of new freedom had been tailor-made for him. He pulled his 'birds' quietly, not flamboyantly, but when others weren't around to overhear him, he came out of his shell and talked about his lifestyle

as a Beatle. In those days, Ringo's tastes were simple. He had no time for gourmet cookery. His idea of the ideal slap-up meal was a plate piled high with chips, plus an overdone steak. Until they had their own flats in London, the Beatles stayed in a series of second-rate hotels, mostly in or near Russell Square. It was fascinating to watch Ringo getting used to his new environment. Just making a phone call to Liverpool from his bedside was a big deal,

and room service was quite clearly a luxury he'd never experienced before. Ringo was the least ambitious of the Beatles. Each of the others had deliberate aims, whereas Ringo was content to be a drummer, not a star. Superficially, he gave the impression that he was thick-skinned and could take any amount of ribbing. But the truth is that he'd always been quite sensitive to criticism, although his face never gave away his real feelings. It's a very distinctive face, with a

ignore Ringo on purpose, but it happened anyway. Underneath it all, Ringo was well liked by John, Paul, George and most of their aides.

Up to a point, Ringo was happy enough, and would amuse himself at studio sessions by settling down in a corner to play poker with a roadie or two and a few EMI aides. During his first few years with the group he knew he had to wait on the sidelines while John, Paul and George worked on each new backing track. Later on, and particularly when they stopped touring, the relationship changed and Ringo would get fed up with any disagreements between the other three. At other times he was clearly cheesed off with being left out of what was happening. It didn't always end in a slanging match. Sometimes Ringo would leave the place without a word and nobody would notice for an hour or more. By then it was too late to get him back. In the touring era this sort of thing seldom happened, although he did go missing once or twice, causing the rest of us to panic in case he failed to show up for the next performance. But he always did.

In the studio, Ringo sometimes felt musically inferior. But when it came to concerts, he was a star. He was always in demand, and there was plenty for him to do, giving interviews to journalists, DJs and local fans, and getting to know their thoughts about the Beatles. I think Ringo enjoyed his touring years much more than the others. He took less notice of the perils and problems, and remained light-hearted rather than intense. He really didn't want to stop doing concerts in 1966, but he had to accept that John and George did. He liked the travelling – as he does today – and he got a real kick out of meeting foreigners when he flew into new places around the world. He'd pick up local souvenirs like a tourist, taking them home to show Maureen. All the boys used cameras, but Ringo was a true enthusiast, collecting new and pricey photographic gear at every opportunity and asking press cameramen for help in using his latest gadgets.

Ringo had a very well developed sense of humour. I remember him as a good listener who'd laugh loudly at a funny story. His responses may have been few and far between, but when he did come back with a

large nose at the centre of it and a couple of slightly sad, droopy eyes. Ringo doesn't waste the slightest muscular energy on making a smile without good cause. When someone comes out with a remark that surprises him, he'll raise an eyebrow or two, but that's as far as it goes.

Wearing such a straight face used to give outsiders the impression that Ringo was worried or upset and feeling sorry for himself. This earned him a whole load of public sympathy. Mostly he was quite contented and without a care in the world, just thinking about something personal, his mind a million miles away. Despite that, most outsiders didn't know that Ringo actually resigned

from the Beatles several times. In the group's later years he made a habit of leaving and coming back again. The problem was that the rest of the boys had things to talk about that were never to do with Ringo. John and Paul, in particular, were rapidly expanding their musical scope, experimenting with new ideas, and writing far more complicated stuff. Until they came to the final part of the process, the actual recording of each new number in the studio, there was no professional need to involve Ringo. After the touring was over and the group began to concentrate entirely upon composing and recording, the friction between Ringo and the rest became increasingly obvious. Nobody intended to

The serious face that Ringo often presented to the world concealed a lively sense of humour. He was never happier than when he was playing on stage.

pungent one-liner it could devastate a roomful of us. When a whole bunch of us had been holding a deep and serious discussion without reaching any acceptable conclusion, Ringo could nutshell everything we'd been saying in a single sentence which would have us rolling about with laughter. Occasionally his wit was quick. More often it took its time, but the waiting was worthwhile. Occasionally Ringo became tongue-tied. He'd worked out what he wanted to say in his head, but somewhere between the brain and the lips, sheer confusion set in. The words he spoke might be near gobbledegook – but they became Ringo's trademark, just like the time he came out with the Beatles' first film title, *A Hard Day's Night.*

Ringo was the least demanding of all the Beatles. The others often appeared to expect the impossible from their closest aides. John, Paul and George spelt out what they wanted, encouraged by Brian Epstein to make full use of NEMS staff when professional help was required. Ringo asked assistants to do things politely, genuinely con-

Ringo enjoying the vocal spotlight during the German tour in 1966.

cerned that he might be causing too much bother, and he'd always have a word of thanks when something had been done for him. He was very aware of the group's status as a foursome of superstars. He made great efforts to look his best in public, smartening himself up before facing outsiders, although he loved to loaf around casually in private.

The thing I really liked about Ringo was that, unlike the other Beatles, he didn't have to be chased up all the time. Once he'd been told to be somewhere at a certain time, he'd turn up promptly whereas the others, and Paul in particular, had to be pushed and prodded by somebody until the last minute. Ringo the Beatle and Ringo the family man were always two different animals. He was a typically old-fashioned chauvinist in his off-duty life, expecting Maureen to behave in the approved way as a housewife and mother, but also expecting her to rival the London girls in a glamorous gown at the drop of a hat if he was escorting her to some 'do'. In later years, after his second marriage to Barbara Bach, he obviously took pride in having such a stunningly beautiful woman on his arm.

In total contrast to Paul, Ringo took great delight in appearing to lead a rich playboy's lifestyle – at least until his well publicised 'clean-up' operation at the end of the 80s. But he still likes the limelight of a movie premiere or big occasion. Once he was out of his depth in second-rate London hotels. Now he moves around the French Riviera or Hollywood's most fashionable haunts, displaying absolute self-assurance. In his youth, almost everything Ringo did was dictated by the Beatles. In maturity, he has found pleasure in controlling his own destiny, and in spending his money exactly the way he wants to. He goes to the world's most expensive, luxurious and fashionable spots, acting blatantly like the multi-millionaire that he is.

It makes a remarkable change from the days when he was perched behind his drum kit, watching John, Paul and George claim most of the applause. Yet for all that, I have always thought that Ringo remains the one and only Beatle who'd like to put the clock right back to the beginning, and relive the whole stormy, stimulating, dangerous and exciting Beatlemania years of the mid-Sixties all over again.   (TB)

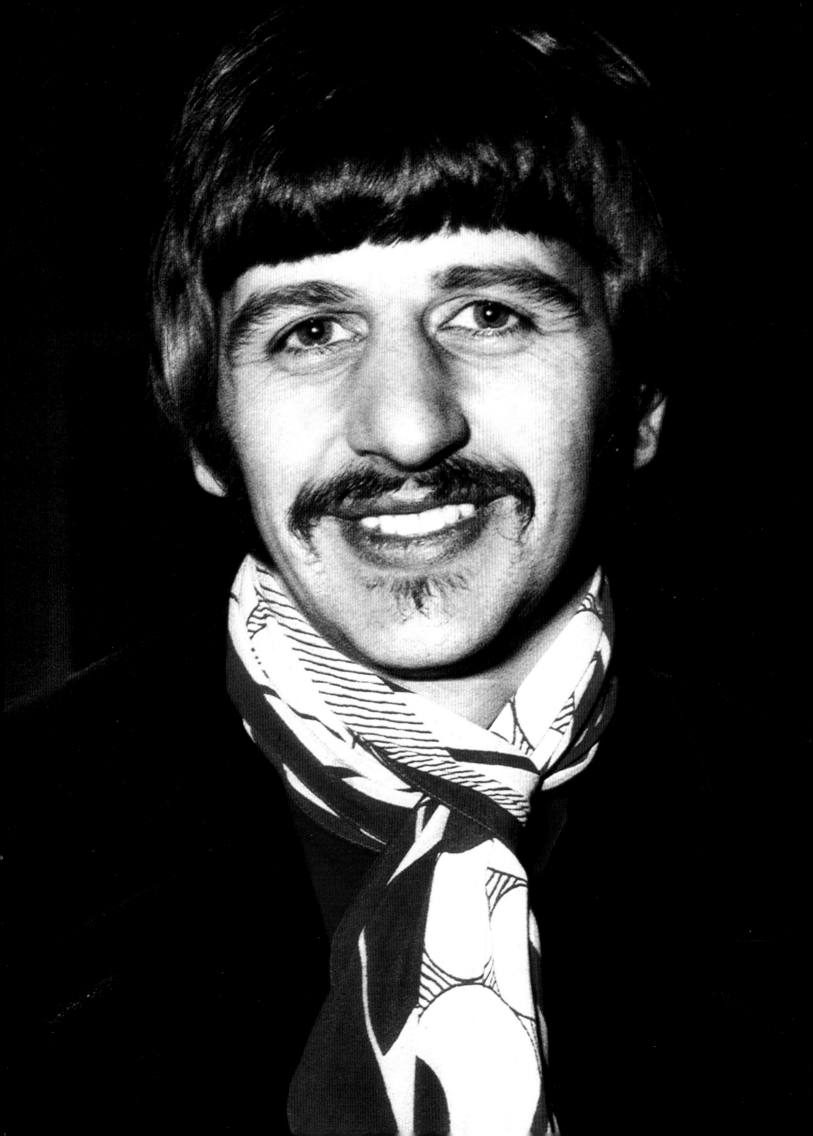

ACKNOWLEDGEMENTS

THE WRITERS

The initials of the original authors are noted in brackets at the end of each article. All uncredited material was written by *The Beatles Book* staff.

THE MAIN CONTRIBUTORS

JD – JOHNNY DEAN
Founded the magazine in 1963, and went on to edit every issue of *The Beatles Book* until the last edition in January 2003. He travelled extensively with the Beatles during the 1960s, and was one of the very few journalists who visited their private homes. He also spent numerous days with them on tour, on film sets and in TV studios. He says that perhaps the most exciting moments were those he spent in the recording studio with the Beatles, watching them record some of their biggest hits.

TB – TONY BARROW
The Beatles' press officer in the 1960s, who accompanied the group on most of their international tours and enjoyed unrivalled access to the boys during the decade. He was the most prolific contributor to the magazine throughout its existence. During the 1960s, he often wrote under the pseudonym of 'Frederick James'. He also acted as ghost-writer for features by the Beatles' roadies, Mal Evans and Neil Aspinall. He continues to write about showbiz matters for newspapers and magazines all around the world.

PJ – PETER JONES
Veteran pop journalist, who not only edited *Record Mirror* in the 1960s but also found time to contribute to all the early issues of *The Beatles Book*, often under the pseudonym of 'Billy Shepherd'. He used that disguise to pen the first biography of the group, *The True Story Of The Beatles*, published by Beat Publications in 1964. He was later the London editor of the prestigious US music magazine *Billboard*.

PD – PETER DOGGETT
Regular contributor to *The Beatles Book* from 1980 to 2003. During much of that time he was also the editor of *Record Collector* magazine. He is now an author and journalist, whose critically acclaimed history of country-rock music, *Are You Ready For The Country*, was published by Penguin in 2000.

OTHER CONTRIBUTORS (in strict alphabetical order)

NA – NEIL ASPINALL
Beatles road manager in the 1960s, who has been the managing director and driving force of their Apple organisation for more than 30 years. He often supplied information to *The Beatles Book* during the 1960s.

AC – ALAN CLAYSON
Prolific pop author who has written biographies of each of the individual Beatles, plus the official tie-in book for the film *Backbeat*.

JE – JOHN EMERY
Beatles Book reporter at the 1964 Christmas Show.

ME – MAL EVANS
Beatles road manager in the 1960s, who remained a close friend and aide to the individual Beatles until his tragic death in 1976, and supplied a lot of material to the magazine during the 1960s.

GG – GILLIAN G. GAAR
Seattle-based rock historian, author and Beatles expert who reported on US concerts and other events during the final years of *The Beatles Book*.

BH – BILL HARRY
Editor of the Liverpool pop paper *Mersey Beat*, who championed the Beatles long before they had a recording contract. He was a close friend of John Lennon and Stuart Sutcliffe during their time at Liverpool Art College. He has since written many books about the group during his long career as a pop and showbiz journalist.

FJ – FREDERICK JAMES
Pseudonym for Tony Barrow in the 1960s (see left).

ML – MARK LEWISOHN
Longtime news editor for *The Beatles Book* during the 1970s and 1980s, who has written several important books chronicling the group's career, and is currently preparing an epic three-volume biography of the Beatles.

PN – PETE NASH
Renowned Beatles memorabilia expert and archivist who contributed regularly to *The Beatles Book* in its final years, and was the magazine's last news editor. He now runs the very informative website: www.britishbeatlesfanclub.co.uk

MOG – MARTIN O'GORMAN
Latter-day news editor for *The Beatles Book*, who now maintains *Q* magazine's online presence.

BS – BILLY SHEPHERD
Pseudonym for Peter Jones in the 1960s (see opposite).

ES – ELIZABETH SACHS
Beatles Book reporter at the premiere of *Help!* in 1965.

SW – SIMON WELLS
Beatles expert who was a roving reporter for *The Beatles Book* during its final years.

THE PHOTOGRAPHERS

Philip Gotlop was commissioned to take shots of the Beatles recording 'She Loves You' in 1963, but Johnny Dean then commissioned Leslie Bryce to take exclusive photographs of the group at Margate. Following that session, Leslie became the official *Beatles Book* photographer, and went on to take thousands of photographs of the group all over the world. Nigel Dickson stood in for Leslie at the so-called 'butcher session' in 1966.

Many other photographers supplied pictures to *The Beatles Book* in the 1960s, including Philip Gotlop, Mr & Mrs Harrison, Dezo Hoffmann, Jim McCartney, Mike McCartney, (Aunt) Mimi Smith, and Mr & Mrs Starkey.

COPYRIGHTS

All photographs Sean O'Mahony Collection, except for the following:

Page 16 (top): ASP
Page 21 (top) © Apple Corps Ltd
Page 23 (top) © Apple Corps Ltd
Page 24: Pan-Foto
Page 32, 33: Decca Records
Page 34 (bottom): Mike Smith collection
Page 35: © Apple Corps Ltd
Page 38: © Apple Corps Ltd
Page 39: © Apple Corps Ltd
Page 74: Christie's
Page 76: Tony Barrow collection
Page 78 © Apple Corps Ltd
Page 86 (top left): Herald-Sun
Page 120: Shea Stadium
Page 123: Press Association
Page 131 (top): Capitol Records

Page 131 (bottom): Barry Plummer
Page 133: Pictorial Press
Page 156: Tony Barrow collection
Pages 157-159: Bob Whittaker/© Apple Corps Ltd
Page 160: Candlestick Park
Pages 162-163: Corbis
Page 170 © Apple Corps Ltd
Page 171: Barry Plummer
Page 200 © Apple Corps Ltd
Page 218 © Apple Corps Ltd
Page 221 © Apple Corps Ltd
Page 229 © Apple Corps Ltd
Page 230 © Apple Corps Ltd
Page 231 © Apple Corps Ltd
Page 234: Barry Plummer
Page 237: Barry Plummer
Page 238: Barry Plummer
Page 239: Barry Plummer
Page 240: MPL
Page 241: Barry Plummer
Page 246: Barry Plummer
Page 247: Barry Plummer
Page 249 London Features International
Page 251: Dark Horse Records
Pages 252-253: Geoff Pugh
Pages 254-257: © MPL Communications Ltd. 2003
          Photographer: Bill Bernstein
Page 259 © Apple Corps Ltd
Pages 262-264: Pete Nash collection
Page 266 (top): Richard Porter
Page 266 (bottom): Simon Wells
Pages 267-270: Simon Wells
Pages 272-277: Corinne Barrow; Cavern City Tours

Every effort has been made to locate the copyright holders of the photographs in this book. The publisher welcomes information about any omissions, so that they can be included in future editions.

Beatles fan clubs & fanzines

The postal and web addresses below were compiled for the first edition of this book in July 2005. Please note the most active fan clubs in each country have been indicated with a star. The publisher welcomes corrections and updates from club organisers and fans for future editions.

UK
★**British Beatles Fan Club** PO Box 756, Bradford BD2 3WY
www.britishbeatlesfanclub.co.uk

ARGENTINA
The Cavern Club Paseo la Plaza (local 47), Av. Corrientes 1660 - CF Buenos Aires. www.thecavernclub.com.ar

AUSTRALIA
★**Across The Universe** PO Box 422, Concord West, NSW Australia 2138

AUSTRIA
★**Beatles Fan Club Oesterreich** Gschwandnergasse 42 / 12Wien, A-117 0 Austria

CANADA
★**Beatlology Magazine** PO Box 90, 260 Adelaide St. East, Toronto, Ontario M5A 1N1. www.beatlology.com
Réseau Québécois des Ami(e)s des Beatles C.P. 37032, 900 Boulevard Rene Levesque Est, Quebec City, Quebec G1R 5PS Canada. www.geocities.com
★**World Beatles Forum** 2440 Bank Street, PO Box 40081 Ottawa Ontario K1V 0W8 Canada. www.beatles.ncf.ca

FRANCE
★**Les Club Des 4 De Liverpool** 43 bis Boulevard Henri IVParis 75004 France

GERMANY
★**Beatlemania** (magazine), Postfach 800538, Erfurt, D-99011. www.beatlemania.de
★**Beatles Beat** Postfach 3247 Kerpen D-50147 Germany
Beatles Club Center Deutschland e.V. Brüeckenweg 2 Niederweimar D-35096 Germany. www.beatlescenter.de
Beatles Club Wuppertal Paulussenstrasse 7 Wuppertal D-42349 Germany. www.beatles-club.de
Beatles File Collection Leitweg 47, Bedburg, D-50181
Beatles Museum "Little Cavern" Postfach 1464, Hattersheim, D-65783 Germany
Beatles Museum Halle Alter Markt 12, Halle/Saale, D-06108 Germany
Beat Archiv August-Bebel-strasse 6, Glauchau, D-08371 Germany. www.beatarchiv.de

IRELAND
★**Beatles Ireland** 37 Glencarrig Drive, Firhouse, Dublin 24 Ireland.www.iol.ie/beatlesireland

ITALY
★**Beatle People Association of Italy** Via C. Biseo 18, Brescia 25124 Italy.www.beatlesiani.com
★**Paul McCartney fan club Milano** via Caroncini 6 Milan 20137 Italy

JAPAN
★**Tokyo Beatles Fan Club** 4-6-14-304 Toyotama-kita, Nerima-ku, Tokyo 00176 Japan

MEXICO
★**Seguimos Juntos** AP 7-1037, Mexico 06700 DF

NEW ZEALAND
★**Friends of the Beatles** PO Box 70041, Ranui, Auckland 1008

NETHERLANDS
★**Beatles Unlimited** PO Box 602, 3430 AP Nieuwegein The Netherlands. www.beatles-unlimited.com
Beatle Fan Next Generation Hovierstraat 8, 1825 AC Alkmaar The Netherlands. www.beatlesfannext.com

NORWAY
★**Norwegian Wood – Beatles Fanclub of Norway** Sandbekkfaret 20, Bloevanstad, N-2006 www.norwegianwood.org

RUSSIA
Back In The USSR M. Kalitnikovskaj 47-A-20, 3509029 Moscow Russia
Beatles Society, ul. Wagorskaja 21, kw. 3400065 Volgograd/Taikinu Russia
Club/Bar/Restaurant "Liverpool" PO Box 123198152 St.Petersburg
Gorky Beatles Fan Club, The PO Box 15103035 Gorky Russia

SPAIN
★**Sgt. Beatles Fan Club** Apartado de Correos 7.250, Zaragoza 50080. Spain. www.beatles.arrakis.es
Club de Fans de Paul McCartney Apartado de Correos 97077, Barcelona 08080 Espania

SWITZERLAND
★**Beatles Fan Club "Fab 4" Schweiz** Postfach 555, Bern 8, CH-3000 Switzerland

USA
★**Beatlefan** PO Box 33515, Decatur, GA 30033 USA. www.beatlefan.com
Atlanta Beatles Club PO Box 2062, Stockbridge, GA 30281 USA
Beatles Fans Unite PO Box 50123, Cicero, IL 60804 USA. www.beatlesfansunite.com
Beatles Video Digest PO Box 13322 Des Moines Iowa 50310-0322 USA
The Beatletter PO Box 13, St Clair Shores, MI 48080 USA
Belmo's Beatleg News PO Box 17163, Ft. Mitchell, KY 41017 USA
Daytrippin' PO Box 408 Beltsville MD 20704-0408 USA. www.daytrippin.com
Drive My Car Beatles Fan Club PO Box 159 Fairfax VA 22030 USA
Good Day Sunshine PO Box 1008, Mar Vista, CA 90066-1008 USA
The Harrison Alliance 67 Cypress St., Bristol, CT 06010 USA
Instant Karma PO Box 256, MI 49783 USA
The McCartney Observer 220 E. 12th St Lacrosse KS 67548 USA
Penny Lane Press 1137 Rogers St.Clarkston GA 30021 USA
St. Louis Beatles Fan Club PO Box 190602, St. Louis, MO USA
The Working Class Hero 3311 Niagara St., Pittsburgh, PA 15213 USA

WEB-ONLY FANZINES & NEWS GROUPS
www.beatlefans.com   www.beatlesfanclub.nl   www.beatlesagain.com
www.beatles.ru   www.beatlesnews.com/   www.brianepstein.com
www.georgeharrison.com   www.instantkarma.com   www.nowhere-land.com
www.paulmccartney.com   www.ringostarr.com   www.thebeatles.com.br
http://aboutthebeatles.com   http://come.to/liverpoolbeatlescene